USTAŠA

Croatian Fascism and European Politics, 1929-1945

SRDJA TRIFKOVIC

USTAŠA

Croatian Fascism and European Politics, 1929-1945

Second Edition

The Lord Byron Foundation for Balkan Studies
Chicago-Ottawa-London
2011

Copyright © Srdja Trifkovic, 2011

All rights reserved

Printed and bound in the United States of America by
The Lord Byron Foundation for Balkan Studies
Chicago-Ottawa-London

ISBN 978-1-892478-01-6

TABLE OF CONTENTS

Foreword
by *Thomas Fleming*   5

Preface   9

I   The Legacy of Premodernity   13
The Military Border 15
The Illyrians 23
Starčević 29
The Serb Question 35

II   The Yugoslav Experiment   38
The Great War 38
Unification 41
An Unconsolidated Kingdom 45
International Environment 52

III   An Émigré Conspiracy   56
Pavelić's Early Italian Contacts 56
Pavelić Goes Abroad 60
Codification of Ustaša Principles 65
The "Military Nucleus" 67
The Ustaša Movement and Fascism 72

IV   Serbs, Croats, and the Axis   78
Aftermath of Marseilles 78
The Rome-Belgrade Axis 81
Hitler's Yugoslav Policy 85
Maček and Italy 91
The Agreement Cvetković-Maček 97

V   The Fall of Yugoslavia   102
Precarious Neutrality 102
Pavelić Reactivated 105
German Pressure 111
Disagreements over the Agreement 115
The Pact, the Coup, the War 119
Germans Seek Croat Allies 127
Tenth of April 136

VI   Croatia in Hitler's New Europe   142
Pavelic's Return from Italy 142
Karlovac: First Signs of Axis Rivalry 146
A Newcomer to "New Europe" 151
Hitler's Croatian Strategy 159
Decision on Dalmatia 165
The Rome Agreements 172

VII   The Ustaša Holocaust   179
Ustašism Unleashed 179
"The Last Bullet for the Last Serb" 184
Pavelić at the Berghof 189
"Intolerance" at Work 193
The Role of the Catholic Church 200
The Ustaša and the Holocaust 208

VIII   The Uprising   218
Causes and Characteristics 218
Italian Response 223
German Response 234
The Dangić Affair 239
German-Italian Discord 243
The Četnik Dilemma 254

IX   Germany Takes the Initiative   257
German Economic Dominance 257
German Generals vs. Pavelić 264
The Wehrmacht Takes Command 275
Weiss and Schwarz 278

X   Accomplices in Coat-Tails   290
Pavelić's Foreign Ministry 290
The Gaffes 294
Areas of Activity 301
Croatian-Hungarian Dispute 304
Partners in the Holocaust 314

XI   The Turning Point   319
German-Partisan Contacts 319
The SS and the NDH 326
Bosnian Muslims and the SS 330
Italian Armistice 338
Neubacher's Mission 347

XII   Decline and Fall   351
Zone of Operations Adriatic 351
Another Croatian Policy Review 356
The "Affair" Lorković-Vokić 363
Glaise Defeated 369
The Last Ally 374
In Search of a Miracle 382

XIII   Conclusion   388

Appendixes   395

Sources and Bibliography   403

Note on Pronunciation

International linguistic authorities continue to regard Serbian and Croatian (as well as their more recent "Bosnian" and "Montenegrin" variants) as one language with some structural, lexical and idiomatic differences. They are mutually intelligible and based on the *štokavian* dialect. The Serbian Cyrillic alphabet was devised by Vuk Karadžić while its Latin equivalent is based on Ljudevit Gaj's reform. The orthography is consistent and reflects the norm "Write as you speak, read as it is written." Serbian and Croatian words and names used in this book are given in the Latin script and commonly should be pronounced as follows:

a – *a* as in f*a*r (long), ab*o*ve (short)
c – ts as in ra*ts*
ć - 'soft' ch, as in Pacino, chilli
č - 'hard' ch, as in chalk, cello
dj, đ – g as in gender, or j as in juice
dž – 'dzh' as in jam, edge
e – as in p*e*t (short), or grey (long)
g – as in go (never as g in 'large'!)
h – 'kh' (gutteral), as in loch
i – as in pin (short) or mach*i*ne (long)
j – y as in yet or yes
lj – li or ly, as in million, halyard
nj – ni as in dominion, canyon
o - o as in up*o*n
s – as in hi*ss*
š - sh as in shawl, sugar
u - u as in rule
ž - zh, as in French *jour*

Foreword
Thomas Fleming

In the course of the 19th and early 20th centuries one after another European people made a bid either to liberate itself from an imperial state, or, as in the case of Italy, to reassemble the fragments of its nationhood that had been scattered and snatched up by foreign powers. Some of the impetus for this nation-building came from the French Revolution, whose leaders preached a militant doctrine of national liberation.

Croatians, who had not enjoyed an independent national existence since the beginning of the 12th century, were far from immune to the spirit of 1848. The ensuing spectrum of nationalist l'political opinion ran the usual gamut, from a nostalgic romanticism that sought a national destiny in the legends and traditions of a subjugated people to the more virulent forms of nationalism that relied on an us-and-them dichotomy that turns neighboring and rival peoples into perpetual enemies or even subhuman demons.

Some attempts at nation-building did not succeed. In the fullness of time it was revealed that such hybrids as Czechoslovakia (whose break-up was precipitated in part over whether or not to include a hyphen in the national name) were sufficiently diverse as to remain unstable, despite the best efforts of flag-designers, anthem-writers, politicians, and visionary intellectuals.

Nations cannot be invented overnight, and it took centuries for the nations of Europe—including France, Britain, Italy, and Germany—to coalesce within national monarchies and legal systems that united diverse regional populations. Italy, which Metternich had derided as a "geographical expression," was so ethnically and linguistically diverse that neither fascism nor mass media could entirely eliminate the distinctive dialects and historic antagonisms that made the *Lega Nord* a political force into the 21st century. Tiny Croatia, with its range of dialects and cultures, was no exception, and it would take no small effort to create a Croatian nation.

To understand the Ustaša state it is necessary to understand the origins and development of Croatian nationalism. For this new edition of *Ustaša*, Srdja Trifkovic has added an opening chapter that is a brief yet essential survey of Serb-Croat relations before 1918. It provides the much needed historical setting for an issue which is routinely treated (when treated at all) as a consequence of the creation of Yugoslavia.

Croatian nationalism has almost always been bound up with a race myth that exaggerates the differences among South Slav nations and defines the

Croatian national character as the opposite of whatever qualities are attributed to Serbs. Even authentic nations, in asserting their identities, rely heavily on myths and fabrications. In the 19th century, astute and learned diplomats of the Dual Monarchy realized that the fabrication of nationalist mythologies, as much as it might threaten the unity of a polyglot empire, could also be incorporated into the most ancient of imperialist strategies summed up by the phrase, *divide et impera*. In turning to the Balkans as the scene of imperial expansion, Austria-Hungary found rich opportunities for mischief-making in the longstanding rivalries of Croats and Serbs, Orthodox and Catholics, Muslims and Christians, Albanians and Slavs, who were encouraged in their search for mythic histories among Scythians, Goths, and Illyrians.

In this context, some Croatian intellectuals would learn to turn away from dreams of South Slavic kinship toward various race-myths that would turn *the Serb* into an ancient and eternal enemy. The groundwork for this myth had already been laid in the attempt of the early-modern Croatian elite to absorb the Serbs, who had been encouraged to settle in Croatia as guardians of the frontier with the Ottoman Empire. As Trifkovic explains, for the upholders of Croatia's tradition of state rights those Serbs were unwelcome and inherently hostile aliens for as long as they insisted on retaining their name, their autonomous socio-economic and legal status, and their Orthodox faith. An obsessive elite resentment at *Grenzer* privileges was passed on from one generation to another, he says, and became 'democratized' after the collapse of feudalism in 1848: "At the historical root of the Ustaša bloodbath in 1941-5 lay a centuries-old striving of the Croatian elite class to impose legal and religious homogeneity and to re-establish political obedience."

Particularly revealing in Trifkovic's opening chapter is the germination of Ante Starčević's distinctly proto-Ustaša "ideology" as early as the 1860's. Starčević's stunning dehumanization of the "Slavo-Serb" and his preference for the genocidal final solution, Trifkovic points out, heralded a new era:

> His *Herrenvolk*-Croatism, Serbophobia and Slavophobia, his often bizarre cultural, racial and historical assertions, make a reader cringe in embarrassment and repugnance. ... There is no inherent reason why a civic Croatian nation-state should not have been able to include Serbs as citizens. Starčević made it so.

Starčević was the spiritual father of the Ustaša movement, Trifkovic concludes, by virtue of providing it with a broad ethno-historical narrative with a radical answer to the unsettled question of Croatian national identity. Seven decades before Pavelić articulated his *Ustaša Principles*, Starčević had established, albeit in a crude form, all key tenets of that narrative.

In the development of a national identity, a certain amount of poetic creativity is always involved. Even authentic nations, in asserting their identities, rely heavily on myths and lies. Up to a point, national myths are harmless and exercise a positive influence. To exaggerate the prowess and honor of one's ancestors is an inevitable temptation, even if the ancestors in question were sheep thieves and brigands. Sir Walter Scott once wrote that he could never find it in his heart utterly to condemn the depredations of his own people, the Border Scots, precisely because they were *his* people. Nationalist myths are not always so naive or so harmless, however: almost a century later, Turks have yet to come face to face with the facts of the Armenian genocide.

Every nation has a record of high crimes and misdemeanors. The Anglo-Saxon nations, which pride themselves on their civilized restraint and sense of fair play, did not exercise those virtues on the Celtic inhabitants of the British Isles, or on the native populations of North America, Africa, and Tasmania. Some of that ancient history has come back to haunt the peoples of Great Britain and the United States.

The Croats are in a similar position; but their crimes against Serbs, Jews, and Gypsies during the Second World War, because they are more recent, are mixed almost inextricably with the myth-making of Croatian nationalism.

The record of atrocities committed by the Ustaša state has been obscured for a variety of reasons. In Tito's Yugoslavia the massacres were swept under the carpet for the sake of 'brotherhood and unity' and to keep nationalist ammunition out of the hands of the Serbs.

In the United States the explanation is partly the historical ignorance of Americans, including those who make foreign policy, and partly the impact of former Ustašas who were recruited as 'anti-communists' during the Cold War by U.S. intelligence and their revisionist descendents. Whatever the reason, not one American in a hundred knows that the war-time Croatian government massacred hundreds of thousand of Serbs. Most American schoolboys are familiar with the names of Himmler and Eichman, but few historians recognize the name of Mile Budak, the Croatian minister who was among the first to state in public his government's policy toward the Serbs: convert a third, expel a third, kill a third.

The Croatian nation will not fully mature until it has reckoned with its past, but one set of propaganda lies cannot be opposed by the anti-propaganda of Serb nationalism or American internationalism. In fact, all propaganda – no matter how superficially attractive – is ultimately lethal to those who believe in it; they are lies covered up in a little truth, like time-bombs wrapped in Christmas paper. Nations are nourished on truth, not lies, and the peoples of the Balkans (and those who would presume to tell them how to live) have an urgent need of the truth that only historical scholarship can provide.

Srdja Trifkovic has written such a book, filled with passion for the truth and for giving justice to victims and to oppressors alike. His examination of the role played by European powers in the disintegration of the Kingdom of Yugoslavia and the creation of a Croatian fascist state blends a meticulous empirical method with clear and perceptive analysis. The result significantly adds to our understanding, not only of the history of southeastern Europe just before and during the Second World War, but also of the genesis of that region's more recent crisis.

Especially revealing is Trifkovic's treatment of the Ustaša ideology, which turns out to be far less complex than its fascist counterparts in Italy and Spain and more akin to Nazism. The evils done by authentic fascists were the crimes of thugs and zealots. Yet fascism offered its adherents some semblance of a coherent response to the crisis of modernity, and to that extent rightist intellectuals like T.S. Eliot found it initially either attractive or, at least, no great threat to civilization. Apart from aping the visual and rhetorical trappings of Italian fascists and German Nazis – whose hatred of the Jews they attempted to outdo – Ustaša propagandists made but the tentative attempt to promote a positive ideology.

The predictable American response to the squabbles in the Balkans has been, for decades, to adopt the position of Henry Ford that 'History is Bunk.' However, as Cicero observed so long ago, those who do not know what happened before they were born remain children forever. Too many Western intellectuals suffer from the sort of infantilism that led one recent American president to dismiss some unpleasant business as 'just history,' and his successor to proclaim that America had no history before the 20th century, when human rights were first guaranteed.

The path to sanity and maturity, both in the Balkans and in the West, must be blazed by scholars and writers who have the courage and stamina to recover the past. That is the reason why this book is so important.

Dr. Fleming is the editor of Chronicles: A Magazine of American Culture

Preface

The history of the Second World War is rich in general overviews and specialist studies. In Southeastern Europe, however, we encounter an exception of long standing. Yugoslavia between the world wars and its *bellum omnium contra omnes* in 1941-5 should be a rewarding area of specialist interest, now that most archives are accessible and travel unrestricted, but both remain curiously under-researched.

The absence of an authoritative corpus in the western academe has been aggravated by two phenomena. One is the reluctance of historians in the successor states of Yugoslavia to come to grips with such delicate subjects as collaborationism and mass murder, or at least their reluctance to do so without ethnic blinkers and revisionist temptations. The other is the tendency of all too many foreign area specialists to view events of 1941-5 through the prism of their current cultural preferences and ideological affinities. In the Yugoslav context this often translates into their predilection for one or another form of nationalist narrative.[1]

This book seeks to help redress this imbalance. Its purpose is to examine the origins, actions and significance of the Ustaša phenomenon in relation to its geographic and political environment, to ascertain its place in the political map of Europe before and during the Second World War, and to evaluate its impact on the political and military developments in the western Balkans during its four years of collaborationist statehood. In a broader sense, this book seeks not merely to broaden our knowledge of the Ustaša phenomenon, but to try to understand it. The job may never get done, the results will never be final, but it is worth trying because we need to move beyond righteous demonization of Ustašism on one side, and its apologetic relativization on the other, to its long overdue historicization.[2]

The problem of Serb-Croat relations, burdened by an ambiguous legacy of earlier centuries, was greatly aggravated by the creation of the Yugoslav

---

[1] There are many recent books on the former Yugoslavia by ambitious non-historians, mostly journalists with a tentative hold on the sources, methodology and local languages, who tend to view the 1940's through a reductionist prism of the 1990's. While often self-styled as *history*, such efforts are outside our purview.

[2] Cf. Martin Broszat's May 1985 essay *A Plea For the Historicization of National Socialism.* (*Plaidoyer fur eine Historisierung des Nationalsozialismus, Merkur* 39/1985)

state in 1918. Those relations probably would have remained ambivalent but tractable had the two nations not been brought under the same roof at the tail-end of their transition to modernity. Yet the disputes between Serbs and Croats, two linguistically similar but historically, ethnically and culturally distinct peoples, are by no means a modern phenomenon.

In the 19th century the Serbs of Serbia, recently emancipated, had no direct or traditional quarrel with the Croats of Croatia, the Habsburg land whose principal concern was with their royal and imperial masters in Budapest and Vienna. The seeds of the perennial Serb-Croat quarrel in the Yugoslav era were sown long before, however. The legal status and privileges of the Habsburg Military Border (*Militärgrenze, Vojna krajina*), with its many Serb Orthodox soldier-farmers, were detested by the Croatian nobility and ecclesiastical hierarchy from the moment the Border was formed in the 16th century to the time it was dissolved in 1881. By that time, the resentment had spread beyond the neofeudal elite and gave rise to the ideology of Croatian state rights (*Pravaštvo*). It included the dual claim that the Serbs in Croatia were, or should be, Orthodox Croats who perforce belonged to the Croatian "political nation"; and that those who rejected such designation were racially inferior subhuman "breed" whose elimination was essential to Croatia's national survival and eventual statehood. The key tenets of this racist, nationalist, and secular ideology were in place more than half a century before the creation of Yugoslavia. Enriched between the world wars with the novel notion of racially distinct Croatdom, it found its radical expression in the *Ustaša* movement of Ante Pavelić.[1]

Yugoslavia's complex relations with Italy and Germany before April 1941 and Balkan rivalries within the Axis camp that surfaced during the occupation will also attract our attention, since they provide the coordinates within which the Ustaša sub-plot unfolded.

"Croatia became during the war a giant slaughterhouse," Ernst Nolte has noted; but this is not a book about the bloodbath as such, and it is not primarily focused on the ideological grounding that made it possible. The enormity of Ustaša crimes against Serbs, Jews and Roma, through which the Independent State of Croatia (*Nezavisna država Hrvatska*, NDH) became infamous, will be treated in so far as such crimes impacted military, political and diplomatic developments in the region and around it. The Ustaša state

---

[1] *Ustaša* means "insurgent," participant in an uprising (*ustanak*). The term first gained wide currency at the time of the Herzegovinian Christian uprising against the Ottoman misrule in 1875. Ironically, as the insurgency spread, the majority of the "Ustaše" (plural form) fighting the Turks were Orthodox Serbs.

was synonymous with mass murder, but today it is necessary to try and understand it as one seeks to understand any other phenomenon from the past. The alternatives are horrified ignorance or creeping apologia.

The Ustašas' genocidal intent and their actual attempt to carry out demographic engineering on a relatively grand scale are not central but are nevertheless very important to this narrative. The intent and its fruits provided a key motive for the regime's striving to carve out as much autonomy of action as possible between its enablers in Rome and Berlin. Its bid to turn a multiethnic and multiconfessional amalgam into an integrated monoethnic state became the main source of military and political instability in the Axis occupation system in the region. It materially affected the outcome of the war by turning the Western Balkans from a potential asset into an actual liability for the Third Reich.

The striving for ethnic, cultural and political uniformity through ethnic cleansing was not uncommon in Nazi-dominated Europe. The remarkable Ustaša bloodlust nevertheless makes the Croatian variety of "native fascism" distinctly *sui generis* and sets it apart from other collaborationist movements and regimes. All of those movements subscribed to "Aryan" racism in some form; all of them claimed a divinely ordained special mission for their particular group; and all were, to some extent and for some time at least, complicit in the Holocaust. All of them had a vision of nationhood that entailed its imposition on the "Aryan" minority groups, ultimately leading to either their assimilation or their removal. Ustašism alone produced a Quisling state with a fully autonomous apparatus of terror and extermination devoted to that end. Proportionate to the number of its victims, the Ustaša apparatus – technologically primitive and bureaucratically underdeveloped though it was – proved only marginally less efficient than the sophysticated Nazi killing machine itself. This fact sets the Ustaša phenomenon apart from other native fascisms. For a historian it makes the "normalization" of the study of Ustašism difficult, just as the Holocaust studies still refuse to be "normalized."

An attempt to advance towards normalization is nevertheless possible and necessary. It need not and must not end up either in trivializing the Ustaša movement's grotesque record or in succumbing to the temptations of the historian's prejudices. Perhaps a barrier will always separate him from the subject – to paraphrase Nora Levin, Jasenovac was indeed another planet – but the effort is intellectually and morally legitimate.

On the seventieth anniversary of the creation of the Axis-sponsored Croatian state, this book will attempt to elucidate an important segment of 20th century southeast European history which is still known in fragmentary and often distorted form. It is presented in the wider hope that post-Yugoslav historiographies will finally grow to be freer from old Balkan feuds and contemporary Balkan rivalries than they are now.

The cause of historical truth in a perennially troubled region can be advanced neither by native mendacity and half-truths nor by the sentimental lapse of seriousness that still characterizes much of the Western discourse on the region.

Chicago, Easter 2011   The Author

I
The Legacy of Premodernity

In November 1942 General Edmund Glaise von Horstenau, the Wehrmacht plenipotentiary representative in Zagreb, made an unscheduled visit to the Ustaša-run prison camp near the city of Sisak, where – as he had been informed by his assistant, Captain Haeffner – many Serbs were being held under appalling conditions. He described the scene in his diary:

> A terrible picture confronted me. There were but a few men, mostly women and children, all of them poorly clad, sleeping on bare stones. Not people, but naked skeletons... The camp commander – contrary to the praises heaped on him later by the *Poglavnik* – was an outright criminal. I ignored his presence. To my Ustaša escorts I commented: 'When a man sees this, he can only vomit – nothing else, my gentlemen!' The worst of all was yet to come: in a separate room, hastily concealed no doubt because of my 'inspection,' along the wall there were some fifty naked children laying on thinly spread straw. Some of them were already dead, and others were dying! ... These houses of horror in Croatia, under their Poglavnik enthroned by ourselves, are the culmination of abhorrence. Jasenovac must be even worse, but no mere mortal can even have a glimpse of that place.[1]

Glaise proceeded to the Serb-inhabited village of Crkveni Bok on the Sava River, where a day earlier he had dispatched a German tank platoon to protect the remaining inhabitants from the Ustašas:

> It is an unhappy place where, under the leadership of an Ustaša lieutenant-colonel, some 500 country folk from fifteen to twenty years old had met their end. They were all murdered, the women raped and then tortured, the children killed outright. I saw in the River Sava a woman's corpse with the eyes gouged out and a stick shoved into the sexual parts. This woman was at most twenty years old when she fell into the hands of these monsters. Away in a corner, some pigs were gorging themselves on an unburied human being. All the houses were looted. The "lucky" inhabitants were consigned to one of the fearsome boxcar trains; many of these involuntary passengers cut their veins on the journey.

As a former Habsburg officer and a gentleman of the old school, Glaise was horrified by the scene, but by November 1942 he could no longer be

---

[1] Peter Broucek, ed. *En General im Zweilicht: Die Erinnerungen von Edmund Glaise von Horstenau*, Vol 3. Wien 1998, p. 167.

surprised by anything. More than a year earlier, in July 1941, he had made his first complaint about the "barbaric" Ustaša methods used against the Serbs who were "fundamentally placed outside the law, outlawed."[1]

Glaise's trip to Sisak came only weeks after a Wehrmacht senior officer serving in northwestern Bosnia, Lt. Col. von Wedel, complained to him of a massacre of Serb women and children witnessed by the Germans. The Ustaša killed their helpless victims "like cattle," von Wedel related, in a series of "bestial executions."[2] At a higher level of command *Obergruppenführer* Arthur Phleps, commander of the 7. SS Mountain Division *Prinz Eugen*, had a similar complaint: "From the start the main Ustaša objective was to annihilate the Orthodox [Serbs], to butcher hundreds of thousands of persons, women and children."[3] Dr. Hermann Neubacher, Hitler's foremost political expert for the Balkans, concurred:

> The prescription for the Orthodox Serbs issued by the leader and Führer of Croatia, Ante Pavelić, was reminiscent of the bloody religious wars of yore: One third must be converted to Catholicism, another third must be expelled, and the final third must die. The last part of the program has been carried out.[4]

General Bader, commanding German troops in Serbia, saw this annihilation as the goal not limited to the Ustaša regime: "There is no doubt at all that the Croats are endeavoring to destroy the entire Serb population."[5] According to a Gestapo report prepared for Himmler, "The Ustašas committed their bestial crimes not only against males of military age, but especially against helpless old people, women and children."[6]

It is unprecedented, even in the traumatized and brutalized Europe of the early 1940's, to encounter a wave of violence so extreme as to shock and awe battle-hardened Wehrmacht and SS officers, Nazi diplomats, and Gestapo operatives. Yet the phenomenon behind that violence, Ustašism remains relatively little known and only scantily researched outside the former

---

[1] Gert Fricke. *Kroatien 1941-1944: Die "Unabhängige Staat" in der Sicht des Deutschen Bevollmächtigen Generals in Agram, Glaise v. Horstenau.* Freiburg: Rombach Verl. 1972, p.39

[2] 714. Division, Operations Staff, "Activity Report: Recent Fighting," NA, T-315, Records of German Field Commands. Translated and quoted by Jonathan Gumz (2008).

[3] OKW *Tagesbuch.* Nr. Ia/545, 44 J.G.

[4] Hermann Neubacher. *Sonderaufrag Südost 1940-1945. Bericht eines fliegenden Diplomaten.* Goettingen: Muster-Schmidt-Verlag, 1957, p. 18.

[5] Karl Hlinicka. *Das Ende auf dem Balkan 1944/45: Die Militärische Räumung Jugoslawiens durch die Deutsche Wehrmacht.* Goettingen: Musterscheudt, 1970, p. 187.

[6] PA, Büro RAM, Kroatien, 1941-42, 442-449. IV/D/4.

Yugoslavia.¹ The usual point of departure for the few non-native historians who have tackled the subject is the aftermath of the Great War, the circumstances surrounding the creation of Yugoslavia, and the Kingdom's failed quest for a viable political system. The results have been invariably unsatisfactory. The acute anxieties of early-modern Croatian nationalists about the Serbs and the possibilities of co-operation between those two nations that had become clearly distinct from each other many decades before 1918, cannot be understood if the record of the preceding decades and even centuries is overlooked.²

1. *The* Militärgrenze

The political history of modern Croatia starts in 1102, when the Croatian nobility reluctantly entered a personal union with the Crown of Hungary. That was the year to which the notion of Croatia's uninterrupted statehood was subsequently backdated. This nominal continuity was reiterated in 1527, after the Hungarian rout at Mohacs, when the title of the slain King Louis II passed to the Austrian Archduke Ferdinand. The complex legacy of the ensuing four centuries of the Habsburg rule contains the key to the horrors of 1941-5.

Ferdinand and his heirs proceeded to establish a fortified cordon that came to be known as the Military Border *(Militärgrenze)* in Croatia-Slavonia and, eventually, points further east. They did so at a time of Europe's supreme peril. The Ottomans had subjugated Serbia, Bulgaria, and most of Hungary, until that time a major European power. They ruled all of the Balkans except an outer fringe of Hungary and a few fortified Dalmatian cities supported by Venice, and they were on the move.

Much of the land the Turks conquered in the western Balkans was remarkably inaccessible until recent times. It was beyond the rule of ancient and medieval states and was a refuge for rebels and resisters until recent times, "an upland universe of contiguous, thinly-populated areas – historically not unlike the Scottish Highlands, but an order of magnitude larger. Into this almost stateless zone the Ottoman state pushed remorselessly in the 15th and

---

[1] There are but a dozen books and major journal articles in English by non-native authors specifically dealing with the Independent State of Croatia or the Ustaša movement. Half a century after being written, the pioneering *Der kroatische Ustascha-Staat, 1941-1945* by Hungarian diplomat and journalist Ladislaus Hory and German historian Martin Broszat (Stuttgart: Deutsche Verlags-Anstalt, 1964) remains unavailable in English.

[2] For a detailed treatment of the subject see Srdja Trifkovic, *The Krajina Chronicle: A History of the Serbs in Croatia, Slavonia and Dalmatia*. The Lord Byron Foundation, 2010.

16th centuries, establishing its control of towns, valleys and fortresses, and offering new religion or new taxes to the new subjects."[1]

As the Turkish raiding parties moved northward, they pushed ahead of them a devastated no-man's land (*serhat*, in a 17th century painting, below). Final attacks were often preceded by years of raiding. This key feature of Ottoman warfare created utter wastelands on both the Turkish and the Christian side of the borders. After the fall of Serbia (1459) and Bosnia (1463), tens of thousands of mostly Orthodox Christians moved into depopulated lands in central and southwestern Croatia, between the Sava River at the southern edge of the Pannonian plain and the Adriatic, that had been ravaged by Turkish attacks.

The Austrians were desperately short of manpower and wanted to deploy the newcomers in defense against Ottoman incursions. To settle them down and give them a stake in the land they were supposed to defend, Vienna was willing to exempt them from feudal obligations and grant them religious liberty in return for military service. The settlers thus became *Grenzers, graničari*, the guardians of the Habsburgs' vulnerable southeastern border, the backbone of the *antemurale Christianitatis*.[2]

This German overlay on the enfeebled Hungarian-Croatian line of defense, established at the moment of the Ottoman zenith, proved successful: the *Grenzer*-reinforced line held. By 1578 the whole Croatian Border from the Adriatic to the Sava River was administered by the *Hofkriegsrat* in Graz. A grant of royal land, exemption from feudal dues to the Croatian-Hungarian nobility, and the right to practice Orthodoxy in return for life-long and minimally renumerated military service, proved an attractive arrangement for the highlanders:

> Mountain air made a man free. More exactly, it offered a distinctive freedom to the head of an extended family of successful stock-herders. They were free from tax and free to move, free to buy and sell. There were freedoms for the young

---

[1] Michael M. Stenton. *Afterword* to Trifkovic, *The Krajina Chronicle*, p. 193.

[2] This title was given to Croatia by Leo X in 1519, just before the storm peaked. (Two years later the same optimistic pontiff hailed England's Henry VIII as *fidei defensor*.)

men who were fit enough, clever enough, and tough enough to keep moving and trading... free of Ottoman beys and pashas and Croat-Hungarian magnates.[1]

In the earliest Habsburg charter for the Border, issued by Ferdinand I Habsburg on September 5, 1538, the settlers were referred to as "Serbs or Rascians" (*Serviani seu Rasciani*). A century later, in 1630, the Grenzer privileges were codified by Ferdinand II in the *Statuta Valachorum,* while other contemporary Austrian documents refer to *Rasciani sive Serbiani atque Valachi*. In the 1660s the Roman Catholic Bishop of Zagreb, Petar Petretić, used the designation "Vlachs or Rascians, better still Serbians" (*gens Valachorum sive Rascianorum vel potius Servianorum*). He also wrote of "Vlachs, or Rascians, or, correctly speaking, Serbs."[2]

The semantic confusion is unsurprising. While many settlers referred to themselves as *Serbs* from the moment of their arrival – which was reflected in their well-documented reverence for the mythologized saga of Kosovo – by geographic origin they were *Rascians*, as soldiers they were *Grenzer*, and as shepherds they were *Vlachs*, members of an upland economy of wandering pastoralists without a fixed locality.[3]

The ensuing debate on the "Vlach" origins of Croatia's Serbs has been as futile and as tainted by political agendas as that on the "Khazar" origins of East European Jews, or on the Iranian (or Gothic, Avar, Celtic, etc.), origins of the Croats. The notion that Balkan peasantries were uniformly *pre-national* before their "awakening" around 1848, or that "bourgeois nationalism" kicked into action to the beat of the *Marseillaise* to astonish an unsuspecting world, is simply incorrect. It is not a primordialist heresy to state that some identities are far older than the continuous documentary evidence for them. In the Balkans, nationality – a name, its memory, and loyalty to a myth – is plainly older than 1789, let alone 1848.[4] They could not be conjured *ex nihilo* back in

---

[1] Stenton, op. cit. p. 193. He notes that the customs and loyalties of the Vojna Krajina are reminiscent of the Anglo-Scottish Border before 1603, and they changed even more slowly.

[2] *Valachi siue Rasciani uel ut verius dicam Serviani nam ex regno Serviae prodierunt*, in a report to the Crown Council dated April 21, 1662. The language they spoke, according to the bishop, was the 'Serbian language, which is by us here known as Vlach' (*Lingua Serviana quae apud nos Valachica dicitur*).

[3] The word *Vlach* in Bosnia is colloquially used by Muslims for Christians regardless of denomination. In Dalmatia it is still used in coastal towns for the people who live inland, regardless of religion or ethnicity. As late as the 1880's the kajkavian speakers of Varaždin referred to all štokavians, Serbs and Croats, as "Vlachs."

[4] The epic of Kosovo has been preserved for centuries in oral tradition all over the Serb-inhabited lands. Confined to the Croatian elite class was the "Hieronymian legend" according

the early 19th century, just as various modern and postmodrn constructs (Macedonian, Montenegrin, Bosniak...) are yet to prove their staying power.

However used or abused by later generations, the foundations of Serb and Croat identity alike rested on real bonds of shared memory and collective experience rooted in medieval times. But the argument applies to both sides of the Serb-Croat equation. No less than their Catholic neighbors, Orthodox *Grenzers* (18th century gravure, r.) had an extensive religion-supported oral history and a grasp of family origins by the time the modern nation-state system was codified by the Peace of Westphalia. They were *Serbs* long before they emerged from the "Vlach" chrysalis. Croat nationalists have tried to apply the "modernist" thory of nations-as-recent-constructs to the Serbs, while reserving the "primordialist" standard for the Croats. The claim that an ethnically undifferentiated Orthodox mélange, formerly Croat or else Vlach in origin, was  "Serbianized" under the influence of the Serbian Orthodox Church and its autonomous schools in the 19th century, has its mirror image is the Serbian nationalist claim that most modern "Croats" are the offspring of Catholicized Serbs. It unintentionally gives credence to the assertion that religious conversion created both Serbs and Croats.[1] This claim, however dubious, is often treated as axiomatic by all too many Western authors.

That Serbs and Croats shared a land is certain, however, and in the late 16th century Croatia was the focus of a double imperative. The first was military: the Grenzers were needed to fight. The second was political: the continued existence of the Croatian Diet (*Sabor*), and the estates it represented, *natio croatica*, were needed in Vienna to help manage Hungary.

The role and status of this "political nation" harked back to the aforementioned events of AD 1102, when after two centuries of existence as a distinct polity under its own prince (*Ban*) and subsequently king (*rex*, the title

---

to which St. Jerome, a Dalmatian Roman, was a Croat who had developed the *glagolitsa* (Glagolitic), the earliest known Slavic alphabet.

[1] As notably claimed by Eric Hobsbawm who saw "Roman Catholicism (and its by-product, the Latin script) and Orthodoxy (with its by-product, the Cyrillic script)" as the most obvious means of dividing Croats from Serbs, "with whom they share a single language of culture." *Nations and Nationalism since 1780*. Cambridge: CUP, 1990, p. 70.

supposedly granted by the pope to Ban Tomislav in 925) Croatia entered a personal union – *Pacta Conventa* – with the Crown of St. Stephen. Austrian monarchs and Hungarian officials were to curtail the degree and geographic scope of Croatia's self-rule on numerous occasions in subsequent decades and centuries. The legal entity of the Kingdom of Croatia nevertheless survived under the Habsburgs, making it one of the chartered *historic nations* of the Empire. The resulting notion of its *state rights* included the key claim that no inhabitants of Croatia were exempt from the jurisdiction of its political and legal institutions.

Although the Croatian nobility continually struggled to maintain control of the region, the Military Border was kept separate from the political, legal and administrative system of "Civil Croatia." This remnant, *reliquiae reliquiarum*, was gradually reduced to the area north of the Sava River inhabited by a generic Slav population on the northern fringe of the original Croatian heartland, and hence known as "Slavonia." Civil Croatia was barely bigger than the Border and even narrower between Karlstadt and Austria. Its writ was explicitly excluded from the Border. Its nobility nevertheless saw itself as the legal and legitimate heir to the 10th century Kingdom of Tomislav, including all the lands it was supposed to have comprised and jointly referred to as *Regna Dalmatiae, Croatiae et Slavoniae*.

For the upholders of Croatia's state rights the Serbs were unwelcome and inherently hostile aliens for as long as they insisted on retaining their distinct name, their autonomous socio-economic and legal status vis-à-vis Civil Croatia, and their Orthodox faith. An obsessive aristocratic resentment at Grenzer priviliges was passed on from one generation to another, and became "democratized" after the collapse of feudalism in 1848. At the historical root of the Ustaša bloodbath in 1941-5 lay a centuries-old striving of the Croatian elite class to impose legal and religious homogeneity and to re-establish political obedience.[1] A culturally homogeneous nation-state could not be created from the diversity of nationalities without ethnic cleansing, however. The notion of a racially distinct national community with an exclusive claim to its land was the necessary ingredient to make such a project emotionally and culturally legitimate and therefore possible. That notion was eventually articulated in the aftermath of 1848, in the period of rapid modernization, with the Serb as the essential 'other' at its center. The old distaste for *the Vlach* of the Croatian Estates was about to spread down the social scale. This happened fairly rapidly, within a generation, in the second half of the 19th century: "The

---

[1] E.A. Hammel, "Demography and the Origins of the Yugoslav Civil War." *Anthropology Today* 9 (1), February 1993.

explanatory slogan *ancient hatreds* of the south Slavic peoples, so often referred to in the Western media, is but a rhetorical screen obscuring the modernity of conflict based on contested notions of state, nation, national identity and sovereignty."[1]

Throughout its history the Border was neither "Serb" nor "Croat," but it provided the framework for the parallel development of a community that was neither of, nor within, Civil Croatia.[2] Such special status was not enjoyed by another large Serb corpus in the *regna,* in Dalmatia. This community was considerably older than the Military Border to its north.[3] Following an Ottoman interlude from the early 1500's until the late 1600's the area remained under Venetian sovereignty until the abolition of the Republic in 1797. Venice's Slavic subjects in the Dinaric hinterland, both Orthodox and Roman Catholic, were collectively referred to as *Morlacchi.*[4] Like the "Vlach" in Croatia-Hungary, this term was originally used to describe the pre-Slavic nomadic population of early-medieval times, but was later used interchangeably with "Serb." Venetian 18th century documents refer to the "Morlachs or Serbs of Dalmatia" (*Morlacchi o Serviani di Dalmazia*) or else to "Morlachs or Slavs, also called Serbs" (*Morlacchi o Schiavoni, detti anco Serviani*), while the Roman Catholic Archdiocese of Zara referred to the *nazione ilirica, morlacca, schiavona, o sia serviana.*[5] In the late 18th century, in his famous travelogue, Abbe Alberto Fortis noted that the *Morlacchi* sang epic poetry in Serbian, to the sound of *gusle,* about Kosovo and the glories of medieval Serbian kings. Fortis also noted some familiar sounding tensions: "A most perfect discord reigns," he wrote, "between Latin [Roman Catholic]

---

[1] Milica Bakić-Hayden: "Nesting Orientalisms: The Case of the Former Yugoslavia." *Slavic Review*, Vol. 54, No. 4 (Winter, 1995), p. 918.

[2] In 1627 the Warasdiner Grenzer asserted that they "would rather be hacked to pieces than separated from their officers and made subjects of the Croatian nobility." Gunther E. Rothenberg, *The Military Border in Croatia 1740-1881.* Chicago-London: University of Chicago Press, 1966, p. 10.

[3] Cf. e.g. Frankish chronologist Einhard's earliest specific reference to the Serbs in the *Royal Frankish Annals* (*Annales qui dicuntur Einhardi*) in 829 AD; Byzantine Emperor Constantine Porphyrogenitus' "On the Serbs and the lands in which they live" in *De Administrando Imperio* (Dumbarton Oaks Texts, 2009), c. 950 AD. The latter work, of uncertain accuracy, also provided an early account on the Croatian migration from "north of the Hungarian lands" to the northern Adriatic, and of their victory over the Avars that made their settlement permanent.

[4] See Larry Wolff. *Venice and the Slavs: The Discovery of Dalmatia in the Age of Enlightenment.* Stanford, California: Stanford University Press, 2001. The territorial militia composed of the Morlacchi was known as the *Craina* (p. 133)

[5] Bishop Nikodim Milaš. *Documenta spectantia historiam Dalmatiae et Istriae a XV usgue ad XIX saeculum.* Zara 1894, pp. 399, 401 and 422.

and Greek [Orthodox] communion, which their respective priests fail not to foment, and tell a thousand little scandalous stories of each other."[1]

All previous Serb migrations were dwarfed by the exodus from southern Serbia, Kosovo and northern Macedonia in 1690, led by Patriarch Arsenije III Čarnojević. Louis XIV threatened the Habsburgs on the Rhine and caused the Austrians to withdraw from the Balkans the forces which had taken Belgrade in 1688. Up to 80,000 Serbs – Austrian volunteers, their family members, and other civilians – withdrew from southern Serbian lands with the Austrian army. Emperor Leopold I (r. 1658-1707) called on them to settle in the Habsburg realm and granted them his first Charter on Privileges on August 21, 1690, with others following in 1691 and 1695. He pledged to take the Serbs "into Royal protection" and recognized their status as a separate political entity (*corpus separatum*), under the authority of the Serbian Orthodox Church. These grants explicitly guaranteed their right to "a free exercise of rite and religion, with no fear, danger, or harm to body or property."

The newcomers regarded the imperial pledge as essential. After the loss of statehood, the Church was the only national institution of the Serbs and the guardian of their collective memories. Religion became central to their identity. The Serbs could not claim to be a "historic nation" of the Empire on the basis of any pre-Habsburg symbol of sovereignty or some ancient constitutional document. The privileges nevertheless enabled them to claim an autonomous status. Unlike other "non-historic nations" of the Empire such as Slovaks, Vallachians or Slovenes, the Serbs were a recognized corporate body with an established legal relationship with the Crown. The reason of state which guided Austria (and at times Venice) in granting such privileges did not shape a full and final religious settlement, however. Toleration conceded in Protestant Europe tended to become permanent. In Catholic Europe it did not gel until after Napoleon.

Faced with a fresh influx of these *schismatics* after 1699, the nobility and clergy of Civil Croatia renewed their insistence on reasserting the feudal privileges of the former and the religious monopoly of the latter. They tried to exercise a double pressure on the *Grenzer:* to turn them into serfs subject to the Croatian-Hungarian nobility, and to force them to accept the authority of the Roman Catholic hierarchy. To that end the *Sabor* passed a special law as

---

[1] *Viaggio in Dalmazia* (1774) was re-published in English as *Travels Into Dalmatia,* New York: Cosimo Classics, 2007. A true man of the Enlightenment, Fortis regarded the superior Italian civilization of Venice as a corrupting influence on the primitive and natural customs and culture of the *Morlacchi* – the noble savages of the Eastern Adriatic.

early as 1608 decreeing that only Roman Catholics could live and enjoy full rights in Croatia.

The hostility gelled over the ensuing century. It acquired sinister overtones in the immediate aftermath of the Great Serb Migration. The overseer of the Zagreb diocesan landholdings, Ambroz Kuzmić, in a report of November 13, 1700, suggested that the "Vlachs" should be "slaughtered, rather than allowed to settle down," as they were "more of a nuisance to the noble state illumined by the Emperor than an advantage... neither the Emperor's radiance nor the noble state will ever be at peace with them."[1] This was the first known proposal for a final solution of the "Serb problem" in Croatia. It was by no means the last.

The number of people eventually known as "Serbs" and "Croats" in the Military Border remains a matter of dispute. In 1785 and in 1797, Austrian census takers counted some 380,000 Orthodox inhabitants in the Border. They and their Roman Catholic neighbors shared some traits of a common *Grenzer* identity – resistance to feudalization and pride in special status – but they lived in separate communites. They shared a common freedom from serfdom and a common history of military accomplishment but they remained Orthodox or Catholic, and thus divided confesionally and culturally. It has been said that the identities of latter-day Serbs and Croats had been "prenational" until the early 1800's; but the speed and irreversibility with which they became identified with their distinct national communities indicates that those identities had been well developed, and important, long before the fall of the Bastille.[2] Throughout the Border (map, above) there had existed a division along confessional lines in a region where local churches and clerics were the backbone of the village society; but what may have been a key cause of differentiation in the early-modern era became no more than its most visible manifestation in the 19th century. The Serbs undoubtedly "found their Orthodoxy to be a major means of maintaining village-level cohesion."[3] It was not the only means, however, and there were few diversified economic interest groups or social classes in the Border that could provide an alternative basis for integration and self-identification. Isolated by geography and

---

[1] *[N]a veksu szu skodu plemenitomu orszagu u czeszarovoi szvetloszti nego haszan... niti czeszarova szvetloszt niti plemeniti orszag snimi nigdar ne bude ztalan niti miran.* Quoted in Vojin S. Dabić, *Banska Krajina, 1688-1751.* Belgrade-Zagreb, 1984, p. 27.

[2] For an example of the opposite, "modernist" view, see Patrick J. Geary, *The Myth of Nations: The Medieval Origins of Europe.* Princeton: Princeton University Press, 2002.

[3] Cf. Lohr Miller's review of Karl Miller: *Freier Bauer und Soldat,* published on Habsburg.com in April 1998.

deliberately kept apart from Civil Croatia by the military administration, the Grenzers of both confessions had acquired recognizably "modern" forms of national consciousness not later than 1848.

The formal end of pressure on the Orthodox was ended in the midst of revolutionary turmoil, when the Crown issued, on March 4, 1849, the Decree on Religious Tolerance, to help secure the loyalty of its Serb subjects. The "Vlachs" and "Morlacchi" disappeared from the anthropological equation, leaving Serbs and Croats. As late as the 1840's, Slovak ethnographer Pavel Jozef Šafárik (1795-1861) treated 391,000 Slavs of Dalmatia as Serbs, regardless of religious affiliation.[1] A generation later such a conflation was impossible. By the late-19th century, Austrian census figures reflected emerging, or finally clarified, ethnic divisions. Pre-modern religious affiliation, early-modern culture and newly-codified language combined to produce modern ethnic identity. The tensions and rivalries had ceased to be ostensibly religious and became openly nationalist.

2. The Illyrians

In the first half of the 19th century the remnants of Croatia's political integrity were threatened by the centralist tendencies of the Hungarian political class. It regarded Croatia as a semi-autonomous province of the Crown of St. Stephen which should accept Hungarian as the official language of the Kingdom. With the rise of Jacobin nationalism in Hungary, starting at fin de siècle and fully mature by 1848, the idea of a unitary Hungarian state from the Carpathians to the Adriatic – inhabited by people whose designations and claimed identities might differ, but all of whom belonged to a Hungarian political nation – became the *leit-motif* in Hungarian politics. It did not diminish after the bloody suppression of the Hungarian revolution in 1849.

In a little under two decades preceding 1848, reaction to Hungarian integralism fostered the rise of the *Illyrian* idea in Croatia. This was a quaint misnomer, coined in the early-modern fashion of giving classical names to contemporary peoples, for the idea of South Slav unity based on the claim of common ethno-racial origins and language.

The notion that Croats belonged to the wider Slavic family of nations was not new, as evidenced by the frequent interchangeable use of *Slovin* and *slovinski* for "Croat" and "Croatian" since early modern times. The idea of Slav unity, from which a distinct Croat nation would derive political and

---

[1] *Slovanský národopis* ("Slavic Ethnology") Prague, 1842. It contains basic data on individual Slavic nations, settlements, languages, ethnic borders, and a map of Slavic *national units*.

cultural support, was developed in the late 17th century by Juraj Križanić, a Russophile Roman Catholic priest. It was elaborated, albeit in a naïve and eccentric form, by Paul Ritter Vitezović a generation later. The novelty of the Illyrian Movement was the notion, by that time well established in the German-speaking *Mitteleuropa*, that language and ancestry define nationhood. Since most Europeans derived that ancestry from one of the three "families" – the Germanic, Romanic, or Slavic – the Croats needed to find their rightful place and plan their future accordingly.

Appealing to a narrow segment of Croatia's educated elite, Illyrism was born out of the perception that the development of a Croat identity needed a broader context in order to assert itself and to withstand the onslaught of stronger, more dynamic and better established nationalisms, Hungarian to the north, Italian to the west, and (less acutely) German to the northwest. The question of language topped the agenda. Resistance to Hungarian could not be based on the defense of Latin, used at the Sabor until 1848. The upholders of the Illyrian idea decided to adopt, in the 1830's, the štokavian (*štokavski*) dialect, already used by many Croats at that time but codified on the basis of the pioneering work of Serbia's language reformer Vuk Stefanović Karadžić. Two distinctly Croat dialects, kajkavian (*kajkavski*), predominant in Zagreb and the Zagorje region of northwestern Croatia, and čakavian (*čakavski*), mainly spoken along the Adriatic coast, were gradually reduced to colloquial regional use.

The Illyrian project engendered the notion of linguistic and cultural unity of South Slavs with proto-Yugoslav political overtones, as manifested by the work of Croatian language reformer Ljudevit Gaj (1809-1872, above). Gaj's choice of the štokavian and his work on the corresponding Latin alphabet was based on a ready-made model. "We do not presume to claim that it is not Serbian but Illyrian language," he wrote. "To the contrary, we are proud and thankful to God that we Croats with our brother Serbs now share one literary language." He expected that the Illyrian designation would eventually result in the convergence of Serbs, Croats and Slovenes under one neutral name and one štokavian standard. He also hoped that linguistic and cultural cement would foster greater political unity, not necessarily within the Habsburg framewok, which he expected would be aided by Russia.

The Roman Catholic Bishop of Djakovo in eastern Slavonia, Josip Juraj Strossmayer (below), was the leading mid-century chamption of the Illyrian idea. He did not go as far as Gaj. When he declared in 1849 that he hoped to bring together all "Yugoslavs," he had in mind cultural and linguistic, rather than political unity. On the latter he assumed that Zagreb would give the tone to a future process of South Slav integration inside the Habsburg monarchy.[1] Getting Croatia-Slavonia and Dalmatia into a single constitutional entity was to be an important step in his attempt to reconcile cultural Illyrianism and political Croatianism. That goal, however, proved unattainable after the *Ausgleich*. Dualism made constitutional reform difficult in theory and impossible in practice.

Strossmayer subscribed to political views firmly rooted in the tradition of state rights. His belief in the linguistic and therefore cultural unity of Serbs and Croats were expressed through the People's Party (*Narodna stranka*), the leading political force in Croatia until it lost support under the long viceroyal tenure of Karoly Khuen-Hedervary. After the Austrian-Hungarian occupation of Bosnia-Herzegovina in 1878, the political side of the equation was no longer tenable. The title over Bosnia was the circle that could not be squared either by Strossmayer the upholder of Croatia's historic rights or by Srossmayer the promoter of "Yugoslav" unity. In the end, politically, he was a Croat first and foremost. Interestingly, even in his later years his pan-Slav spiritual sentiment occasionally veered into syncretism hardly compatible with the vocation of a prince of the Church of Rome.[2]

---

[1] "We Croats can truly say that in this small group of Slavic brothers we represent the 'Tuscan element'," Strossmayer wrote to William Gladstone "We were able in a short period of time to build the institutions which give us the right to lead others toward cultural advances and great ideas." (Quoted by R.W. Seton Watson: *Die sudslavishe Frage im Habsburger Reiche*, Berlin 1913.) Strossmayer shared with Gladstone a negative view of Islam and the Ottomans. The Turks in Europe were a gangrene, Strossmayer held, which should be cut out from the body.

[2] On 27 July 1888, during the celebration of the 900th anniversary of Russia's Christianization, Strossmayer sent a telegram to the rector of St. Vladimir University in Kiev that caused an international sensation. It was remarkable for an Austrian subject and a Catholic bishop to say,

Both Serbs and Slovenes stayed aloof from the lure of Illyrianism, however. From Belgrade or Ljubljana it appeared too Zagrebian in spirit if not intent, and too parochial in its political preoccupations. In Belgrade, Ilija Garašanin's *Načertanije* ("Draft," 1844) outlined a long-term program of unification of Serbs into a single state. The document, written as a private brief for Prince Aleksandar Karadjordjević, was not published until 1906; but both then and at the time of its writing the concept had clarity and was readily understood. This was hardly the case with an amorphous Croatocentric Yugoslavism advocated by a Russophile Roman Catholic bishop with a German name.[1] In Ljubljana, Slovenian revivalists were busy codifying a linguistic standard of their own: the first novel in modern Slovene was published as late as 1866. This language could have been conceivably harmonized with the *kajkavian* dialect of Croatia's Zagorje, but not at all with the *štokavian* standard promoted under an anachronistic, Illyrian label.

Far from leading to a long-term Serbo-centric amalgamation feared by some critics of Gaj's reforms,[2] the adoption of *štokavian* had the opposite effect. In the second half of the 19th century the Illyrian heritage failed to bring the South Slavs together, but it provided the Croats with the linguistic base for their very own national integration. It was well-nigh unattainable for as long as coastal čakavians, Dinaric štokavians and Zagorje kajkavians could barely understand each other, let alone share a common sense of destiny. It also enabled the nationalist intelligentsia, in the fullness of time, to claim the heritage of distinctly non-Croat traditions (including self-avowedly Serbian-speaking Dubrovnik writers), and accordingly to stake bold territorial and ethnic claims based on the spread of the "Croatian" language.[3]

The category *Croat* was seldom used in many parts of today's Croatia, let alone in Bosnia-Herzegovina, until after the Illyrian Awakening. The Hungarian 1840 census listed 504,000 Serbs in Croatia-Slavonia and a total of 1.6 million "Serbs of both Orthodox and Roman Catholic faith" and 1.3 million Croats, in the Monarchy as a whole. Mid-19th century Austrian

---

inter alia, "God bless Russia and give it, through living faith, exemplary life, the help from above and Christian heroism, with all its other duties, that greatest of all worldly duties, destined by God's providence to be fulfilled with fortune, salvation and triumph." Later that year, in Bjelovar, he was loudly rebuffed for this gesture by Emperor Francis Joseph.

[1] Garašanin himself evolved toward Yugoslavism in the 1860's when he established contact with Strossmayer and revised his earlier aversion to a common state with the Croats.

[2] E.g. Count Janko Drašković, the author of the 1832 "Dissertation," arguably the first attempt at devising a Croat national program.

[3] On the Dubrovnik (Ragusan) tradition, language and identity see Count Louis Voinovitch. *Dalmatia and the Yugoslav Movement.* London: George Allen & Unwin, 1920.

sources also did not register any Croats in Dalmatia, which was listed as 96.18 percent Serb.[1] Within a generation, however, the fruits of the Illyrian linguistic *legerdemain* became visible in the rising number of self-declared Croat-speakerss in the Habsburg censuses between 1880 and 1910.[2]

The adoption of the štokavian form written in Latin script as the Croat linguistic standard was a formula to claim that all Roman Catholic Slavs using that standard and variously known by their regional affiliation as *Bunjevci, Slavonci, Dalmatinci*, etc, were all in fact Croats. The process was aided by the Austrian authorities, which in 1843 sought to suppress the use of the term "Illyrian" as a potentially subversive euphemism for centrifugal South Slavdom. The "Croat" designation readily stepped into the vacuum, and eventually became the cornerstone of a nascent "imagined community."

The process was still far from complete when the revolution of 1848 shook the Habsburg Empire. During the revolution the provincial authorities in Zagreb, supported by Vienna, propagated the Serb-Croat commonalities and common interests. Reversing earlier negative attitude to "Illyrism" was a small price to pay for the willingness of both Serbs and Croats to fight for the Austrian Crown under Ban Josip Jelačić (l.). One notable decision he made in 1848 was to allow the use of Cyrillic script in elementary schools in Croatia and Slavonia. This was a major step towards the recognition not only of the Serbs' religious rights but also of their cultural, and therefore national, distinctiveness.

In the aftermath of the revolution, however, the idea of the "political" Croatian people – a carbon copy of the detested Hungarian claim – gained prominence in Croatian politics. Whereas in feudal society only the gentry, often tenuously "Croat" by blood, made up the "political" people, after 1848 all inhabitants of Triune Croatia (i.e. Croatia, Slavonia and Dalmatia), irrespective of their socioeconomic status or self-perceived national identity, were supposed to constitute the Croatian "political nation." No one inside the territory claimed for Croatia was to belong to any other political nation: modernization demanded cultural uniformity and political homogenization.

---

[1] Joseph Hain, *Handbuch der Statistik des österreichischen Kaiserstaats*, Vienna 1852-3.
[2] Census-takers used the criterion of *Umgangsprache*, the "language of daily use," in Austria, and mother tongue, *Muttersprache*, in Hungary.

In a well-established state this is not a problematic doctrine; inside a multiconfessional, ethnically complex territory of potential nation-states, it is a call to controversy. Young Croatian nationalism in the 1850's was rapidly becoming both democratic and assimilationist. This process matured at the end of the absolutist regime of Alexander von Bach and the rise of liberal institutions in the Monarchy, following the military defeats of 1859. The Serbs in Croatia subsequently were given civic rights, but their right to national individuality continued to be challenged.

Hungarian resistance to centralism, after the setback of 1849, was crowned almost two decades later with the Compromise (*Ausgleich*) of 1867 which created a confederalized *Austria-Hungary*. Within the Dual Monarchy Hungary was effectively left to deal with its multiethnic, multilingual plurality of non-Hungarian subjects of the Crown of St. Stephen as it deemed fit. The ensuing Croatian-Hungarian "Agreement" (*Nagodba*) of 1868 governed Croatia's political status as a province of Hungary for half a century until the end of the First World War. It recognized Croatia-Slavonia as a distinct political unit with its legislative *Sabor,* but it also confirmed its subordination to Hungary. Key elements of statehood, including most budgetary issues as well as foreign and defense policy, remained in Pest and Vienna.

The Agreement was seen as a defeat by most supporters of Croatian self-rule. For the upholders of the principle of state rights it contained a welcome sop, however. Its Article 59 asserted that "the Kingdoms of Croatia and Slavonia are made up of one single political nation." Constitutionally, it could be argued, *there were no Serbs in Croatia*: under Article 59 they formed an integral part of the Croatian political nation. Accordingly, in later years in official statistics the Serbs were not identified by their national name but according to their religious confession ("Greco-Easterners") and the Serbian Orthodox Church in Croatia was described as Greco-Eastern or "Greco-non-Uniate" (*grčko-nesjedinjena crkva*), which implied its provisional status.

These developments coincided with the demilitarization (1871) and final abolition (1881) of the Military Border, which after the occupation of Bosnia-Herzegovina by Austria-Hungary in 1878 no longer served any military purpose. Its integration into Croatia-Slavonia led to a significant increase in the number of Serbs in the expanded *Banovina.* The Border's abolition presented the Serbs with the task of articulating their political and cultural interests and aspirations as a distinct group. Their old goal of seeking national recognition, religious equality and educational autonomy soon faced new challeges. The main challenge – to their very name and identity – was not to come from Vienna or Budapest, however, but from Zagreb.

3. Starčević

The notion of Croatia's state rights inspired a radical form of Croatian nationalist ideology which was to veer far from the legalistic roots of the original doctrine. That ideology was articulated by publicist and political activist Ante Starčević (1823-1896). His nationalism did not recognize the existence of any distinct nations in the western Balkans. They were all Croats, including not only Slovenes and Bosnian Muslims, but also – primarily in fact – those people "mistakenly called *Serbs*" who should come to their senses and return to the Croat fold; while those who refused to do so were fit for extermination.

Starčević adopted for his own purposes the Hungarian claim, launched at the end of the 18th century, that domicile in a particular polity rather than national culture defined nationhood and that on the soil of Hungary there existed only one "political" people. Starčević and his heirs likewise proclaimed that in Croatia there was only one "state-bearing," constitutive nation: the Croatian nation. His views were soon expressed in the political arena. The *Party of Rights* was founded in 1861 by Starčević and his leading follower Eugen Kvaternik with the slogan *Neither Vienna nor Pest, but a free and self-governing Croatia*.

The Party of Rights demanded sovereign statehood and territorial expansion to the Drina River. It asserted *sui generis* Croatianism and adamantly rejected Yugoslavism and any other from of "Slavism." It imagined Croatia as a western civilizational and racial bulwark against a theatening, barbarian east (yet claimed Bosnian Muslims as "pure Croats" in genetic terms). All along, its defining trait was an extreme antagonism, determinist, racist, and ultimately exterminationist, towards the Serbs.

Starčević's animus, unprecedented in sentiment, language and intent, harked back to "problem" of the Serbs' special status. They were successful in preserving their name, privileges, and religion. By the time the Military Border was abolished, they accounted for over a quarter of the population of today's Croatia and constituted a majority in over a third of its territory. In the final decades of the 19th century the Serbs were making inroads into the professions and commerce, competing with the young Croat bourgeoisie. If their presence and separate status had been a permanent irritant to the Croatian-Hungarian feudal nobility and clergy in the 17th and 18th centuries, it was an even more acute thorn in the side of 19th century nationalists who denied that those people were *Serbs* in the first place.

Starčević (below) argued that the essence of Croatian nationhood was woven into the totality of the nation's historical experience. The *Ancient Rights,* denuded of context and nuance, were to be the political foundation. The language, as restructured by the Illyrians and now called *Croatian*, was to provide the cultural and emotional identity. Starčević treated the resulting *Nation* as a distinct, homogenous, organically structured entity. Its members had to see themselves as members of the corporate entity. Any disagreement with his model was either an expression of "deformity" caused by the long period of foreign rule, or else treason. His messianic zeal led him to claim that only the Almighty was fit to judge his actions: "God and the Croats" (*Bog i Hrvati*), his slogan from the 1860's, has found resonance ever since.

Starčević saw the Serbs as the main obstacle to the fulfilment of his vision, and tried to resolve it by asserting that the Serbs did not exist: they were "a geographic term," not a people.[1] By their very nature and even by name (*Serb-Servus-Slavus*, "Slavo-Serbs"), he wrote, they were a "breed" of slaves, a mongrel melange of Vlach and Gypsy blood predestined for criminality or slavery and unworthy of human designation.

Starčević used similar language to describe the Jews: "They are the breed, but for a few, without any morality and without a homeland, the breed of which every member strives for his personal gain, or to the gain of his kin. To allow the Jews to participate in public life is dangerous: throw a speck of mud into a glass of crystal-clear water, and all of it will be polluted." He ranked the Serbs even lower, however: "The Jews are less harmful than the Slavoserbs. For the Jews care for themselves and their people ... but the Slavoserbs are always for the evil."[2]

To Starčević, all Muslims of Bosnia-Herzegovina – including those who lived outside the confines of "Turkish Croatia" supposedly belonging to the Crown of Tomislav – were racially "the purest of all Croats" and culturally untainted by western decadence. Even their conversion to Islam was, to

---

[1] Cf. Ferdo Šišić, "O stogodišnjici Ilirskog pokreta." *Ljetopis Jugoslavenske akademije*, Zagreb, Vol. 49 (1936).

[2] For a detailed study of Starčević and his impact see Mirjana Gross, *Izvorno pravaštvo – ideologija, agitacija, pokret.* Zagreb: Golden marketing, 2000.

Starčević, the commendable proof of their aristocratic preference for lordship over faith and their determination to maintain the purity of their blood.[1]

Starčević's anthropological claims were patently ridiculous (e.g. that the Serbs had no concept of land ownership and were therefore devoid of "human dignity, love for the home and law" which it engenders), yet his language was painfully "modern" in its rhetorical flair and its implications:

> There are three levels of perfection: that of the animal, that of comprehension, and that of reason. Slavo-Serbs have not quite reached the first level, and cannot rise above it. They have no conscience, they cannot read as humans, they are not teachable... Some call a magnitude of Croatia's populace 'Serbs,' and a piece of Croat land 'Serbia,' all based on a name they don't understand.[2]

Starčević's antisemitism was perhaps unremarkable by Central European standards of the time, but the word *genocide* was over seven decades from being invented when he declared the Serbs fit for extermination: "Give this beast breed a little bread, then strike it with an axe and skin it to the bone," was his final dictum.[3] Such language was a distinct novelty in the discourse of the 19th century Europe. His stunning dehumanization of the "Slavo-Serb," his colorfully expressed preference for the genocidal final solution, heralded a new era, that of the *Völkischer Beobachter*.[4] His *Herrenvolk*-Croatism, Serbophobia and Slavophobia, his bizarre racial and historical assertions, make a reader cringe in embarrassment and repugnance. Shallow, chaotic often repetitive, filled with non-sequiturs, the writings of Ante Starčević are the ramblings of a provincial auto-didact with a cause. *Mein Kampf* comes to mind, for style and emotion rather than substance. Devoid of coherent methodology, they nevertheless resonated even before the echoes of social Darwinism and the later notion of *Rassenkampf* reached Zagreb. As Croatian ethnographer Vladimir Dvorniković remarked in 1939, "Never before had a

---

[1] Starčević had a soft spot for Islam as such and for the Ottoman legacy in particular, in contrast to the *Antemurale* tradition of the upper crust.

[2] Ante Starčević, *Razgovori*. Djela, Vol 3. Zagreb 1894, p. 213.

[3] Starčević's opus had earned him the title of "the Father of the Nation" among his followers. This designation has been approvingly revived: there is hardly a town, in today's Croatia, without a street or an institution named after him. His portrait was depicted on the obverse of the Croatian 1000 *kuna* banknote, issued by Tudjman's government in 1993.

[4] The fact that Starčević's mother Milica Bogdan was an Orthodox and his father of Serb origin from Herzegovina adds an interesting Weiningerian dimension to his personality. Likewise, all over central-eastern Europe, most ardent antisemites often had a significant admixture of Jewish blood in their veins.

tribal, atavistic urge entered with such irrational force into the world of political formulas and programs as it did with Starčević's all-Croatness."[1]

There is no inherent reason why a civic Croatian nation-state should not have been able to include Serbs as citizens. Starčević made it so. He was the father of distinctly Croatian integralism which defined itself by treating the Serbs as either traitors or aliens. The fact that Illyrians and Slavophiles were the first to think in ethno-linguistic and "racial" terms is irrelevant: The Czechs had their own, more recently based and more solidly grounded "state rights" tradition, as well as their own, enormously influential pan-Slavs and Slavophile integralists. Nevertheless, the lively hothouse of diverse ideas and theories that was Prague in the mid-1800's did not produce a Czech Starčević who would seek to dehumanize Sudeten Germans, say, let alone call for their extermination. On the other hand, "striking the Slavoserb beast with an axe" was a sentiment that harked back to Ambroz Kuzmić in the year 1700.

Starčević was the spiritual father of the Ustaša movement by providing it with an ethno-historical narrative and with a radical answer to the unsettled question of Croatian national identity.[2] Seven decades before Pavelić's *Ustaša Principles*, Starčević had established nine key tenets of that narative:

1. The assertion of ethno-cultural, linguistic and spiritual uniqueness of the Croat nation, with some uncertainty regarding its supposed racial makeup but with a strong emphasis on its authenticity and distinctiveness vis-à-vis other nations – above all Serbs – and other ethno-lingustic groups (Slavs);

2. The novel demand for the establishment of a fully sovereign Croatian nation-state, and the elevation of the ideal of statehood to the cult status;

3. Extravagant territorial claims for that state based on its alleged historical and ethnic rights, starting with the mythologized "right by conquest" of the early-medieval Croatian heartland 14 centuries ago;

4. Specific claim to Bosnia-Herzegovina, and the related assertion that Bosniak Muslims are pure Croat by blood, and are (or ought to be) "Croats of Islamic faith" by sentiment;

---

[1] Vladimir Dvorniković. *Karakterologija Jugoslavena*. Beograd: Gregorić, 1939, p. 894.

[2] Some Croat historians have tried to absolve Starčević of this charge by claiming that he "cannot be held accountable for the racist policies of the NDH, policies that would have been anathema to a man who shared the pacifist aversion to political violence common to most Croatian political leaders." (Nevenko Bartulin. "The ideology of nation and race: the Croatian Ustasha regime and its policies toward minorities in the independent state of Croatia, 1941-1945." PhD Thesis: University of New South Wales, School of History, November 2006). Ideas have consequences, however. Whether Starčević would have approved of the Ustaša state's specific policies is both impossible to know and irrelevant. Whether his ideas have contributed to the articulation and execution of such policies is not.

5. The insistence that only Croats by blood, born into the organic entity that is the Croat nation, and proudly conscious of their birthright, are the heirs to the state rights of Croatia and thus its sole lawful citizens;

6. The demonization and dehumanization of *the Serb* as the ultimate "other," the "breed of impure blood," the defining counter-model to the Croat and an existential threat to his survival and self-realization[1];

7. The advocacy of either assimilation of "Orthodox Croats" or elimination of racially inferior and morally depraved Serbs ("with an axe"!) as the final solution to the problem of Croatia's ethno-religious heterogeneity;

8. The adoption of anti-Semitic slogans and imagery;

9. The claim that radical acts committed in pursuit of these objectives are not to be judged by any conventional moral standard.

Pushing his *Untermensch* rhetoric about the Serbs aside for the moment, Starčević's immediate heirs preferred to adopt the assimilationist position that "in Croatia, whatever religion one wants to be, whatever name one calls himself, everyone is born a Croat... regardless of calling himself a member of another nation."[2] Vjekoslav Klaić, the foremost *fin-de-siècle* nationalist historian, held that "the true national name" for all people between Istria and Bulgaria was *Croat*, while *Serb* was to him but a "tribal name": every Serb is a Croat, Klaić wrote, but a Croat is not a Serb.[3] In the same vein, Frano Supilo, a leading *Pravaš* who later became a proponent of Yugoslav unity,[4] argued in the 1890's that "every honest Croat must be quite clear about the so-called Serbian question": admittedly there *are* Serbs, "but in our lands there are no Serbs.[5] Those in Croatia-Slavonia and Dalmatia who call

---

[1] A member of Pavelić's inner circle, *Doglavnik* Miško Račan, remarked in 1944 that whenever citizens questioned the Ustaša treatment of Serbs, he would respond by quoting Starčević's views about them. "Only 'Starčevićism', Pavelić himself maintained, 'is the bearer of Croatdom...Starčevićism is a racial matter, only it carries Croatdom and the state idea'." Bartulin, op. cit. p. 342.

[2] Mihovil Pavlinović: *Misao hrvatska i misao srbska u Dalmaciji, od godine 1848 do godine 1882*. Zadar, 1882.

[3] Vjekoslav Klaić: "Hrvati i Srbi." *Vienac*, 1893, ch. 2, p. 25.

[4] Such volte-face was untentionally implicit in Starčević's views. He argued that all people living west of Bulgaria and southeast of the Alps were Croats, that is, of one common stock.

[5] Starčević's followers also advanced extravagant territorial claimes. The Party of Rights paper *Hervatska* thus asserted (No. 6 of 1871) that "the lands to which Croatia's state rights apply, in terms of history and nationality, extend from Germany to Macedonia, from the Danube to the sea, and by their separate provincial names they are: Southern Styria, Carinthia, Carniola, Gorizia, Istria, Croatia, Slavonia, Krajina, Dalmatia, Upper Albania, Montenegro, Hercegovina, Bosnia, Rascia, Serbia – have one true name – the State of Croatia. These lands extend over four thousand square miles and their inhabitants number up to eight million people."

themselves Serbs, are not Serbs but Orthodox Croats."[1] Starčević's legacy ensured that, after the *Ausgleich* of 1867 and the *Nagodba* of 1868, the Serbs in Croatia-Slavonia would be reluctant to support the Croats in resisting Hungarian domination.

One of Starčević's successors distilled his vehement anti-Serbism into the determining feature of "Croatness" itself. This was the leader of the Pure Party of Rights (*Čista stranka prava*, ČSP), Josip Frank (r.), who had split from the Rightist mainstream shortly after Starčević's death. Memorably described by Croatian writer August Šenoa as "that infamous political louse,"[2] Frank was a German-speaking Jewish convert to Roman Catholicism who became a fully-fledged Croat in his adulthood. Unlike Starčević, who was a confused visionary antipathetic to the Habsburgs, Frank was an opportunist and an avid Austrophile. He tied his brand of chauvinism to the black-and-yellow mast of Habsburg loyalism and clericalism. In  contrast to Starčević, who shied away from direct action, Frank's *Pure Party of Rights* was an instigator of periodic anti-Serb riots, in 1895, again in 1899, and most notably in 1902. To Frank and his followers, the Serbs – *all* Serbs, including those east of the Drina – were "a rabble of Cincars, Gypsies, Albanians and Vlachs" of allegedly Semitic origin. An unbridgeable gap separated them from Croats. Any notion of their unity, under whatever name, was impossible *ab initio*.

Frank's position on the Serb question made the Party of Pure Rights a marginal force in the early 1900's. In the first decade of the new century it was left with only one partner. It was the Croatian People's Peasant Party (HPSS) of Stjepan Radić – state-rights Croat, agrarian, anti-capitalist, and anti-Semitic, culturally Slavophile and Germanophobic, but unyielding on the issue of the Croat "political nation." Their agreement on joint political action, drafted by Radić in August 1909, stated that both parties were imbued with Croatian state rights "and will never depart from it even for the sake of the

---

[1] *Crvena Hrvatska* (Dubrovnik), V, br. 26, 29. V. 1895.

[2] Miroslav Krleža, ed. "FRANK, Josip." *Enciklopedija Jugoslavije*. Vol. III (1st ed.). Zagreb: Leksikografski zavod FNRJ, 1958, p. 387.

necessary and desirable popular accord with *that portion of our people who for various reasons call themselves Serbs.*"[1]

The term "Frankist" (*Frankovac*) came to denote a mood and an outlook, rather than political affiliation. It was the mood of virulent lower-middle-class Serbophobia characteristic of the shopkeepers of Zagreb's Vlaška Street and provincial students at the Law School, often subsidized village boys from the poor Dinaric regions of Lika and western Herzegovina. Their numbers were modest but their zeal knew no bounds.[2] The resulting atmosphere was summed up by a Croat *Rightist* historian in the aftermath of a wave of anti-Hungarian and parallel anti-Serb riots that accompanied the visit of Emperor Francis Joseph to Zagreb in 1895: "Nowhere in Europe is there more animosity between peoples who speak different tongues than in this country between those who speak the same language."[3]

4. The Serb Question

Starčević died only months after those lines were written. The continuity of his life's work was assured, however. It exacerbated the dilemma of the Serbs in Croatia through the centuries, which may be reduced to the question "Who will grant us our rights in return for our loyalty?" From the time of Emperor Leopold I until the abolition of the Military Border the essence of the question had not changed. It reemerged in a stark form after Ban Ivan Mažuranić closed Serb Orthodox schools. He was a secularist who wanted to centralize education in state hands, rather than an anti-Serb, but many Serbs regarded the Croat-controlled educational system with a centralized curriculum as an inherently assimilationist device.[4]

In the early 1880's, as further old Grenzer privileges were eroded, the answer to the Serb dilemma of rights-for-loyalty seemed clear. The former was offered by Croatia's new Ban, Karoly Khuen-Hedervary. This Hungarian

---

[1] Bogdan Krizman, *Korespondencija Stjepana Radića, 1885-1918* (Zagreb, 1972), vol. I, p. 471 (emphasis in the original). Also in 1909, Radić wrote that "from the ethnic and linguistic point of view, all Slavs are in reality one people and belong to one nationality." Croats were a branch of the Slav trunk, but no Serbs in Croatia were to belong to any other branch.

[2] Their slogan in anti-Serb demonstrations in Zagreb in 1902 reflected the mindset: *Udri, udri in der štat, Slavo-Srbom štrik za vrat!* (loosely, "Go, go, gung-ho, hang the Serb by the neck!")

[3] Pero Gavranić, *Politička povjest hrvatskog naroda od prvog početka do danas*. Zagreb 1895, pp. 325-326.

[4] One of the most important figures in Croatia's cultural life in the mid-19th century, Mažuranić was the poet of a famous epic (*Smrt Smail age Čengića*, 1845) and an accomplished linguist, as well as the first Ban to have been born a commoner.

magnate of Slavonian stock arrived in Zagreb from Budapest in 1883 determined to enhance Croatia's integration into the political and economic structure of Hungary. He developed a strategy in line with the Habsburg practice of distributing or withholding rewards and privileges among the competing national groups and provinces. The Serbs, with a quarter of the population and a large block of seats in the *Sabor*, were a key element in Khuen's equation. In return for their support he would give them a stake.

Two important laws were passed under Khuen, the legalization of the Serbian language and Cyrillic alphabet and the restoration of Serbian educational autonomy (1887-8). Both were vehemently denounced by the Croat nationalist opposition. For the Serbs that merely proved that working with Khuen (r.) was a matter of politics as the art of the possible, if not an imperative of national survival itself. Many Croats, on the other hand, saw in their *mađaron* ("Hungarian-serving") attitude nothing but additional evidence of their inherent treachery. The circle was thus closed.

In the late 1890's a new generation of political activists started to emerge on both sides of Croatia's ethnic and confessional divide. They were known simply as "the Youths" (*omladina*). The discourse of the *Omladina* came to be characterized by the avoidance of old-style nationalist rhetoric, by political pragmatism, and by heightened concern for social and economic issues. On the Croat side its members, subsequently known as the *Progressive Youth*, were ready to discard the old Rightist denial of the Serbs' existence and identity. On the Serb side they were ready to accept the notion of Croatian statehood and civic identity as the framework for joint political action. This was the formula that eventually produced the "New Course" in Croatian politics. It key novelty was the notion that the individual, rather than the corporate entity, was the basic political actor.[1]

The crisis of dualism in the early 1900s and the unprecedented violence of the anti-Serb demonstrations in Zagreb in 1902 had an electrifying impact across Croatia's political spectrum. The Hungarian hegemony could not be resisted, many Croats realized, unless the Serbs were offered some form of

---

[1] Miller, op. cit. (1997), p. 51.

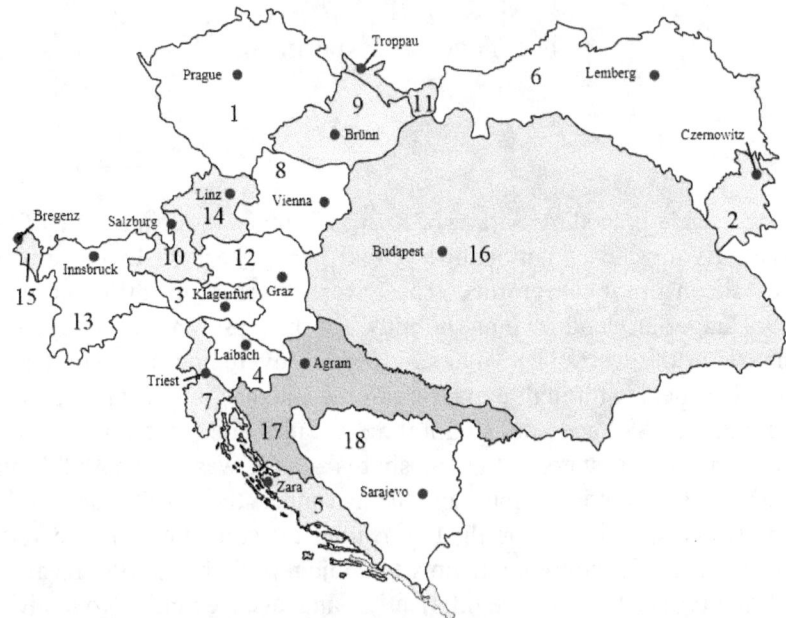

rights-for-loyalty. The resulting *New Course* formula paved the way for the establishment of the Croat-Serb Coalition, the leading political force in Croatia in the years before and during the Great War. It remained in power until the momentous events in late 1918. It also created the intellectual and emotional climate for the rise of a modern, post-Illyrian Yugoslav sentiment.

In the early 1900's it appeared that Croatia's political elite was able to devise a workable *modus vivendi* with the Serbs. It hardly reflected the sentiment of the common people, however. Croatia's political scene under the Habsburgs was limited to a narrow social base and excluded the vast majority of Croatia's population, its peasantry. Its views and aspirations were assumed by the political class, rather than articulated.[1] There was, therefore, less than met the eye in the New Course and the Croat-Serb Coalition.

On the eve of 1914 the traditions and aspirations of the two communities, similar in appearance and language, were based on different sets of values, distinct political philosophies, and largely incompatible historical experiences.

MAP LEGEND *Empire of Austria (Cisleithania):* 1. Bohemia, 2. Bukovina, 3. Carinthia, 4. Carniola, 5. Dalmatia, 6. Galicia, 7. Küstenland, 8. Lower Austria, 9. Moravia, 10. Salzburg, 11. Silesia, 12. Styria, 13. Tyrol, 14. Upper Austria, 15. Vorarlberg; *Kingdom of Hungary (Transleithania):* 16. Hungary proper 17. Croatia-Slavonia; *Austrian-Hungarian Condominium:* 18. Bosnia and Herzegovina

---

[1] See Josip Horvat. *Živjeti u Hrvatskoj: Zapisi iz nepovrata.* Zagreb, 1983.

II
The Yugoslav Experiment

1. The Great War

In the decade preceding Sarajevo, Austria-Hungary was in a state of latent crisis. Its mosaic of nationalities could hardly be held together without radical constitutional reforms.[1] These were opposed, for different reasons, by the Hungarian land-owning nobility in the east and by the German nationalists in the west. The Monarchy tried to overcome domestic tensions, among other means, through expansion in the Balkans, by occupying Bosnia-Herzegovina in 1878 and annexing it three decades later. In doing so it turned Serbia from a client state of the Habsburgs – as it was in the 1880's under King Milan Obrenović – into an enemy under the rival Karadjordjevic dynasty, which was restored to the throne after the coup d'etat and regicide of May 1903. The Monarchy's attempts to subjugate Serbia by the means of a tariff war (1906-1911) proved ineffective and even counter-productive, by enhancing Belgrade's links with Paris and St. Petersburg.

The immediate trigger of the European war in 1914 was the desire of Austria-Hungary to settle accounts with Serbia once and for all, with Germany's protection vis-à-vis Russia. The essential precondition for the chain reaction was Berlin's *cheque blanche* to Vienna, which reflected Germany's desire to force a preventive war on Russia before its anticipated growth into a first-rate economic and military colossus. The reckless risk included the assumption that Britain would stay out of the war, even though the Shlieffen Plan entailed the violation of Belgian neutrality.

Such issues were hardly considered in Vienna, where the murder of Archduke Francis Ferdinand was seen as an opportunity to neutralize Serbia's perceived *Piedmontism*. When Austria annexed Bosnia, the streets of Belgrade seethed with anger. In 1908-9 Russia was weak and Serbia did nothing, but Serbia's impressive and, to many, unexpected victories in 1912-13 awakened the Yugoslav sentiment in the Monarchy. Vienna watched with consternation the triumph of Serbian arms against Turkey, then Bulgaria, and the doubling of its territory (map: borders fixed by the Treaty of Bucharest

---

[1] A group of scholars around the heir to the throne, Archduke Franz Ferdinand, suggested the creation of the 'United States of Greater Austria' (*Vereinigte Staaten von Groß-Österreich*), a federation of autonomous units based on language and ethnicity. The specific proposal was drafted by a Rumanian scholar from Transylvania, Aurel Popovici, in 1906.

ending the Second Balkan War in 1913). July 1914 was neither an accident nor a tragedy beyond human control. With its blank check hastily granted from Berlin, the Monarchy presented Serbia with an ultimatum with extravagant demands. It was not meant to be accepted: Austria-Hungary *willed* a Balkan war, and Germany *wanted* an European war. With the march on Liège they ended up fighting a world war that destroyed Europe.

The popular Viennese jingle of August 1914, *Serbien muss sterbien*, suggested that Croatia's Frankist bile had been approved in the *Mitteleuropa*. The consequences were dire for the Serbs of Croatia. Frankist-led rioters once again took control of the streets of Zagreb, this time with the assistance of the police. The atmosphere of pogrom was fuelled by the nationalist press, which, as a Croat deputy in the Austrian parliament recalled, "published invented accounts of attempts made by Serbs to use bombs to wreck trains, railway lines, ships, and other means of communication, in order to justify the draconian measures adopted by the authorities."[1] "I'll never forget the horrible scene at the end of the first day of mobilization," another Croatian politician recalled, "when a huge bonfire was burning at Jelačić Square fuelled by furniture and household items looted from the shops and homes of the Serbs of Zagreb, surrounded by a screaming Frankist mob ... chanting 'Hang the Serb on a willow tree' [*Srbe na vrbe*]."[2] In Zagreb, "thousands of people poured into the streets, festive mood everywhere, Croatian flags flutter

---

[1] Speech by Dalmatian deputy Ante Tresid-Pavičić in the parliament in Vienna, as quoted in *Novosti* (Zagreb), October 25, 1918.

[2] Dr. Ivan Ribar, *Iz moje političke suradnje, 1901-1965*. Zagreb: Naprijed, 1965, p. 133.

from every house, slogans ... demanding the destruction of Serbia."[1] Thousands of prominent Serbs were arrested and summarily deported, and dozens killed, even before the war against Serbia was declared. The Serbs were saved from wholesale massacre thanks to the commendable *sang-froid* of the ruling Serb-Croat Coalition administration domestically, and the sobering news of the Habsburg armies' military debacles externally. Austria-Hungary was forced to evacuate Serbia by the end of the year.[2]

In 1915 the Monarchy shifted its focus to the Russian front; but after the Allied landings at Gallipoli in April 1915, Germany could no longer ignore Serbia and proceeded to open the Danubian link to Turkey. In October German Field Marshal August von Mackensen led the attack from the north, while Bulgaria joined the war and cut off Serbia's southern flank. The campaign crushed it but it did not destroy the Serbian army, which, though cut in half, marched across Albania to the coast. Allied ships evacuated 150,000 Serbian soldiers. Following recuperation and complete rearmament by the French, these troops re-entered fighting on the Salonika Front where they won a decisive victory against Bulgaria in October 1918. On the other side, for the remaining three years of the war Austria-Hungary deployed its South Slav conscripts mainly on the Italian front. Serbs, Croats and *Bosniaken* fought hard to prevent Italy from gaining the borders promised by Entente powers, which included most of Dalmatia. In an ironic twist, both Serbs and Croats fought the Italians under the Habsburg banner, although for different ends.

As the war entered its decisive stage in early 1918, the future of the Monarchy was becoming uncertain. The Allies were prepared to see Serbia expand, after the war, into Habsburg lands with large Serb populations, such as Bosnia and Vojvodina. Until the final months they did not envisage the creation of a Yugoslav state or a thorough dismemberment of Austria-Hungary. Even President Woodrow Wilson's Fourteen Points provided for "autonomous development" for the Monarchy's nationalities rather than full sovereignty outside its framework.[3] Wilson's was a revolutionary doctrine that could not be contained, however. It accelerated competing aspirations among the smaller nations of Central Europe and the Balkans that hastened the collapse of transnational empires and gave rise to ethnic conflicts and territorial disputes that still remain unresolved.

---

[1] Isidor Kršnjavi in *Oesterreichische Rundschau*, October 1, 1914.

[2] In Company 10 of the 'Devil's Own' (Vražja) regiment of the Zagreb Corps, a sergeant was decorated for bravery on the Serbian front. He was Josip Broz, later known as Tito.

[3] Ivo Lederer. *Yugoslavia at the Paris Peace Conference*. New Haven and London: Yale University Press, 1963, Chapters 1 and 2.

2. Unification

The unification of Serbs, Croats and Slovenes came several decades too late. Had it happened during the era of Germany's and Italy's unification, it might have proved more enduring; but the powers rushed to defeat Russia in 1854-6 and to obstruct her again in 1877-8. Over the ensuing decades the opponents of the political concept of South Slav unity had an upper hand in the Balkans, in Vienna naturally enough, but also in Serbia itself during the turbulent reign of the Austrophile King Milan Obrenović. Half a century after the Congress of Berlin, the process of separate cultural and political development and formation of separate and even competing "Yugoslav" national identities, had gone too far to be recalled. The fusion, based on the myth of ethnic kinship which was supposedly only masked by religious and political diversity, would not happen because local enthusiasts wanted it to happen, or because a handful of Allied scholars thought they grasped the "South Slav" destiny better than their Viennese counterparts. In chaotic times, when sound policy is needed, it is pretty ideas and tempting concepts that rule, however good or bad they may be. The supra-national, cultural Yugoslav model, founded on the ideas of the Enlightenment and mixed afterwards with the experiences of a romantic era, was itself a myth based on blood kinship, anachronistic and obsolete by the time it was applied:

> Both Serbs and Croats used linguistic nationalism in the form of a Yugoslav idea... as an auxiliary device in respect of their own national integrations. Within the framework of their different political and socio-economic backgrounds, the Serbs and the Croats used it with fundamentally different interpretations of its real content.[1]

The Yugoslav idea was imagined as a 20th century rendering of the 19th century concept constructed on the basis of Europe's tripartite ethno-linguistic division as devised by the romantic mindset of 1848. As articulated by Count Lujo Vojnović of Dubrovnik shortly after the Great War, the new Kingdom remained a political *idea*, an imagined community par excellence, rather than a viable and practical political *project*: The Serbo-Croat difference bore no national aspect, he claimed:

---

[1] Dušan T. Bataković. "The National Integration of the Serbs and Croats: A Comparative Analysis." *Dialogue* (Paris), No. 7-8, September 1994.

It was brought about by the historical divorce of the two branches of the nation and by their belonging the one to the Western and the other to the Eastern Church (though there are Orthodox Croats as well as Catholic Serbs). Both these facts are due to the circumstance that fate placed the Serbo-Croat nation at the meeting-place of two worlds, which incidentally explains the eagerness of the Germans to secure a passage to the East over the dead body of our nation... Neither religious considerations, nor the characters of the alphabet, neither facial type nor complexion, nor the high-sounding names of noble houses, can be invoked with impunity in support of any solution of the problems of our race, save the one and only natural solution — Union.[1]

The manner in which Yugoslavism was embraced by the political elite of Serbia, a mere four months into the war, remains mystifying even a century later. On December 7, 1914, after a brief and almost perfunctory debate, the Serbian National Assembly (*Skupština*) approved a government statement on the country's war aims that envisaged the "liberation and unification of our unfree brothers Serbs, Croats and Slovenes."[2] Those were the heady days after Serbia's early victories, when it appeared that the downfall of the Dual Monarchy was only a matter of time. It was partly calculated to weaken the fighting zeal of the Croat regiments by removing the Austrian argument that they were defending Croatia's eastern border from a "Greater Serbian" project. The adoption of such a radical program at such an early stage of the war was nevertheless an ill-considered act of bravado. It created a host of potential and actual difficulties for the Serbs as well as their Allies – even before Italy's claims came into play in April 1915 – by reducing the prospects for a separate peace with Austria-Hungary.

Serbia's Prime Minister Nikola Pašić claimed that "South Slav unity" would bring peace and stability to the Balkans by creating "one national state, geographically sufficiently large, ethnically compact, politically strong, economically independent, and in harmony with European culture and progress."[3] Pašić's estimate was not only flawed in asserting an imaginary ethnic homogeneity, but also wildly optimistic. He nevertheless went out of his way to win over the Allies for the South Slav project. To that end in early 1915 a "Yugoslav Committee" came into being, composed of Croat, Serb and Slovene political émigrés from Austria-Hungary in Western Europe. Their

---

[1] Count Louis Voinovitch, op. cit., p. 243.

[2] The declaration was adopted in the city of Niš, in southeastern Serbia, where the government and the assembly were temporarily located (*Niška deklaracija*).

[3] Alex N. Dragnich, *Serbs and Croats: The Struggle in Yugoslavia*. New York: Harcourt, Brace. 1992,, p. 23.

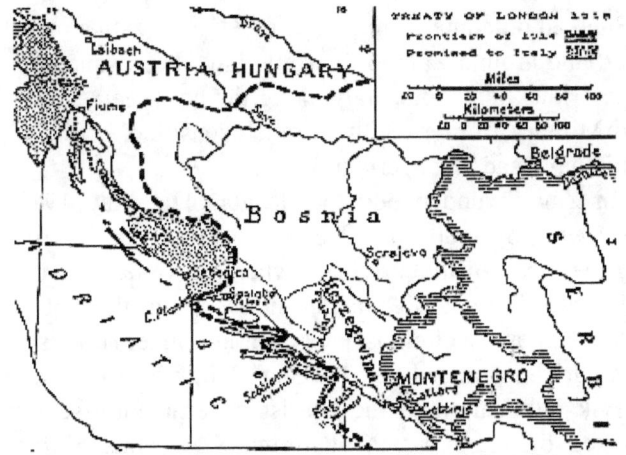

main purpose was to lobby the Allies for "Yugoslavia." On the other hand, Serbia's considerable national dynamism in the early 20th century was chiefly directed at liberating *Serbs* from foreign rule, and resulted in a doubling of the Kingdom's territory in 1912-13. The wider South Slav issue, in so far as it figured at all among common people, was perceived as an extension of that task. Millions of Serbs in the devastated, occupied Serbia, and hundreds of thousands in the Serbian Army overseas or in captivity, wanted a resurrected and enlarged *Kingdom of Serbia*. They had no idea what their leaders were planning – and they were not going to be asked. Further millions of South Slavs in Austria-Hungary did not know that a "Yugoslav Committee" existed, let alone that it presumed to negotiate settlements of far-reaching significance on their behalf.

The Corfu Declaration of 1917, agreed between the government of Serbia and the Yugoslav Committee, proposed the creation of a "constitutional, democratic, and parliamentary monarchy headed by the house of Karadjordjević," to be called the Kingdom of the Serbs, Croats and Slovenes. Under its terms Serbia was not to have a privileged status or veto power in the new state, such as had been granted to Prussia in 1870: both Serbia and Montenegro were supposed to cease their existence as sovereign states. This outcome was a major political success for the Croats on the Committee.[1] The decision of the Serbs to reject the Treaty of London, sign the Declaration, and present it to the Allies as their official program – even though a "greater Serbia" was probably available – was an act of political shortsightedness of which the Serbs were to prove the main victims. Britain and France would have preferred the "small" solution, which would consist of a greatly enlarged Serbia united with Montenegro, Bosnia and Herzegovina, and the Adriatic coast south of Split. This solution could be accommodated with the Treaty of London (see map above), under which Italy was to get

---

[1] Ibid. p. 25.

Dalmatia north of Split. Such an outcome would have left Croatia with a mere "four counties" of its heartland around Zagreb. It would have been squeezed between two enlarged, victorious neighbors, Italy along the coast and Serbia south and west of the old Military Border. Without much coastline, bereft of friends or mentors, it would have had an uncertain future.

The political class in Zagreb understood the danger. The May 1917 Declaration (*Majska deklaracija*) of South Slav deputies in Vienna heralded a new trend, by demanding the union of the provinces where Slovenes, Croats, and Serbs lived in a single state. The qualifier 'under the scepter of the House of Habsburg' was obligatory under the circumstances, but no longer seriously meant. The new wave was driven primarily by the fear of Italy's ambitions, confirmed by the Bolshevik publication of the Tsarist government's secret treaties, and well publicized by the press in all South Slav lands, if the collapse of Austria-Hungary caught Croatia alone.

As the Monarchy crumbled in the autumn of 1918, the ruling Croat-Serb Coalition was the driving force behind the founding in Zagreb of the National Council of Croats, Slovenes and Serbs, an *ad hoc* body that proclaimed the "joint people's sovereign State of Slovenes, Croats and Serbs" in the South Slav lands of the Monarchy as the first step toward their eventual union with Serbia and Montenegro. The vote in the Sabor to sever all links of Croatia with Hungary and Austria on October 29, 1918, (r.) came amidst a mix of panic and euphoria.[1]  A plea for the preservation of Croatia's state rights was hardly to be heard.

When external military and political developments presented the unification of South Slavs as an immediate and necessary prospect, the decision-makers in Croatia could claim but a limited mandate for the fateful steps they were taking. The political enfranchisement of Croatia's peasantry took place only after 1918, in the Yugoslav state. That state might have had a happier start if the unification had not been rushed, but at the time of fear, exshilaration and confusion in the fall of 1918 Croatia's political leaders

---

[1] Cf. Bogdan Krizman. "Stvaranje Jugoslavije" in *Zbornik: Iz istorije Jugoslavije, 1918-1945*. Belgrade, 1958, pp. 147-164.

could see no alternative to an urgent union with Serbia on the basis of the Corfu Declaration. They acted under intense pressure from a combination of events and forces over which they had no control. In addition to the Italian problem, "Yugoslavia became the only way to prevent Serbia from taking its pick of former South Slav lands. To this extent, Yugoslavia was a Croatian political choice, however painful, which cannot be explained at all without... Croatia's Serbian Question."[1]

In the Zagreb Diet one significant dissenting voice was that of Stjepan Radić, the Croatian People's Peasant Party leader. He was not opposed to the establishment of the common state in principle but objected to its form. In particular he was opposed to the looming predominance of Belgrade and interruption of Croatia's notional statehood. He objected to the haste and warned the 28 delegates, as they were departing for Belgrade, that they had no mandate for what they were about to do: "You are roaming like geese in the fog!" Radić's quip about *guske u magli* became famous, but at the time he was isolated and rebuked by other Council members. Their main concern was to get the Serbian army in, to keep the Italians out, and to keep the Reds down. The delegates left for Belgrade and on December 1, 1918, presented Regent Alexander Karadjordjević with an Address informing him of the National Council's decision in favor of the unconditional union. The Regent accepted the offer and proclaimed the establishment of the Kingdom of the Serbs, Croats and Slovenes.

3. An Unconsolidated Kingdom

From the moment of its creation until its disintegration Yugoslavia was beset by national problems. They were dealt with in different ways and with different intentions, on average once every decade: from the triune centralism of the Vidovdan Constitution of 1921 to King Alexander's integralism of 1931; from the quasi-federalism of the Serb-Croat Agreement of 1939 to Tito's Stalinist model (DFJ) of 1945; from federalism of the 1953 FNRJ constitution to the proto-confederal Socialist Federal Republic (SFRJ) of 1968; and finally, from the institutionalized chaos of Tito's last period, embodied in the Constitution of 1974, to the doomed attempt of his successors to keep the edifice together amidst the collapse of communism and the

---

[1] Stenton, op. cit. p. 197. "Yugoslavia was a country desired by the few, not the many," he notes. "It would have been possible, before 1914, on Austrian terms if Vienna had felt able to break with Hungarian privileges. But Vienna refused to base its imperial survival on the loyalty of South Slavs and therefore, in a sense, chose to be afraid of little Serbia."

emergence of the short-lived unipolar world order following the end of the Cold War.[1] Structural deficiencies of each Yugoslavia, as a state and as a polity, were fundamental and precluded the emergence of a viable political system. This was the root cause of its speedy, inglorious collapse in 1941 and of its final, violent disintegration in 1991. The issue of Serb-Croat relations was at the core of the problem. Those relations, already made delicate by the legacy of the Military Border, were poisoned by the creation of a common state based on the fiction of ethnic unity derived from linguistic similarity. They would have remained ambivalent but tractable had the two nations not been forced under the same roof. It is unlikely that they could have been any *worse* than they have been over the past century.

The collapse of Austria-Hungary presented the South Slavs with their unification as a fact of practical politics that did not allow any delay. All parties were forced to improvise. This created a problematic legacy for the new state's internal development, just as its territorial disputes created the potential for conflict with its neighbors. Neither internal solutions, based on the openly centralist Constitution of St Vitus's Day (*Vidovdanski ustav*, June 18, 1921), nor external settlements, based on the Paris treaties, were effective in providing stability at home or security abroad.

On the Croat side, signs of discontent were visible as soon as the new state was proclaimed. On December 2 Frankist demonstrations broke out in Zagreb that quickly turned violent and several people died in the ensuing clashes with the National Council authorities. Within days an increasingly active Stjepan Radić, who also opposed unification – albeit not in principle but in its unitarist form – attempted to involve foreigners in support of his demand for a plebiscite and the establishment of an independent Croatian republic. He sent messages to President Wilson and other Allied powers seeking help in the creation and recognition of a Croatian republic. In subsequent months and years Radić appealed to, or otherwise attempted to involve, Lloyd George, the League of Nations, France, Austria, Italy, and the Soviet Union (where he subsequently joined the Peasant International). His attempts to internationalize the Croat problem, though unsuccessful, aggravated the fragile internal situation.[2]

---

[1] For a brief survey of various constitutional and – especially – economic models tested over almost exactly seven mostly unhappy decades, see John R. Lampe. *Yugoslavia as History: Twice There was a Country*. Cambridge University Press, 2000.

[2] Cf. Alex N. Dragnich. *The First Yugoslavia: Search for a Viable Political System*. Stanford: Hoover Institution Press, 1983, p. 19.

The results of the first election, held on November 28, 1920, displayed a sharp division between Serbs and Croats. In the electoral districts of today's Croatia the Serb vote was divided between the Radical Party of Nikola Pašić, which was perceived as supportive of specifically Serbian interests, and the newly-created Democratic Party of Svetozar Pribićević, who stood for the "state-enhancing" centralism. The Croats, on the other hand, gave their votes *en masse* to Radić's HPSS, which was rapidly turning into a political representative of the nation as a whole. It gained 230,000 votes in 1920, and doubled it at the general election three years later. Radić declared that his success was tantamount to a referendum in favor of a "neutral Croatian republic" he advocated at the time, and defiantly changed the party's name to the Croatian *Republican* Peasant Party (HRSS). He continued to boycott the constituent assembly, insisting on a prior "Croatian constitutional pact" that would lead to a deal with Belgrade – an arrangement, presumably (con)federal, based on the "historical boundaries" of Croatia prior to the act of December 1, 1918.

Radić's views on the Yugoslav idea and the state itself were complex and often contradictory. Before the war he maintained that all Slavs were in reality one nation and one people ethnically and linguistically. Among them the South Slavs were one "tribe" and Serbs and Croats "one nation" within that "tribe." At the same time Radić regarded the Croats as a distinct people (*narod*), with a sense of identity rooted in the historic state rights. This implied that Croats and Serbs *from Serbia* could be regarded as one nation, but *within Croatia* all Serbs were "political Croats." His position on the Croatian identity and territorial aspirations actually hardened with the creation of the Kingdom. His demands for a "neutral Croatian republic" based on its "historical boundaries" were even less realistic in 1919 than his trialist hopes had been before 1914.

The Radical-Democrat coalition, which formed the government after the election, rejected Radić's federalist demands without ado and supported the unitary model. That model was not universally popular in Serbia either. Nikola Pašić opposed any solution that fell short of the Serbs' unification within a single political entity. He was not *a priori* against the federal model, but insisted that it would have to be based on the principle of ethnicity, "and then we can draw boundaries and make a federation."[1] In contrast to Pašić, Pribićević preferred the unitary model without provincial boundaries, in which Serbs, Croats and Slovenes would rule "equally and with equal rights

---

[1] In a letter to Milenko Vesnić. *Narodni glas*, April 29, 1926, 1-2.

over the entire state." That position was embodied in the *Vidovdan* Constitution, which was adopted by the Constituent Assembly with a simple majority of votes.[1]

The institution of French-style parliamentary democracy, well known to Serbia prior to 1914, did not provide an adequate venue to Croat politicians groomed under the Habsburgs. They tended to assume an *us-and-them* posture in all dealings with the state authority, with Radić as the embodiment of such attitude. The inheritance of the past became apparent in an almost reflexive treatment of Belgrade as if it were Budapest. The result was a deadlock, framed by the 1921 Constitution and sealed with the general election of 1923.

In retrospect it is clear that a federal model, with its implied recognition of ethno-historical individualities, would have been a more functional solution. It would have clarified the issue between Serbs and Croats, which had always been not only cultural but also territorial – perhaps *primarily* territorial. Few other European nations have encountered similar difficulty in determining the physical extent of "their" lands. If the Banovina model of 1939 (see p. 96) had been applied in 1921 the Yugoslav experiment may have failed anyway, but not as acrimoniously and bloodily as it has done.

To most Serbs outside Serbia the creation of the Yugoslav state was greeted as an act of deliverance pure and simple. Many Croats, especially the middle classes and intelligentsia, had accepted the new state out of necessity rather than conviction, however. An even greater number – the peasantry – were more inclined to complete the process of Croatian national integration before even considering the wider project. With Radić's electoral success it became clear that both groups would have preferred a sovereign state of their own, just as most Serbs – had they been asked – would have preferred an expanded, strong and secure Serbia to the new amalgam. The Serbian political establishment failed to grasp this. By opting for the centralist concept it made a grave error, compounded by the crude and insensitive methods of its enforcement.

Challenges of nation building, of defining and defending recognized borders, of establishing a single currency, of regulating economic, educational and judicial systems, and above all of solving issues of multi-ethnicity, were immense. They were temporarily concealed behind the fiction of one nation with three names, which increasing numbers of Croats saw as a misnomer for Serbian hegemony. The army remained thoroughly Serbian in spirit and appearance, the eastern (*ekavian*) variant was informally but visibly promoted

---

[1] Gligorijević, op. cit. p. 302.

as the proper "Yugoslav" idiom, the gendarmerie occasionally resorted to corporal punishment unknown in the Habsburg lands for the previous half-century. The political class in Belgrade lacked tact and imagination, and a budding new generation of Serbian leaders – more enlightened, better equipped to deal with the challenges and complexities of the new state – was decimated on the battlefields of the Great War.[1] The legacy of different cultural, political and religious traditions was underestimated. This legacy could not be overcome by a centralist constitution and unitarist slogans.

Belgrade was inclined to view the new state as a continuation of pre-1914 Serbia. It advocated centralism on the premise of national, that is, "Yugoslav" unity. The Croats, in turn, knew historical rights and legal agreements, contracts, *Pacta*, *Ausgleichen* and *Nagodbas*... devices based on a long tradition of seeking greater self-rule in opposition to the centralist concept. The Croat advocates of Yugoslav integralism were revealed, after 1918, to be devoid of a strong popular base, except to some extent in Dalmatia which was threatened by Italian irredentism. To common people of different origins the slogans of [Yugoslav] national unity did not make much sense. Many Serbs accepted them half-heartedly and parroted them dutifully; most Croats not at all. Their final national integration was to take place within the new Kingdom. In preceding decades ordinary Serbs and Croats, 98 percent of non-voters in pre-1914 Croatia, had lived side by side or in mixed communities, often uncomfortably but in peace. After 1848 at the latest they did not consider themselves one and the same people.

Assimilationist claims by Starčević and his heirs only served to deepen the gap: they forced the Serbs to accelerate their integration and to articulate and assert their distinct political goals. Likewise, after December 1918 the royal centralism enhanced national integration on the Croat side and bred opposition not only to the government in Belgrade but to the very concept of the new state. That opposition ranged from "soft," autonomist, to "hard," openly separatist.[2] Its resilience belies the pleasingly moderate view is that Croatia and Serbia only began to quarrel in 1918, when they started having disputes within and about the new Yugoslavia without which they would have had nothing to quarrel about:

---

[1] Serbia lost 28 percent of its population in 1914-18. Military losses exceeded 50 percent. Barely one-third of its junior officers, which included educated reserve subalterns, lieutenants and captains, survived the war.

[2] See Ivo Banac. *The National Question in Yugoslavia: Origins, History, Politics*. Ithaca: Cornell University Press, 1984.

In a narrow sense this view is true of pre-1914 Serbia. It is not, however, true of all Serbs, and it is not true of Croatia. One may indeed refuse to accept that any conflict is immutable, still less genetic, ineradicable, essential or, more recently, 'anthropo-geographical.' But, on the territory of today's Croatia, there is a Serb-Croat quarrel which happens to be rather old. It is certainly not modern in origin: Croatian hostility to the Military Border can be traced back at least to the early 17th century. It became worse, not better, with time and ended up by infecting Yugoslav politics.[1]

The Serbs in Serbia were unaware of this complex dynamic. They were told by their leaders that the creation of Yugoslavia was the fulfilment of everyone's aspirations. The result was their national demobilization, leaving it up to the unifying state itself to take care of everyone's supposedly bundled quasi-post-national interests. Proclaiming one's Serbdom too loudly was frowned upon because the integralist paradigm demanded sacrifice of particularism on all sides – but only the Serbs fell for the propagandistic slogans of their leaders.

By an ironic contrast, Stjepan Radić was only beginning a national mobilization focused on the idea of a sovereign Croatian state. Belgrade's ill-advised and futile attempts to enforce King Alexander's (r.) ill-conceived concept of national unity served other projects well. Improvized and never seriously applied, they do not even hint "that the Serbian royalist regime did intend, on the basis of Greater Serbian ideology, to eradicate a separate Croatian national identity, through the assimilation of the Croats to 'pure Slavic' Serbian nationhood."[2] Quite the contrary: the "royalist regime" – predominantly but by no means exclusively "Serbian" in its composition and assumptions – provided the institutional framework for the process of national integration and political mobilization of the Croat nation in the 1920's and 1930's that would have been unimaginable before 1914. The Serbian political establishment continued to behave as if the Croat storm would blow itself out, as if Radić were merely an opposition politician in pre-

---

[1] Michael Stenton, op. cit. p. 195.
[2] Bartulin, op. cit. p. 133.

1914 Serbia with whom a regular give-and-take deal could be struck. Both sides thus contributed to an almost permanent political crisis throughout the first decade of the Kingdom, even after Radić's apparent *volte-face* in 1925. While visiting Moscow at the end of 1924 he joined the Bolshevik-controlled "Peasant International" – for reasons of practical politics, rather than out of ideological kinsahip – and was duly arrested on his return home under the 1920 Decree (*Obznana*) which outlawed the Communist Party. After a few months in jail, in March 1925, he decided to accept the legitimacy of the state and the fact of union, erased "republican" from the Party name, and joined government as a coalition partner of the Radicals. The parties proved incapable of developing a viable model of political cooperation in a flawed political entity, however: the coalition between Radić and Pašić collapsed in April 1926; Pašić died only months later.

Having gone into opposition, Radić entered into another unlikely alliance in 1927, this time with none other than Svetozar Pribićević, the veteran leader of the Serbs in Croatia and an advocate of centralism in the early years after unification. By the late 1920's, embittered and disillusioned by the Serbian political establishment which he accused of undermining the state by its hegemonistic preferences, he was in opposition both to the Radicals and to King Alexander himself. The new Peasand-Democrat Coalition (SDK) brought together two parties with fundamentally incompatible programs and objectives, but with one common foe: the Radicals of Serbia Virulent recriminations and scenes of mayhem in the *Skupština* became a frequent spectacle. They culminated in bloodshed in June 1928, when a Radical deputy from Montenegro, Puniša Račić, shot five HSS deputies, including Stjepan Radić. Two were killed on the spot, including Radić's nephew Pavle. The HSS leader was wounded and died two months later. His funeral turned into an impressive display of Croat defiance and unity.

The carnage caused shock and outrage in the country and abroad. All SDK deputies departed from Belgrade for Zagreb. They met at the Sabor building on August 1 and adopted a resolution demanding reorganization of the state on the basis of equality and respect for national distinctions.

By the end of the year a near-complete paralysis had set in. On January 6, 1929, King Alexander suspended the Constitution and assumed personal rule, thus effectively acknowledging the failure of a decade-long attempt to devise a workable political system based on the model of parliamentary democracy imported from Paris. That failure, with the Croatian question at its core, was profoundly important for the country's future. For six subsequent years the Kingdom was run on authoritarian lines in an effort to develop from above a feeling of "Yugoslav" national unity. A new, even more centralist constitution was enacted by the King in the fall of 1931. Organizations based on religion or nationality were banned or suppressed. The personal power of the King was now given a formal framework. It was exercised through the civil service, with the army always present in the background.

The Croatian political leadership, headed by Radić's successor Vladko Maček, initially supported the King's decision to assume personal rule ("the waistcoat is finally unbuttoned" was Maček's comment on hearing the news), but not for long. The HSS was opposed to the formal change of the name of the state to *Yugoslavia* and to the introduction of the administrative system based on nine *banovinas*, units that bore no relation to historic provinces and cut across traditional and ethnic lines. The King's insistence on the concept of the "Yugoslav nation" was seen in Zagreb as a further step away from federalism that would respect the individuality of Croatia.

For almost three years Maček nevertheless refrained from high-profile political activities opposing the "royal dictatorship." In November 1932, however, he presided over a gathering of Croat politicians from different parties. They signed a list of demands known as the *Zagreb Resolution* (the *Punktacije*) demanding the return of parliamentarianism and the solution to the Croat question through reorganization of the state along federal lines. This open challenge earned Maček a three year prison term.

4. International Environment

The boundaries of the new Yugoslav state, determined at the Paris peace conference after a long and arduous dispute with Italy, gave it an ostensibly viable territorial base. They did not bring the longed-for stability, however. As a "beneficiary of Versailles" Yugoslavia eventually had to cope with an array of the discontents within (Croatian separatists, Bulgaro-Macedonian "autonomists," Albanian *Kachaks* in Kosovo) and with three revanchist states on three sides of its borders: Italy, Hungary, and Bulgaria.

It is an irony of Versailles that the settlements of 1919 (above) eventually proved to be a major source of weakness for those who appeared to have gained the most. Poland's eastern territories beyond the Curzon Line and its corridor to the Baltic, Czechoslovakia's possession of the Sudetenland, and Romania's doubling in size in Transylvania, Bukovina and Bessarabia, created a constant source of revanchist malevolence among the losers who exacted their revenge two decades later.

The newly-created South Slav state found itself in a similar position. The most acute problem concerned Italy. The Italians were unwilling to give up what had been promised to them in London in 1915: Dalmatia with most Adriatic islands. To their dismay, in December 1918 the Italians found that this enemy territory became, by the act of unification, an "Allied" land. Rome came to regard the Yugoslav state as an unwelcome successor to Austria in the eastern Adriatic, a rival and potential enemy, even though Mussolini regretted the ascendancy of Croat Italophobia over what he assumed was traditional Serb affection for Italy.[1]

The rise of Mussolini was welcomed by many Italians not because of the ideological appeal of fascism, which was still vaguely defined at the time, but because it seemed to offer practical solutions to two specific problems: the 'red menace' at home and the 'mutilated victory' abroad. Yugoslavia was seen as a leading culprit for the latter. The "injustice" meted out to Italy in 1919 was a potent sentiment, as illustrated by D'Annunzio's Fiume adventure. This event, its theatrics notwithstanding, also reminded Mussolini

---

[1] *Documenti diplomatici italiani* (DDI), 7 ser. IV, No 59. Bodrero to Mussolini, 7 July 1925; No. 73; 24 July 1925.

that if he did not assume the role of the nationalist hero, someone else would. He understood, and from the outset Italy's international status was perceived as the criterion by which the Fascist experiment would stand or fall. Initially Mussolini insisted on his friendship for Serbia as a means of securing a sympathetic audience in Belgrade. At the same time, he made a sharp distinction between Serbia and Yugoslavia, expressing his admiration for 'Serbia and her army':

> During the Great War you will find in my articles so much admiration for Serbia and the heroic Serbian Army... Towards Serbia [I'll keep] the same, friendly policy. As for Yugoslavia, our relations will be good... especially if Serbia takes the correct road, which history has determined. Geographically, it takes her not to the Adriatic, but to the Aegean Sea. In the history of Serbia there is no other direction but towards Macedonia.[1]

Belgrade still hoped to appease Rome after Mussolini came to power and grudgingly accepted D'Annunzio's *fait accompli* in Fiume, codified in the Rome Treaties of January 1924. A chance to stem the tide of deteriorating relations came with the signing of the Nettuno Conventions accepting the Adriatic frontier as permanent (July 1925). This was the swan song of the Yugoslav foreign minister, Momčilo Ninčić, as it coincided with the entry of Stjepan Radić into the Belgrade cabinet. Radić was an opponent of the policy of friendship with Italy, which he accused of suppressing Croat minority rights in Istria. Belgrade realized the damage that Serb interests would suffer from his wrath, incurred on behalf of the Croats. Nevertheless, the Serbs were forced to acquiesce in Radić's anti-Italian tirades as a price of his long-awaited acceptance of state institutions. Losing the elusive good will of Rome was seen as a price worth paying for the long-awaited rapport with the Croats.

The Croats' agitation against Italy in the *Skupština*, in the press, and in the streets was analogous to the role of a few vocal Italian Slavophobe nationalists from Venezia Giulia in Rome.[2] An Italian author scornfully noted "the coterie of Triestines, Istrians and Dalmatians who, blinded by their parochial hatred of the Slavs, preferred Italy to have to her eastern frontier a mosaic of little states, open to German influence" instead of a South Slav state able to defend itself against Germany in concert with Italy.[3] But far from seeking an understanding with Yugoslavia, Mussolini upped the ante with a

---

[1] Franko Potočnjak. *Kobne smjernice naše politike spram Italije*. Zagreb 1925, p. 97.

[2] Cf. Dennison I. Rusinow. *Italy's Austrian Heritage*. Oxford: Clarendon Press, 1969, p. 196.

[3] Gaetano Salvemini. *Mussolini Diplomatico*. Bari, 1952, p. 209 f.

"friendship and security" treaty with Albania (the *First Tirana Pact*, November 1926). It touched a raw nerve in Belgrade, which regarded Albania as a zone of prime strategic interest. Momčilo Ninčić, long identified with the policy of seeking friendship with Rome, had to go. His successor Vojislav Marinković (1927-1932) negotiated a friendship treaty with France in November 1927, which included a secret annex on military cooperation. While ready to reach an understanding with Rome, King Alexander could not accept Italian dominance in Albania.[1] When indirect negotiations indicated that on this issue the King would not give way, Mussolini finally embarked on the policy of anti-Yugoslav subversion. In this he eventually came to utilize the Ustaša movement of Ante Pavelić.

Mussolini subsequently found himself in the contradictory role of supporting and even actively sponsoring Yugoslavia's enemies in the Balkans, while remaining staunchly anti-revisionist on on the issue of the Brenner frontier, Habsburg restoration, and Austrian independence. His restlessness paid no dividends: it "inexorably led to the Axis and a German triumph in the Balkans that could not stop short of Trieste."[2] Belgrade reacted by forging links with two states that had most to fear from revanchism and revisionism, Romania and Czechoslovakia. Failed attempts by the former emperor-king Charles to return to the throne in Hungary (March and October 1921) prompted the creation of a military and political alliance among Belgrade, Prague and Bucharest (August 1922) that came to be known a decade later as "The Little Entente."

Although focused on an issue with which Italy could agree, the prevention of a Habsburg restoration, the new alliance caused further resentment in Rome because it was perceived as a French-inspired attempt to create a counterweight to Italy's influence in Central Europe. Mussolini responded by strengthening relations with Austria and Hungary and by becoming more closely identified with the revisionist camp in the Danubian Basin.[3] His move coincided with the coming to power in Berlin of a revisionist *par excellence*.

---

[1] Jacob B. Hoptner. *Yugoslavia in Crisis, 1934-1941*. New York: Columbia University Press, 1962, p. 19

[2] Rusinow, op. cit., pp. 185-186.

[3] Cf. Konrad H. Jarausch. *The Four Power Pact 1933*. Madison, Wisconsin, 1965.

III
An Émigré Conspiracy

1. Pavelić's Early Italian Contacts

With the meteoric rise of Stjepan Radić and his party, other Croatian political groups either ceased to exist or were pushed to the margins of the political spectrum. The Party of Rights (*Hrvatska stranka prava*, HSP) was reduced to only two deputies in the Belgrade *Skupština*. Resolutely opposed to the new state but devoid of significant membership and popular mainly among the lower middle class in the city of Zagreb, the *Frankists* (as the HSP supporters were known) felt frustrated by what they regarded as Radić's inconsistency, manifest in his willingness to accept the legitimacy of the Yugoslav state, the Crown, and the Vidovdan constitution (1925). This was anathema to them, but they were powerless to challenge Radić's unassailable status among the majority of Croats.

With the onset of the royal dictatorship one option for the hard separatists was to abandon the political process altogether and to engage in subversion and violence. This was the path eventually chosen by one of the two HSP deputies, lawyer Ante Pavelić, the founder of the Ustaša movement.

After the Axis powers made it possible for Pavelić to take power in Croatia in April 1941, Ustaša propagandists claimed that the movement had come into being even before he went into self-imposed exile in January 1929. The claim is based on scant evidence. In the aftermath of the bloodshed in Belgrade, some members of the HSP youth wing (*Hrvatska pravaška revolucionarna omladina*, HPRO) contemplated creating clandestine armed groups. In October 1928 they founded a self-styled sport society, *Hrvatski domobran*, which was supposed to provide a cover for paramilitary training and terrorist actions. On December 1 they disrupted the celebrities marking the tenth anniversary of Yugoslavia's unification and engaged in a bloody clash with the police. Two Frankist activists directly involved in this incident, HPRO leader Branimir Jelić and HSP secretary Gustav Perčec, had to flee the country to avoid arrest.

Pavelić initiated clandestine contact with the Italian government as early as 1927 – that is, well before the crisis that followed *Skupština* shootings, Radić's death, and the imposition of King Alexander's personal rule. As a parliamentary deputy for the city of Zagreb, Pavelić was part of the delegation representing Croatia's capital at the Congress of Cities in Paris in 1927. On his way he stopped in Vienna and met two staunchly anti-Yugoslav Croat émigrés, former high-ranking Austro-Hungarian officers, Ivo Perčević and Stjepan Sarkotić. Knowing of their anti-Yugoslav views and their links with the Italian embassy, he told them of his wish to visit Rome on the way back from Paris and talk to a high-ranking Italian official.[1]

This initial contact was simultaneously organized on two tracks. The Italian minister in Vienna, Auriti, informed Mussolini on 22 June 1927 of Pavelić's request. It was passed to the Italian military attaché in Vienna by the two Croat ex-officers.[2] At the same time, a former Frankist deputy of the Croatian *Sabor*, Ivica Frank – who lived in Budapest as an émigré – sent Pavelić's memorandum for Mussolini to the Italian minister in Hungary. It contained an appeal for Italy to support the cause of Croat independence. Frank's covering letter informed the Italians that Pavelić would seek contact in order to discuss the possibilities, and stated that "it is our axiomatic conviction that Italy is the only salvation for the Croats."[3] The Italian minister informed Mussolini of Pavelić's one prior attempt to establish similar contact with the government of Hungary, which the authorities in Budapest refused fearing a provocation.

The Italians were not so circumspect and accepted the offer. Their relations with Yugoslavia had reached a new low point at this time and Mussolini was ready to explore the possibilities. Arrangements were made, and on his return from Paris Pavelić stopped in Rome and met Robert Forges Davanzati, a prominent journalist who was a member of the Grand Council and former Fascist Party secretary. According to Davanzati's lengthy note on this meeting, Pavelić handed him a memorandum identical to the one that had already arrived from Frank in Budapest.[4] The salient features of both documents Davanzati summarized as follows:

> 1. Deep contradictions between Italy and the Yugoslav state give hope to the Croats that they may soon get rid of the "Serb yoke."
> 2. Italian support for the Croat struggle is of importance for "the European culture" and for the enhancement of Italy as a great power.
> 3. The Croat nation had lost its autonomy "against its will" at the time of the collapse of Austria-Hungary. It demands sovereign statehood independent of either Serbia or Yugoslavia.

---

[1] Jere Jareb. 'Šest dokumenata o postanku NDH.' *Hrvatska Revija*, Vol. 20, Dec. 1970.

[2] DDI, VII serie, Vol. V, p. 280, No 286; Auriti to Mussolini, 22 June 1927.

[3] DDI, VII, V, pp. 270-271, No 273; Ivo Frank to Durini di Monza, Budapest, 13 June 1927.

[4] DDI, VII, Vol. V, pp. 303-305, No 313; Durini di Monza to Mussolini, 2 July 1927.

4. The Croats demand all lands "where they have a majority," i.e. Croatia-Slavonia; Dalmatia, "in the frontiers *indicated below"* (the map that Pavelić had enclosed is lost), and Bosnia and Herzegovina.
5. The new Croatian state, as "an outpost of Western culture," would seek particularly close ties with Italy and Hungary.
6. Croatia would "unreservedly recognize Italy's predominance in the Adriatic" and enter the Italian sphere of influence politically, economically and militarily.
7. Croatia would refrain from having a navy if Italy undertakes to protect its coast. It would "cede" Cattaro (Kotor) and accept Italy's right to use military installations along the eastern Adriatic.
8. Croatia would grant Italy economic concessions and privileges and refrain from building a commercial port, so as not to undermine Fiume.

In case of war between Italy and Yugoslavia, the memorandum promised active Croat sabotage and armed action against the Serbs and provision of intelligence to the Italian military. Finally, Pavelić requested the Italians to strengthen their propaganda, and weaken that of the Serbs, by refraining from any statements on their aspirations to Croat territory.

The memorandum of 1927 was the first formal approach by Pavelić to Mussolini. It is of key importance for the understanding of later events, as it is eminently *collaborationist* in spirit and substance. Pavelić was willing to accept Croatia's eventual limited sovereignty under Italian tutelage and to make major concessions incompatible with any conventional understanding of the national interest of the Croatian people. Both the tone and contents of the memorandum were to find their logical conclusion in the Rome Treaties, fourteen years later, when he accepted the amputation of Dalmatia and at least nominal Italian predominance in the NDH.

On the territorial issue two details are significant. It is striking that Pavelić (in the middle, on a 1926 photograph, above) mentions Dalmatia "in the frontiers indicated below," which presumably refers to a map prepared by him and attached to the original memorandum. Such qualification indicates that Pavelić had always intended to cede at least some Dalmatian territories to Italy as an inducement for its support, or else he could have simply mentioned Dalmatia or "Dalmatia presently belonging to Yugoslavia" (i.e. excluding the city of Zara and the island of Lagosta). Secondly, Pavelić requested that the Italians refrain from making irredentist statements merely in order to "strengthen their propaganda," and not because he expected or urged them to give up such claims. When he met Davanzati in Rome and presented him with the above document Pavelić did not have any mandate to speak on behalf of Croatia or the Croat people. The party to which he belonged was a marginal entity; Stjepan Radić and his HSS were the acknowledged representatives of the majority of the people. There is no hint that Radić knew of Pavelić's action, let alone condoned it. In any event, Radić was a staunch opponent of Italian ambitions in the Adriatic, as was manifested in his opposition to the Nettuno Conventions in the Belgrade *Skupština* in 1927.

Anti-Italian sentiment was rampant in Croatia at that time. Violent anti-Italian demonstrations in Dalmatia and in Zagreb contributed to the tension between Belgrade and Rome. Apprehension over Italy's designs was one of the factors that influenced Radić's decision to make his U-turn in 1925. There can be no doubt that Stjepan Radić, his aides and eventual successors, and the majority of the Croat people would have rejected Pavelić's initiative out of hand, had it become known. Even to those Croats unhappy with the Yugoslav experience – probably the majority by the late 1920's – Croatia's "independence" at the price of becoming an Italian satellite would not have been considered acceptable.

Pavelić's memorandum illustrates the difference between the HSS and the separatist fringe. Both Radić (above) and later Maček sought reconciliation with Belgrade and a place for Croatia within the Yugoslav framework when they concluded that external dangers, such as the rise of Mussolini in the early 1920's, or the approaching European war in 1939, might leave Croatia vulnerable. Like the Croatian political elite in the fall of 1918, they considered the Yugoslav solution not out of conviction but as a means of protecting Croat interests. For all their rhetoric, the HSS leaders knew that *the Serbs* did not seriously hope to extinguish Croat identity. They could be insensitive to Croatia's peculiarities and concerns, they were heavy-handed, corrupt, boastful of their glorious past and recent sacrifices, even "primitive" from a *Mitteleuropisch* vantage point; but as Radić once exclaimed, "You can quarrel with a Serb, you and he will insult one another, maybe even fight; but afterwards, he will slap you on the shoulder and ask you to have a drink with him. Don't all brothers do that among themselves?"[1]

The Frankists and their offshoot, the soon-to-be founded Ustaša movement, postulated a different, darkly demonic concept of the Serb. It was the cornerstone of their entire outlook, of their very Croatness. Such outlook made any compromise with Belgrade impossible by definition. Therefore every alternative to Yugoslavia – amputation of Croatian territory and limited sovereignty for the Croatian state included – appeared tolerable, and certainly preferable to the continuation of the Yugoslav framework. Pavelić's peculiar view of Croatia's interests was consistent with his basic assumptions.

2. Pavelić Goes Abroad

Italian willingness to accept clandestine contact was prompt and it encouraged Pavelić to consider a sustained campaign in favor of an independent Croatia that would rely on foreign governments unfriendly to Belgrade. In January 1929, after the King proclaimed personal rule, Pavelić decided to test the possibilities. As a prominent opponent of the Yugoslav state and advocate of Croatia's sovereign statehood he had reason to fear arrest. On the night of January 19-20 he eluded police surveillance and boarded a train for Vienna, taking advantage of the fact that his passport had not been confiscated.

The capital of Austria seemed a convenient location, favored by assorted conspirators, revolutionaries, anarchists and spies from many parts of Europe. This motley crew included the Communist Party of Yugoslavia (which had its headquarters there) and the openly terrorist pro-Bulgarian "Macedonian Internal Revolutionary Organization," VMRO. In Vienna Pavelić could rely on his previously established Croat contacts (Perčević and Sarkotić). The secretary of the Party of Rights, Gustav Perčec (with Pavelić, sabove), arrived in Austria six weeks earlier and soon joined him in Vienna.[2] The leader of the

---

[1] Dragnich (1992), p. 67.

[2] Statement by Ivo Perčević to Yugoslav interrogators (3. January 1947) contains details of his early assistance to Pavelić and Jelić, including the provision of a fake journalist pass for Pavelić. A-VII, NDH, I.O.9 5/6 1-82.

Party's youth wing, Branimir Jelić, also emigrated in December and initially settled in Graz with Perčević's help.

Pavelić's first public gesture, with which he effectively burnt the bridges behind him, did not take place in Vienna but in Sofia, which he visited with Perčec in April 1929. Enthusiastically greeted by their VMRO hosts they exchanged rabidly anti-Serb and anti-Yugoslav toasts with president of the Macedonian National Committee Stanišev and signed a declaration on joint struggle against Belgrade.[1] Pavelić also conferred in private with the leader of the VMRO, Ivan-Vančo Mihajlov, who subsequently provided much needed assistance to the Croat émigré group. (Below: Pavelić, second from left in the middle row, with his Bulgarian hosts).

Belgrade reacted with a protest note to Sofia. Bulgaria replied that it regretted the events surrounding Pavelić's and Perčec's visit and that it would prevent their repetition.[2] Three months later Pavelić and Perčec were sentenced *in absentia* to death in Yugoslavia. The Court for the Protection of

the State in Belgrade found them guilty of sedition and high treason. (It was the first such sentence; Pavelić was sentenced to death again after the killing of King Alexander.) Pursuant to diplomatic pressure from Belgrade, Pavelić was denied further hospitality by the Austrian government on his return from Bulgaria. After an unsuccessful attempt to obtain a Hungarian visa he went to Germany. The Weimar authorities cultivated friendly relations with Yugoslavia, however, declined contact and ordered him to leave the country.

Just before leaving Munich, devoid of other options, Pavelić turned to the Italians. The Italian consulate consulted Rome and issued him a passport with which he went to Italy and temporary arrangements were made for him to settle in Verona. For the first time he encountered open support of the host country and funds were put at his disposal. From his new base, Pavelić started agitation in the cause of Croat independence. Relying on a small network of supporters and sympathizers of the Party of Rights abroad, he started setting up recruiting points and front organizations in Western Europe and the

---

[1] *Povodom trogodišnjice "Sofijske deklaracije."* Izdanje "Grič" (an émigré publication, quoted by Krizman, 1978, pp. 54-58.)

[2] AJ, Ministarstvo unutrašnjih poslova, fasc. 33

Americas. Since there were few potential recruits in the two countries where Pavelić could expect support, Italy and Hungary, the initial activity was taking place under the label of mutual assistance and cultural organizations in six countries with Croat expatriate communities (Belgium, France, Germany, Argentina, Canada and the United States).[1] Pavelić's sympathizers started printing newsletters and brochures in Croatian and host-country languages and sending them to Croatian churches, community centers, clubs, and mutual-help societies.

While Pavelić concentrated on political work, Gustav Perčec, as a former Habsburg officer, was given the task of preparing military action. Before leaving Zagreb he had developed a network of Frankist youths willing to carry out terrorist actions. They were activated in the spring of 1929. Their first act of terrorism was the murder of a pro-Yugoslav newspaper editor, Toni Schlegel, in Zagreb on March 22, 1929. The second was a bomb explosion outside a gendarme barracks, also in Zagreb, and the shooting of two police agents who were attempting to arrest the suspects. As a result of his activities Perčec, too, had to leave Austria. He went to Hungary and with the funds provided by his contacts in the Hungarian military intelligence rented an isolated estate, Janka Puszta, located near the Yugoslav border. This was to be the training camp and base for future actions which, over the ensuing four years,  amounted to eleven explosions on trains and public places in northwestern Croatia and some half-dozen assassinations. While Pavelić's "nucleus" in Italy grew slowly, its limited ability to act meant that the highlight of Ustaša pre-war activity – the assassination of King Alexander and French foreign minister Louis Barthou in Marseilles – was largely due to the Janka Puszta group. Its members were more experienced in direct action, and the trigger of the murder weapon (above) was pulled by one of Vančo Mihajlov's VMRO professionals.[2]

Even before Perčec established his base at Janka Puszta, Hungary had enjoyed the reputation of a country sympathetic to the cause of Croat separatism. In the 1920's this was reflected in the help it gave to émigrés such as Ivica Frank and in the official tolerance of several Hungarian nationalist

---

[1] E.g. *Hrvatski savez* in Belgium had as its stated objective "struggle against illiteracy"; cf. Krizman, 1978, p. 73.

[2] See Vladeta Milićević. *A King Dies in Marseilles: The Crime and its Background.* Bad Godesberg, 1959. For a survey of sources on the affair, cf. Krizman (1978), Chapter III.

groups devoted to the revision of the Treaty of Trianon. In 1921 one such organization (*Awakened Magyars*) included the "liberation of Croatia" in its program, and counted among its members several Croat officers who remained in the Hungarian service after 1918.

The initial support for the émigrés was provided by the Hungarian military intelligence. Official circles were reluctant to be visibly involved, as evidenced by their refusal to issue Pavelić an entry visa in 1929. In early 1931 several Ustaša émigrés were quartered at the barracks in Pecs. They moved to the estate at Janka Puszta in the autumn of that year. The location was selected for its proximity to the Yugoslav border and for its inaccessibility to undesirable visitors. This group eventually grew to about forty men who were subjected to military regime and discipline.

The Yugoslav authorities were well informed about the existence and activity of Perčec's group, however. The counterintelligence center in Vienna, headed by the Yugoslav police expert on Ustaša affairs Vladeta Milićević, obtained detailed information from Perčec's mistress Jelka Pogorelec who acted as a double agent.[1] Starting in 1931 the Yugoslav government lodged a series of well documented protests against such activities to Hungary; but they proved of no avail. Due to its growing ties to Rome the Hungarian government had grown less circumspect about its links with the Croat separatists than it had been in 1929. In March 1933 the Hungarian foreign ministry arranged a meeting between Pavelić and the leader of the Albanian "Kosovo Committee" Hassanbey Prishtina. They signed an agreement on cooperation between Croat and Albanian separatists "against the common enemy" in Belgrade.[2] Pavelić also suggested the signing of an agreement between the Albanian group and the VMRO, but this proved impossible due to their differences over the future of western Macedonia.

Yugoslav complaints against Hungary at the League of Nations were answered by the Hungarian delegate in Geneva, Tibor Eckhardt (above). At

---

[1] She eventually returned to Yugoslavia and published her memoirs filled with salacious details. In 1941 Ustaša police located her in Sarajevo. She was tortured and killed on specific orders from Pavelić. Pavle Ljumović, "Atentat u Marselju: Kralj na nušanu." *Večernje novosti*, Belgrade, 29 September 2004.

[2] Krizman (1978), p. 116.

the same time he was president of the Hungarian Revisionist League, an organization openly devoted to overthrowing the Versailles order. In that capacity he signed an agreement on cooperation with Pavelić in July 1933.[1] In this document Pavelić agreed to a plebiscite in the Medjimurje (Muraköz, a historic Hungarian county awarded to Yugoslavia in 1919) to decide if it would belong to Croatia or Hungary. He also agreed to Hungary's annexation of southern Baranja, which had a Croat plurality. As in his initial contact with the Italians in 1927, Pavelić proved ready to trade parts of the "ethnic and historical" territory of Croatia for foreign support.

Italy's treatment of the Ustašas was different from Hungary's because the Italians expected to obtain different results from hosting them. In Italy Pavelić and his group were supplied and controlled through a network of foreign ministry and police officials, with the latter supervising the training of early recruits (r.) The chain of command went operationally to Inspector Conti and politically the top of the hierarchy of state authority, to Mussolini himself. The Ustašas were meant to be an auxilliary instrument of Italian policy and their activity limited to whatever was deemed by the Duce to be within the parameters of that policy. They were denied autonomous decisions on what actions to take.

In Hungary the goal of the military intelligence service sponsoring the émigrés was simply to destabilize the Yugoslav state, rather than use such destabilization to some strategic end. The Janka Puszta group was not a tool of any specific state policy. The military intelligence appears to have acted independently of other organs, before 1933, at least. In the early days Regent Horthy may have been unaware of its existence. In a similar vein, Serbia's military intelligence under Colonel Dragutin Dimitrijević-Apis had acted independently vis-à-vis the Young Bosnia group and without Prime Minister Pašić's knowledge or approval, in the run-up to Sarajevo in 1914.

Political pressure from the League of Nations and from individual countries, international outcry, and the results of French police investigation after Marseilles compelled Hungary to liquidate the Janka Puszta camp. The remaining dozen Ustašas were sent to Italy. Their transfer coincided with a

---

[1] A-VII, NDH, Kut. 233, Br. Reg. 17/8.

general clampdown on Pavelić's supporters throughout Europe. In Belgium the Ustaša front organization was disbanded and its activists expelled.

The perpetrators of the *attentat* in Marseilles had regarded the King as the last remaining "Yugoslav" institution and expected that his removal would clear the way for a speedy collapse of an unnatural state edifice devoid of staying power. This was not to be, however. Yugoslavia was unconsolidated, but states seldom "fall" by themselves, even when they seem ripe; the long dotage of the degenerate Ottoman Empire is a case in point. The weaknesses inherent to the Yugoslav kingdom ensured that its few remaining years would be tense internally and turbulent externally, but its eventual collapse was caused by an overwhelmingly powerful attack from without, not by disintegration from within.

3. Codification of Ustaša Principles

Having settled in Italy Pavelić decided that the objectives of his group needed to be defined and its principles codified. By late 1931 he had attracted the first batch of volunteers. They were constantly told that the beginning of insurgency in Croatia was imminent. Some fifty Croat guest-workers from Belgium, France and Germany responded to the initial round of recruiting leaflets and word-of-mouth appeals. The first Ustaša camp was established in the winter of 1931-2 in Bovegno, in the Lombard province of Brescia. Pavelić set up his headquarters there (*Glavni Ustaški Stan*, GUS) and promulgated the

founding documents of the Ustaša, Croatian Revolutionary Organisation (*Ustaša, hrvatska revolucionarna organizacija*, UHRO). The UHRO Statute of 1932 and the Ustaša Movement Principles (*Načela Ustaškog pokreta*) of 1933 were meant to give the still rudimentary movement its formal structure.[1]

When initiated, an Ustaša swore before a crucifix, a hand grenade, a knife and a pistol to uphold the *Principles* which had 17 articles. They asserted that the Croat nation is "a people by itself, not the same as any other, not a part or tribe of any other nation." The Croat nation had never given up its right to statehood, nor transferred that right to anyone else, but in 1918 "alien force" prevented it from exercising its sovereign rights. The Croat people have the right to realize their sovereign

---

[1] *Hrvatska pošta* (émigré publication), Vol. 1, No. 1. A-VII, NDH, Kut. 85f and 290.

power in the entire ethnic and historical area of Croatia, and in their exercise of that right they are not bound by any present or past international, legal or other obligations contrary to this principle. In the affairs of state and nation only "a Croat by blood" can take part in the making of decisions. While "peasantry is the foundation and source of the Croat people," the document continued, all social strata of the nation form one national entity, for as long as their members have Croat blood. All material, spiritual and natural resources are owned by the Croat people, who are solely empowered to use them. A hint of "leftist" radicalism was present in the assertion that "the source of all value is labor, and the source of all right is duty. Labor will be the criterion of value of each individual in the Croat state, and his duty to the state." All holders of public office are accountable by their life and estate. Duty and responsibility to the whole are to be the basis of all activity in every person's private life. Independent Croatia will provide "good life for honest work," and not "wealth for capitalists." The goal of the state would be to secure harmonious growth of all national parts.

The key features of the *Principles* were the centrality of ethno-racism and the concomitant denial of legal and property rights to non-Croats in the future state, a quasi-mythological historical narrative, the assertion of continued statehood, the claim to sovereignty over the entire "ethnic and historical" territory, patriarchal collectivism, and organic nationalism. Pavelić's repeated insistence on distinct "blood," coupled with his assertion that the Croats were ethnically and racially distinct from their Slav neighbors, marked a major ideological departure from earlier traditions. The Croats were distinct not only politically and historically but also genetically.

The *Principles* remained substantially unchanged until April 1941. After the proclamation of the Independent State of Croatia Pavelić made some alterations to the *Principles* and took an oath on them as *Poglavnik, in lieu* of a constitution.

The Ustaša Statute promulgated a year later, in 1933, dealt with the command structure of the organization. It postulated complete blind obedience to the *Poglavnik*. The last founding document, "Military Regulations" (*Službovnik ustaške vojske*, 1933), was to provide a manual to the Ustašas organized into active service units. In its first article the Regulations reiterated the key objective of the Ustaša movement:

> ... to liberate Croatia from the foreign yoke by armed insurrection, so that it is independent in all its ethnic and historic territory. [...] When that goal is achieved, the Ustaša organization will defend the independence of Croatia and the individuality of the Croat people. It will struggle to ensure that only the

Croat people will ever rule the Croat state, and that it will be the sole master of all actual and spiritual wealth in the country.¹

Over the years these founding documents constituted the normative basis of the Ustaša movement. They were the basis of the movement's "ideology." Their chief practical value to Pavelić was in the proclamation of the *Führerprinzip* attached to him personally (*Poglavnik*). The spirit of these documents, the claims to ethno-racial distinctiveness notwithstanding, is more reminiscent of a secret nationalist society in the tradition of pre-1914 Bulgaria or Serbia, than of a modern mass movement of the 1930's bent on taking power by force. The exortation to armed struggle and violence was at its core, in line with Pavelić's aim to mold a new racial "Croatian man" characterized by an uncompromising warrior spirit and the readiness to rely on violence: "The knife, revolver, machine gun and time bomb, these are the bells that will announce the dawn and resurrection of the Independent Croatian State."² The Ustaša emblem was supposed to reflect this spirit: a burning cannonball with  the checkboard coat of arms in the middle within a *serif* letter "U," which was developed into cap badge design (l.) According to Pavelić, an Ustaša had to be be severe and merciless, "for his duty is to lessen the pain of the Croatian people with fire, iron and blood, to crush with force the neck of the foreign parasite and so liberate his homeland."³

4. The "Military Nucleus"

The Italian government formally approved the establishment of Pavelić's "militarily organized" center in 1932; thereafter it was referred to, in Italian documents, as the "Ustaša military nucleus." The response to Pavelić's recruitment efforts proved disappointing, however. At its peak (1935) the group's number was around five hundred.⁴ They were recruited overwhelmingly from among the peasants who had left underdeveloped areas in the Dalmatian hinterland, Lika and western Herzegovina in search of work abroad, the coal and steel basin of eastern Belgium being a favorite destination. Mainly poor and uneducated, from areas plagued by chronic rural

---

¹ A-VII, NDH, Kut. 85f, 28/6.

² Bartulin, op. cit. p. 161.

³ Krizman, 1978, p. 86.

⁴ A detailed list of 508 Ustaša émigrés was submitted by Inspector Milićević to the Yugoslav interior ministry. AJ, Ministarstvo unutrašnjih poslova, Kut. 33.

over-population, they were naturally prone to radicalization.[1] Over 70 percent came from the arid mountains of the Adriatic hinterland.[2] About a fifth were from the coast (Dalmatia and the Croatian Littoral); barely ten percent came from the most populous and developed areas of Croatia-proper and Slavonia. The group included only a small number of urban workers and artisans, and a mere handful of students and professionals.

This pattern subsequently repeated itself on a much greater scale after 1941. While the Panonian plains remained largely loyal to Maček, and while Dalmatia was unsurprisingly the breeding ground of Yugoslavism (both royalist and Titoist), the Ustaša regime could count on the loyalty of the "Dinarites" until the bitter end. It confirmed Pavelić's well-known preference for the Dinaric "wolves and lions" over the supposedly "softened" Dalmatians and docile, pacific Pannonian plainsmen.

Pavelić's recruiting efforts were scant at first. They were aided to some extent by the economic crisis in Western Europe, which caught many expatriate Croat workers in the dilemma between looming unemployment and an unwished-for return to their impoverished homes in Yugoslavia. Their response to Pavelić, while ostensibly based on a nationalist sentiment, was probably combined with their personal economic predicament, but the data is not available to draw conclusions. Their latent radicalism could turn both Left and Right, as illustrated by the fact that that in the main recruiting center for Pavelić' organization – among the Croat workers in the Belgian industrial city of Seraing near Liège – the Communist Party of Yugoslavia was able to recruit some two hundred volunteers for the Republican cause in Spain.[3] Even among the Croat diehards who came to Italy, the loyalty to Pavelić was not absolute. The claustrophobic life of regimentalized émigrés (shown in their Italian-supplied surplus gear in 1935, opp. p.) proved conducive to irritable factionalism and internal squabbling.[4]

The changing fortunes of the émigré group also enabled Pavelić to test the endurance and devotion of his early followers. Those who proved single-mindedly faithful and fanatical, Pavelić trusted in later years more than

---

[1] A similar socio-economic and geographic stratum provided the most fanatically devout Serb and Montenegrin recruits to the Communist Party of Yugoslavia throughout the 1930's. On problems of rural overpopulation see: Jozo Tomasevich. *Peasants, Politics and Economic Change in Yugoslavia*. Stanford University Press, 1955.

[2] Krizman, 1978, pp. 564-574.

[3] Uroš Kulić in *Večernje novosti*, Belgrade, 16 March 1972.

[4] Cf. detailed report by Stjepan Marušić, an Ustaša émigré who returned to Yugoslavia in 1938, addressed to the HSS leadership. Krizman, 1978, pp. 575-579.

anyone else. In a sense he was right: his veterans from the early days, people like Lisak, Herenčić, Moškov and Boban – having thrown in their lot with Pavelić when the attainment of his objectives seemed very distant – were unlikely to desert him thereafter. Like most dictators and many democratic politicians, Pavelić valued personal loyalty above all other qualities. This enduring trait eventually caused divisions within his régime and tensions with his allies. The coterie of old émigrés around Pavelić eventually turned into a major informal power center in the NDH. They behaved like feudal warlords, accountable only to their chieftain, and were accordingly nicknamed *Rasovi*. The struggle against the *Ras* influence was a feature of many Axis officials' daily life in the NDH after April 1941.

Pavelić was completely dependent on the Italian government. He was  receiving money, arms, supplies and logistic support through Inspector Ettore Conti, the man who remained in charge of the group until the end of its stay in Italy in April 1941. Instructions concerning policy and organizational matters came from the Foreign Ministry in Rome. Conti's equivalent in the Ministry was the head of a special "Croatian Department," Paolo Cortese, to whom all Pavelić's requests had to be addressed. Italian expenses for the Ustaša operation in the early 1930's were 100,000 Lire a month.[1] The life in Pavelić's Italian camps was hard. Many of his followers later commented that their daily lot was not different from that of common prisoners. Hundreds of young men joined in the hope of seeing some action, but instead they were forced to spend years together in a confined space, often arguing, with no end in sight. There gradually emerged a divide between the Dalmatian minority, who were even in those early days suspicious of Italian intentions and Pavelić's obligations to his hosts, and the majority from Lika and western Herzegovina.[2] They were all supposedly bonded by Pavelić's ideology of radical Croatism but their faith was severely tested in a state of enforced idleness. Their basic military training, a welcome

---

[1] On the logistics behind Italian support for Croatian émigrés see Teodoro Sala. *Basi italiane del separatismo croato 1929-1940*. Ancona, 1977.

[2] On continuing squabbles between the factions, see A-VII, NDH, *Zapisnik saslušanja A. Moškova*, I.O.9 1/4 1-117 (Ante Moškov's statement to the Yugoslav authorities.).

distraction from the grim daily grind, was frequently curtailed for extended periods by the Italians to make the group's presence less conspicuous.

The authorities in Rome pretended that the Ustaša "nucleus" did not exist. Even before the scrutiny of the outside world was attracted by the assassination of King Alexander, the Italians moved Pavelić's camp whenever they had reason to believe that the Yugoslav authorities had obtained information about its location. In 1933 alone, Pavelić and his followers were moved from Bovegno to Borgo Val di Taro, then on to Vischetto (Emilia), and soon thereafter – in January 1934 – to Oliveto in Tuscany. In the summer of 1934 the Italians suspected that Yugoslav diplomats at the Vatican had obtained information on the camp at Oliveto. They hurriedly split the group in three and dispersed it to isolated locations in the Appenines (San Demetrio ne'Vestini, Fontecchio and San Lorenzo), taking arms in store first.[1] Such transfers often followed high-profile Ustaša actions, such as the attack on a gendarme outpost in Lika or the capture of King Alexander's would-be assassin Oreb in Zagreb.[2]

An attack was launched on the gendarme outpost at Brušani, just north of the Italian frontier near Zara (Zadar), on the night of November 6-7, 1932 by ten Ustašas infiltrated from Italy abetted by four local sympathizers. The attack, commanded by Juraj-Juco Rukavina[3] ended in failure: after a shootout lasting half an hour the attackers withdrew and there were no losses among the gendarmes. During the subsequent chase one attacker was killed, several local supporters were captured, and the rest of the group promptly withdrew to the Italian territory. It was a terrorist attempt, plain and simple. In its aftermath the Yugoslav authorities, uncertain of the magnitude of the conspiracy, carried out an extensive search of the area using methods of interrogation which embittered the local population. The official over-reaction did more to promote Pavelić's cause among the local people than the attack itself, inappropriately labeled the *Lika Uprising* by the Ustašas. The incident was given extensive coverage in the Italian and Hungarian press, which tried

---

[1] Pavelić pretended that transfers were arranged of his own will, and accompanied them with "orders" to his followers; e.g. Order of 16 July 1934. A-VII, NDH, Kut. 85f.

[2] *Zapisnik saslusanja A. Moškova.*

[3] Rukavina was subsequently captured, sentenced to death, had had his sentence commuted to 12 years' imprisonment, and pardoned in 1939. While in the Mitrovica penitentiary he developed close personal links with a number of imprisoned senior Communists, including Andrija Hebrang and Milovan Djilas. In April 1941 Pavelić appointed him the commander of the Ustaša militia. In June he organized and personally led Ustaša flying squads which murdered thousands of Serb civilians in Lika and northern Dalmatia. Surrendered by the British to Tito's forces at Bleiburg in May 1941 he was sentenced to death and shot on June 7.

to present it as the harbinger of a looming civil war in Yugoslavia and a decisive escalation of the Croat resistance to the Serb-dominated regime. In fact it remained an isolated incident and its repercussions were confined to a narrow geographic area.

The incident marked a fresh deterioration in Italo-Yugoslav relations. Behind the scene, however, an exchange of messages between King Alexander and Mussolini had continued for almost three years, with Albania always the sticking point. This contact was severed at the end of 1933, following the capture of Petar Oreb, an Ustaša infiltrated from Italy with the task of killing King Alexander in Zagreb. A small-time smuggler fallen on hard times, Oreb crossed into Italy and joined the Ustaša in the summer of 1933. He attended training camps in Borgo Val di Taro and Vischetto. As a crack shot he was selected to assassinate the King on the occasion of his visit to Zagreb on December 16 for his birthday celebration. Oreb bungled the

plan, however, and in the end made no attempt on the sovereign's life. The Zagreb police were alerted to his presence, however, and during a check-up Oreb shot one officer and wounded another. He was subsequently caught and told the police every detail of his stay in Italy.[1] In March 1934 he was sentenced to death by hanging, along with his two aides Josip Begović and Antun Pogorelec. Oreb and Begović were executed in May. The duplicity of Rome infuriated the King and prompted him to sever further contacts.

Mussolini's exact goals in taking Pavelić under his aegis remain unclear. In his memoirs published posthumously (l.), Italy's powerful under-secretary for foreign affairs (1932-1936), Fulvio Suvich, maintained that Mussolini did not intend to use Pavelić for "aggressive purposes," but rather as a means of calculated pressure on Yugoslavia.[2] This view is supported by another senior official, Rafaelo Guariglia, who wrote that both the Croatian and Albanian card were used by Rome as "instruments of pressure to coerce Belgrade to accept *faits accomplis*."[3] This may have been Mussolini's intention at first, but in 1934 the émigré group was used to

---

[1] See Tonko Barcot. "Nesuđeni atentator na kralja Aleksandra: Petar Oreb Mijat i njegov put do vješala." *Časopis za suvremenu povijest*, Zagreb, 3, 2006.

[2] Fulvio Suvich. *Memorie 1932-1936*. Milano: Rizzoli, 1984.

[3] Guariglia, op. cit. p. 74.

kill King Alexander – an act which Pavelić would not have been able to launch without prior Italian approval. This act went well beyond the presumed original design. The weakening and eventual disintegration of Yugoslavia had itself become an objective of Italian policy.

The trigger that killed King Alexander and French foreign minister Louis Barthou in Marseilles on October 9, 1934, was pulled by a Bulgarian, Veličko Kerin, but the conspiracy that made the *attentat* possible was the work of the Ustašas. The group planning the operation was headed by Pavelić's young assistant Eugen-Dido Kvaternik and included émigrés Mijo Kralj, Ivan Rajić and Zvonimir Pospišil. Czech and Hungarian forged documents for Kralj (r.) and others were prepared at Janka Puszta. They were all arrested in France except for Kvaternik, who managed to cross the border into Italy and evade capture. At their trial at  Aix-en-Provence (November 1935-February 1936) they were given long prison terms. The culpability of Hungary and Italy was obvious, which had immediate repercussions for the émigré "nucleus" in Italy. As masterminds of the operation Pavelić and Kvaternik were sentenced to death in absentia in a separate trial.

The King's death produced an international scandal and forced Mussolini to remove his Croatian protégés from public view to the Lipari Islands off Sicily, a traditional place of banishment since the Roman times. Pavelić and Kvaternik were kept in jail in Turin from October 1934 until the end of April 1936. Pavelić remained upbeat, however, telling Kvaternik that the assassination in Marseilles was "the only language the Serbs understand."

5. The Ustaša Movement and Fascism

The collapse of the parliamentary system and the imposition of royal dictatorship in Yugoslavia in 1929 coincided with the period of growing political radicalism all over Europe and the beginning of a worldwide economic crisis. Each development was a necessary condition but none by itself sufficient for the rise of a Croat separatist movement that was not only nationalist but also racist, and violent. It cannot be termed "fascist" without qualification, however. Only its subsequent evolution and final manifestations place it into the group of political phenomena in Central and Eastern Europe known as "native fascism."[1] Among several varieties of fascism in Europe between the wars, a salient feature common to all was their celebration of a glorious past of a particular nation and the promise of a correspondingly glorified future, based on that nation's alleged particular qualities and its mission ordained by "history," "providence," or God. There was also the virulent opposition to Marxism and the reliance on the dynamism of violence and direct action. Fascism was born out of the crisis of European liberalism, when traditional political forces were delegitimized by war, shaken by internal instability and scared by the revolution in Russia. Its early recruits were the radicalized veterans who wanted revenge and restitution, having been "stabbed in the back" at home (the *Heimwehr*) or having had their victory "mutilated" by foreign enemies (D'Annunzio's Fiume Legion).

The forerunners of the Ustašas, by contrast, were Croat military officers, Habsburg loyalists, who refused to come to terms with the creation of Yugoslavia in 1918 and preferred to live in Vienna or Budapest as émigrés. They could not be compared in numbers or influence to those German or Italian veterans who provided the backbone of the black or brown shirts in the 1920s. The circle around General Stjepan Sarkotić von Lovćen (l.) in Vienna was bourgeois to the bone. It was *reactionary* in the literal sense of wishing for the return of a previous order, rather than revolutionary; it was conservative rather than radical; and it was neither activist nor populist. It provided the initial means of communication between Pavelić and the Italians in 1927 but its impact was limited, both before and after 1941.[2] A decade later, in the late 1930s, the same spirit was in evidence in Zagreb: many middle and upper-middle-class *Agramers*, nationalist but not radical or prone to violence and on the whole supportive of the HSS mainstream, found the Ustašas "coarse and frankly repulsive."[3] By the abandonment of the traditional codes of behavior in the struggle against the communist threat, Italian fascism and Nazism aped their

---

[1] The term was coined by the late Peter F. Sugar in *Native Fascism in the Successor States, 1918-1945*. ABC-CLIO, 1971.

[2] A-VII, NDH, I.O.9/5, 1-82. Perčević's statement to interrogators of January 3, 1947.

[3] Branko Pešelj to the author, Washington D.C., May 1989.

red opponents. They used not only its slogans of social justice and the vocabulary of simplified clichés, but also its social base. This tendency was less apparent in the case of national fascisms of south-eastern and eastern-central Europe because of those countries' different social structures.

Pavelić did not propose an "Ustaša" solution to the problem of governance and integration that preoccupied Hitler and Mussolini. He proposed the Ustaša solution to the problem of Croat identity. Ustašas' anti-Serbism was not merely a component of their ideology; it was its very essence. Their notion of an organic national community of Nordic-Dinaric stock, eternally bonded by its undiluted blood and ancient conquest, the vengeful *wolves and lions* eager to give up their *tamburas* for guns, bombs and knives in an all-out struggle against Serbs, took precedence over all social and political concerns. It was a rough and ready solution to the problem of insecurity. The resulting imagined community was presented in contradictory terms. By the early 1930s both Nazism and fascism had developed their responses, however improvised, to the challenge of modernity. The attempted response to that challenge by a leading Ustaša intellectual, Mile Budak, was painfully bland. His anti-capitalist, anticommunist and anti-Semitic rhetoric notwithstanding, his distinctly premodern nostalgia for the patriarchal extended family evoked the language and imagery of an earlier era:

> Communism and capitalism are but two forms of slavery of the soul, liberty, pride and dignity... The leaders of both are always the same, the same blood, and race, which has been following its objectives for centuries... A Rockefeller or a Stern is replaced by a Trotsky a.k.a. Bernstein ... Our old family *zadruga* offered a better, happier and richer life than today's households. Families may prosper or fail, but the essence of the *zadruga* should be secured in perpetuity.[1]

Budak glorified the rural, Dinaric Croat in his fiction. His best known novel, *The Hearth*, archaic in language and imagery, was light years away from the sophistication and sensibility of Pound, Marinetti, Brasillach, Henriot, Malaparte, or Wyndham Lewis. Budak came from the rugged Adriatic hinterland, an ethnically and religiously mixed area where family collectivism went hand-in-hand with a mystical sense of one's ethnic and religious affiliation defined by antagonism towards "the other." The Croat peasant of Lika and Herzegovina could be receptive to Pavelić's brand of *Volksgemeinschaft,* which marked him off vis-à-vis the Serb, but that hardly made him a "fascist."

---

[1] Mile Budak's pre-World War II 1938 pamphlet. A-VII, NDH, Kut. 289, Reg. No. 1/1.

Starčević's tirades against the *breed of Slavo-Serbs* fit for slaughter were given a modern facelift by Milan Sufflay, a Zagreb historian and amateur anthropologist assassinated by police agents in 1931. Sufflay's main thesis was that there could be no union between Croats and Serbs owing to the inherent biological and racial differences between them. A millenium of divergent development had turned Croatia into a Western nation, by virtue of its religion, culture, and modes of thought, while Serbia leaned to the East, to Orthodoxy, and to Russia as Byzantium's successor.[1] Sufflay claimed that such differences were genetically insurmountable and racially determined, Croats being a fair race with some Mongolian blood and Serbs being a darker race of paleo-Balkanic origin. Writings of this sort were common in Europe between the wars, but there was an important difference. While to a Nazi *the Jew* was a necessary social and political concept, to the heirs of Starčević and Frank, to Pavelić and his disciples *the Serb* was much more: he was the key element of their very Croatness and its defining feature.

The Successor States' culture after 1918 inculcated in the young the belief in a divinely sanctioned and structured sense of values. It shaped a young person's outlook even when the original religiosity – well eroded even before 1914 – was no longer present. The result was a strong receptiveness to fascist phenomena.[2] But such *mitteleuropaeisch* receptiveness was absent among the Croat extended families of the Balkan badlands. In its place there existed an *intuitive* hatred of the Serb, a raw sentiment that was at best proto-fascist. It was ideologically underdeveloped but it needed no ideology because its grounding was not in the realm of codified concepts. Fascists respected the irrational as a reality but for the most part were not themselves swayed by wilfully irrational considerations. The Ustašas' outlook and program was built on them, which brings them closer to National Socialism.

The Ustaša ideology was entirely focused on the *creation* of a nation-state – for and by those belonging to the Croat community of descent, mystically linked by the blood of its alleged ancestors – and not on that state's supposed salvation from the "Bolshevik menace," or "plutocracy," or its engagement in the quest for a metaphysical higher goal. While an Ustaša perceived an ethno-racially pure nation-state as his supreme objective, a German Nazi or an Italian fascist saw the state as a ready-made instrument of his *Wille zur Macht*. Fascism and Nazism were dynamic, ruthlessly modernizing movements, as manifested in a dramatic poster glorifying

---

[1] Milan Sufflay. *Hrvatska u svjetlu svjetske historije i politike*. Zagreb, 1928.

[2] Fritz Fellner. "The Background of Austrian Fascism"; in Peter F. Sugar, Ed. *Native Fascism in the Successor States 1918-1945*. Santa Barbara: ABC-Clio, 1971, pp. 17-18.

Mussolini (above). The Ustašas were essentially static: they aimed for a "stable" situation, the creation of a nationally homogeneous, Serb-free Croat state. They had no coherent "mission" for that state once it came into being.

By virtue of conspiratorial action and exiled leadership the Ustašas also fell outside mainstream fascism, which relied on publicity and street action. The class context was also different. Devoid of a sufficiently strong popular base, the Ustaša movement did not carry out a "national revolution" in 1941, which would demand cooperation with the established political and economic forces. The state from its inception was to be the Ustaša state: unlike

Mussolini in the 1920's or Hitler in 1933-38, Pavelić did not feel he needed allies among the conservative forces to stay in power. After April 1941 he sought to *absorb* them (starting with the right wing of the HSS) or to silence them. The movement lacked the class basis provided elsewhere in Europe by coalitions between the traditional nationalist Right and Fascism in the struggle against Communism. Ustaša propaganda and pamfleteering was a substitute for ideology, forced mobilization a substitute for participation. The notions of a "Dinaric" race with its allegedly inherent superior qualities were a minority interest between the wars, confined to a narrow circle of Zagreb's amateur historians-cum-anthropologists.[1]

In the 1930's the Ustaša movement was only tentatively "fascist," and it underwent fascization of sorts after beng installed in power. Its ideology was rudimentary, and secondary to its main focus: "Anti-Serbdom had always been central to Ustaša ideology; in the words of one prominent Ustaša, it was 'the quintessence of the Ustaša doctrine, its *raison d'être.*'"[2] A man could not be *bona fide* Ustaša without embracing the exterminationist anti-Serb canon, even if he accepted all other elements of Ustaša "ideology" (anti-Semitism, the cult of peasantry, corporatism, Nordic-Dinaric racism, Muslims-are-Croats etc.). Conversely, it *was* possible to be lukewarm on all non-Serb-related ideological tenets but to adhere to genocidal anti-Serbism, and still to be a fully-fledged, *bona fide* Ustaša. A decade after coming into being, having reached power through the intervention of its external mentors, the Ustaša movement translated its *raison d'être* into practice. It and destroyed half a million human lives by unimaginably savage means.[3] That fact remains the most enduring legacy of the movement and its founder.

---

[1] Sufflay relied on an obscure book by a long-forgotten Swiss anthropologist, Eugen Pittard (*Les peuples des Balkans*, 1917) to stake his claim of the racial superiority of Croats over Serbs. Cf. Milan pl. Šufflay, *Izabrani eseji, prikazi i članci*. Zagreb: Darko Sagrak, 1999, p. 132. This was further elaborated by Filip Lukas a decade later (*Hrvatska revija*, No. 10, 1937).

[2] Mark Biondich, "Persecution of Roma-Sinti in Croatia, 1941-1945." United States Holocaust Memorial Museum – Center for Advanced Holocaust Studies, *Roma and Sinti: Under-Studied Victims of Nazism*, Washington D.C. 2002, p. 33.

[3] The killing of roughly 400,000 Serbs (approximately one-fifth of the NDH population) was a case of *attempted* rather than accomplished genocide. It was not completed due to the Serbs' armed resistance and Italian and German restraining policies rather than for the want of Ustaša zeal. The killing of 30,000 Jews (75 percent) and 25,000 Roma (90 percent) was indeed *genocide*: both groups were substantially eradicated beyond the possibility of recovery.

IV

Serbs, Croats, and the Axis

1. The Aftermath of Marseilles

The new course of Italian diplomacy, starting in 1926, was evident in Italy's readiness to support Pavelić and to become involved in the Marseilles conspiracy. It reflected Mussolini's consolidated hold on both internal and external policy. He did not need to rely on the old liberals any longer, and heralded the one-party dictatorship in the speech of January 3, 1925. In his foreign policy he was no longer subjected to the tutelage of the career diplomats who had assisted him in the early days to the point of grooming him in the finer points of table manners. The diplomats were keen to oblige him at first. His goals, after all, corresponded to Italy's *nationalist*, rather than specifically fascist objectives: annexation of Fiume, a foothold in Albania, expansion in the Mediterranean. Those objectives had been supported all along by the senior foreign ministry establishment, whose members subscribed to the notion of a "mutilated victory" of 1918.

The resumption of a hard-line approach to Yugoslavia in 1926 symbolized the new, "fascist" course at the Palazzo Chigi. The appointment of Dino Grandi, a *squadrista* leader from Bologna, as under-secretary for foreign affairs was meant to reflect the new course. But Mussolini's activism reflected a limited grasp of foreign affairs, which went beyond his impatience with old diplomacy. He had no strategy: his emphasis on means, in fascist parlance on "action," packed together ends and means in semantic imprecision until the means, the acquisition of strength, became an end in itself. "When the rhetoric of the regime became identified with a statement of ends, Italian policy became the prisoner of that rhetoric."[1]

To the career diplomats of Palazzo Chigi a dispute with Belgrade over Albania, or with France over Tunisia, did not preclude equable relations. Not so to the Duce; his activist policy got him linked to a motley band of European discontents, from Austrian corporatists to Hungarian revisionist diehards and Croatian separatists. The worsening relationship with Yugoslavia after 1926 was linked to the problem of Italy's relationship with France; periods of closeness between Belgrade and Paris coincided with new strains in Yugoslav-Italian relations.

---

[1] C.J. Lowe and F. Marzari. *Italian Foreign Policy, 1870-1940*. London and Boston: Routledge & Kegan Paul, 1975, pp. 209-210.

This need not have been so. Italy and France shared an interest in maintaining the system codified at Versailles, since any upset was more likely to work to their detriment than to their advantage. Both had grounds to fear a resurgent Germany, on the Rhine as well as on the Brenner. But this common ground could be maintained only if Italy went along with France's security concerns and accepted its bilateral alliance with Poland and its sponsorship of the Little Entente (Czechoslovakia, Romania and Yugoslavia, map below) which were supposed to offer a substitute for the pre-1914 alliance with Russia as the safeguard against Germany. Mussolini's change of approach to the Adriatic problem – after 1926 a "problem" only of his own making – and his parallel courting of revisionist forces in Central Europe exemplified his confusion of ends and means.[1]

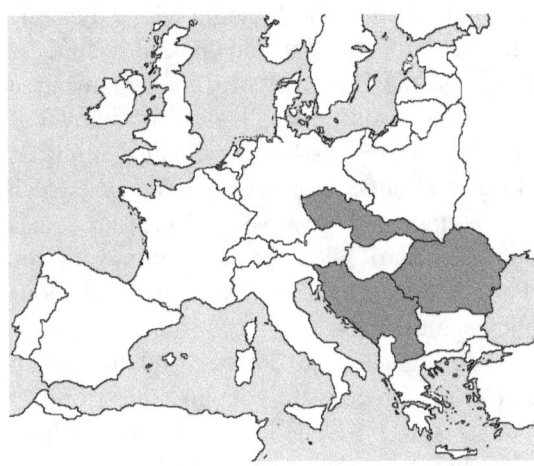

On the other hand, by striving to keep Austria and Hungary under Italy's influence at the time of the rise of Hitler and taking a defensive posture in the Danubian basin, Mussolini acted as a defender of the existing order. The abortive Nazi coup in Vienna and the dispatch of four Italian divisions to the Brenner in 1934 made Italy look like a defender of the European status quo. This was the basis for Laval's pact of January 1935. King Alexander was killed in Marseilles three months earlier but Yugoslavia did not disintegrate. Left with what looked like a losing Croatian card, amidst international disapproval and potential embarrassment at the League of Nations which was about to launch an enquiry, Mussolini put it on a back burner. The Duce also understood the potential menace that the new regime in Berlin posed to Italy's position in the Danubian basin in general and to its long-term hold on the former Austrian lands in particular. The first half of 1935 could have been the turning point in Italy's foreign and security policy, making it a guardian of Versailles.

---

[1] In fairness to Mussolini it should be added that the French were welcoming hosts to anti-Fascist Italian émigrés, the *fuorusciti*, and often unwilling to take Italy seriously as a power with aspirations no less legitimate than France's own.

Everything changed with Ethiopia. Planned as an old-fashioned colonial expedition, it escalated into an international crisis. Mussolini responded in his fashion: by changing the substance of his foreign policy and thus altering the political map of Europe.

The softening of Mussolini's attitude to Belgrade in early 1935 coincided with the revival of political life in Yugoslavia. As Regent until 11-year-old King Peter's coming of age, Prince Paul Karađorđević – the late King's cousin – released Maček from jail and called elections for May 1935. The Croat leader headed the United Opposition list, which included the HSS and several Serbian political parties opposed to the regime. Maček's Serbian partners accepted the principle of reforming the state and adopting a new constitution. The United Opposition did well at the polls but the Government List gained more votes and Prince Paul asked Milan Stojadinović, a dynamic Radical Party politician, to form the new government. This he did in June by bringing the Slovene People's Party and the Yugoslav Muslim Organization into coalition with the Radicals. The new coalition was henceforth known as the Yugoslav Radical Alliance (JRZ). A year earlier, as finance minister, Stojadinović had established close economic ties with Germany, which became Yugoslavia's chief trade partner on the basis of clearing deals favorable to Belgrade. He acted in accord with the mastermind of the country's foreign policy, Prince Paul. The Regent believed that good relations with Berlin were an insurance policy against Italy.[1]

In late 1935 France encouraged Yugoslavia to improve relations with Italy. Hoping to engage Mussolini in a joint front to contain Hitler, French diplomacy under Pierre Laval put pressure on Belgrade not to accuse Italy directly for the murder of King Alexander at the League of Nations but to limit its indictment to Hungary. Laval reiterated to Stojadinović the need for Belgrade's reconciliation with Rome when the new Yugoslav premier visited Paris in September 1935.[2] On the other side of the Rhine, at about the same time, Hitler advised Ciano to improve relations with Yugoslavia.[3] Both Prince Paul and Stojadinović understood that the *Anschluss* was merely a matter of time after Mussolini announced the creation of the Rome-Berlin Axis on November 1, 1936. They agreed that stability on the Kingdom's western border was an urgent necessity.

---

[1] Krizman. *Vanjska politika* (1975), p. 84

[2] Milan Stojadinović. *Ni rat ni pakt*. Rijeka: Otokar Keršovani, 1970, pp. 368-369.

[3] *Ciano's Diplomatic Papers*. London, 1946, p.58.

2. The "Rome-Belgrade Axis"

Belgrade regarded the folding up of the Ustaša organization in Italy as a priority and indicated that its liquidation was a precondition for better relations.[1] Rome responded favorably. Initial steps were taken by Mussolini with the imprisonment of Pavelić and the internment of his followers. Stojadinović responded by sending two negotiators to Rome in December 1936 to discuss overall improvement of relations. Political issues were entrusted to an experienced diplomat, Yugoslavia's delegate at the League of Nations, Ivan Subbotić. His agenda included four items: a Yugoslav-Italian treaty, the status of Albania, the position of South Slav minorities in Italy, and the Ustaša problem.[2] Subbotić had five negotiating sessions with senior foreign ministry officials, Gino Buti and Leonardo Vitetti. In his report to Stojadinović, he wrote that Buti would advise Ciano of the need to deal with the Ustaša issue *before* the agreement with Belgrade was signed and independently of any such agreement.[3] Buti further suggested a clause in the political agreement obliging both sides not to tolerate on their territory any activity directed against the security of the other party.

When Ciano received Subbotić at Palazzo Chigi on January 16, 1937, he was even more emphatic on the Ustaša issue than his officials had been: "We shall remove some of them from the country: we shall send them to Africa or let them go far away from Europe, while others will be kept under strict police surveillance in the country. In brief: we shall disband them and make their action impossible!" In his second round of talks with Subbotić, on March 3, Ciano said of Pavelić, "I am not interested in him or the likes of him. I've had enough of them."[4] He expressed willingness to offer a verbal note to the Yugoslav government pledging to ban "all organizations and activities of persons whose activity is directed against the territorial integrity and established order of the Yugoslav state." He added that the pledge was not contingent on the outcome of negotiations and said that the émigrés would be "sent as laborers to Italian colonies." Italian police would inform its Yugoslav counterparts of places where remaining émigrés were interned or confined and supply names of those who wished to return to Yugoslavia.

---

[1] Krizman. *Italija u politici kneza Pavla*. pp. 65-68.

[2] For an account of Subbotić's mission in Rome see Živko Avramovski. *Balkanske zemlje i velike sile 1935-1937*. Belgrade, 1968, p. 267; Krizman (1978), pp. 271-279.

[3] AJ, Fond M.M. Stojadinovića, fasc. 14

[4] ibid.

Ciano's desire to reach a major agreement, which he said could go well beyond all previous drafts, impressed Subbotić. His final report contained a vivid sketch of the Italian foreign minister's personality and style: "I have the impression that Ciano is very keen to come to Belgrade and create a sensation. It looks like he wants to perform that visit in a 'hussar' style: he'll fly in and out, he'll stun the whole world."[1] Three weeks later Ciano did go to Belgrade "hussar style," where he and Stojadinović signed the Italian-Yugoslav Treaty on March 25, 1937. The negotiations were kept secret and the treaty came as a surprise to the world, just as Ciano had desired. It consisted of the political agreement and a supplementary trade agreement. The gist of the political agreement was that common frontiers would be respected in perpetuity. If one side were to become a victim of unprovoked attack by a third party, the other would refrain from any action favoring the aggressor. The two sides also undertook "not to tolerate on their territory, nor to assist in any manner," any activity directed against the other.

The Italians made no secret that their readiness to compromise was partly based on their apprehension of Germany. Ciano's blunt statement to Subbotić on March 6, 1937, sounded like a far cry from the Axis principles announced by Mussolini four months previously:

> I am a friend of Germany but, *entre-nous*, Germany is not only a dangerous adversary to her enemies, but also a difficult friend to her friends. I do not think that we need to organize against Germany now, but we must bear in mind that your and our position vis-à-vis Germany will improve if we stick together. Our 42 million and your 15 million will mean more together than apart... I don't think we should turn against Germany, but we must – between ourselves – organize our cooperation with her.[2]

The discrepancy between Mussolini's loyally pro-Axis rhetoric and Ciano's stated misgivings reflected a fundamental, and ultimately fatal, contradiction in Italy's foreign policy in the late 1930's. Hitler's repeated renunciation of any aspirations in South Tyrol demanded Italy's acceptance of the *Anschluss* in return. But even if Alto Adige was safe for Italy, its interests in the Danubian area and the Adriatic were not. Hitler had sacrificed the South Tyrolese to the Italian alliance; but it was uncertain whether the same applied to *other* Italian gains dating from 1918. The bleak possibility was that "Hitler the anti-Habsburg and the anti-Marxist was ready at the same time to

---

[1] Quoted in Krizman (1975) p. 97.

[2] AJ, Fond M.M. Stojadinovića, fasc. 14.

hazard [the Italian] alliance by sponsoring a German drive on Trieste which could only be based on Habsburg tradition and economic determinism."[1]

Hitler wanted an alliance with Italy, but at the same time he sought the end of Italian influence in the Danubian basin. Hitler's Danubia ultimately included the eastern shore of the Adriatic. By assuming sovereignty in Austria, Hitler could not avoid inheriting its strategic concerns. As his *Gauleiters* and commanders in the Adriatic Operations Zone proved after September 1943, the logic of the Habsburg inheritance functioned sometimes regardless of Hitler's deliberate design. That logic was behind Mussolini's attempt to make a friend, and perhaps even an ally, of Yugoslavia. As Ciano put it, "once the *Anschluss* is an accomplished fact, all those countries that must oppose the German descent towards the Adriatic or along the Danube valley will polarize around the Rome-Belgrade axis. This bloc which will arise will be such as to dissuade the Germans from any mad attempt."[2]

In the context of such considerations Pavelić and his five hundred followers paled into insignificance. They were not even negotiated about: Ciano offered their neutralization upfront.[3] On his return from Belgrade he acted immediately. Less than a week after the signing of the Yugoslav-Italian Treaty, on April 1, Pavelić issued an order releasing all his followers from "active duty." He announced that all Ustaša camps on the territory of the Kingdom of Italy would be dispersed and all activity would cease. Trying to put a brave face on what was obviously the low point of his movement he promised that the struggle was not over: "From now on we shall continue to be prepared to do our duty, even at the price of our lives, when the moment comes and the homeland calls. That moment will come, and we shall respond to the call, wherever any of us may be."[4] To the members of the "nucleus" his words could not conceal that this was tantamount to their project's *finis*.

The leaders of the Ustaša nucleus, about sixty men, were confined in pairs in small towns throughout southern Italy. Pavelić and three of his closest aides (Vjekoslav Servatzy, Mile Budak and Eugen Kvaternik) were kept apart from each other in four northern Italian towns. A delegate of the Yugoslav interior ministry, Sava Ćirković, arrived in Rome and was given files on all Ustašas in Italy. He established initial contact with some two-dozen dissidents

---

[1] Rusinow, op. cit. p.226.

[2] *Ciano's Diplomatic Papers*, p. 100.

[3] His contemptuous disdain – he'd ship them to Italy's colonies "as laborers" – was evident in his later diary entries, e.g. "Pavelić... and his band of cutthroats" (April 25, 1941)

[4] A-VII, NDH, Kut. 85f.

from Dalmatia who had asked to be separated from the main group in Lipari because of mutual tensions. The Italians wanted to repatriate as many Ustašas as possible, and Conti insisted that this could be done "without any fear" regarding their future behavior. Ćirković agreed: the rank and file was "demoralized and leaderless."

To facilitate repatriation the Italians requested the dispatch of a higher-ranking person, equivalent to Ettore Conti, to assist with the processing of applications for return to Yugoslavia.[1] Ćirković's place in Rome was taken by Vladeta Milićević, an expert on Ustaša affairs. Prior to his posting in Rome he had headed the delegation of the Yugoslav Interior Ministry in Vienna, the chief center for gathering intelligence on Croat émigrés. Experienced and ambitious, Milićević established personal contact with numerous Ustašas. He told those who requested repatriation that their return would depend not only on their promise of good behavior and co-operation with the authorities, but also on their readiness to give signed statements with every minute detail they knew about the organization and its key figures. Within weeks Milićević was able to build a comprehensive dossier. His *coup* was to arrange the return of Mile Budak.[2] In his reports to Stojadinović he hinted that Budak's presence might have a bearing on Maček's posture by making the latter more flexible. The arrangement was facilitated by Budak's assurances to the Yugoslav authorities that he had been unaware of the conspiracy to kill King Alexander, having spent the critical months in 1934 in Berlin.

The Italians discarded the Ustašas – albeit temporarily, as it turned out – in favor of a new strategic design in the Balkans. In May 1938 Mussolini assured the Yugoslav minister in Rome, Hristić, that "the Croats cannot do a thing any more."[3] Both sides saw the agreement as beneficial. It settled disputes almost two decades old. The main concession Belgrade made was to accept Italy's dominant role in Albania. Mussolini could derive satisfaction from the fact that the agreement implied a shift in Yugoslavia's foreign policy, away from France and the Little Entente. Ciano hoped that this represented but a first step towards the full alliance, "which Stojadinović considers natural and inevitable."[4] The Yugoslav premier, for his part, adopted the rhetoric of the "Belgrade-Rome Axis" and to express his

---

[1] Ćirković's reports from Rome are in: AJ, Ministarstvo unutrasnjih poslova, fasc. 33.

[2] Cf. Ljubo Boban. "Nekoliko izvještaja o povratku Mile Budaka iz emigracije (1938)." *Zbornik Historijskog instituta Slavonije*, 1970, 7-8, pp. 510-514.

[3] Hristić to Stojadinović, 29 May 1938. AJ, Fond M.M. Stojadinovića, fasc. 24.

[4] *Ciano's Diplomatic Papers*, pp. 98-105.

misgivings about the League of Nations in Geneva, his hopes for expanded trade with Italy, and his contempt for England's "bluffs" over Ethiopia, Ciano was delighted. Somewhat optimistically he concluded that "Italy will shortly be able to take the place in Yugoslavia of France herself."

3. Hitler's Yugoslav Policy

The new Germany, intent on revising the Versailles order, could hardly be regarded as a natural friend of Yugoslavia. From his earliest days in power Hitler nevertheless sought to woo Belgrade, rather than subvert it. This was in sharp contrast to his policy towards another "Versailles creation," Czechoslovakia. His policy was pragmatic. He understood that the cement keeping the Little Entente together, and its members close to France, was their fear of Hungarian revisionism. To undermine the Little Entente and to diminish the influence of France in the Balkans, he needed to restrain Budapest vis-à-vis Belgrade and to turn its energy against Prague. Soon after coming to power Hitler made this position clear to the Hungarian Prime Minister Gyula Gőmbős. Hungary's revisionism could count on Germany's support, he said, but only against Czechoslovakia.[1] Germany sought to bring Yugoslavia and Romania into its sphere of influence by economic means, he added, and to isolate them from Paris and Prague. To that end he needed Hungarian help.

In the aftermath of Marseilles foreign minister Konstantin Neurath also urged the Hungarians to improve their relations with Belgrade.[2] The foreign ministry instructed other government ministries to regard Italy's policy of anti-Yugoslav subversion as detrimental to Germany's interests. Within the Nazi leadership a notable supporter of pro-Yugoslav policy was Hermann Göring, who took a special interest in the Balkans. In October 1934, after returning from King Alexander's funeral (above), Göring spoke of the

---

[1] DGFP, C, Vol. 2, Minutes of Hitler's meeting with Gombos.

[2] DGFP, C, Vol. 3, No. 269. Memorandum by the Foreign Minister, 25.10.1934.

need for a strong and friendly Yugoslavia. This theme became a salient feature of German diplomatic documents in the 1930's.[1]

A small branch of the Ustaša organization was founded in Germany at the end of 1931.[2] Vladeta Milićević's reports from Vienna noted "activity in Berlin" in early 1932, but nothing much happened for the rest of that year.[3] After Hitler came to power, however, some German officials – apparently acting without instructions and separately from each other – responded favorably to several Croat émigrés' requests for help. In October 1933 the *Reichswehr* Ministry suggested supporting Branimir Jelić and his associates who were short of funds to maintain publication of two pro-Ustaša papers. The military proceeded from the reasonable assumption that in the event of a future European war Yugoslavia would side with Germany's opponents and that therefore émigrés hostile to Yugoslavia could be useful assets.

The Foreign Ministry retorted sharply on November 3 that German diplomacy "steered clear" of all Croat issues and that the Reich wanted good relations with Belgrade." Through the existence of the two Croatian papers in Germany these relations were being injured and we are anxious that a final ban should be declared," the reply went on. "Continued publication of a paper by the name of 'Independent Croatian State'... on German soil is totally impossible."[4]

Two weeks later the Foreign Ministry rebuffed an attempt by Branimir Jelić to present a memorandum on the situation in Croatia addressed to Hitler. The Ministry noted that it was "the special wish of the Reich Chancellor" that relations with Yugoslavia be given "especially careful treatment."[5] The Ministry followed this with a further letter suggesting action to curtail émigré activities. Sent to the Prussian Ministry of the Interior on November 29, 1933, it noted "in confidence" that Hitler had given specific instructions on the need to improve relations to Viktor von Heeren, Germany's newly appointed Minister to Belgrade.[6]

---

[1] Dušan Biber. "Ustaše i Treći Reich: Prilog problematici jugoslovensko-nemačkih odnosa." *Jugoslovenski istorijski časopis*, No 2, p. 44.

[2] The leading members of the group were Branimir Jelić, the Frankist youth leader who emigrated shortly after Pavelić in 1929; Mladen Lorković, son of a prominent prewar politician; Josip Milković, eeditor of "Croatia Press"; and Stijepo Perić. They were financed by a businessman from the Ruhr, Mijo Gavranović.

[3] AJ, Ministarstvo unutrašnjih poslova, fasc. 33.

[4] DGFP, C, Vol. 2, No. 43. Memorandum by Department II, 3 November 1933.

[5] DGFP, C, Vol. 2, No. 72. Bülow to State Secretary Lammers, 16 November 1933.

[6] DGFP, 6065/E448791-93.

The Foreign Ministry reacted even more resolutely to block an attempt by the Nazi Party Foreign Policy Department to save Jelić's newspapers from the police ban. The issue was sensitive because the Foreign Ministry under Neurath – a lukewarm Nazi himself – was determined to assert its authority *in principle* as well as in practice over the NSDAP on all issues concerning foreign affairs. The Wilhelmstrasse obtained necessary support from Hitler, who declared that "we have no interest whatsoever in tolerating or indeed encouraging this activity in any way."[1] Faced with such strong hint from the top, the NSDAP foreign policy department chief Alfred Rosenberg (l.) quickly revised his position: within weeks his office prepared a long memorandum on the *desirability* of strong and friendly relations with Yugoslavia.[2] Belgrade was the pivotal point of any southeastern policy, it said, in view of Yugoslavia's central position, its participation in regional treaties, and its problems with Italy (which was still regarded as Germany's rival). King Alexander's death changed little since Prince Paul's policy was not different. Internally "the country is firm" and the Croat issue does not threaten it. On balance, it concluded, "stronger links are both possible and necessary, starting with economics and ending with politics." This was ultimately Hitler's policy. Any deviation from could only come from the uninformed lower echelons.

Two weeks after the assassination of King Alexander the Foreign Ministry sent a circular to all German legations, instructing them to reject any claim that Germany tolerated the activities of Croat émigrés as "utterly tendentious" and calculated to divert attention from the real culprits.[3] The Ministry quoted police measures taken throughout Germany against known and suspected Ustaša activists. They included cooperation with the Yugoslav authorities, whose requests for surveillance of Croat émigrés in Germany were forwarded to the police and the results of all inquiries passed back to the Yugoslav Legation.[4] Goering personally demanded the arrest of two

---

[1] DGFP, C, Vol. 2, No. 92. Lammers to State Secretary Bülow, 30 November 1933.

[2] Krizman (1975), pp. 82-83.

[3] DGFP, C, Vol. 3, No. 268. Foreign Ministry circular of 25 October 1934.

[4] In order to expedite investigation of Ustaša activities in the Reich, the Yugoslav government asked the Germans on 27 October 1934 that the Legation in Berlin be allowed to communicate directly with the police authorities. Foreign Ministry under-secretary Koepke asked Goering to

prominent Croat émigrés, Lorković and Cihlar. They were released in February 1935, but only after signing statements that while in Germany they would refrain from all political activity. In March 1935 the Foreign Ministry instructed its consulates in Italy not to issue a new visa to Branimir Jelić for his return to Germany, since he was politically undesirable.[1]

The remaining suspected Ustašas were placed under police surveillance and subjected to preventive arrest. When two Croat activists, Mladen Lorković and Andrija Artuković, evaded tails and disappeared in June 1937, the search for them was given such priority that the chief of Section III at the State Security Directorate, Heinrich Müller more commonly known as "Gestapo-Müller" (r.), was personally involved in the investigation. Lorković was eventually located and arrested. Extensive correspondence with other émigrés uncovered in his lodgings was presented to Mogorović for examination.[2]

Faced with rejection but uncertain of its source, Pavelić tried to approach the Wilhelmstrasse directly. In October 1936 he addressed a lengthy memorandum, "On the Croatian Question" (*Die Kroatische Frage*) to the German Foreign Ministry.[3] Declaring himself an enemy of Versailles and ideologically close to National Socialism, he asserted a community of interests and culture between Croats and Germans.[4] Serbs and Croats were worlds apart, he wrote, the latter being culturally and racially superior by virtue of their "Gothic," rather than Slavic origins.[5] Tailoring the pitch to the

---

grant this request, which the latter did immediately. Goering also assured the Yugoslav Minister, Balugdžić, that he would extend every help to the Yugoslav police delegate, Ivan Mogorović, when he arrived in Berlin.

[1] Biber, op. Cit., pp. 44-45.

[2] AA, PA, Buero Staatssekretär, Jugoslawien, Bd. 3.

[3] The document was sent in October 1936, but it was not received at the *Wilhelmstrasse* until early April 1941, by which time the Reich was about to attack Yugoslavia. It was sent to Mladen Lorković in Berlin, who forwarded it to Professor Carl von Loesch, head of the institute for the study of southeast European affairs in Munich.

[4] A copy of Pavelić's memorandum in Croatian is in: A-V.I.I., NDH, Kut. 85e.

[5] This claim was repeated by Pavelić on various *ad hoc* occasions in the years to come, notably during his first meeting with Hitler in June 1941. It was not based on any distinctly Ustaša "theory," however. Different claims of Iranian, Sarmatian, Illyrian, Celtic or Avar origins were

audience, Pavelić listed among Croatia's enemies, besides the Serbs, "international freemasonry, Jewry and Communism." The masons "invented" Yugoslavia in 1918, while the Jews controlled its trade and banking. The Jewry (*Judentum*) eagerly greeted the creation of Yugoslavia. "In the chaos of nationalities is the Jew's empire," Pavelić went on. "A Croat national state was not to the Jews' liking because the founder of modern Croat nationalism Dr. Ante Starčević was an enemy of Jewry and an antisemite. And indeed, Yugoslavia has developed just as the Jews had predicted, as a veritable El Dorado for the Jewry."

Just as worryingly, according to Pavelić, Yugoslavia was fertile ground for Communist agitation. The Serbs, having been "a long arm of tsarist Russia" in the past, were naturally prone to Bolshevism. While Yugoslavia upholds the Versailles order, and will therefore remain an ally of France, a free Croat state would trust "those to whom it is close culturally and economically":

> The model for all Croats is the German nation, with the Great German Reich at its center, embodied in its greatest and best son Adolf Hitler. In its struggle for freedom and independence against the imposed peace treaty, the Croat nation asks for the support of Hitler's Germany, in which it sees the mightiest warrior for natural rights, true culture and higher civilization.

Pavelić's memorandum had no impact. The Italians almost certainly had no knowledge of this document. In view of its tone and contents Pavelić had every reason to keep it well concealed from his paymasters, who were adverse to any German involvement in Croatian affairs. If Pavelić had hoped to induce the Germans to change their attitude, he was disappointed: throughout 1937-8 police surveillance and periodical imprisonment of his supporters made their activities impossible. Shortly before Stojadinović's visit in 1937 all known Ustaša sympathizers in Germany were interned, and suspects confined to their places of residence where they had to report to the police three times a day.[1]

Throughout this period Germany's vigorous economic penetration of the Balkans was proceeding unhindered. By 1936 Germany was taking a greater share of the Balkan countries' exports than all other powers together. Since trade was based on barter, those countries had to increase their imports from Germany in order to equalize the balance; Yugoslavia's surplus in 1936 was 21 million Reichsmarks. The trend was cemented with the Anschluss in

---

made at different times by Ustaša authors, often on the basis of scant scientific evidence – but always with the objective of asserting the racial distinction between Croats and Serbs.

[1] AJ, fond M.M. Stojadinovića, fasc. 20.

March 1938, which made the Reich Yugoslavia's neighbor, and with the absorbtion of the remnant of Bohemia-Moravia in March 1939. Both had been Belgrade's important trading partners and the economic dominance of the greatly enlarged Reich thus became unassailable. With his Balkan policy firmly on track and paying dividends, Hitler had no reason to take risks by dealing with Croat separatists.

The policy of wooing, rather than destroying Yugoslavia was not the only reason for Germany's attitude. There was also the need to maintain Germany's budding alliance with Italy, which was made possible and perhaps unavoidable by the Abyssinian war. This affair preoccupied the Western powers and Italy for more than a year and it helped conceal the nature of the real threat to peace in Europe. Unwittingly, Italy did a favor to Hitler by drawing attention away from him. In the end, the split between Italy and her former allies was beyond repair, with Hitler as the chief benefactor. Mussolini's accession to the Anti-Comintern Pact (initially signed by Germany and Japan), his withdrawal from the League of Nations and his invention of the "Rome-Berlin Axis" added a few sturdy nails to the coffin of the Europe of Versailles.

Italy's strategic shift was not wholehearted, as Ciano indicated to his hosts in Belgrade, and fear of Germany's rising power necessitated the definition of an exclusively Italian sphere of influence. During the tenure of Stojadinović it seemed to Mussolini that Yugoslavia was being drawn into such a sphere. The premier's fall in February 1939 placed Mussolini's entire Balkan strategy in doubt. Unexpectedly it transpired that his "Belgrade-Rome Axis" hinged too much on the authority of one man. Germany's seizure of the rump of Bohemia and the proclamation of an independent Slovakia the following month were received in Rome with alarm. It was feared that Croat activists not connected to Pavelić may engineer a replay of the Slovak scenario in Zagreb under German tutelage. Such fears grew with the news that Maček's deputy was coming to Bratislava on a "private" visit.

Mussolini wanted an explicit German guarantee of his sphere of influence in the Balkans.[1] Ciano told Mackensen of "rumors" that Maček intended to proclaim Croat autonomy under German protection, and asked for unambiguous reassurance. Hitler was only too pleased to oblige and reiterated his disinterest in Croatia. To additionally reassure the Italians, Ribbentrop sent a letter to Ciano which included an unequivocal statement that "in all Mediterranean questions the policy of the Axis is to be determined by

---

[1] Ciano, *Diary*, 16 and 17 March 1939.

Rome."[1] Ribbentrop added that "just as the Duce declared his lack of interest in Bohemia, we ourselves are disinterested in the Croat question, and if we acted at all in this matter it would only be in the closest cooperation with Italian wishes." While acknowledging that unnamed Croat representatives had approached the Germans, Ribbentrop said that they were told that Germany's position on the issue depended on Italy. He followed those assurances with a circular to all state ministries and diplomatic missions. "Italy's intentions should exert a decisive influence on Germany's attitude" in all Mediterranean issues, it said. Specifically, "in the interests of German-Italian relations, connections with Croat organizations must on no account be maintained."

Judging by Ciano's record, Hitler's gestures achieved the desired effect. Ribbentrop's letter induced Mussolini to declare "We are not whores, we cannot change our policy."[2] He was to succumb to the spell of his brutal friend on many other occasions in the remaining six years of their lives. Hitler's reiteration of Italy's Mediterranean and Balkan primacy averted a crisis in Axis relations, but the alleged strategic community of interests between Italy and Germany remained unclear. This ambiguity was to have grave consequences. In pursuit of his relatively limited objectives Mussolini was frequently erratic and inconsistent. He eventually limited his options to the point where he played a subordinate role to the German dictator whose long-term goals were dangerously open-ended, but who displayed skill and – until June 1941, at any rate – rationality in their pursuit. The two (above) differed in world outlook, basic assumptions, strategic objectives, temperament, and above all in the degree of moral depravity. Mussolini's failure to grasp the implications cost him his life and reputation, and his country many lives and much suffering.

---

[1] DGFP, D, Vol. 6, No. 94. Circular of the Foreign Minister, 25 March 1939.
[2] Ciano, *Diary*, 20 March 1939.

4. Maček and Italy

The fall of Stojadinović created a stir in Zagreb: outside support for "the Croat cause" appeared feasible once again. Such expectations were not groundless. Within days the German minister in Belgrade, Heeren, recommended a fresh look at the Croat issue: "The new situation created by the fall of Stojadinović's government gives us back complete freedom of action to use such favorable circumstances to regain the Croats' friendship."[1] Germany did not follow this course, primarily because it was at odds with Hitler's established Yugoslav policy; the respect for Mussolini's sensibilities was very much a secondary consideration. Te Croats were not to know this, however. If a diplomat of Heeren's stature and experience saw a change of policy as reasonable under the circumstances, it was unsurprising that similar expectations grew among Croatian separatists.

The leader of the Croatian Peasant Party Vadko Maček (below) decided to explore the possibilities. On February 12, 1939, one week after Stojadinović's fall, a man claiming to be his envoy visited the Führer's headquarters in Berlin and asked for German help in solving the Croat question.[2] He said that after gaining independence Croatia would establish closest possible co-operation with Germany and join the Anti-Comintern Pact. In line with Ribbentrop's circular, however, the German official remained reserved. State Secretary Weizsaecker responded to Heeren on February 22 and warned him against any encouragement of separatist expectations in Croatia.

The proclamation of Slovakia's independence by Monsignor Jozef Tiso nevertheless fanned many hopes in Zagreb. Maček's deputy August Košutić immediately left for Bratislava and Prague, ostensibly on private business, but the trip was interpreted as a signal that the HSS was interested in following the Slovak example.[3] The impression was reinforced by foreign press reports which drew a parallel between Czechoslovakia and Yugoslavia. There were rumors of secret contacts between Maček and Hitler and of Germany's

---

[1] DGFP, D, Vol. 5, No. 300, p. 401. Heeren to Weizsäcker, 22 February 1939.

[2] PA, Pol. IV, 61, Bd. 2, 12 February 1939. A note of 12 February 1939.

[3] On Prince Paul's reaction to Košutić's trip, see AJ, Fond J. Jovanovića.

alleged readiness to assist the cause of Croatia's autonomy if not full independence.[1] HSS publications added to such atmosphere by staring to publish articles favorable to Germany and full of praise for Hitler's supposed support for the self-determination of peoples.

Maček's envoys made a fresh attempt in Berlin and approached Hermann Goering but he gave them a short shrift.[2] He sarcastically remarked that if they had to discuss political issues with foreign governments rather than their own, they should go to Rome, not Berlin. And to Rome they did go.

"With the removal of Stojadinović," Ciano wrote of his friend, "the Yugoslav card has lost for us 90 per cent of its value."[3] The loss induced him to accept Croat overtures which would have been unthinkable only a few months previously. For the final two years of the existence of the Kingdom of Yugoslavia, the attitude of Italy would be consistently hostile. This was reflected in its receptiveness to contacts with two secret envoys from Croatia.

On March 9 Count Josip Bombelles, a country gentleman from Slavonia, asked to see Ciano. At first Ciano thought that this was a courtesy call, since the two had met at a hunt with Prince Paul in Yugoslavia, but Bombelles declared that he came as Maček's confidential envoy.[4] He talked of the "gulf" between Serbs and Croats and the impossibility of an agreement. An independent Croatia headed by an Italian prince would be the best solution, he said, or in personal union with Italy. Without presenting any demands, he warned Ciano that the policy of Belgrade was becoming increasingly pro-Western after the fall of Stojadinović.

Ciano cautiously replied that Italy's policy was in the spirit of the Treaty of 1937, but agreed to retain contact ("whenever the situation changes we might listen to the Croat point of view in deciding our political attitude"). The situation did change with the German liquidation of the rump of Czechoslovakia and the occupation of Prague. Mussolini's initial reaction was to postpone his planned occupation of Albania. He feared that by shaking up Yugoslavia, it could lead to the proclamation of Croatia's independence under German protection. He even advised Prince Paul to speed up negotiations with Maček.[5] Ciano's suspicions about German intentions in Croatia induced

---

[1] AJ, Fond M.M. Stojadinovića, fasc. 37, letter by A. Balinić dated 18 February 1939; fasc. 39, report by Stražičić dated 27 February 1939.

[2] DGFP, D, Vol. 6, No. 178, p. 248. Erdmannsdorff to Weizsäcker, 7 March 1939.

[3] Ciano, *Diary*, 7 February 1939.

[4] ibid. 9 March 1939.

[5] ibid. 19 March 1939.

him on March 19 to confide to his diary some of his harshest lines he had ever written about Hitler, referring to him as "unfaithful and treacherous."

The following day, March 20, yet another visitor claiming to be Maček's secret envoy came to see Ciano. This was Amadeo Carnelutti, a Croat construction engineer of Italian origin. He had first met Ciano in late 1938, when he presented the Italian foreign minister with a private memorandum advocating Croatian independence.[1] This time Carnelutti went further, asserting that the Croats were enemies of Germany but would nevertheless ask for its help if rebuffed by Rome.[2] If negotiations with Belgrade did not result in autonomy for Croatia, Carnelutti suggested that within six months there would be an uprising. An appeal for Italy's help would be sent, leading to an alliance between Croatia and Italy, customs and monetary union, and finally personal union with Italy.

In his diary entry Ciano noted that Carnelutti "repeated what had been said by Bombelles: negotiations to obtain concessions toward autonomy from Belgrade" would be tried first. But unlike Bombelles, Carnelutti came with concrete proposals. After consulting Mussolini, Ciano gave him the reply the following day: "First, seek an agreement with Belgrade if for no other purpose than to gain time; second, if this should fail, and you revolt, we shall intervene at the call of the Croat Government; third, abstain from any contact with Berlin, and forewarn us of your actions."[3] In the aftermath of the German entry into Prague Italy was loath to risk the Yugoslav status quo; hence Ciano's reference to the need to continue negotiations. If an uprising in Croatia were to take place in any event, Italy would respond to an appeal for help, if only in order to pre-empt the Germans. But by the time Carnelutti returned to Rome on May 18 Ciano was less restrained. Italy had occupied Albania in early April. Closeness between Germany and Italy had been re-established, and Ciano was about to depart for Berlin to sign the Pact of Steel. Prince Paul's visit to Rome, only days earlier, bore little fruit for either side. During their second encounter, the nature of Carnelutti's proposals and Ciano's reaction to them were remarkably uninhibited:

> 1. Maček no longer intends to come to any agreement with Belgrade; 2. he will continue his separatist movement; 3. he asks for a loan of 20 million dinars; 4. within six months, at our request, he will be ready to start an uprising. I make an

---

[1] Boban (1974), Vol. 1, p. 438.

[2] Ciano, *Diary*, 20 March, 1939.

[3] ibid. 21 March 1939.

appointment with him following my return from Germany, in order to continue our negotiations.[1]

The next day Ciano went to Berlin and Carnelutti returned to Zagreb. On May 26 they met again. Carnelutti informed Ciano that Maček had decided to reject agreement with Belgrade. On the basis of their previous discussions they prepared a memorandum with the following points:

> 1. Italy will finance Maček's Croat revolt with 20 million dinars; 2. he undertakes to prepare the revolution within four to six months; 3. he will quickly call in the Italian troops to insure order and peace; 4. Croatia will proclaim itself an independent state in confederation with Rome. It will have its own government but its ministries for foreign affairs and of national defense will be in common with Italy; 5. Italy will be permitted to keep armed forces in Croatia and will also keep there a lieutenant-general, as in Albania; 6. After some time we shall decide on the possibilities for union under a single head.

Mussolini approved the memorandum, Ciano added, and was generally "taken up with the idea of breaking Yugoslavia to pieces and of annexing the kingdom of Croatia."[2] Only four days later, however, Ciano learned of Maček's refusal to sign the memorandum which Carnelutti had taken with him back to Zagreb. This information reached him from both Carnelutti and Bombelles, but it did not dissuade Mussolini from talking about the Italian protectorate over Croatia as an objective to be attained in the future.[3]

In his memoirs and statements after the war Maček denied that he had initiated any contacts with Rome.[4] He also denied that he had authorized Carnelutti to negotiate on his behalf. In a letter to Cvetković written after the publication of Ciano's *Diary*, Maček insisted there was "nothing conspiratorial" in his indirect contacts, which he claimed were but a way of seeking information. Maček also maintained that the Ciano-Carnelutti draft agreement did not contain any reference to an uprising or to financial assistance from Rome; he claimed that it simply stated that in case of war the Croats would invite in the Italian army.[5] Maček's claims cannot be taken at face value, however. In the spring of 1939 he was dispatching envoys all over

---

[1] ibid. 18 May 1939.

[2] ibid. 26 May 1939.

[3] ibid. 31 May 1939.

[4] Vladko Maček, *In the Struggle for Freedom*. Pannsylvania University Press, 1968, p. 187; Hoptner, op. cit. pp. 139-140.

[5] Dragnich, op. cit. p. 119 (quoting from Cvetković Papers).

Europe. Even if the role of Bombelles was dubious, Carnelutti's *bona fides* were indisputable. Ciano and Mussolini would not have entered into potentially compromising arrangements with him had they not been assured of his credentials. It is inconceivable that an anonymous building contractor would try to mislead the foreign minister of a great totalitarian power and Mussolini's son-in-law (second from left, below), or that he would conceive the idea to misrepresent himself and go to Rome without a mandate from Maček. In addition, both sides had a motive for contacts. Mussolini and Ciano were apprehensive of German intentions in March of 1939; the Duce became aggressive towards Yugoslavia in May. They naturally welcomed an approach from the party which was far more credible local partner than their own Ustaša protégés. Maček's envoys had attempted to sound Berlin, too, but encountered a firm rebuke.[1] Having concluded that, in Axis relations, the Italians had the last word on Croat issues, it was not unreasonable for Maček to explore Mussolini's intentions. We know how far he went in those probings, but how serious were the implications? Did Yugoslavia's soon-to-be Deputy Premier came close to high treason?

Prima facie the Camelutti episode makes Maček appear not all that different from Pavelić in methods and objectives. There was one major difference, though: while Pavelić rejected any Yugoslav solution *a priori*, and in the end consummated his Italian connection at the cost of Dalmatia, Maček always allowed the possibility of an accord with Belgrade. His separatist alternative, and foreign arrangements necessary for its realization, were kept as contingency options if no agreement proved possible. Maček's contacts with Rome and his failed attempt to gain some traction in Berlin during the spring of 1939 need to be seen in the context of his negotiations with Prince Paul and the new post-Stojadinović government which were under way at that time. Both the outcome of those negotiations, and Maček's subsequent decision to sever contact with the Italians, indicate that his primary goal was internal: to strengthen his position in relation to Belgrade.

---

[1] Ilija Jukić. "Hrvatska u burno proljeće." *Hrvatski glas*, Winnipeg, 15 March 1954.

5. The Agreement Cvetković-Maček

Prince Paul replaced Stojadinović partly out of concern that the premier's policy of friendship with the Axis powers had gone too far, but this was not the main reason for his unexpected decision. In view of the deteriorating situation in Europe more significant was Stojadinović's inactivity on the Croat question. His self-confidence appears to have increased increased after the December 1938 election. Shortly afterwards he wrote to the Prince:

> That which now gives me the greatest concern is the situation in the Savska and Primorska Banovina (Croatia), where Maček is not only master in the majority of districts, but is, in addition, now beginning to command the state civil servants. To elevate the authority of the state in those regions, it seems to me, becomes the first order of business in the future program.[1]

Stojadinović occasionally made statements which indicated his readiness to solve the Croat question. After almost four years in office, however, he had not done so. His freedom of maneuver, he later claimed, was limited by the decision of the Regent not to change the 1931 constitution based on the concept of Yugoslav unitarism until young King Peter II came of age.[2] At the same time he was unmoved by international events. The treaty with Italy neutralized the only power that offered some hope to the Croat cause. Wooed by Germany, friendly with Italy, still nominally allied with France and the Little Entente, he believed he was building a strong external position.

Maček maintained that the Constitution had to be abolished so that the boundaries of the future Croat unit within Yugoslavia and its constitutional status could be clearly determined. Maček expected the rising tension in Europe to work in his favor by making Belgrade readier to grant concessions. He regarded Prince Paul as a more suitable partner for negotiations than the premier, having stated on more than one occasion that he only recognized the Crown and the Yugoslav state. The only known meeting between Stojadinović and Maček (January 1937) ended without results and no progress was made during Stojadinović's remaining two years in power. Although the two continued to maintain contact until mid-1938, with Maček's private secretary Branko Pešelj acting as an intermediary, the sticking point was the HSS insistence that the Constitution be abolished right away.[3] Stojadinović

---

[1] The Cvetković Papers (Hoover Institution Archives); Dragnich, op. cit. p.112.

[2] Stojadinović, *Ni rat ni pakt*, p. 514

[3] Branko Pešelj to the author, Washington D.C., May 1989.

refused, but offered instead to form a coalition with Maček and to sign a provisional agreement on the basis of Article 116 of the Constitution, which provided for emergency measures in case of a threat to the country. This was less than Maček would accept at that time.

To reach an agreement with the Croats which he regarded as essential, Prince Paul concluded that he needed someone other than Stojadinović. He also knew that by the end of 1938, Maček demanded the Prime Minister's removal as his *conditio sine qua non*. The Prince therefore selected Dragiša Cvetković, a politician from Niš and former justice minister, as Stojadinović's successor. Cvetković was reputed to be an advocate of agreement with Maček, but his lack of authority and independent power base also meant that the new premier would not be too much his own man. On the debit side, it was unlikely that the new government would enjoy any great credibility among the Serbs.

Prime Minister Cvetković announced his intention to negotiate with Maček in a speech to the Skupština on 10 March 1939. He recognized the individuality of Croatia as a fact predating Yugoslavia. Having received an encouraging reply, Cvetković arrived in Zagreb on 3 April, not only as Premier but also as Prince Paul's envoy. His talks with Maček proceeded smoothly. On April 22 a tentative agreement was reached, amended on April 27 and sent to Prince Paul for approval. The proposed arrangement was reminiscent of the Austro-Hungarian *Ausgleich* of 1867. The draft was short and simple: an autonomous Croat province (*Banovina*) was to be created, embracing two *Banovinas*, Savska and Primorska, parts of Bosnia-Herzegovina with a Croat majority or plurality (the Sava valley in the north, western Herzegovina and southern-central Bosnia around Travnik in the South), and Dubrovnik with the coastal strip to the entrance into the Bay of Cattaro (Kotor). Several districts in the new Banovina in the old Military Border had a large Serb majority. The final boundaries were to be decided by a plebiscite in a few contested municipalities. Banovina Hrvatska would enjoy wide autonomy. Defense, foreign affairs and common finances would remain in the jurisdiction of the central government in Belgrade. A joint government would be formed to see the agreement (*Sporazum*) through. The deal was to be legally based on

Article 116 of the 1931 Constitution, which provided for emergency measures in case of a threat to the country's security.

The draft was not approved by Prince Paul (with Cvetković, opp. p.). He was under intense pressure from several quarters to reject it in the given form. The sticking point concerned areas to be subjected to plebiscite and the way this would be carried out.[1] Determined resistance came from the Bosnian Muslim JMO party, led by Mehmed Spaho, opposed to the division of Bosnia-Herzegovina. Also opposed were senior generals, who regarded the proposed solution as detrimental to the defence capability of the country. Further negotiations were temporarily discontinued.

Frustrated by the delay, on May 8 a convention of HSS deputies met in Zagreb and granted Maček full powers "to make the necessary decisions commensurate with the attitude of the Serb people and political situation in Europe," and to undertake all actions in domestic and foreign policy which he found necessary to resolve the Croatian question. This resolution looked *prima facie* as authorization to Maček to go ahead with Carnelutti's mission to Rome, which followed soon thereafter; but the deputies were not told of any such plans at the time.

During his visit to Berlin in June 1939 Prince Paul became convinced that war in Europe was both unavoidable and imminent. He resolved to revive the talks. Some contact between Cvetković and Maček had been maintained through intermediaries, and formal negotiations resumed by the end of June. The agreement was reached quickly and the resolution of several finer points was entrusted to a team of legal and financial experts of both sides. The final version of the text was submitted to Prince Paul on August 24.[2] He signed it immediately.

The Agreement opened with the statement that "Yugoslavia is the best guarantee of the independence and progress of Serbs, Croats and Slovenes." The Banovina of Croatia comprised rather more territory than envisaged in

---

[1] Boban (1974) Vol 2, pp. 49-50.

[2] Ibid. Vol. 2, pp. 62-63.

the draft agreement of April 27 by including several districts of Bosnia and Herzegovina (map below). The new unit enjoyed extensive legislative, administrative and judicial autonomy. The government in Belgrade, which the HSS joined as a coalition partner (Maček's swearing in, l.), retained control over national security and defence, foreign affairs, and cenral finances. Ivan Šubašic became Ban (governor).[1] Šubašić's appointment was acceptable to Prince Paul and Cvetković as he had the reputation of a pro-Yugoslav moderate. He was responsible to the Crown on the one hand, and to the *Sabor* (local legislature yet to be elected) on the other. Laws and decrees pertaining to the Banovina would be signed by the King and countersigned by the Ban. The 1931 Constitution was still in force but the principle of state and national unitarism was dead. The Kingdom of Yugoslavia was being federalized.

The ensuing HSS strategy was twofold. On the one hand, Maček expressed his devotion to Yugoslavia and to Prince Paul personally. He argued that the jurisdiction of the Banovina and its final territory ought to be increased, but within the framework of Yugoslavia. On the other hand, local activists and the party-controlled press talked of the Agreement as but "a bare minimum," "only the first step," and hinted that the final objective was nothing short of full independence.[2] This two-track approach reflected genuine differences of opinion within the Party ranks, with Ivan Šubašić, Branko Pešelj and Maček acting more moderately than August Košutić, Juraj Krnjević, and many HSS middle-ranking officials and local activists.

The Ustaša organization within Yugoslavia violently opposed the Sporazum. The number of sworn Ustaša members was not greater than a thousand, but their impact was disproportionate to their numbers. The "home" group was led by Slavko Kvaternik (Eugen's father) and included Pavelić's future senior officials Ivo Oršanić, Mirko Puk, and Jozo Dumandžić. It used a

---

[1] Until 1918 this title designated the highest executive office representing the Crown in Croatia-Slavonia. It was also the designation of provincial governors under King Alexander's administrative division of the country.

[2] ibid. Vol. 2, pp. 217-220.

"mutual assistance society," *Uzdanica*, as its front for political lectures, collection of subscriptions for the ultra-nationalist *Hrvatski narod* ("Croat People"), and a semi-legal student organization.[1] The members of this group hoped to create a counterweight to Maček's claim to undisputed leadership with an all-out attack on the Agreement. Their agitation in 1939-40 was not without effect, and some party faithful were worried that the HSS political monopoly was being eroded.[2] The Ustašas contended that the deal obtained very little for the Croats and that it represented Maček's capitulation to Belgrade. Their real opposition was not to the terms of the *Sporazum* but to *any* agreement with Belgrade which would fall short of independence and leave Croatia within Yugoslavia.

Particularly virulent was the radicals' attack on Maček on the account of his "failure to take advantage of the unique international situation" to ally the Croat cause with the victorious Axis forces. The vow that "Croatia must not be on the losing side in another war" was often repeated by Pavelić's supporters in 1939-40.[3] Pavelić reacted to the Agreement with a circular from his "headquarters" in which he accused the HSS of illegitimately presuming to represent the people but "not saying or doing what the Croat people demanded of them." Pavelić specifically attacked the *Sporazumaši* ("Agreementers") for their failure to support "the two greatest and most powerful nations," Germany and Italy, opting instead to serve the "Masonic capitalist policy of international Jewry."[4]

As the only unit constituted on the principle of nationality and named after the nation which comprised a majority within it, the *Banovina* came close to resembling a nation-state. The *Sporazum* which created it was similar in spirit and in several important clauses to the Austro-Hungarian *Ausgleich* of 1867. It was the type of agreement which could have satisfied Radić two decades earlier. In the summer of 1939 the accord came too late. To the hard separatists it was a sellout by Maček. To the soft ones, it was a step in the right direction rather than a permanent solution. And in Belgrade some prominent Serbs, such as Professor Slobodan Jovanović and his disciples at the Serbian Cultural Club, thought that by "solving" the Croat question in this manner Prince Paul had merely helped create the Serb question.

---

[1] Slavko Kvaternik to interrogators. A-V.I.I., NDH, I.O. 9 6/9 1-104

[2] Branko M. Pešelj. "Serbo-Croatian Agreement of 1939 and American Foreign Policy." *Journal of Croatian Studies*, Vol. I, p. 29.

[3] Jere Jareb. *Pola stoljeća hrvatske politike*, p. 72.

[4] *Pro--glas hrvatskom narodu.* Leaflet dated 1 July 1940. A-VII, NDH, Kut. 85f.

V
The Fall of Yugoslavia

1. Precarious Neutrality

The fall of Stojadinović was an unpleasant surprise for Hitler and Mussolini. When Göring met Mussolini in Rome in April 1939 he remarked that unsettled internal conditions provided ample room for pressure: if Belgrade were to lean too far in the direction of Paris and London, it would be enough to encourage the Croats and the country would be paralyzed.[1] Ciano and Ribbentrop met in Milan on 6 and 7 May and agreed on their joint interest in preserving the Yugoslav status quo.[2] Ribbentrop expressed the opinion that in case of war Yugoslavia would remain neutral and reaffirmed Italy's primacy in the region.

Yugoslav diplomacy tried to reassure both Axis powers. Foreign minister Aleksandar Cincar-Marković told Ciano in Rome on April 22 that in case of war Yugoslavia would be neutral and continuie normal economic relations with Italy and Germany. He accepted the Italian *fait accompli* in Albania, which had  previously been a major source of friction between the two countries.[3] From Rome Cincar-Marković proceeded to Berlin, where he had talks with Ribbentrop and Hitler on 25 and 26 April. The Germans stressed the importance of continued good relations between Rome and Belgrade, to which the minister reiterated Yugoslavia's desire to remain neutral and her intention to avoid any arrangements directed against the Axis.[4]

When Ciano went to Berlin in the second half of May to sign the Pact of Steel (above) he expressed distrust of Prince Paul as a well-known

---

[1] See DGFP, D, 6, pp. 248-250, 252-253, 263. Memoranda on conversations between Göring and Mussolini, 15 April 1939.

[2] DGFP, D, 6, No. 341. Record of talks between Ribbentrop and Ciano, 18 May 1939.

[3] Ciano, *Diary*, 22-23 April 1939.

[4] DGFP, D, 6, No. 262, p. 325. Record of talks between Ribbentrop and Cincar-Marković, 25 April 1939; No. 271, p. 340. Record of Hitlerćs talks with Cincar-Marković, 26 April 1939.

Anglophile.[1] He suggested that during the Prince's forthcoming visit to Berlin he should be asked to leave the League of Nations and join the Anti-Comintern Pact. A few days later, on 30 May, Mussolini prepared a confidential memorandum for Hitler in the same vein.[2] He wrote that the Axis powers should not be satisfied with Yugoslavia's professions of neutrality but should occupy the entire Danubian basin and the Balkan Peninsula as soon as war broke out. Ciano's comments and Mussolini's memorandum heralded a new phase in Yugoslavia's relations with the Axis powers. Italy reverted to its anti-Yugoslav posture of the years before Stojadinović's rise, while Germany restrained Mussolini and vetoed any Italian action against Yugoslavia.

In his memorandum of May 30 Mussolini talked of war as an imminent European prospect, but not before the end of 1942. Hitler did not reply: he was preparing to attack Poland and planning to escalate the Danzig crisis as a first step. He and Ribbentrop assumed that Britain would not go to war over Poland, which Mussolini rightly doubted. Aware of his Axis partner's concerns Hitler had kept him in the dark until he told Ciano of the forthcoming attack on August 12.

During their visit to Berlin in June Prince Paul and Cincar-Marković were treated to an impressive display of German might, including a parade that included an entire tank division. Hitler went out of his way to impress and intimidate his royal visitor (l.). French foreign minister Georges Bonnet described the visit as being "worthy of the mightiest of monarchs": nothing was missed to create the impression of popular enthusiasm and to provide evidence of the value that the Reich attached to Yugoslavia's friendship. And yet, Bonnet pointed out, "the Prince remained true to his promises, given to our Minister prior to the trip to Berlin, and he refused to make any concessions."[3]

---

[1] PA, Büro Staatssekretär, Italien, Bd. 1. Ribbentrop's talks with Ciano, 23 May 1939.
[2] Krizman (1978), p. 322
[3] Georges Bonnet. *Fin d'une Europe*. Geneva, 1948, pp. 244-245

Indeed, Prince Paul resisted Hitler's pressure to take Yugoslavia out of the League of Nations or to replace the Balkan Pact with an explicitly anti-British arrangement.[1] Germany put a brave face on the slim results of the visit; the Foreign Ministry called it "mutually completely satisfactory."[2] Prince Paul's enduring impression was that war could no longer be avoided. During his subsequent visits to France and Britain he told the Western powers that it was essential for Yugoslavia to remain neutral in case of war.

The outbreak of war in September 1939 was immediately followed by Yugoslavia's declaration of neutrality. For over a year Belgrade's position was accepted by both belligerent sides. The Western allies her supplies of food and raw materials needed for the war effort continued to arrive as before. Prince Paul was privately sympathetic to Britain, and most Serbs regarded France as a natural ally, but Minister Viktor von Heeren (opp. p. r.) accurately reported that Germany had no reason for concern: her quick victory over Poland, while the French remained passive behind the Maginot Line, created a deep impression in Belgrade.[3] Talking to Ciano on October 1 Hitler calmly

---

[1] DGFP, D, 6, No. 474. Ribbentrop's note on talks with Prince Paul, 7 June 1939.

[2] PA, Buero Staatssekretär, Jugoslawien, Band 1, 9 June 1939.

[3] DGFP, D, 8, No 155, Heeren to the Foreign Ministry, 28 September 1939.

remarked, "for the time being nothing new is going to happen in the Balkans." With the confidence of a senior partner, he repeated the usual assurances of his lack of political interest in the area.

Italy's position was ambiguous. In August 1939, after Ciano's visit to Ribbentrop and Hitler, Mussolini briefly toyed with the idea of attacking Yugoslavia.[1] He decided to see the Allies' reaction to Hitler's attack on Poland first. Since they declared war, Mussolini was caught between the fear of war and the fear of revealing his fear of war.[2] He settled for the improvised policy of non-belligerency. The period both before and after September 1939 displayed the extent to which Italy's foreign policy had lost its sureness of touch and its freedom of action.

2. Pavelić Reactivated

Once the "Phony War" took hold Mussolini decided to make the policy towards Yugoslavia more assertive. Having encountered German opposition, he did what he could do without Berlin's approval: he reactivated the Ustaša organization in Italy, after six years of its inactivity and isolation. He decided to resuscitate Pavelić only after his attempts to strike a deal with Maček through Carnelutti had failed to produce results. Had Maček approved the agreement with Italy, the Italians would not have needed Pavelić. Their ambitions would have been satisfied, and backed by the authority of a popular political leader, not an émigré with marginal influence. Maček's refusal to become an Italian protégé disappointed Ciano, who suspected that Maček was plotting an arrangement with the Germans.[3]

After his final meeting with Ciano in May Carnelutti disappeared from the scene. The ubiquitous Count Bombelles came back, however, though no longer "on behalf of Maček." He now claimed to represent the Ustaša movement within Yugoslavia. The Italians allowed him access to Pavelić and gave him some money.[4] He told Ciano that conditions in Croatia were ripe for

---

[1] Ciano, *Diary*, 21 August 1939; DDI, viii, 13, No 162.

[2] Lowe and Marzari, op. cit. p. 340.

[3] For a detailed account of Maček's foreign contacts, see Boban (1974), II, pp. 108-119.

[4] Ciano, *Diary*, 20 September, 12 October 1939, 21 January 1940.

action because the Agreement was unpopular and the Serbs could no longer count on the support of France. He also urged Ciano to meet Pavelić. On January 22, 1940, Mussolini approved the meeting and the following day Ciano summoned Pavelić for talks.[1] After almost six years of post-Marseilles disgrace the Ustaša leader was back.

Italian expectations, as stated by Ciano, were essentially the same as the proposals he forwarded through Carnelutti to Maček. The focus was on a monetary and customs union leading to personal union between Croatia and Italy. The meeting on January 23 was not followed by any concrete steps, however, and there is little mention of Croatia in Ciano's diary entries in February and March 1940. It was easy for Ciano to deal with Pavelić, but Mussolini was not able to overcome German veto of his wished-for action against Yugoslavia. Things did not change by April 9, when after a lengthy pause Ciano returned to the theme of Croatia. Mussolini's "hands fairly itch," he wrote, and he is worried that if Italy does not act soon, Germany might.

The second meeting between Ciano and Pavelić took place on 10 May.[2] They discussed the location of his followers and their needs prior to Italian intervention, the date of which was left open. In the event, Germany vetoed Italian plans and Pavelić's "nucleus" remained dispersed and inactive until April 1941. Yet although he was finally received by a top official and promised some significant role in the events to come, Pavelić's predicament had hardly changed. Unlike Maček he was in no position to say "no" to anything. His chances, however slim they appeared at times, depended on his compliance with his hosts' and paymasters' demands.[3] Their ability to deliver, however, depended on the Germans.

Pavelić's contacts with the home Ustaša group were still scant. His absence, somewhat paradoxically, helped enhance his position because it enabled his followers to ascribe to him the views and intentions dear to themselves. Among the separatists in Croatia the Pavelić myth was enhanced by the very absence of the hero himself: by not being on the spot, he could not get involved in factionalism, and he could not make visible mistakes.[4]

---

[1] Ciano's *chef du cabinet* Anfuso kept minutes of the meeting; see Appendix.

[2] Ciano, *Diary*, 10 May 1940.

[3] Pavelić lived in a villa in Florence with a monthly allowance of 5000 Lire, "more than an Italian army corps commander or a provincial prefect." Eugen-Dido Kvaternik. "Ustaška emigracija u Italiji i 10 travnja 1941." *Hrvatska Revija*, Buenos Aires, 1952, p. 210.

[4] The reputation of another terrorist, Josip Broz, was greatly enhanced among his fellow Communists during his spell in prison, chiefly because he could not be involved in bitter factionalism riddling the Party at that time.

According to one of his closest aides, confidence in him and devotion to him knew no bounds: "Any thought that he may not properly represent Croat interests [vis-à-vis the Italians] was a priori excluded... We regarded Belgrade propaganda concerning Pavelić's promises to the Italians as the usual Serbian slander."[1] Yet the "slander" was true. The Italians did have territorial aspirations, and Pavelić did conspire with Ciano to satisfy them.

The exact terms were left vague: "How much of the Croatian coastline Italy would take and how much control she would exercise over the Croatian state were issues which were perforce glossed over for as long as possible."[2] His talks with Ciano on 23 January 1940 were not the cornerstone of his obligations to Italy but only an episode in a continuum that culminated in May 1941. Pavelić set the tone and defined the framework of the relationship in his first memorandum to Rome as early as 1927. The extent of territorial concessions he had to make to Italy in 1941 went beyond anything previously discussed, but the difference was merely that of a degree.

Pavelić's two meetings with Ciano in January and May 1940 were an accurate indicator of his relationship with the Italians. He was unexpectedly summoned, confirmed the nature of his obligations, and was put on ice again, until the coup in Belgrade radically changed the equation. He came to Palazzo Chigi not to negotiate but to listen to Ciano's terms and to endorse them. He might express a view, raise a point or two, but when it came to an issue of substance, to Croatia's post-independence status, to the customs, monetary and personal union with Italy, or Italian control over its defense and foreign affairs, Pavelić could do no more than ask that the details be kept secret "at first" for public relations reasons.

From the outset, Pavelić's reliance on Fascist Italy was a marriage of convenience. There was no natural affinity, cultural, ideological or geopolitical, between Croatian ultra-nationalism and Italian fascist irridentism. They needed each other only because they expected to obtain some advantage from the other. This fact remained implicit in all of Pavelić's dealings with the Palazzo Chigi. Well aware of the uncomfortable and potentially compromizing implications, Pavelić preferred to deal with the Italians strictly on his own. This arrangement had an advantage and a disadvantage for the Italians. By dealing only with the émigré leader they ensured that deals could be struck behind the backs of his followers. The danger lay in the fact that Pavelić alone was the guarantor of their designs.

---

[1] Kvaternik, op. cit.,. p. 211.

[2] Stevan K. Pavlowitch, *Unconvential Perceptions of Yugoslavia, 1940-1945*. New York: Columbia University Press, 1985, p. 107.

It is noteworthy that from among several hundred Ustaša émigrés who had spent some time in Italy over a decade, the Italians had not recruited any *other* Ustaša assets. Unlike other totalitarian powers, which actively recruited, promoted and trained two or more teams of potential collaborators in different countries – some motivated by ideology, others by more mundane reasons – the Italians *alienated* most Ustaša émigrés and turned some into their sworn enemies. Animosity towards Italy is present in many statements and writings by the members of Pavelić's group. There was no "pro-Italian faction" in the Ustaša leadership except for Pavelić himself. Accordingly Mussolini and Ciano had to rely on Pavelić, and him alone, when the time came to consummate the relationship. When he paid the debt with the Rome Treaties in May 1941, there was nothing left to bind him to Italy or the Italians to him.

The news of Ciano's first round of talks with Pavelić on January 22, 1940, soon reached Belgrade, probably through Count Bombelles. Yugoslav Minister Hristić visited Ciano on 7 March to express concern over renewed Ustaša activity. Ciano gave him "at once the most ample assurances."[1] Hristić was not reassured,. In April he visited his German colleague and told him of rumors that Italy was preparing military action against Yugoslavia.[2] Ambassador Mackensen said that it was in the interest of Germany, as well as Italy, that peace should reign in the Balkans.

As Ciano met Pavelić for the second time on May 10, Mussolini was in a belligerent mood. He ordered General Gambarra's recall from Spain so that he could take command of Italian troops earmarked for action in Croatia. Ciano noted that the Duce circled "a day in early June" in his calendar. On that same day, however, the Wehrmacht started its Blitzkrieg in the west. By May 13 Mussolini was so impressed by the pace of the German offensive in France that he told Ciano he would not be attacking Yugoslavia after all. Attacking it, he said, would be "a humiliating fallback."[3]

---

[1] Ciano, *Diary*, 7 March 1940.

[2] PA, Buero Staatssekretär, Jugoslawien, Bd 1, No 785 of 30 April 1940.

[3] Ibid. 13 May 1940.

On June 10 Mussolini declared war on France and Britain in an address to a rapturous crowd from his balcony at Piazza Venezia (opp. p. l.). His decision to join Hitler's side had been long in the making. In April and May, as Germany scored one success after another, his caution – so apparent between August 1939 and April 1940 – melted as quickly as the French divisions. Even Ciano's Germanophobia seems to have been pushed aside. The King and the army tried to stem the tide. The chiefs of staff admitted their inability to conduct a war even on a limited scale. Marshal Badoglio made the amazing admission that Italy's intervention could only be considered "if the enemy was so prostrated to justify such audacity."[1] In the end German victories in France made "the enemy" utterly prostrated,[2] and his fear that the spoils would be all Germany's forced Mussolini's hand.

The spoils proved meager. Extravagant Italian demands of France- Nice, Corsica, Tunisia, Savoy – were firmly toned down by the Germans at Mussolini's meeting with Hitler and Ribbentrop in Munich on June 18. Hitler wanted to offer armistice terms which would make it easier for France to break with Britain and end all resistance. Italy was allowed only to occupy a symbolic thirty-mile belt of French territory. Its ambitions in French North Africa were ignored. Mussolini was left in no doubt who was calling the shots. He therefore turned his attention to the Balkans yet again. The southeast appeared the only area where he could enjoy some freedom of action, and where he could compensate for the success of his brutally dominant friend.

On July 4 Mussolini ordered his General Staff to prepare plans for a simultaneous attack on both Yugoslavia and Greece. To this end an appeal for Italian intervention was procured from Zagreb and signed by a fictitious "Croatian National Committee."[3] This document was drafted by the "home Ustaša" group, probably with Pavelić's approval. [See Appendix] In the summer of 1940 Yugoslavia's neutrality still suited German interests, however. When Ciano expressed belligerent intentions towards Yugoslavia in a conversation with Hitler on July 7, he received a firm rebuke:

> The Führer replied that the decisive question ... was whether it was a matter of indifference to the Duce and Italy which country had the possession of the

---

[1] Lowe and Marzari, op. cit. p. 368.

[2] . Even so Italian Alpine soldiers were unable to make any progress against the French – demoralized by the defeat against the Germans as they were – and remained deadlocked at the border at the time of the Armistice.

[3] DDI, Ser. 9, Vol. 4, No 848, pp. 631-632. "Croatian National Committee" to Foreign Minister Ciano, Zagreb, 10 June 1940.

Dardanelles and Constantinople. If Italy should attack Yugoslavia, Hungary would immediately fall upon Romania ... [and] the Russians would also no doubt bestir themselves again, cross the Danube, and seek to establish a connection with the Straits.[1]

Hitler's concern over Italian restlessness was shared by the military. On May 27, at the height of victorious operations in France and Belgium, Generalfeldmarschall Walther von Brauchitsch, commander in chief of the German land forces felt sufficiently alarmed by the possibility of an Italian move against Yugoslavia that he made the unusual move of appealing on the foreign minister of the Reich to ensure "that chaos did not develop in the Balkans owing to Italy's attitude."[2] On July 9 the German military attaché in Rome, General Emil Rintelen, reported his disquiet after talks with General Roatta, chief of Italian army intelligence.[3] Roatta said that the Italian General Staff had been given the task of preparing plans which included attacking Yugoslavia's *northern* border from Austria – that is, from the territory of the Reich. The General Staff in Rome, Roatta went on, was "under the impression" that this had been politically cleared in Berlin. Hitler replied angrily that an attack on Yugoslavia was out of the question, that he wanted peace on his southern border, and that "the English" should not be given an opportunity to create bases in Yugoslavia.

To preclude any further surprises, Ribbentrop spelled out the German position to the Italian ambassador in Berlin, Dino Alfieri (r.) on August 16. The struggle against England should come first, he insisted. The Serbs were good soldiers and Italy would need considerable forces to defeat them. More worryingly, British bombers would certainly come to help Yugoslavia, which would inevitably involve the Luftwaffe just as the air war against Britain was becoming imminent.[4]

---

[1] DGFP, D, 10, No 129. Minutes of conversation between Hitler and Ciano, 8 July 1940. Hitler added the usual assurance that the Yugoslav issue should be resolved "in the Italian sense" when the time came.

[2] DGFP, D, 9, No 328. Memorandum by Etzdorf, 27 May 1940.

[3] DGFP, D, 10, No 343. The Foreign Intelligence Department of the Wehrmacht to the Chief of the OKW, 9 August 1940.

[4] DGFP, D,10, No. 353, pp. 408-410. DDI, Vol V, No.431, pp.414-415. Alfieri to Ciano, 17 August 1940.

Mussolini and Ciano accepted German admonitions but Hitler was still worried. He sent Ribbentrop to Rome to make sure that all was well. Talking to Mussolini on 19 September Ribbentrop repeated the familiar German line: Greece and Yugoslavia were in the Italian sphere of interest, and it was up to Italy to decide how to deal with them.[1] All such matters had to be left aside for the time being, however. The Germans put another veto on Italian plans, and Mussolini could do nothing; or so it seemed.

3. German Pressure Begins

Hitler and Mussolini met at the Brenner two weeks later, on October 4. Hitler talked of his plans concerning Spain, France and Britain, but he concealed the fact that he had already issued orders for the entry of German troops into Romania. When this happened only days later Mussolini was outraged. Not for the first time, and certainly not for the last, he complained that Hitler always faced him with a *fait accompli*.[2]

He decided to respond with a defiantly unilateral action of his own. On October 28, 1940, Italian troops in Albania attacked Greece. The attack made the geostrategic and political position of Yugoslavia even more precarious than it had been. The government in Belgrade was concerned about the future of Salonika in case of a swift Italian victory; the strategic importance of the Aegean port was enhanced by the memories of the Great War.[3] Only a day after the Italian attack, on October 29, Heeren reported to Berlin that the issue of Salonika figured prominently in the political circles in Belgrade.[4] In the first week of November, the Yugoslav military attaché in Berlin, Colonel Vladimir Vauhnik – an exceptionally capable intelligence officer (above) – paid two visits to the German Army High Command, as instructed by the Ministry of War acting on the request of foreign minister

---

[1] DDI, V, No.617, pp. 598-601. Minutes of talks between Ribbentrop and Mussolini, 19 September 1940.

[2] Ciano, *Diary*, 12 October 1940.

[3] On the Crown Council session after Italy attacked Greece, see Radoje L. Knežević, "Kako se to zbilo: grčko-italijanski rat, Solun i Jugoslavija," *Poruka*, London, No. 4-5, October 1951.

[4] See Bogdan Krizman. "Odnosi Jugoslavije s Njemačkom i Italijom 1937-1941." *Historijski zbornik*, Vol. 17, Zagreb, pp. 235-236.

Cincar-Markovic.[1] He brought up the issue of his country's interests in Salonika, and hinted that Germany could ask certain favors of Yugoslavia if it supported Yugoslav interests there. At the same time Belgrade nervously waited to see whether the latest conflict would remain localized. When this appeared probable after the first few days of fighting, which went badly for the Italians, the Yugoslav government issued a statement on November 2 affirming its policy of neutrality and expressing hope that it would be respected. Yugoslav reliance on Germany in restraining Italian aggressive intentions during the summer of 1940 also gave rise to expectations in Belgrade that similar German benevolence would continue in 1941.[2] This was not to be.

Hitler was furious and only grudgingly accepted Mussolini's *fait accompli*. Two factors were to play a decisive role in shaping his policy in the Balkans: British military commitment to Greece, which started with the establishment of RAF bases in Crete, and Italian military defeats. When Hitler

---

[1] Minutes of Vauhnik's visits: DGFP, D, 11, No 320, November 11, 1940.

[2] On Yugoslav expressions of concern see: DGFP, D, 10, Nos. 232 and 395.

talked to Ciano on November 18 he asked what Italy was ready to offer to Yugoslavia to placate it, and immediately added that Salonika would be "an appropriate inducement." His assertiveness in the matter was apparent in the way Hitler brushed aside Ciano's remark that this would be "difficult" for Mussolini to accept. In his ensuing letter to Mussolini on November 20 Hitler stressed the need to cultivate Yugoslavia, which had to be encouraged to change its policy and enter into real co-operation with the Axis. In his reply of November 22 Mussolini declared readiness to let the Yugoslavs have Salonika and to guarantee their frontiers, but only if Yugoslavia joined the Tripartite Pact and if it demilitarized the eastern Adriatic coast.

Italian setbacks in Greece forced Germany not only to become more directly involved in the Balkans, but also to have a more explicit final word in this nominally Italian zone. Faced with military reverses at the hands of the small but determined Greek army, Italy had to accept a further erosion of its role within the Axis. As had become usual, Italy's weakened position was the result of a self-inflicted wound.

Some pressure from Berlin on Belgrade could be felt even before Mussolini's Greek fiasco. Initially this took the form of demands that the government of Yugoslavia should bring under firmer control anti-German papers and publications, which were conspicuous in Belgrade. A hint of the new German posture was felt in a report Heeren sent soon after the fall of France, to the effect that the new reality "requires an unconditional and candid adjustment of Yugoslav policy to the situation created by the German victory in the West."[1] In July Heeren reported with indignation that the arrival of the Soviet minister in Belgrade had stimulated pro-Russian and pro-Communist circles.[2] The diehard Francophiles, too, hoped that a Soviet-German conflict sooner or later was inevitable, he added, and that a Soviet-German war would ease the situation for the Balkans in general and for Yugoslavia in particular. By the end of August Prince Paul felt compelled to indicate to Heeren that Yugoslavia would increase its reliance on Germany.[3] The Prince did not conceal that this was a choice imposed by the circumstances.

As an inveterate Anglophile, in the early months of the war Prince Paul could take some comfort in the fact that there had been little discrepancy between the policy of Yugoslavia and British interests. His *soirees* with successive British ministers in Belgrade, his readiness to keep them well

---

[1] Heeren's report of 21 June 1940. DGFP, D, 9, No. 517.

[2] Heeren's report of 23 July 1940. DGFP, D, 10, No. 215.

[3] Heeren's report of 26 August 1940. DGFP, D, 10, No. 395.

informed at all times, had been prompted not only by his desire for kindred companionship, but also by a deeper reverence for what he assumed were British "standards" and values. In the words of a British Foreign Office official, "in fact Paul's trust of British representatives abroad was so profound that it was invariably taken for granted in official circles, and occasionally even taken advantage of by individuals..." His posture reflected a mood of deep shock which the fall of France caused in Yugoslavia, especially among the traditionally Francophile Belgrade elite. To many, the final predominance of Germany in Europe seemed assured: the liberal democratic idea was nearing the end of its era, and a new order was emerging. Its pillars were to be two totalitarian Axis powers.

During the latter half of 1940 the Balkans became the focal point of conflicting interests of Germany, Italy, Russia, and Great Britain. Since Germany obtained vital oil and food supplies from the Southeast, Hitler went out of his way to preserve peace in that part of Europe and avoid any incident which might lead to Great Britain's direct intervention. It was no easy task to synchronize many divergent political actions at a time when Germany was contemplating the invasion of the British Isles and subsequently planning, as alternate measures, the capture of Gibraltar, the occupation of Egypt and the Suez Canal, and the attack on Russia.

Once its hand was forced by the Italian action in Greece Germany proceeded with great determination, no longer to woo Yugoslavia to its side but to bully it into submission. The pressure was not only political but also economic.[1] By mid-1940 Yugoslavia's trade was totally dependent on Germany. As a result of the sheer weight of events and the feeling that a new era was approaching, a debate commenced within Yugoslavia about the need for internal adjustment which would bring the country more into line with the anticipated new order. Prime Minister Cvetković also aired such views. In June 1940 he talked of the need to reform social policy in line with "the experiences of other great states."[2] He indicated that Italian experiences would be applied in carrying out labor and social reforms.[3] Cvetković also encouraged debate on the introduction of planned economy.[4] The Government daily *Vreme* wrote often in this vein in the weeks and months following the fall of France. Such views were also present among the HSS and the Slovene

---

[1] Cf. DGFP, D, 9, No. 442. Director of Economic Policy Dept. to Heeren, 15 June 1940.
[2] *Politika*, Belgrade daily, 21 June 1940.
[3] *Politika*, 28 June 1940.
[4] *Politika*, 6 July 1940.

People's Party. A few weeks after the fall of France, breaking with his image of a "democrat" in the western mien, Maček declared: "It is obvious that the peasant democracy which we promote has nothing in common with the bourgeois democracy of Western Europe."[1]

4. Disagreements over the Agreement

After August 1939 there developed an increasing divergence of views between the HSS mainstream, now firmly in power within the Banovina, and the advocates of separatism. Within the HSS a strong separatist streak viewed the *Sporazum* as a means to the goal of total separation. Among the Ustaša sympathizers it encouraged a feeling that, for once, they had a chance to challenge Maček more effectively than before by attacking his "capitulation to the Serbs." The effectiveness of such attacks was enhanced by the activities of several high-profile returned émigrés, with Mile Budak in the position of prominence. In February 1939 he started publishing an openly separatist, pro-Axis weekly, *Hrvatski narod* ("The Croat Nation"), which in its first issue paid handsome tribute to "Our Glorious Neighbors," Germany and Italy. It became the focal point of the Home Ustaša group. Its contributors included several top officials of the subsequent NDH regime, notably Slavko Kvaternik, Ivan Oršanić, Vilko Begić and Mladen Lorković. In numerous editorials and commentaries they claimed that Maček betrayed "the Croat cause" because of his vanity coupled with a naïve trust in the Serbs. Other Frankist publications echoed the theme and alleged that his "so-called autonomy" could be taken away by those who had given it to him "by a stroke of the pen."[2] Maček was attacked not only for being "pro-Yugoslav" but also for not being fascist, attuned to "our great and powerful neighbors, who are determining the fate of Europe today."[3]

In 1940 the Ustaša activity aimed at penetrating local HSS branches, recruiting new members among the party's right wing, and fanning internal rifts. In this they had some success, especially among students. Maček's supporters were aware of the trend but comforted themselves with the thought that he remained "the master in the villages." On the whole the response of the HSS leadership was ambiguous. Maček was reluctant to acknowledge any schism within the Croat camp, which had been solidly united behind him and

---

[1] *Hrvatski dnevnik*, No. 1495, 26 June 1940.

[2] *Nezavisnost* (a Frankist paper edited by Stjepan Bućć), No. 1, 12 January 1940.

[3] ibid.

the HSS prior to the *Agreement* of August 1939. He was reluctant to deal too harshly with the separatists and worried about the extent of their infiltration of the Party, and especially of its paramilitary organizations, the Village Guard and the Citizens Guard (*Seljačka zaštita, Građanska zaštita*; picture below :a *Zaštita* bugler at a 1940 rally).[1] Only when the Frankist-Ustaša agitation turned violent under the auspices of the illegal *Matija Gubec Society* the HSS-controlled Banovina authorities decided to clamp down on all fringe groups, Communist as well as separatist. In early 1940 fifty known Ustašas and their sympathizers were arrested and interned at a camp at Kruščica near Travnik, in an area of southwestern Bosnia incorporated into the Banovina.[2] Two leading separatist papers, Budak's *Hrvatski narod* and *Nezavisnost* (*Independence*), edited by a self-styled "Croatian National Socialist," Stjepan Buć, were banned. Ustašas responded by attacking Maček in clandestinely distributed leaflets and in newssheets published abroad, such as the

Domobran, "Home Defender," smuggled from Argentina (p. 117, overleaf). Maček was depicted as a traitor: his Banovina was a pathetic remnant of what belongs to Croatia by historical right and he was destroying Croatia in order to save Yugoslavia, "which is but another name for the Greater Serbia."[3]

The profile of the leading Ustaša activists reflected the social context of the movement's relative strength in the legal profession. The study of law in Austria-Hungary and elsewhere in Central Europe had had for its primary purpose social advancement. The graduate's traditional career path was in the civil service. In this field many Croats felt that they were at a disadvantage in the Kingdom of Yugoslavia, not least because of the need to accept and identify with the values of the state in order to serve it with distinction and and advance in its hierarchy. The Zagreb business class, prominent in Yugoslavia's financial and industrial life, did not have that problem: most top Croat bankers and enterpreneurs were known for strong pro-Yugoslav views.

---

[1] ibid. pp. 188-189.

[2] The list of internees read like a partial *Who Is Who* of the subsequent Ustaša regime: Ivan Oršanić, Mladen Lorković, Jozo Frković, Juco Rukavina... Also interned were "Croatian Hitlerites," the self-styled national-socialists led by Slavko Govedić, who were seen as potential rivals and treated accordingly by Pavelić and his followers.

[3] E.g. undated leaflet (spring 1940) in A-V.I.I., Pop. 17, Kut. 32, Reg. 31/1-8.

To the lawyers, however, the Ustašas bore the promise of the fulfillment of nationalist values in an explicitly *Croat* state bureaucracy. The potential for social advancement, political participation and job security in the future independent Croatia was an alluring package, however uncertain its prospects.

The ambivalence of the HSS was apparent in its twin efforts to maintain its leading position among the people and at the same time to play the role of a responsible partner in the governing coalition in the midst of a major war. On the one hand, the HSS-controlled press kept repeating that the *Banovina* was not the final solution of the Croat question but only the first step toward such solution: many areas of authority were ill-defined, the argument went, and various territorial and financial arrangements still remained to be finalized. This gave rise to rumors that the *Sporazum* itself was a cunning ploy by Maček, whose final objectives were no different to those of Pavelić. A secret party circular to that effect, supposedly written by the HSS leadership, fanned Serb suspicions.[1]

On the other hand, Maček stated repeatedly that he had made the strategic decision to accept the Yugoslav solution of the Croat question. He heaped extravagant praise on Prince Paul during the latter's visit to Zagreb in January 1940. In April he gave a strongly loyalist statement to a visiting French journalist:

---

[1] On the alleged *Okružnica* see Boban (1974), Vol. 2, pp. 217-227.

Twenty years after the war, within the Kingdom of Yugoslavia our demands were recognized.... We are rejoicing that our aspirations encountered a cordial response with Prince Paul. Foreign propaganda seeks to frustrate fulfillment of our ideals, but we, and our kinsmen the Serbs, will not fall for any intrigues.[1]

Maček was trying to square a circle: to extend the Banovina autonomy internally, while providing broad support to the government in its foreign relations. This assessment of his ambivalent position was supported by foreign observers. The British consul in Zagreb, Rapp, reported that Ilija Jukić, Maček's chief of staff at the Office of Deputy Premier, insisted that his boss was "a totally loyal Yugoslav" who had "special confidence in Prince Paul" and who would not engage in any intrigues with other countries.[2] In December 1940 the Italian minister in Budapest, Vinci, reported that the Hungarian foreign minister, Imre Csaky (r.) told him of Maček's conversation with a visiting Hungarian dignitary. Maček is supposed to have declared that the Croats would fight "to the last man" if Italy intervened in Yugoslavia in any way.[3]

The HSS press promoted the view that Maček had a special role in preserving the neutrality of Yugoslavia and shaping its pragmatic foreign policy. There were hints that Yugoslavia's diplomacy would have been less stable if left entirely to the Serbs. The HSS also stressed the link between the deteriorating international situation and the need for swift application of the *Sporazum*.[4] In fact there was no disagreement between Prince Paul, Cvetković and Maček on foreign issues. As the architect of the country's foreign policy, Prince Paul could count on Maček in presenting the image of a united Yugoslavia to the outside world, which after all was the Regent's key objective in engineering the *Sporazum*. In view of Yugoslavia's worsening geopolitical situation in the autumn of 1940, Prince Paul was in need of all the support he could muster.

---

[1] As reported in *Hrvatski dnevnik* and *Politika* on 20 April 1940.

[2] F.O. 371, f-24884, R 617. Shone's report to Nichols of 7 January 1940; Rapp's report to Shone was dated 6 January.

[3] DDI, 9, II, 595, Vinci to Ciano, 30 December 1939.

[4] See Boban (1974), Vol. 2, Chapter 3.

5. The Pact, the Coup, the War

By the end of November 1940 a notable reversal of roles in the relationship between Yugoslavia and the Axis was taking place. For the best part of the previous two years Italy was aggressive towards its eastern neighbor, while Germany exercised a moderating influence. As the year drew to its close, German pressure on Belgrade increased, while Italy had stopped contemplating any aggressive action against Yugoslavia. Bogged down in Greece, it welcomed the establishment of discreet contact between the two countries through a prominent Belgrade lawyer and legal advisor of the Italian Legation there, Vladislav Stakić.[1] On November 11 Stakić visited Ciano who told him that Mussolini supported the idea of an Italo-Yugoslav entente. Ciano added a personal thought:

> I always considered an attack on Yugoslavia a difficult undertaking and not useful for the future equilibrium of Europe. Instead of bringing under our roof a mass of nervous and untrustworthy Croats, I believe it is better to create a solid basis of understanding with Yugoslavia.[2]

The prospects for Pavelić were becoming bleak again. His status as a dispensable tool of dubious value was strikingly underlined by Ciano's words.

While Stakić was in Rome, another Yugoslav secret emissary was sent to Berlin. This was Danilo Gregorić, an agile Slovene journalist in his 30s who edited the center-right Belgrade daily *Vreme*, close to the government.[3] During his two visits to Germany in as many weeks he attempted to find out informally but authoritatively what the Germans really wanted. Told that a non-aggression treaty would satisfy the Reich, Gregorić promptly responded that Belgrade would comply. He arranged for the foreign minister, Cincar-Marković, to come to finalize the treaty.

Cincar-Marković left for the Berghof and was received by Hitler on November 28. At first Hitler suggested that Yugoslavia sign a non-aggression treaty with Germany and Italy, as expected.[4] He promised German backing for a consolidated Yugoslavia if it entered the new European order, and mentioned Salonika as an inducement. But then Hitler omenously added that the future relationship could go further, alluding to the possibility of

---

[1] See Vladislav Stakić. *Moji razgovori sa Musolinijem*. Munich: Iskra, 1967, pp. 86-87.
[2] Ciano, *Diary*, 11 November 1940.
[3] On Gregorić's approaches to the Germans: DGFP, D, 11, No. 324 of 12 November.
[4] Record of Hitler's talks with Cincar-Marković: DGFP, D, 11, No. 417.

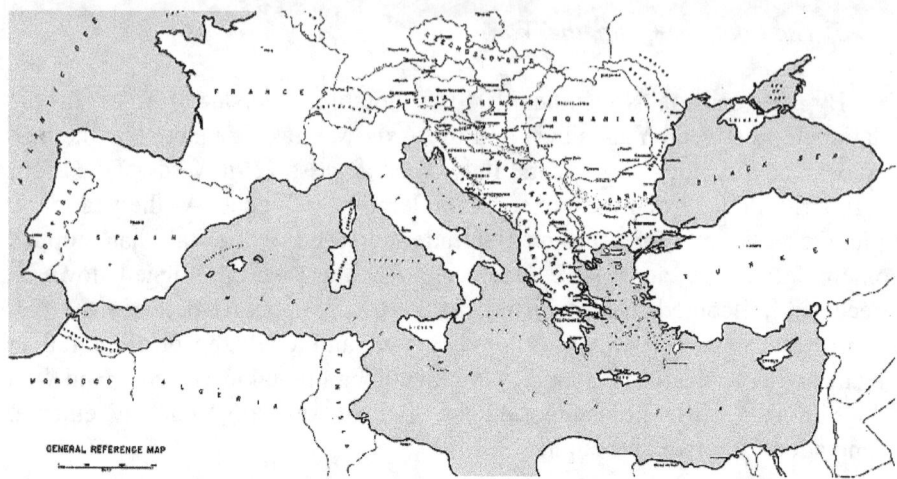

GENERAL REFERENCE MAP

Yugoslavia joining the Tripartite Pact. Cincar-Marković returned to Belgrade to present Hitler's proposal, still confident that a suitable formula could be found for the proposed treaty that would satisfy Hitler and safeguard the country's neutrality. Assuming that he would be appeased with the Yugoslav acceptance of the non-aggression treaty – especially since it was *he* who had proposed it – the Yugoslav government replied on December 7 that it was prepared to sign such a document, "based on the Italian-Yugoslav Treaty of March 1937."[1] Hitler suddenly raised his demands, however. After two weeks' silence he replied that a non-aggression treaty "would not satisfy" the need for closer links between Yugoslavia and the Axis, since it would still "leave open" the issue of its accession to the Tripartite Pact.[2]

Prince Paul and the government were taken aback. Hitler had simply changed his mind, which was in his power to do anyway. Throughout this period Germany's combined diplomatic and military pincer movement had continued. One by one, Yugoslavia's neighbors to the north and east were joining the Pact and accepting German troops on their territory. Hungary signed the Pact on 20 November 1940; Romania on 23, and Slovakia on 24 November. Bulgaria waited until the Germn troops could cross the Danube from Romania and signed its accession on March 1,1941.

During the conferences between Hitler and Mussolini (January 18-20) the Italians were told about the intended crossing into Bulgaria and forthcoming attack on Greece so as to prevent the British from gaining a foothold. Bulgaria was to be protected against the Soviet Union or Turkey.

---

[1] DGFP, D, No. 238, 10 October 1941, No 467. Heeren's report dated 7 December 1940.

[2] DGFP, D, 11, No. 549, 21 December 1940; DGFP, D, 11, No. 551, 23 December 1940.

The inviolability of what remained of Romania would be guaranteed by the presence of German forces. Each objective required strong forces whose assembly would take time. Precautions had to he taken that the German plans would not be revealed prematurely. For this reason the crossing of the Danube would have to be delayed as long as possible and, once it was executed, the attack on Greece would have to be launched at the earliest moment.[1]

Hitler's strategicy objective was to prepare his southern flank for the Barbarossa. In the process Yugoslavia found itself encircled. Most of Germany's new Balkan allies had actual or potential irredentist claims against it, which left the country vulnerable militarily and psychologically. In the Balkans, in the winter of 1940-1941, it was not easy to enjoy the distinction of being the last "Versailles state" to have its 1919 frontiers still intact.[2]

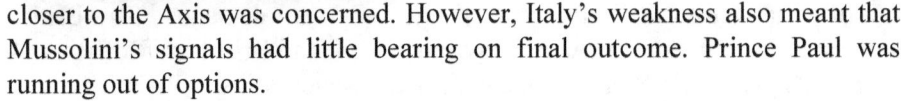

It is ironic and indicative of the desperate predicament of Prince Paul and his government, that a respite was sought in Rome. Sensing that the difficulties in Greece had rendered Italy harmless to Yugoslavia and sensitive to Germany, the Belgrade government hoped to win Mussolini over to the idea of a bilateral or trilateral treaty based on the 1937 model. Stakić went to Rome again in early 1941 and was pleased with Mussolini's encouraging response.[3] The Duce suggested that such treaty would suffice as far as the demand for Yugoslavia's drawing closer to the Axis was concerned. However, Italy's weakness also meant that Mussolini's signals had little bearing on final outcome. Prince Paul was running out of options.

---

[1] Department of the Army Pamphlet 20-260, The German Campaigns in the Balkans (Spring 1941). Washington D.C. 17 November 1953.

[2] The Baltic states and Poland were wiped off the map in 1939-40; Finland lost territory (Karelia, Vyborg) to the Soviets in 1940; Czechoslovakia finally ceased to exist in March 1939, having already lost much of its original territory to Germany (Sudetenland), Hungary (southern Slovakia, Ruthenia) and Poland (Teschen, or Ciesynski Slask); Romania was mutilated by its "friends" in two arbitrations, ceding most of Transylvania to Hungary and south Dobruja to Bulgaria; in addition it had lost Bessarabia and Bukovina to the Soviets.

[3] Stakić, op. cit. pp. 92-100.

The Italians duly informed Berlin of their talks with Stakić. Hitler would have none of this. He had serious business on his mind: getting Greece out of the way and settling scores with Stalin. There was no room for *combinazioni* any longer, and on a subsequent visit to Berlin Gregorić was firmly told that Cvetković and Cincar-Marković should come to Berghof to clarify the issue. They arrived there on February 14, 1941. Ribbentrop (with Cvetković, opp. p. l.) and Hitler cut short their preliminary suggestions of a "neutral bloc" in the Balkans. For Yugoslavia it would be best to join the Tripartite Pact, Hitler said, and so to ensure her proper position in the New Europe.[1] Hitler's tone left no doubt that joining the Pact was the only option. Cvetković and Cincar-Marković were also told that Prince Paul himself needed to come for talks.

Aware that he was going to face a determined German assault, the Prince tried the Italian card once again.[2] This time the Germans intervened, asking the Italians not to accept any overtures and to let Berlin know immediately of any eventual Yugoslav proposals.[3] The door was shut. When Prince Paul presented himself at the Berghof on March 4, he was alone in every sense. What followed was a five-hour "massage" by Hitler, in Prince Paul's own words to Ban Šubašić.[4] In spite of intense pressure the Prince evaded a final answer, saying that he could not make a decision of such magnitude as joining the Pact without consultations. This was his way of saying that he was *unwilling*, rather than unable, to make that decision alone. He returned to Belgrade on March 5, still undecided but aware that the time was running out. For the following day he called a session of the Crown Council, an *ad hoc* body not provided for in the Constitution, which included the other two regents and key government ministers.

In the meantime, British and American diplomats in Belgrade were making last-minute efforts to dissuade the Yugoslav government from signing the Pact. Both ministers, Arthur Bliss Lane and Ronald Ian Campbell, went out of their way to make Prince Paul reject German demands.[5] The British suggested consultations between Yugoslav, Greek and British staff officers. A representative of the Yugoslav General Staff, Major Milisav Perišić, flew to Athens and met senior Greek and British officers on March 8 and 9, 1941. He soon established that Yugoslavia could expect no help from the British, who

---

[1] Record of talks at Berghof: PA, Buero Staatssekretär, Jugoslawien, Bd 1, 56.
[2] See PA, Büro Untersekretär, Jugoslawien, Band 1, No. 129; Stakić, op.cit.
[3] PA, Buero Untersekretär, Jugoslawien, Band 1, No. 133 of 28 February 1941.
[4] Krizman (1976), p. 145.
[5] Dragiša Cvetković. *Istina o 25 i 27 martu*. Paris, 1951, p. 31. F.O.371, f-30207, R 2926.

ПОЛИТИКА

УТВРЂИВАЊЕ ОДНОСА ИЗМЕЂУ ЈУГОСЛАВИЈЕ, НЕМАЧКОГ РАЈХА И ИТАЛИЈЕ

ЈУГОСЛАВИЈА ЈЕ ПРИСТУПИЛА ПАКТУ ТРИЈУ СИЛА ПОД УСЛОВОМ ДА ЗА СВЕ ВРЕМЕ ТРАЈАЊА РАТА НЕМАЧКА И ИТАЛИЈА НЕ ТРАЖЕ ПРЕЛАЗ НИТИ ПРЕВОЗ СВОЈИХ ТРУПА ПРЕКО ЈУГОСЛОВЕНСКЕ ТЕРИТОРИЈЕ

Немачка и Италија потврђују своју одлуку да ће суверенитет и територијални интегритет Југославије свагда поштовати

were in need of help themselves.[1] Yugoslavia was asked to sacrifice itself by refusing all German demands, plunging into war, and actually starting it by attacking the Italians in Albania.[2]

After hearing bleak reports from Prince Paul and Cincar-Marković on the political situation and from the war minister on the country's desperate military position, the Council unanimously decided to sign the Pact with certain provisos. The following day (March 7) Cincar-Marković informed Heeren of the decision and asked for written assurances from Germany and Italy on three key points:

1. Yugoslavia's sovereignty and territorial integrity would be respected;
2. No military assistance or troop transfers would be sought; and
3. Yugoslav interests in Salonika would be considered.[3]

Belgrade was demanding special treatment. Typically, shortly after a new member had signed the pact a German military mission would cross its border and gradually assume control over communications, airfields, and internal security. Ribbentrop reluctantly accepted all Yugoslav demands however, and even agreed that the first two of those provisions be made

---

[1] For the bankruptcy of the British war-fighting strategy in 1940-41, see A.J.P. Taylor, *English History, 1914-1945*. New York and Oxford: Oxford University Press, 1965, p. 515.

[2] In February 1941 President Roosevelt sent a message to Prince Paul asking him to make the plunge: "I most earnestly wish to point out that the United States is looking not merely to the present but to the future. I wish to convey to you my feeling that the world in general regards with very real sympathy any nation which resists attack, military or diplomatic, by the predatory powers." Roosevelt cited the example of Abyssinia, China, and Norway: each had resisted, and those that succumbed would be restored after the war. He added the threat that in the eventual peace settlement the treatment of a nation's claims would depend on its earlier attitude to the "predators." The U.S. was not at war at that time.

[3] DGFP, D, 12, No. 131; Heeren to the Foreign Ministry, 7 March 1941.

public, to placate the public opinion. This provided the Yugoslav government with the media pitch in its presentation of the Pact to the Serbian public, as evidenced by the headlines in the leading Belgrade daily *Politika* (opp. p.).

After an agonizing fortnight of further discussions in Belgrade and an exchange of messages on technical details between Belgrade and Berlin, the final decision to sign the Pact was made at the Crown Council on March 20 and confirmed at the Council of Ministers the following day. On March 23 Prince Paul cut the knot and sent Cvetković and Cincar-Marković to Vienna to sign the Pact. This outcome was not an expression of the Prince's political will, but it was the best the Serbs could get after a brave show but they could not maintain their opposition for ever: "The growing concentration of German troops in Rumania spoke a stronger language than moral exhortations from England's friends... [Hitler's concessions were] a great victory for the Serbs... By dragging their feet for so long, they had shown unequalled courage in the face of a state so much stronger than themselves."[1]

The signing ceremony (r.) was described by a participant as "reminiscent of a funeral." The leaders of Yugoslavia hoped that the watered-down version of the Pact – grudgingly accepted by Hitler – would calm public opinion at home. This failed; the government of Cvetković and Maček, and Prince Paul himself, did not enjoy the confidence of Serbian public opinion, which felt that the regime did not have the mandate to take such a decision.[2]

In the early hours of March 27, 1941, a group of Serb officers took power in an almost bloodless coup in Belgrade. Its apologists claimed that, for all its awful consequences, it enabled Yugoslavia to avoid the allegedly inevitable slide into the Axis war camp. This sentiment was echoed in the streets of Belgrade and other Serbian cities in the slogan of "Better grave than

---

[1] Martin van Creveld. *Hitler's Strategy 1940-1941: The Balkan Clue*. Cambridge University Press, 1973, p. 139.

[2] Prince Paul was shabbily treated by the British in later years. He had done his best to avoid the kind of catastrophe which befell his country after 27 March 1941. He died in Paris in 1976, convinced until the end that *any other outcome* would have been preferable to what had come to pass after March 27, 1941.

a slave" (*Bolje grob nego rob*) and "Better war than the Pact" (*Bolje rat nego pakt*). It was an explicit rejection of realism for transcendent goals. The conspirators reflected a certain Serbian tradition that at its best harked back to the *hajduks*, and at its worst culminated in the ignominy of the regicide of 1903. In 1941 the motives of the self-appointed upholders of that tradition had little to do with any notion of "national interest", rationally defined and prudently pursued. Its proponents "knew" what had to be done and sought legitimacy in the alleged support of an excitable mob (below). Their coup was

an incoherent, inarticulate act of protest, all the more destructive for its heartfelt sincerity. There was no plan on what to do afterwards.[1] During his discussions with Yugoslav leaders in Belgrade on April 1, General Sir John Dill, Chief of the British Imperial General Staff, found nothing but confusion and paralysis. Political leaders repeatedly stated that Yugoslavia was determined not to take any steps that might provoke a German armed attack. They failed to realize the imminence of their country's peril. Their mood and outlook left Dill under the impression that they believed they would have months to make their decisions and enforce their plans.

The *a posteriori* claim that the coup and the subsequent German attack contributed to victory over Nazism, allegedly by forcing Hitler to postpone his attack on Russia by six weeks, was proven to be false. The postponement had been made inevitable by the unusually wet spring of 1941 which made the roads of Belarus, Ukraine and western Russia impassable for German armor until mid-June at the earliest.[2]

---

[1] Cf. an eyewitness account by Lovett F. Edwards, BBC Radio, 27 March 1951, Studio 6A, BHRP Ref. No. Slo 86936.

[2] The only factor which may have contributed to a delay – had May 15 remained unaffected by floods – would have ben the need for all units, and in particular the armored and motorized infantry divisions, to be refitted after the Balkan campaigns. This rehabilitation, which was estimated to take a minimum of three weeks for the mobile units, had to be performed within Germany in the vicinity of major repair shops and spare parts depots.

In spite of the work of the British intelligence the coup was not "imported" from without.[1] Just as intensive Western pressure and propaganda was not sufficient to dissuade Prince Paul and the government from signing the Pact, so British and American efforts would not have sufficed to pull off the officers' revolt.[2] The coup was a Serb affair. It prompted Hitler's immediate decision to destroy Yugoslavia, starting with a furious, vengeful bombing of Belgrade, and ending in the collapse of the country.[3] Unconsolidated Yugoslavia – or, rather, disoriented Serbia – may have "found its soul" (Churchill), but in doing so it headed straight for the heavenly kingdom in the tradition of Prince Lazar, martyred at the Battle of Kosovo in 1389. It has not recovered since.

In Berlin the news of the coup in Belgrade caused shock. Hitler had an attack of fury. He saw the coup as an act tantamount to the declaration of war and as a personal blow. Without waiting to hear of the new government's composition or intentions, he decided to smash Yugoslavia.[4] He would do it with assistance from Italy, Bulgaria, and, a few days later, Hungary.[5] The turn of events forced Hitler to improvise, however. Having avoided contact with Croat separatists prior to March 1941, let alone supporting them, he had no contingency alternatives prepared in advance. At the conference on March 27 Hitler mentioned that Croatia would be granted "autonomy" but his thoughts seem to have been vague at first. In a letter to Mussolini the following day, informing him of the decision to attack Yugoslavia, Hitler did not mention Pavelić and his Ustaša followers.[6]

---

[1] Churchill either believed or pretended otherwise in the immediate aftermath of the coup: *Roosevelt and Churchill: Their Secret Wartime Correspondence*, Doc. 48: Churchill to Roosevelt, March 27, 1941, p. 136.

[2] David A.T. Stafford. "SOE and British Involvement in the Belgrade Coup d'Etat of March 1941." *Slavic Review*, Vol. 36, No. 3.

[3] But Roosevelt and Churchill greeted the news of Yugoslavia's collapse with perfect sang froid: ibid. Doc. 52: Roosevelt to Churchill, May 1, 1941. P. 139.

[4] Cf. DGFP, D, 12, No. 217. Minutes of a Conference on Yugoslavia, 27 March 1941. Hitler declared that the coup had drastically changed the entire political situation in the Balkans. He maintained that Yugoslavia must now be regarded as an enemy and must be destroyed as quickly as possible despite any assurances that might be forthcoming from the new Yugoslav Government. Hungary and Bulgaria were to be induced to participate in the operations by extending to them the opportunity of regaining Banat and Macedonia, respectively. By the same token, political promises were to be extended to the Croats, promises that were bound to have all the more telling effect since they would render even more acute the internal dissension within Yugoslavia.

[5] Cf. *The Confidential Papers of Admiral Horthy*. Budapest: Corvina Press, 1965, p. 176.

[6] Hitler to Mussolini, letter of 28 March. DGFP, D, 12, No. 224

In his reply Mussolini hastened to remind Hitler that "besides Bulgarian, and above all Hungarian cooperation, we should count on the Croats' separatist tendencies, which are represented by Dr Pavelić and his group. Pavelić himself is located in the vicinity of Rome."[1] His investment finally seemed about to yield some dividends.

6. Germans Seek Croat Partenrs

The ensuing ten days show that the stance of Mussolini had far less bearing on the future of Croatia than the intentions of Germany and the posture of Maček. The Germans hoped that he could figure in their plans; after all, it was he who had exclaimed *"We are Yugoslavia's Sudeten Germans!"* only three years previously.[2] Their desire to bypass Pavelić – in spite of Mussolini's pleas and Italy's nominal primacy – was due to three factors. Maček was the undisputed leader of his people and any scenario concerning Croatia's future would have far better prospects with him than

without him. Secondly, Pavelić's stock in Germany had never been high; he was regarded as an Italian puppet, and his movement as far too weak either to make a contribution to Yugoslavia's fall or to form a viable government. Finally, Maček's initial negative reaction to the coup in Belgrade may have given Germany some reason to believe that he could be won over because he would grasp the futility of cooperating with the people capable of making such a stupendous blunder.

Maček's attitude to the government of General Simović (l.) depended on two questions: what would be its relations with the Axis powers, and what would be its position on the *Sporazum* of 1939. It was obvious in the streets of Belgrade that the coup had brought to the fore pent-up dislike of Prince Paul's regime and its overall policy, both external and internal. It could have been interpreted as a revolt against the *Sporazum*, as well as against the Tripartite Pact. The military were reputed to take a dim view of the *Sporazum*, and Simović's government included some of its well-known opponents, such as

---

[1] Mackensen to Berlin. DGFP, D, 12, No. 226.

[2] At the HSS Congress in Zagreb, 15 January 1938. Boban (1974), Vol. 1

the second deputy-premier, Slobodan Jovanović. The new government nevertheless tried to provide continuity on both fronts. The attempt initially focused on the inclusion of both Maček's HSS and the Slovene People's Party in its ranks. Those two parties had strongly favored the signing of the Pact in the weeks prior to the coup. Their inclusion would help maintain the degree of unity of the country and send a signal to Berlin and Rome that the coup was not directed against them. Desperate to gain time, and unaware that the decision in Berlin had been made anyway, the putchist government went out of its way to appease the Reich. It issued a formal statement of its respect for international treaties, including the Pact.[1]

Maček gave his approval from Zagreb that HSS ministers join the government on the morning of March 27. He reserved the right, as deputy premier-designate, to wait and see how things would develop before accepting the post.[2] He decided to remain in Zagreb and to sound out the Germans on their intentions. On March 28 he spoke to a German geologist, Michael Derffler, who ostensibly came to Zagreb on a business assignment but was actually working for the Abwehr center in Vienna. Maček asked him to travel to Berlin and find out what were Germany's plans.[3] Simultaneously Maček instructed *Ban* Šubašić (r.) and another senior HSS figure, finance minister Šutej, to talk to Heeren in Belgrade. On March 28 Heeren reported that they assured him of Maček's desire not to change the foreign policy course and asked for German patience.[4]

On March 31 Ribbentrop instructed the Consul-General in Zagreb, Alfred Freundt, to give a reply to Maček. It boiled down to an unconditional appeal to him and other Croat leaders not to co-operate with the Belgrade government, but to "maintain contact" with Germany.[5] On the same day Freundt received another cable from Ribbentrop; he was to inform Maček that "provision would be made for an independent Croatia within the new order" if

---

[1] Cf. DGFP, D, 12, No 225, 28 March 1941; 234, 29 March; and 235, 30 March.
[2] See Boban (1974), Vol. 2, pp. 388-389; Maček, op. cit. pp. 216-218.
[3] Canaris to Ribbentrop, ADAP, 12, 1, p. 349; A-VII, mikrofilm Bonn 1/1032-34
[4] DGFP, D, 12, No. 236 of 30 March 1941.
[5] Ribbentrop to Freundt, 31 March 1941. DGFP, D, 12, No. 238.

Yugoslavia collapsed.[1] Freundt replied on April 1 that one of his officials had warned Maček not to participate in the new Yugoslav government.[2] Maček told the official (Otto Mitterhammer, press officer at the Consulate-General) of his conditions laid down to the Simović government, which included the recognition of the Tripartite Pact and adherence to its spirit.

In the evening of March 31 Maček received an explicit German warning from Derffler not to cooperate with Simović. Derffler later described Maček's reaction as that of "a completely broken man." The following day Derffler visited Maček again and pressed him not to go to Belgrade under any circumstances. Maček appeared hesitant and complained that many people came to him claiming to be German emissaries with all sorts of vague offers. The complaint was not unfounded: it is possible that Derffler's and Mitterhammer's efforts were not coordinated, although there is no evidence of any other German emissaries talking to Maček before April 1.

Maček was in the near-impossible situation of trying to preserve peace and stave off a German attack by assuring Nazi representatives that the new government would observe the Pact, even though he had only suggested such observance as his condition for joining the putschist government. His eventual decision to go to Belgrade he presented to the Germans as the policy that served their interests as well.[3] He did not know that the die had been cast

By April 1 the Germans realized that they had to broaden their options. It was far from certain whether Maček would heed their advice and stay away from Belgrade. They nevertheless continued to maintain contact with him but also reluctantly decided to prepare a reserve option with the extreme Croat nationalists. On April 1 Freundt was informed that two German officials were coming to Zagreb to get in touch with "influential Croat personalities."[4] The two were Walter Malletke of the NSDAP Foreign Department (headed by Rosenberg) and SS-*Standartenfuehrer* Edmund Veesenmayer (l.), who was seconded to the Special Operations unit of the Foreign Ministry.

---

[1] Ribbentrop to Freundt, 31 March 1941. DGFP, D, 12, No. 239

[2] DGFP, D, 12, No 241. Malletke's report quoted in Hoptner, op. cit. p. 272.

[3] A-VII, Bonn 2/231, cable received in Berlin 2 April at 8 p.m.

[4] Ministry to Freundt, 1 April 1941. DGFP, D, 12, No 243.

Malletke was supposed to keep pressure on Maček, while Veesenmayer's task was to create links with the separatists.

The leading figure among the "radicals," as German documents referred to the Ustašas within Croatia, was Slavko Kvaternik. In the days after the coup he had numerous meetings with three right-wing HSS deputies (Tomašić, Berković, Kuvedžić) trying to find out whether Maček intended to go to Belgrade. Kvaternik also attempted to influence the HSS leader through those intermediaries, asking him not to join the Simović government.[1] The first contact between Kvaternik and the Germans was established through an unnamed German consular official. Their conversation was limited to mutual exploration of intent. Kvaternik, unsurprisingly, recommended the Ustaša solution but the German said that they had confidence in Maček, who could "if he wanted, save the country [Croatia] from occupation." The role of Kvaternik and his group apparently became more important in German eyes on April 3. That morning Maček spoke to Malletke and finally rejected the idea of helping establish an independent Croatia under German protection.[2] By that time Maček had already made up his mind to go to Belgrade, where he arrived by the end of the day and was immediately sworn in as vice-premier. He appeared more determined and self-assured than during his earlier meeting with Derffler. He reiterated his readiness to assume personal responsibility for negotiations with the Reich on any outstanding issues, if Germany so desired.

Also on April 3, following the failure of Malletke's efforts, Veesenmayer was introduced to Kvaternik. Veesenmayer did not conceal his distaste for Pavelić. He told Kvaternik that *only Maček* enjoyed credibility in Berlin and made disparaging remarks about the Ustašas and Pavelić personally, saying that he was completely in Mussolini's hands and that even his mental health was in doubt.[3] Either Veesenmayer was not fully aware of Kvaternik's allegiance to Pavelić, assuming him to be an independent separatist leader, or else he wanted to induce Kvaternik to start acting on his own account – in which case the Germans would finally have *their own man* in Croatia. Kvaternik replied that Pavelić could not be bypassed in any combination because Mussolini trusted nobody but him and "it was well known that Germany and Italy had made an agreement which left Croatia in the Italian sphere of interest." At the same time, Kvaternik was forced to admit to

---

[1] Kvaternik's statement to interrogators, 1946-47. A-VII, NDH, I.O. 9 6/9-104.
[2] Report from Zagreb dated 4 April 1941, referring to 3 April. DGFP, D, 12, No. 262.
[3] A-VII, mikrofilm Bonn 2/259-260, cable No 33 of 3 April 1941.

Veesenmayer that "the radicals" lacked strength to start any action on their own. He saw the solution in the Germans' swift arrival.[1]

Veesenmayer's talks with the "radicals" convinced him of the chasm between them and Maček, whom they regarded as a traitor to the Croat cause. In view of Maček's refusal to accept Derffler's and Malletke's advances, Veesenmayer told Ribbentrop that further attempts with the HSS leader made no sense and requested approval of his efforts to unite "all important Croat groups who reject Maček's conduct of affairs."[2] The next day, April 5, Veesenmayer reported that he was successful in creating a broad front of nationalists, including right-wing HSS dissidents, with a written program.[3] He added that signatures were being collected for an appeal addressed to the government of the Reich (see Appendix).[4]

This "appeal" raises intriguing questions about German intentions. If the Germans were serious about the principle that Croatia belonged to the Italian sphere of interest and influence – as they had been repeating *ad nauseam* for years – then it would not have been necessary for their many agents to be involved. Least of all would it have been necessary to get appeals addressed to the Reich Government. The decision to destroy Yugoslavia was Hitler's own, made on the grounds of strategic grand design and the need to vent his anger. But the details of internal arrangements to befall the defeated country theoretically should have been left to the Italians: Mussolini was quick to remind Hitler of his own candidate for the Croat solution, Pavelić, as soon as the German ambassador woke him up with the news of the Führer's decision to attack. There are three likely motives for the German behavior.

The statement could provide a pretext, or one of them, for German attack. It did not carry much conviction ("Yugoslavia has ceased to exist"), but it could be used in the same way the "attack" on the radio station at Gleiwitz, by "Polish" soldiers on the night of August 31, 1939, was used. More likely the statement was meant to justify German involvement to the Italians. Hitler habitually applied the practice of presenting the Italians with *faits accomplis* and justifying his action by the need to act rapidly and to exploit the situation, which supposedly made prior consultation impossible. It is also possible that the statement was meant for public consumption in

---

[1] PA, Büro Staatssekretär, Jugoslawien, Bd 2, 34. Veesenmayer to Ribbentrop, 3 April 1941.

[2] Freundt to the Foreign Ministry, 4 April 1941. DGFP, D, 12, No. 263.

[3] Consulate in Zagreb to the Foreign Ministry, 5 April 1941. DGFP, D, 12, No. 270.

[4] From Veesenmayer's cable it is obvious that the signatures for the above statement were only collected on the day of its dispatch to Berlin, i.e. 5 April, but for political reasons it was antedated to "31 March 1941."

Croatia, as a means of making it more susceptible to Axis propaganda once the attack started.[1]

Maček's actions in the months before April 1941 and in the days between the coup and the capitulation of Yugoslavia were consistent with his principles. In 1939 he saw the Yugoslav solution as the least undesirable one under the circumstances. While opening or accepting lines of communication to different external and internal parties (e.g. Carnelutti's mission to Rome in the spring of 1939), he nevertheless displayed a degree of steadfastness in this basic stand. Only when Yugoslavia all but collapsed would he adopt a more ambivalent line.

The position of Kvaternik and the "radicals" was also ambiguous. They vastly preferred Germany to Italy as the dominant factor in Croatia. To their chagrin, however, the Germans were less willing than the Italians to treat them as viable contenders for power. Veesenmayer approached them only as second best, after Maček's refusal to cooperate. Even then he could hardly conceal his disdain for Pavelić and his movement. However much they disliked Italy, Kvaternik and his group had found it useful to point out to the Germans that Pavelić could not be bypassed since "Germany accepted that Croatia was in the Italian sphere of influence." They could also entertain hope that – if Germany turned out to be the dominant party – Hitler still might give power to *them*, and not to Maček, that "traitor of the Croat cause" and who snubbed the Germans anyway.

Pavelić had no part in the proceedings. With events unfolding at an ever faster pace, the contact between the "home" group around Slavko Kvaternik and their *Poglavnik* was non-existent. Eugen Kvaternik, who was with Pavelić most of this time, described the lack of links with Zagreb as well-nigh total, stressing that those links "had been always the weakest point of the Ustaša organization in Italy."[2] Occasional letters from supporters in Croatia contained information about who was doing what to whom, but there is no evidence of any instructions from Pavelić coming back to them.

---

[1] The Germans had expected tougher resistance by "the Serbs" than encountered once the attack started. According to the 1953 U.S. Department of the Army history of the Balkan campaign (op. cit.), "When the German forces struck, the mobilization and concentration of Yugoslav defense forces had hardly begun. Instead of massing their forces around strategic points and behind natural terrain barriers in an effort to conserve strength and operate along interior lines of communication, the Yugoslav command chose to scatter its forces and spread them along the entire perimeter of the country's frontier. Thus, by attempting to hold everywhere, the Yugoslavs lost everything."

[2] Cf. Eugen-Dido Kvaternik. "Ustaška emigracija u Italiji i 10 travnja 1941." *Hrvatska Revija*, Buenos Aires, Vol. 2 (1952), No. 3, p. 217.

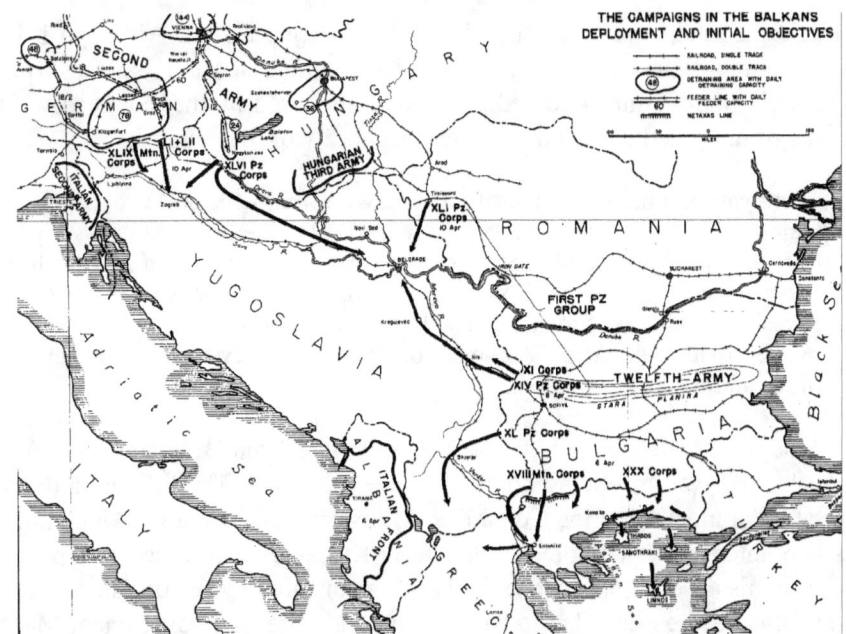

The radicals in Croatia had had some difficulty in squaring the circle of supporting Pavelić on the one hand, and fearing or despising Italy on the other. They understood the contradictory nature of Pavelić's endeavor from the beginning: that the marriage between Croat and Italian chauvinism would entail territorial concessions of the former to the latter. The separatists tended to brush such fears aside because they trusted Pavelić to find a solution. There was an implicit assumption among the "home Ustašas" that he would use the Italians to get installed in power, and then turn his back on them and enjoy the protection of Berlin. This view was reinforced by the appearance of German agents who were urging separatists to get organized and send appeals to Berlin, without any reference to Italy. Aware of Italy's position as the junior Axis partner, the Ustašas could hope that Germany was preparing to turn Croatia into its own satellite – just as it had done with Romania and Bulgaria, two Balkan states originally said to be in Rome's zone of interest.

The first four days of the war marked a curious interregnum in Zagreb. Life appeared normal, newspapers were published, all essential services were functioning. The apparatus of state authority was gradually disintegrating, however. Veesenmayer's "radicals" were in hiding, waiting for the arrival of German troops. The only significant military operations were taking place in Macedonia where General List's XII Army was about to cut off Yugoslavia from Greece. After three days the Wehrmacht established contact with the Italians near Ohrid. Militarily, Yugoslavia was already defeated on April 9.

Leaderless soldiers were surrendering without firing a shot. Although it had been common knowledge that considerable ethnic tension existed within Yugoslavia, the Germans nevertheless were surprised by the extent to which the lack of unity had eroded the defense capability of the country:

> There can be little doubt that the rift between the Serbs and Croats played a major role in the rapid collapse. Whereas the Serbs vigorously opposed cooperation with Germany, as demonstrated by the uprising on 27 March, the Croat element of the population thought it wiser to compromise with Hitler than to resist in the face of tremendous odds. This feeling was naturally also shared by the Croats in the Army. A number of Croat officers even went to the extreme of committing acts of treason.[1]

Maček retreated with Simović's government from Belgrade on 6 April while the city was still being bombed by the *Luftwaffe*. The following day he presided at a meeting of the Council of Ministers, at which a working cabinet was appointed. Maček suggested that Juraj Krnjević be co-opted to represent Maček in his absence or incapacity. This was inspired by the decision already made some days earlier, that in case of war and retreat of government Maček would not leave the country and Krnjević would take his place.[2] On April 7 in the evening Maček left the government in retreat by car and arrived at his farm in Kupinec the following morning. During a halt in Zagreb he wrote a proclamation calling for order and discipline.[3] His reference to the Yugoslav military, with the implicit call on his followers to defend the country, made little difference.[4] The collapse of Yugoslavia was under way.

Pro-Ustaša activity contributed to an air of defeatism and encouraged desertion, but it was not its cause.[5] Ustašas later made claims to the effect that

---

[1] The U.S. Department of the Army history of the Balkan campaign (op. cit.), p. 68.

[2] See Ljubo Boban (1974), Vol. 2, pp 397 and 409.

[3] *Hrvatski dnevnik* and *Jutarnji list*, 9 April 1941.

[4] "Croatian people! Brothers and sisters! I am back among you, amidst the greatest misfortune that can befall any nation, and that is war. This evil can be mitigated only through unity and discipline. You have listened to me until now in all the difficult moments, and I am certain you will do so now. I shall stay with you and share good and evil as before. Naturally, in each particular instance I shall give instructions in the usual way, either through our organizations or through special envoys, deputies or other generally well known leaders of the party. At this moment I demand from you complete order and discipline, be it at home or in the military."

[5] The one "mutiny" on record – the defeatist meltdown of an infantry regiment in Bjelovar – was afterwards claimed to be a major Ustaša achievement, but it was mainly due to the Communists' anti-war agitation. Cf. Stevan K. Pavlowitch. *Unconventional Perceptions of Yugoslavia*. New York: Columbia University Press, 1985, p. 145 (f.10).

the "revolution" of the Croat people "contributed considerably to the speedy fall of Yugoslavia."[1] The primary cause of the speedy fall of Yugoslavia was, in fact, in the overwhelming military-strategic superiority of the German Reich[2]. Even if the country had been united in the will to resist, and politically more consolidated, the defense would have been hopeless under the given circumstances. With or without Ustaša action, in April 1941 there were no military, economic, geographic, political or psychological foundations for a sustained defense of the Yugoslav state. The Ustaša fifth-column activity was merely a symptom of the malaise which turned military defeat into collapse.

Maček's message to the people of April 8 showed that he would not change his mind on the refusal to accept the German offer of an "independent" Croatia headed by him. The question of who would take over therefore remained open.[3] Immediately after Maček's broadcast this issue was supposed to be resolved at a conference called by Consul-General Freundt, who was also in hiding. The discussion was acrimonious. Both Tortić and Veesenmayer were still unwilling to accept that Pavelić would become the leader. Veesenmayer repeated to Kvaternik his view that Pavelić was an Italian tool with "precise obligations" to Mussolini. Unable to come up with an alternative, Veesenmayer finally accepted that the proclamation of independence would be made by Slavko Kvaternik acting on behalf of Pavelić, and instructed him on the course of action when the first Wehrmacht units approached the city. The outcome was an improvisation caused by Berlin's uncharacteristic lack of contingency plans. This uncharacteristic lack of preparedness indicated that Germany had expected the signing of the Pact on March 25 to "resolve" the issue of Yugoslavia's status.

---

[1] Mladen Lorković, in his speech to the Sabor in 1942.

[2] It was an exclusively German victory. According to the 1953 U.S. Department of the Army history of the Balkan campaign (op. cit.), "During the Yugoslav campaign the German command was confronted by the problems of coalition warfare for the first time. It became obvious from the very start that the German units would have to be the driving spirit and carry the brunt of the fighting during the operations. The participating allied and satellite forces achieved success only when they were under German command. Both commanders and troops of the Italian Second Army lacked aggressiveness and initiative. Moreover, the Italian command demonstrated little tactical know-how and failed to comprehend German strategic concepts. Its intelligence system was poorly developed and often tended to overestimate enemy strength and capabilities. During the entire campaign the Italians, as well as the Hungarians, displayed great reluctance to attack until the enemy had been soundly beaten and thoroughly disorganized by the Germans." The same pattern was to be repeated during the counter-insurgency operations in subsequent years.

[3] Dragan Mirković. "HSS u vladavini NDH." *Hrvatska misao*, Buenos Aires, No. 32, p. 27.

7. The Tenth of April

Early on April 10, 1941, General Maximilian von Weich's Second Army started its final push along the entire northern Yugoslav front. Before the end of the day its 14th armored division entered Zagreb without encountering any resistance.[1] The German high command had received prior information that Croat nationalists were ready for the coup and the Wehrmacht was cordially greeted in the city.[2] Between 8 and 9 in the morning Kvaternik felt secure enough to proceed with the coup as instructed by Veesenmayer.[3] He arrived at the office of the *Hrvatski radiša* co-operative, his provisional headquarters.[4] From there he phoned the commanders of gendarmerie, General Tartalja, police, Josip Vragović, and the HSS *Zaštita*, Colonel Kovačević. As they arrived Kvaternik asked them to take an oath of allegiance to the Croat state "which would be proclaimed later in the day"; they obliged. He ordered them to maintain law and order, to take control of radio stations in Zagreb and Velika Gorica, of electricity and waterworks, railway stations, post and telegraph offices, and the Sava bridges. This was a classic *coup d'etat*, except that there was no longer an *etat* to oppose it. The officials accepted Kvaternik's command, knowing that the city would be occupied soon anyway and having no other instructions from their superiors. Kvaternik described them as "initially frightened" on arrival at his office, which suggests that they had not been privy to his plot. Kvaternik proceeded to the Viceroyal Palace (*Banski Dvori*), where he read an ad-hoc proclamation of Croatia's independence at or shortly after 1 p.m.[5] This was a modest event: surrounded

---

[1] In addition to the overall hopelessness of the Yugoslav position, the speed of the German advance was enhanced by the self-defeating defense plan known as R-41. It called for a fairly even distribution of all available forces along the extended frontiers of the country. In adopting a cordon defense the Yugoslav high command deprived itself of reserves and enabled the Wehrmacht to fan out at will once the initial breakthrough had been achieved.

[2] A-VII, mikrofilm Bonn, II, notes by Hans Kramarz, Berlin, April 9, 1941.

[3] The paralysis of the remaining Yugoslav forces in the area was aided by the sabotage activity of a senior Croat officer, Colonel Franjo Nikolić. As chief of staff of the First Army Group he had secretly placed himself at Kvaternik's disposal. Nikolić helped disperse remaining Yugoslav soldiers by telling them that an armistice was in effect, and prevented the demolition of two bridges on the Sava. Kvaternik was free from danger that could be presented by the retreating Yugoslav troops. Colonel Nikolić alone did more to sow confusion and defeatism than all other recorded pro-Ustaša activity in the Yugoslav rear.

[4] Kvaternik's statement (cf. F. 52)

[5] This document was, according to Kvaternik, the same as the one he read on Zagreb radio later that same day. Ibid.

by a few companions, Kvaternik read the statement – without a loudspeaker – in front of a small crowd of bystanders at Mark's Square.[1] This event, noted by a few Ustaša enthusiasts who insisted that the proclamation had occurred *before* German units entered the city, was politically irrelevant; Veesenmayer did not even mention it in his reports.[2]

The news of the arrival of German troops to the outskirts of the capital and their cordial welcome by the population (above) reached Veesenmayer in early afternoon. He went to see Kvaternik immediately at 3 p.m., told him the time had come to go ahead with the proclamation of independence, and that he (Veesenmayer) would visit Maček and ask him "to resign." The news delighted Kvaternik, Veesenmayer noted, "since this issue was his greatest concern and he did not feel quite up to dealing with it." Kvaternik did not go with him to Maček right away, but agreed to join them later. Veesenmayer's conversation with Maček between 3:30 and 4 p.m. achieved its objective: Maček agreed to accept Kvaternik's takeover and make a signed statement confirming the decision. This news, Veesenmayer noted, "created great delight among the nationalists, and [Kvaternik] went to see Maček immediately." Veesenmayer went on with Kvaternik to the radio station.[3]

---

[1] Vjekoslav Vrančić. *Branili smo državu*. I. Barcelona: Knjižnica Hrvatske Revije, 1985, p. 196

[2] Veesenmayer's report to Ribbentrop, 11 April. DGFP, D, 12, No 311.

[3] ibid. Re. Veesenmayer: CA Potsdam: Nuremberg Trial Papers, Case 11, Band 892.

Kvaternik read the proclamation at 5:45 p.m. whereupon an announcer read Maček's proclamation to the people. (See *Appendix*) By 8 p.m. a special edition of the *Hrvatski Narod*, with the text of both proclamations was on the streets (next p.). Maček's account is broadly similar.[1] Two Germans visited him in the afternoon on April 10 as he was preparing to leave Zagreb for his farm in Kupinec.[2] One of them was Doerffler, while the other's name he could not remember [obviously Veesenmayer]. They came to tell him that "the German Army" had entrusted all power in Croatia to Kvaternik and asked him to relinquish the leadership of the HSS and of the Croat people, which he refused to do. After an argument they agreed that he would issue a proclamation to the Croat people simply appealing for the acceptance of the new situation, to which there was no alternative. This he accepted, and the two called Kvaternik to come to Maček's apartment and take the text of the proclamation to be read on the radio.

The question of the precise time of Kvaternik's proclamation of the NDH and Maček's message to the people is of peripheral importance. It has been of interest to Ustašas, however, who regarded the timing as crucial to their argument that the proclamation of independence occurred "spontaneously" and *prior* to the arrival of German troops in Zagreb. In fact there would have been no proclamation of any kind were it not for the German Army, which attacked Yugoslavia on April 6 and had its army defeated by the tenth. The role of the Germans was indispensable, not only in providing the basic precondition – external attack – but also in creating the practical framework for it. Edmund Veesenmayer was the key player in effecting the change. He got the "radical elements" together and stage-managed Kvaternik's activity. Veesenmayer's efforts induced Maček to sign his endorsement. As a result, some time between 4 p.m. (according to Kvaternik) and 5:45 p.m. (Veesenmayer) the NDH "formally" came into being.[3]

Maček's statement, with his call on all HSS authorities "sincerely to cooperate with the new government," was not made under duress, as claimed later by some of his supporters.[4] Various accounts, including Maček's own, do not support the claim. Veesenmayer went to him to "ask" for a statement.

---

[1] Maček, op. cit. pp. 228-229.

[2] Maček's son-in-law and HSS official August Košutić was also present. According to him Veesenmayer arrived to see Maček, without Kvaternik, at around 4 p.m. Kvaternik came only after an agreement on the statement had been reached. Maček agreed to give up authority, but refused to hand over "the leadership of the people" as originally requested.

[3] *Narodne novine*, Zagreb daily, 11 April 1941; *Hrvatski narod*, 10 April 1941.

[4] Boban (1974), Vol. 2, p. 411-412, quoting *Hrvatski dnevnik*, No 1781, Easter 1941.

Neither Veesenmayer nor Kvaternik were in the position to *order* him to do so, and they did not. Maček could have flatly refused to make *any* statement, without fear of immediate consequences. He did not do so because he felt that *some* statement was necessary, in view of his position of the informal leader of the nation, HSS president, and vice-Premier. He returned to Croatia "to be with his people," and being with them entailed communicating.

Maček would have needed to make some statement even without Veesenmayer's intervention. Its form and its mode of delivery would have been different, but essentially it would have been a call for the acceptance of the new situation. On 8 April Maček called on his followers to do their duty and obey orders on military service and at home; two days later he essentially told them the same thing, although the context had changed. Maček could go along with Kvaternik's act or resist. He did not want to resist since it would be equal to resisting the Germans. The impression created by Maček's statement on his followers, however, and its far-reaching consequences went well beyond the mere acceptance of *faits accomplis* created by the occupying power. In the minds of Maček's followers, his statement sounded like an endorsement of, and identification with, the new order. Apart from its contents, the form of the message, read right after Kvaternik's proclamation, created the impression of Maček's willing stamp of approval. He had also agreed to drop the original formulation concerning the Germans' "handing over" power to Kvaternik. The rest of the statement was Maček's own, notably his call on his followers not only to accept the situation created by the Germans, but also "sincerely to cooperate with the new government."

The effect of Maček's broadcast was augmented by the decision of the head of the Catholic Church in Croatia, Archbishop Stepinac (r.), to welcome the new regime in his Easter sermon at the Zagreb Cathedral on April 12. He compared the creation of the new state to the resurrection of Christ. In his pastoral letter of April 28 he called upon his flock to follow Pavelić, in whom there was "God's hand in action." In his diary Stepinac wrote of his first meeting with Pavelić on April 16, "If that man rules Croatia for ten years... Croatia will be a paradise on earth."[1]

These two exhortations provided great assistance to the rudimentary Ustaša power structure in the first few weeks. 220-odd returnees and a thousand domestic supporters, inexperienced in running state structures, could rely on the HSS apparatus, on its *Zaštita* units and local administrators while establishing their power. It is immaterial whether Maček's statement reflected his opportunism, his admission of weakness in the face of debacle, or his covert identification with the new order. The consequences of the statement were independent of Maček's intentions. The Ustašas initially exploited advantages offered by Maček, but soon afterwards they were no longer satisfied by mere "cooperation." They wanted complete eradication of the HSS and its dissolution in the Ustaša state. By that time, Maček was no longer able to alter his initial stand:

---

[1] Stepinac had viewed the coming storrm without trepidation, as is revealed from entries in his diary; in 1940 he wrote that "the Serbs have not learned anything... and in the end they will lose everything.... If nothing can teach them a lesson, distress will."

When the Ustaša authorities increased pressure on the HSS too, Maček became totally passive and he personally had no role in resisting it... He spent the war under greater or lesser surveillance of the Ustaša authorities, which apparently suited him. By not confronting them, he did not invite repercussions. This secured his personal comfort, and also suited his ideological orientation.[1]

Maček's role reflected the polirical and social forces that he represented and led. The peasantry and small town folk, mainly in the Pannonian part of Croatia north of the Sava River. provided the backbone of his support. These farmers and artisans, had never been given to the "Dinaric" feats of audacity and potential violence. Their leaders acted in the manner expected by, and acceptable, to the rank and file. Some HSS supporters went over to Pavelić more or less enthusiastically in April 1941 e.g. *Zaštita* guards, l.). Some decided to join Tito's Partisans when the writing was on the wall, after September 1943 hesitantly and in the summer of 1944 more eagerly.

The overwhelming majority hedged their bets and waited. The *attentisme*, especially after Germany's crisis at the gates of Moscow and the entry of the United States into the war in December 1941, was based on the premise that the Allies would eventually land in Dalmatia. In April 1941 Maček effectively abdicated his ability proactively to influence events and let the course of Croatia's history be dictated by others.

Such considerations still belonged to an uncertain future on the evening of April 10, 1941, when Slavko Kvaternik received the seal of state from a representative of the Banovina administration at the Ban's Palace. True to form, he subsequently greeted Veesenmayer with a hearty "Heil" and by inviting the attendees to do likewise.[2] Close to midnight, as Kvaternik was driven home after a long day, peace and quiet reigned in the city. Joint sentries of policemen and *Zaštita* activists guarded public buildings, railway stations and road junctions. Maček's radio address was bearing fruit.

---

[1] Boban (1974), Vol. 2, p. 412.

[2] ibid. p. 414.

VI
Croatia in Hitler's New Europe

1. Pavelić's Return from Italy

The events in Zagreb in the first ten days of April 1941 were unfolding without Pavelić's direct participation and his two hundred-odd followers who were still left in Italy. At the time of the signing of the Pact in Vienna on 25 March 1941, Ustaša émigrés were in a position similar to that during Stojadinović's honeymoon with Italy in 1937. They were politically passive, dispersed throughout the peninsula, and demoralized. In early March Anfuso's chef de cabinet, de Ferraris, reiterated the need for total political and organizational inactivity of the Ustašas, in view of the impending signing of the Tripartite Pact by Yugoslavia.[1]

Scant news from the "home" Ustaša reached Pavelić but there were rumors that they increasingly looked to Germany as the key to the future of Croatia. They despised Italy for its military weakness, blatantly obvious in Greece. They also feared it because of Italy's suspected designs on the eastern Adriatic shore. Warned of such sentiments, Pavelić reacted impatiently: "What do they know; we belong to the Italian sphere!"[2] Nevertheless, his standing among the followers remained high. Suspicion of Italy was counterbalanced by the belief that Pavelić would outsmart his hosts and that Rome would not have the last word anyway.

On March 28, upon learning of Hitler's decision to attack Yugoslavia, Mussolini decided to talk to Pavelić right away, and informed Mackensen of his intention. After twelve years on Italian soil the Ustaša leader would finally meet his chief mentor. Two meetings between them took place in the two weeks between the coup in Belgrade and Pavelić's departure for Croatia. The first took place on March 29 1941 in Mussolini's private residence in Rome, Villa Torlonia. Acting foreign minister Anfuso was the only other person present (Ciano was with his air force unit at that time), and he gave an account of the meeting in his memoirs. Anfuso's testimony carries special weight since he had been closely involved in the Croat issue for years and attended all key meetings the Italians had had with Pavelić in 1940-1941.

---

[1] Eugen-Dido Kvaternik, op. cit. (1952), p. 209. Kvaternik's article is the only first-hand account of Pavelić's actions before his return to Zagreb. By 1952 the author had become Pavelić's opponent, arguing that he had betrayed Croatia's interests in his dealings with Italy.
[2] Ibid.

According to Anfuso, at the first meeting between Mussolini and Pavelić it was already clear that Italy wanted Dalmatia, and that Pavelić was prepared to sign it off in s-pite of the anticipated objections of his fellow countrymen:

> [Pavelić] confirms earlier obligations to Italy; he guarantees that he will carry them out; he disperses any doubts about his loyalty. [...] The essence of the problem is Dalmatia. Will Pavelić be able, and how far, to restrain the aspirations of his compatriots against Italian irredentism? Pavelić does not conceal that this will be difficult.[1]

Anfuso (below) registered that Pavelić suggested an Italo-Croatian union to ease the Dalmatian problem. He also noted that the prospect of taking political power appeared more pressing to Pavelić than that, or any other issue. "He is afraid that some unforeseen changes in German posture may cost

him the throne," Anfuso noted. "Mussolini is at the verge of solving the Adriatic issue, which does not come to him unexpectedly, since it has been on his mind for years. But this solution is too enticing and radical to disperse fears that behind guarantees given by Pavelić there may be a postponement of the Dalmatian issue or total transfer of an "independent" Croatia to German authority, which would make void all agreements reached with the Croat agitator."[2] Anfuso's overall verdict on Pavelić's talks with Mussolini was that "of these two men of politics discussing their nations' problems, one is fatally returning to his country as a traitor." Pavelić knew all too well what reaction his agreement with Mussolini would produce among his followers, Anfuso added, but his concern was only "to avoid the impression of being a renegade."

Pavelić was unwilling to open the cards even to his closest collaborators. On his return to Florence he told young Kvaternik that an accord had been reached between Italy and Germany over Croatia. Specifically asked about Dalmatia, according to Kvaternik he replied that there was no mention of it during the talks.[3] Instead, Pavelić talked at some length about technical matters that were also discussed, such as the planned concentration of Ustašas

---

[1] Filippo Anfuso, *Roma Berlino Salo* (1936-1945). Milano: Edizione Garzanti, 1950.

[2] ibid, p. 186 on

[3] Kvaternik (1952), p. 217

in a camp in northern Italy and his forthcoming propaganda broadcasts to Croatia on Florence radio.

The ensuing days were tense for Pavelić. All lines of communication with Croatia were severed. Concentration of dispersed Ustašas at Pistoia was slow. There was uncertainty regarding German intentions, especially after the news of Germany's attack on Yugoslavia. Pavelić was making broadcasts and issuing "bulletins" on Florence Radio, ostensibly "from the battlefield," a myth cultivated by propagandists throughout the war.[1] His only source of information about the course of the campaign came from Italian newspapers and foreign radio news. Slavko Kvaternik's proclamation on April 10 caught Pavelić by surprise. Earlier in the day he was in a pensive mood and irritated by a question concerning the imminent entry of German troops into Zagreb.[2] That evening, the news of the proclamation produced an icy atmosphere in the room. According to Eugen Kvaternik, who lived in Pavelić's villa, a German broadcast announcing the entry of "victorious German units into Zagreb, enthusiastically greeted by the jubilant people of Croatia" (r. and opp. p.) produced a shattering effect on Pavelić. Pale, without a word, he went to the telephone, called Ettore Conti, and asked to talk to Anfuso.[3] When the latter called back some minutes later Pavelić asked to come to Rome the following morning.

Kvaternik-*fils* accompanied Pavelić on the trip to Rome but was not allowed to be present at any of his ensuing meetings with Anfuso or Mussolini. No minutes of his talks would ever be presented to any of his aides, and in any event did not exist in any form other than Anfuso's confidential notes. His verbal accounts of what came to pass, given to his circle of trusted followers, were always vague and in later, émigré years contradictory. The only available testimony again comes from Anfuso. Even more than before, he wrote, Pavelić's goal was to get to Zagreb as soon as

---

[1] Mijo Bzik, *Ustaška pobjeda*, Zagreb 1942; Krizman (1978), p. 392 ff. "Use your weapons against the Serbian soldiers and officers," he appealed to Croats in the Yugoslav army, "We are fighting shoulder to shoulder with our German and Italian allies."

[2] Kvaternik (1952) p. 223

[3] ibid, p. 232

possible and thus to preempt other outcomes that could cost him power. The Italians shared his concern:

> Although Hitler has given us repeated assurances that all actions in the Mediterranean and – with more justification – in the Adriatic concern only Italy, the campaign waged by the Germans in the Balkans altered the situation and created fear that they would change their position.[1]

The second meeting with Mussolini, on the morning of April 11, confirmed the agreement on Italy's right to annex Dalmatia's "Italianate cities" reached two weeks earlier. The logistics of getting Pavelić and his group into Zagreb was an urgent issue to both sides, neither of which had any control over events. The Italians made the arrangements; Pavelić left Rome for Trieste on the same day and arrived at 11 p.m. His men arrived from  Pistoia the following day. On April 12 at 10 p.m., with just over two hundred followers, Pavelić left Trieste in a convoy of municipal buses provided by the district military commander General Ambrosio. They crossed the old Italian-Yugoslav border at Sušak shortly after 2 a.m. on April 13. After more than twelve years Pavelić was back in Croatia.

The group passed through the area of Gorski Kotar without firing a single shot or encountering any resistance. The war was over. The mood of the returning émigrés was jubilant: they believed that they were the true creators of the emerging state. Pavelić tended to reinforce that view, thus sowing early seeds of discord between the émigrés and the "home Ustašas."[2] In the first town on their way, Delnice, Pavelić stopped to call Slavko Kvaternik in Zagreb by telephone; this was their first direct contact since before the coup in Belgrade. They agreed to meet in Karlovac, 40 miles southwest of Zagreb, at 4 p.m. that same day, April 13. The progress was slow, however. In the small town of Srpske Moravice, the first settlement with a significant Serb population, Pavelić's entourage disembarked and seized

---

[1] Anfuso, op. cit. pp. 189-190

[2] Kvaternik (1952) p. 235

some two hundred confused inhabitants. They were lined up, verbally abused, threatened, and eventually set free: this was, after all, only the first day. The spectacle was repeated at Ogulin, where the Roman Catholic parish priest, Fr. Ivan Mikan, addressed the captive Serbs with some choice words: "Now there will be some cleaning.... Scoot you dogs over the Drina."

At Duga Resa, between Ogulin and Karlovac, a German officer approached Pavelić and asked him to proceed to Karlovac immediately because the Germans were expecting him. It was already 8 p.m. Pavelić arrived in Karlovac about an hour later. After a brief speech at the city square he went to the barracks of the old Austrian officer school. Slavko Kvaternik and Edmund Veesenmayer were waiting for him there.

Kvaternik-père took Pavelić aside immediately to ask him if he had any "outstanding obligations" to the Italians. Pavelić assured him that he was free from any such commitments and that Italy had no territorial designs in Croatia. On Kvaternik's specific request, Pavelić confirmed this with a solemn word of honor.[1] Kvaternik was satisfied and relieved. Immediately thereafter Pavelić was introduced to Veesenmayer and told him that he hoped for an early formal recognition from Hitler, which Veesenmayer supported. Tuning his pitch to the audience, Pavelić talked of the Croats' admiration for Hitler and of their link to the German people "by blood and race."[2]

2. Karlovac: First Signs of Axis Rivalry

Pavelić was expected by all to continue his trip to Zagreb, now firmly in German hands and only an hour's drive away, early the following morning. In anticipation a welcome ceremony was being prepared at the entry into the capital. Yet Pavelić behaved as if he wase in no hurry to consummate his success. He got up late and went for a solitary walk in a park. At lunch he complained of a slight cold and gave it as the reason for his hesitation to complete the journey. His entourage was baffled and impatient, but nobody dared hurry him up. Eugen Kvaternik realized later that the delay could only be explained by the news that Anfuso was coming from Rome to see Pavelić.

Anfuso's journey to Croatia to meet Pavelić again, only three days after his meeting with Mussolini in Rome, was the product of Mussolini's restlessness and his worry that the Germans would try to double-cross him:

---

[1] A-VII, Statement by Slavko Kvaternik, I.O. 9 6/9, 1-104.
[2] Kvaternik (1952) pp. 238-243.

Once Pavelić and the Ustašas had left, we had little or no news about them. The first question Mussolini put to me during the morning report [on 14 April] was 'What do you know about Pavelić?' I replied that I did not know much beyond the fact that he had returned to Croatia and that the Wilhelmstrasse was willing to recognize his government. Mussolini then changed his question. 'Dalmatia?' he asked next, not mentioning Pavelić by name. I did not know the answer.[1]

Anfuso tried to calm Mussolini by pointing out that even before the meeting at Villa Torlonia (March 29) Pavelić had made precise and specific promises regarding Italy's Adriatic aspirations; and by assuring him that the Croat leader was worthy of trust; but the Duce was not convinced:

The issue [of Dalmatia] must be placed on the agenda and resolved before the Germans create an irreparable situation. I can trust Pavelić's word, but what will he do if he is faced with a German veto himself? Pavelić is the only pawn we have on the Balkan board, and we must not allow them to take it away from us.

The lack of reliable information was so grave that Anfuso was not certain whether the airport at Zagreb, where he was heading later that day, was in German, Croat, or hostile Yugoslav [sic!] hands. He left with Mussolini's clear instructions: "To obtain from Pavelić, before Italy recognizes his government, a public and solemn statement which would oblige him to determine the new state's frontiers, taking into special account Italian interests in Dalmatia."[2]

To Mussolini such a statement was important in order to preempt any claim by Pavelić that he could not keep his promises – previously made in private – because of the supposed pressure from his own supporters, or due to some intervention by the Germans, or both. Pavelić was not about to resist, however. Any thought he may have had of double-crossing the Italians by virtue of his apparently secure position – which could have been sealed by a "triumphant" entry into Zagreb – was offset by his own uncertainty about the Germans. It was necessary for him to keep the Italian card lest alternative arrangements – with Maček, for instance – were imposed from Berlin behind his back. He rejected urgent appeals from Slavko Kvaternik and Veesenmayer to proceed to Zagreb at once.[3]

When Anfuso finally arrived in Karlovac at 2 p.m. Pavelić even asked Veesenmayer and both Kvaterniks to hide from view, and they exited by a

---

[1] Anfuso, op. cit. p. 190.

[2] Ibid., p. 191.

[3] Krizman (1978) p. 409

back door.[1] When they were seated, alone, Anfuso immediately started talking about Dalmatia and Mussolini's concern about their agreement. Pavelić appeared incredulous that the Italians had any doubts about his loyalty to them and his readiness to keep his word:

> He gave me a surprised look from head to toes and swore that nothing had changed in his intentions. Busy establishing the first contact with the Croat people, he did not have time – he told me – to carry out in a concrete form his obligations to Mussolini; but he said he would not be late doing so.[2]

For the second time in two days Pavelić swore to two very different things. In the meantime, Veesenmayer and the two Kvaterniks were nervously waiting for the end of Pavelić's talks with Anfuso. After about half an hour Pavelić emerged with the draft text of a telegram. It was addressed to Mussolini and written in Italian:

> The Croat people express their deepest gratitude to the glorious Italian forces for the liberation of Croatia. Croatia will enter the new European order under the care and protection of Fascist Italy. When deciding the frontiers of the new state, attention will be paid above all to the Italian rights in Dalmatia.[3]

Veesenmayer rejected the styling with an undiplomatic outburst: "This is impossible; what about us, and we took the heaviest burden?" He promptly drafted another telegram, addressed to both Hitler and Mussolini and requesting both governments' recognition.[4] This draft was given to Pavelić and Anfuso in the other room. After a few minutes Pavelić reappeared and said that Anfuso could not accept the new draft, which made no mention of "Italy's rights in Dalmatia," without consulting Mussolini. He was therefore waiting for a telephone call to Rome. Upon hearing this, Veesenmayer jumped and literally ran to the post office, manned by German Army telephone operators. He ordered them to disconnect all lines immediately.

While waiting, Anfuso agreed on the satisfactory text of the telegram from Pavelić that satisfied his instructions. It could only be prepared when he was left alone with Pavelić, without the implicit pressure of Veesenmayer's

---

[1] Eugen Kvaternik (1952), p. 239. Slavko Kvaternik said that he and Veesenmayer arrived in Karlovac *after* Anfuso, and were asked to wait while Pavelić and Anfuso conferred (A-VII, NDH, I.O. 9 6/9, 1-104).

[2] Anfuso, op. cit. p. 193.

[3] Krizman (1978) p. 409

[4] Kvaternik (1952) p. 240

presence.[1] The result was "a message which blended irredentist zeal, fanned in Palazzo Venezia, and reserves, imposed on Pavelić by the tutelage of Germany and her Croat admirers."[2] It is notable that Anfuso does not blame *Pavelić* for any "reserves" about Dalmatia, but stresses that attempts to change the telegram were "imposed" on him. Pavelić's request for recognition, containing due reference to the frontiers, was taken by Italian army messengers to Fiume and conveyed to Rome by 9:30 p.m. on 14 April.[3]

The Karlovac episode is significant as an early manifestation of two sources of conflict. One was the tension between Germany and Italy and the Italians' chronic mistrust of Germany, based on a long history of German unilateralism in those regions that had been formally recognized as its zone of interest. Mussolini's fear of yet another surprise from Hitler prompted him to dispatch Anfuso to Karlovac so soon after his last meeting with Pavelić. By that time the Italians may have learned of German attempts to win over Maček in early April. Had they succeeded, the Germans would have presented Mussolini with their own decision regarding Croatia's future – and Mussolini did not know that no such deal was struck.

Italian apprehension was justified in the light of Veesenmayer's role. He did not think his mission was over with the proclamation of independence. He wanted to secure German influence in the new state regardless of the Italians – and as his behavior in Karlovac indicated, in spite of them if necessary.

In this endeavor Veesenmayer enjoyed the support of Kvaternik (still in a semi-civilian outfit at that time, l.) and the "home Ustaša" group, Germanophiles and Italophobes without exception. They regarded Pavelić's dealings with Italy as a matter of expediency and temporary necessity which would not mark the long-term future of Croatia.

---

[1] PA, Buero RAM, Kroatien. Note dated 14 April; Veesenmayer reported that Pavelić assured him that "Anfuso had not requested any unilateral change of the telegram"!

[2] Anfuso, op. cit. p. 197.

[3] DGFP, D, 12, No 348.

Immediately after the proclamation on April 10 Slavko Kvaternik requested German recognition and conveyed his request to Berlin through Veesenmayer.[1] No such request was sent to the Italians, however, and the telegram to Berlin made no mention of Italy. It contained extravagant praise for the German army and Hitler personally, and ended with a "*Heil* to the Führer of the German people!" Unaware of Kvaternik's request, Pavelić sent his own message to Hitler from Rome on April 11 expressing his gratitude to the Germans, but also taking care to mention both dictators and both Axis powers.[2] This telegram was not a request for German recognition, since the Italians did not want it to happen unless and until after Pavelić was secure in his position in Zagreb. Oblivious of Pavelić's actions, two days later Slavko Kvaternik sent a new recognition request to Berlin, routed through German military channels (and again none went to Rome).[3] It is clear that Kvaternik was acting under Veesenmayer's guidance. Reporting to Ribbentrop on the proclamation of the NDH on April 11, Veesenmayer described accurately (if not modestly) the events of the previous day.[4] He ended the report in the manner of a budding *Reichskommissar*:

> The initiative and execution during the hours described were exclusively in my hands. [...] Since Kvaternik took over the Government I have been at his side constantly and I am assisting him inconspicuously. I intend to continue to do this so that any danger can be overcome more easily.

In his reply Ribbentrop approved of Veesenmayer's action, but asked him to leave further measures "up to the Croats" and to remain aloof himself because "[i]n the further treatment of the Croatian question we now intend to let the Italians have precedence entirely."[5] Ribbentrop's warning to Veesenmayer was at odds with the visible firmness with which Germany dictated the pace in connection with Croatia, and Italy toed the line. Mackensen woke up Mussolini early in the morning on April 14 to tell him that, in the opinion of Hitler and Ribbentrop, the time had come to recognize the Croatia without delay.[6] To Mussolini's added chagrin, Mackensen brought

---

[1] DGFP, D, 12, No 311. Veesenmayer to the Foreign Ministry, 11 April.

[2] DGFP, D, 12, No 317. Memorandum by the Chief of Protocol, 12 April

[3] DGFP, D, 12, No 324. The Consulate General at Zagreb to the Foreign Ministry. Kvaternik also requested approval for the establishment of a Croat armed force.

[4] DGFP, D, 12, No 313. Veesenmayer to the Foreign Ministry, 11 April.

[5] DGFP, D, 12, No 328. Ribbentrop added in his hand *ganz* on the draft.

[6] See DGFP, D, 12, documents 336, 337 and 338.

with him a telegram supposedly sent by Pavelić to the Germans from Karlovac.¹ It probably contributed to Mussolini's decision to dispatch Anfuso to Croatia without delay.

A few hours later, on Ribbentrop's instructions, Mackensen requested another meeting with Mussolini to press for simultaneous recognition of Croatia by Germany and Italy. The reason for such German haste was military rather than political. The war in some parts of Yugoslavia was still not over, although its outcome was clear. The OKW assumed that the act of recognition would induce any remaining Croat soldiers in Yugoslav ranks to surrender.

Mussolini tried but failed to establish telephone contact with Anfuso in Karlovac. He resisted German demands for immediate and simultaneous recognition, saying that he first needed formal commitment on the territorial issue from the Croats.² At around that time Pavelić complied with Anfuso's request for a telegram making such commitment. He was equally ready to provide assurances to Veesenmayer and to Kvaternik about the innocuous nature of Italian demands; but it was the Italian card that he trusted most.

3. A Newcomer to the "New Europe"

Both Axis notes recognizing the new Croat state contained a clause demanded by Mussolini: that they were looking forward to reaching an agreement on frontiers "in a free exchange of views with the Government of Croatia." The announcement was made in Berlin on 15 April at noon, in Rome two hours later. That same day, at the crack of dawn, Pavelić finally drove through the deserted streets of Zagreb and took possession of the Ban's Palace. The following morning, accompanied by Kvaternik, he inspected his émigré companions (below and opp. p.) who were to provide the backbone of the new regime. The NDH thus became the latest addition to the "New

---

¹ DGFP, D, 12, No 343. Dateline was 'Zagreb, 14 April' although Pavelić was still in Karlovac at that time.

² DGFP, D, 12, No 345. Mackensen to the Foreign Ministry, 14 April 1941.

European Order." It was not a fully-fledged member because its legal status was dubious. Its creation was a direct outcome of the German attack, and military facts on the ground could be legalized only by a peace treaty at the end of the war. It it did not qualify for general recognition under the Stimson Doctrine.[1] The action of Germany and Italy in carving up Yugoslavia and setting up the NDH could not acquire such status for as long as the Royal Yugoslav government continued to function in exile, which it did. Croatia was recognized only by Germany, Italy, and their satellites. The prevalent recognition by other states, as a constitutive factor of its legal existence, was absent. It was always clear that the survival of the NDH depended entirely on the victory of the Axis.

Ustaša authors have attempted to bypass this obstacle by ignoring the prevalent standards for legal sovereign statehood under public international law *per se*, and instead by stressing the unequal position of different parts of the territory of Yugoslavia after capitulation.

> [Unlike Serbia] Croatia was the subject of international law, it had territory, people and authority as its elements of statehood.[...] Croatia signed international treaties, it was recognized by other states and recognized them, it received and sent diplomatic representatives, it had its own army, which obeyed only its state leadership.[2]

The comparison with Serbia is correct but irrelevant. Croatia was an allied "state" in Hitler's New Order while Serbia was not, but that hardly enhanced its international legality. While Croatia was recognized by *some* states, their number fell far short of at least prevalent recognition. The number of states (including all neutrals and even the Vatican) that had continued to recognize Yugoslavia was much greater throughout the war. Up to one half of Pavelić's state was subsequently occupied by the Italian army for extended periods and regardless of his wishes. Nobody in Zagreb ever pretended that

---

[1] Charles Rousseau. *Droit international public*, Paris 1953; the author mentions Croatia along with Georgia, Armenia (1918-1921) and Manchukuo (1931).

[2] Milan Blažeković. "NDH u Stepinčevom procesu." *Hrvatska revija*, Vol. 10 (1960), p. 677.

the Second Italian Army garrisoned the NDH in 1941-1943 because its government so desired. There were other large areas theoretically under NDH sovereignty that were controlled by various insurgents (Četniks, Partisans). In many instances the regime felt compelled to reach accommodation with such insurgent groups and formally to recognize their control over certain areas. Finally, in 1942 the Croatian armed forces were placed under German supreme command.

The NDH was not a state in terms of the international law, but as a collaborationist entity it possessed certain attributes of *de facto* statehood. They were sufficient to qualify it as an actor in terms of foreign policy analysis. The traditional distinction between foreign and domestic policies is admittedly blurred in the case of the NDH. Most facets of its brief existence included some sort of relationship with various German or Italian military or civilian authorities, often outside the sphere of conventional diplomacy. The NDH was nevertheless a *de facto* state in some part of its territory for some of the time. Both the territorial quantity and decision-making quality of its statehood kept diminishing as the war went on, but the NDH was an "actor," in the sense of not being a mere extension of either Italy or Germany.

The existence of divergent interests of those two Axis powers enabled the NDH to have, for the first 18 months at least, more "statehood" than would have been the case without that rivalry. A case in point is Pavelić's behavior in the first two days following his return. Immediately upon meeting Veesenmayer in Karlovac he gave him extravagant assurances of his admiration for Hitler, Germany and the Wehrmacht.

According to Veesenmayer, who was temporarily rather charmed by the display, Pavelić said he "did not intend to conduct any foreign policy at all – Adolf Hitler was doing that – and he only wanted to raise up his people and to prove that the Croats were not Slavs, but profess themselves, in the last analysis, as being German by blood and race."[1] Only one day later Pavelić gave Anfuso unequivocal assurance of his loyalty and determination to keep his promises about Dalmatia, and appeared surprised that any concern existed about his sincerity.

To his followers, finally, throughout this period Pavelić continued giving assurances about Italy's benevolence; to Slavko Kvaternik he gave his word of honor to that effect. His almost conspiratorial rapport with Anfuso was not due to his "loyalty" to Italy, but to his concern for his own position. Over the ensuing four years Pavelić's priorities indicated the same pattern. This was as

---

[1] DGFP, D, 12, No. 341. Veesenmayer to Ribbentrop, 14 April 1941.

apparent in April 1941 as it was in the summer of 1944 or in May 1945. His range of options was limited and his resources modest, but his policy was neither Germany's nor Italy's, nor for that matter Croatia's; it was strictly Pavelić's own.

The *Poglavnik* never shared his innermost thoughts and long-term plans with anyone. Both during his émigré years and later in Zagreb there was no heir apparent, no single trusted aide who would be privy to Pavelić's inner world. The decision-making process was structured so that he was in full control of all external contacts, which he conducted literally single-handed. Pavelić lacked the paternalistic charisma of Mgr. Tiso, or the morbid mystique of Ferenc Szálasi – let alone the magnetism of Hitler or Mussolini – but he was an accomplished manipulator of his followers. As the leader of his movement, on which he relied to the exclusion of all other forces, he went out of his way to equate "Croat" and "Ustaša." This ambition, the salient feature of his propaganda throughout the war, postulated the *Führerprinzip* from the outset as inviolable and sacrosanct.

The Ustaša variety of *Volksgemeinschaft* made autonomous political and other institutions suspect and unnecessary. Its ideological underpinnings were distinctly nihilistic. The glorification of the racially pure Nordic-Dinaric Croat peasant, his murderous rage justified by parallels from the animal kingdom, his social-Darwinian "natural justice" his only guidance, produced a cult of unbridled bloodlust and pure hatred. Pavelić's "nation of wolves and lions" was a clumsy mix of Nazi brutality and quasi-racism, fascist irrationality, and above all "oriental" primitivism. It soon turned Croatia into a pandemonium of anarchy and genocide. Thanks to Pavelić and his followers, for four years the "Western" side of Croatia's cultural and political legacy was swept aside and its "Eastern" heart of darkness was exposed in all its awfulness.

The NDH was the exact opposite of a *Rechtstaat*. It never had a constitution; instead, on April 16 Pavelić swore an oath on the the *Ustaša Principles* (opp. p.) and proclaimed them "the supreme law" of the state. Numerous "laws" introduced in the first weeks were not enacted through an assembly because no such body existed: the *Sabor* was convened briefly in early 1942 and lasted for a few weeks as an irrelevant talking shop. Legislation was reduced to a series of decrees and ordinances, signed by Pavelić or issued on his orders. He had the sole right of appointing and dismissing ministers, secretaries of state and heads of state directorates (the "Law" of June 24, 1941). Pavelić thus "legitimated" his personal power and created a quasi-constitutional framework in which he combined all authority. All ministers were directly responsible to him.

The government was not a body in its own right. Cabinet sessions were rare and Pavelić dealt with his ministers one-on-one. In addition he created separate "directorates" (*Ravnateljstva*) which overlapped with ministerial briefs and competed for authority. Eugen-Dido Kvaternik, Slavko Kvaternik's son and Pavelić's close émigré companion, thus became Director for Public Order and Security (*Ravnatelj za javni red i sigurnost*, RAVSIGUR), an institution separate from the interior ministry that launched a campaign genocidal terror against Serbs, Jews, Roma, and political enemies.

The establishment of the institutions and structures of the new state was focused from the outset on the apparatus of repression. It contained an ominous hint of what the transformed Croatian society ought to look like. For the Ustašas, *the State* itself was the highest goal. The immediate aftermath of its achievement displayed their mono-dimensional concept of the Croatian man and society. The avowed goal was to turn the NDH into an Ustaša-state (*Ustaška država*). Pavelić took this to mean his personal power unhindered by a constitutional framework and supported by a growing personality cult. His unlimited authority was occasionally exercised through the largely fictitious Supreme Ustaša Headquarters (*Glavni ustaški stan*, GUS), which was nominally the supreme organ of the only legal political organization, the

Ustaša movement. The GUS consisted of the Poglavnik, his close advisors (*Doglavnici*) constituted into a sort of Politbureau (*Doglavničko vijeće*),[1] as well as his reliable aides (*Poglavni pobočnici*) and trustees (*Povjerenici*). The GUS was only formally a decision-making body. In practice all of its constituent parts were devoid of any real power. It was exercised by the Poglavnik in direct liaison with his subordinates. The most influential among those were a small circle of émigré veterans who belonged to Pavelić's most trusted inner circle until the end.

The *Gleichschaltung* in all spheres of social, political and economic life started a week after Pavelić's return to Zagreb. On April 22 an edict placed all civil servants and other employees of the former Banovinas and municipal authorities at the disposal of the government. The media, education, cultural institutions, professional bodies, were all Ustašized; but because of the small

---

[1] This body initially consisted of seven members: Mile Budak, Ademaga Mešić, Jozo Sunarić, Marko Došen, Slavko Kvaternik, Luka Lešić, and Andrija Betlehem. A total of eight new members were coopted over the years (Mate Frković, Lovro Sušić, Ljudevit Šok, Vilko Begić, Stipe Matijević, Ivan Ćelan, Janko Tortić and Jure Pavičić); four were eventually expelled, including one of its original members, Slavko Kvaternik.

initial number of activists, this provided a haven for careerists and a hotbed of corruption. A network of Ustaša plenipotentiaries (*povjerenici*) was sent to the provinces and charged with recruiting new, politically reliable local and regional officials to replace the *Banovina* apparat. The new state appointees often doubled as Ustaša officials.

The state was divided into 22 counties (*velike župe*), headed by prefect (*župan*). These units were far smaller than King Alexander's banovinas, but similar in one important respect: they crossed traditional boundaries, notably between Croatia and Bosnia-Herzegovina, and had the unstated yet obvious objective of preempting any autonomist tendencies among the Muslims of Bosnia (see map opp. p. 1.).[1] The duality of the NDH political system was reflected from the outset in the parallel replication of state institutions within the Ustaša organization itself. Political bosses at the level of municipalities (*tabornici*), districts (*logornici*) and counties (*stožernici*) were more powerful than their civilian equivalents, and they could rest assured that this was exactly how the Poglavnik wanted it to be.

Some attempts were made to introduce a corporate economic system, limit ownership rights and mimic some socialist notions present in early Fascism and Nazism, but they were half-hearted and short-lived. In a speech on May 21 Pavelić stated that he would establish "such social order which would not lead to the gap between the rich and the poor, those who work and those who enjoy the fruits of others' toil, those who rob and those who sweat [...] Croatia's Independent State is, and will remain, the edifice which serves Croatia's peasants and working people."[2] In practice this pledge amounted to a rapid wholesale confiscation of Jewish assets and property, with the loot divided mostly among the regime's top brass.

---

[1] The formal takeover of institutions in Sarajevo took place in the last week of April.

[2] As reported by *Hrvatski narod*, Zagreb, Vol. 3, No. 99, 22 May 1941. See Appendix.

The first NDH government, appointed by Pavelić on April 16, 1941, was an all-Ustaša affair.[1] He rejected suggestions that it would be opportune, at least initially, to seek partnership with the HSS. Slavko Kvaternik suggested that three or four ministerial portfolios should be set aside for the HSS "in the interest of national unity and peasant support."[2] Pavelić preferred total control. His government members were gathered for the swearing-in ceremony (previous page) but they were rarely brought together in the months and years that followed. There was no "cabinet," the government did not function as a collctive body and did not hold regular meetings. Various *ad-hoc* sessions were called mainly to rubber-stamp decisions already made. The Croatian variety of the *Fuehrerprinzip* was spelled out in Pavelić's first major speech: "I shall bear responsibility to the entire Croat people for all [government] acts, while all state organs, officials and employees will be responsible to me – and you know that I am not joking."[3] To disperse any doubts about Pavelić's seriousness, an elaborate apparatus of political indoctrination, internal control and outright oppression was quickly established. On May 10 the Ustaša movement formally constituted an armed militia, *Ustaška vojnica,* commanded by Juco Rukavina. Independent of the military arm were the powerful Ustaša Supervisory Service (*Ustaška nadzorna služba*, UNS) and the Ustaša police (*Ustaško redarstvo*). Separate from all of them stood the dreaded Directorate for Public Security, headed by Kvaternik-junior with its own network of agents and armed units. The speed with which those bodies were set up and the human and material resources set apart for their establishment were indicative of the shape of things to come.

The first weeks of the NDH were a period of intense consummation of various outward attributes of statehood. Flags, coats of arms, titles, administrative rearrangements with the creation of medieval-sounding "counties," initially blurred the fact that the question of frontiers remained unsettled. This was an issue that Italy wanted to settle as soon as possible.

---

[1] Prime minister and foreign minister: Ante Pavelić; Vice-Premier: Osman Kulenović (the only Bosnian Muslim in Pavelić's first government); commander of the armed forces and minister of the home guard (Domobranstvo, i.e. defence): Slavko Kvaternik (in Karlovac Pavelić conferred on Kvaternik the title of *Vojskovodja*, or "Marshal"; Kvaternik was also supposed to take over Pavelić's duties in the event of the latter's absence or incapacity); justice: Mirko Puk; interior: Andrija Artuković; health: Ivan Petrić; national economy: Lovro Sušić; religion and education: Mile Budak; forestry and mining: Ivica Frković; labor: Jozo Dumandžić; and legislative commission: Milovan Žanić.

[2] Izjava Slavka Kvaternika. A-VII, NDH, I.O. 9 6/9, 1-104.

[3] *Hrvatski narod*, 22 May 1941.

4. Hitler's Croatian Strategy

Immediately following the successful completion of operations in the Balkans Hitler paid scant attention to the newly conquered area. Initially (March 27) he envisaged Croatia in some sort of union with Hungary or as an "autonomous" state, but probably under Hungarian "influence."[1] A few days later (April 12) the OKW Provisional Guidelines on the partition of Yugoslavia mentioned an "independent Croatian state" but with the specific exclusion of Bosnia-Herzegovina.

Limited interest in the area in general and in Croatia in particular was also apparent in Hitler's instructions given to his newly-appointed plenipotentiary military representative in Zagreb, General Edmund Glaise von Horstenau, who was destined to become one of the most influential and observant foreign figures in the newly-founded state. Suave, erudite and eloquent, with a doctorate and a solid reputation as a military historian, Glaise belonged to a diminishing circle of aging Austrian officers who had managed to combine an intense nostalgia for the old Habsburg Monarchy with Nazi sympathies. As time went on, his views grew increasingly divergent from Hitler and Nazism.[2] That time was still distant on April 14, 1941, when Glaise reported to Hitler at his special train in Southern Austria (somewhat ironically called *Amerika*) to receive instructions. He recorded his initial impressions:

> From the beginning of the Axis policy there has been an arrangement between Germany and Italy according to whicht only Hungary and Romania belonged to the German sphere of interest, while everything further south belonged to the Italian sphere... As for Croatia, the task is to get the place swiftly consolidated so that German troops can withdraw. I will need the Second Army in another place soon, the Fuehrer remarked significantly, and he did not need to explain where that could be. This would be our political objective in Croatia; everything else the country would have to do by itself, while taking into account Italy and her aspirations.[3]

---

[1] DGFP, D, 12, No 291. Unsigned memorandum, date unknown, initialled by Foreign Ministry officials Ritter and Woermann on 6 April 1941.

[2] Glaise's diary is an invaluable primary source on German policy in Croatia. Together with other papers from his tenure in Zagreb it is kept in the War Archive in Vienna (KAW B/67). It was published in 1988 as the final volume of Broucek's trilogy.

[3] Glaise's diary, 14 April 1941; Vasa Kazimirović, *NDH u svetlu nemačkih dokumenata i dnevnika Gleza fon Horstenau*. Belgrade: Nova knjiga-Narodna knjiga, 1987.

Asked by Glaise (below) about the future frontiers of Croatia, Hitler indicated the Drina river in the east, the Drava-Danube line in the north, and the old boundary between Croatia and "Southern Styria" (i.e. Steyrmark, part of Slovenia annexed by the Reich) in the north-west. The coastal strip remained "an open issue" depending on Italy's aspirations.[1]

Similar instructions were given to the newly appointed German minister in Zagreb, *SA-Obergruppenführer* Siegfried Kasche. He was a newcomer to diplomacy, drafted by Ribbentrop into the Foreign Ministry to infuse it with a little more Nazi spirit.[2] Kasche (in SA uniform, opp. p., top, upon arrival in Zagreb in April 1941) was warned on the eve of his departure for Zagreb that the Croats and Italians were not likely to get on well, and that the former would probably appeal to Kasche, hoping to turn him into an arbiter. As long as the war was going on the German side was obliged to respect Italian sensibility without reserve. Thus any mediation would have to result in support for Italy, which would only alienate the Croats. Therefore, the German Minister should "stay aloof" and allow the Italian predominance in Croatia to be as strongly felt as was in line with the Reich's interests.

The occasion to settle the "open issue" of Italy's aspirations and to coordinate Axis policy came in Vienna on April 21 and 22, at a meeting between Ciano and Ribbentrop and their staffs. The meeting was arranged on German initiative. In his telegram to Mackensen, instructing him to invite Ciano to the proposed meeting, Ribbentrop indicated that the talks on dividing spoils in the Balkans would also cover the frontiers of the newly created state "in accordance with Italian interests."[3] The Germans undertook thorough preparations for the meeting in order to coordinate the views of military, political and diplomatic circles. At a conference in Vienna on April 18, Ambassador at the Foreign Ministry Karl Ritter said that the overriding interest of Germany in the Balkans was to

---

[1] Rudolf Kiszling, *Die Kroaten*, Graz 1956, p. 172.

[2] See Hory and Broszat, op. cit. pp. 60-61; Nachlass S. Kasche, PA, Nachlässe.

[3] DGFP, D, 12, No. 368. Ribbentrop to Mackensen.

receive as many raw materials from the Yugoslav lands as before. Ritter expressed ignorance of Italy's territorial demands, but correctly predicted that they would extend to Dalmatia and the port complex near Fiume, at Sušak. He added that the recognition of Croatia did not preclude the possibility of Germany's future involvement in order to influence its political course.[1] In the ensuing discussion, participants expressed preference that the territories rich in minerals and raw materials to be given to countries *other than Italy*. Especially important to Germany were bauxite mines near Mostar (in Herzegovina) and lead and zinc mines at Trepča near Mitrovica, in Kosovo. The latter was excluded by German fiat from Mussolini's "greater Albania" and left within rump Serbia under German occupation.

When he heard of the forthcoming talks between Italy and Germany Glaise returned to Hitler's headquarters. Three days earlier, during his first audience, he expressed his opposition to Italy's annexation of Dalmatia and urged Hitler to let Croatia have the same coastal strip as Yugoslavia.[2] On April 17 Glaise tried again. He apologized for making his reappearance so quickly and explained that this seemed necessary in view of strongly pro-German sympathies he encountered in Zagreb, which were in sharp contrast to the Croats' hatred of Italy. He asked if Germany had already accepted certain obligations regarding Italy's plans for territorial rearrangements along the eastern Adriatic. Hitler interrupted him and said that no specific promises had been given, but that Italian interests had to be given priority:

---

[1] Krizman (1978), p. 447.

[2] Kazimirović, op. cit. p. 88.

This is a matter that concerns primarily the Italians and the Croats. South of the Drava Germany has only purely economic interests. He personally did not want in the deepest corner of his soul to be lured to the Adriatic coast. If he were to allow that, and then went to the Mediterranean, then would he really be stuck in a local sea. The nation, however, needed to be oriented to the North Sea.

Then Hitler turned to Dalmatia. He said that its handing over to Italy could be useful because it created "a permanent basis for conflicts between Italians and Croats, whereby Germany could always reserve the role of an arbiter." This remark was in apparent contradiction to the instructions given to Kasche by Weizsäcker (at his 1947 trial, r.) on the eve of Kasche's departure for Zagreb.[1] On that occasion Ribbentrop's deputy specifically warned Kasche *against* accepting the role of an arbiter. Hitler's statement to Glaise went contrary to the official Foreign Ministry line and reflected his real purpose: to prevent long-term stabilization  of Croatia as an Italian client. He was going to achieve this by letting Italy follow its annexationist course, which was bound to cause resentment among the Croats. In addition to the pending Croat-Italian strife Hitler also envisaged the flaring up of internal conflicts between Serbs and Croats, which would prevent stabilization of the new state and result "in a permanent schism between nations which had been within one state until now." The effect on the future role of Germany would be the same: by creating discord between Croats and their neighbors, the Germans ensured their presence and enhanced their influence.

This theme Hitler was to repeat often in later years, to the chagrin of German generals who regarded the Ustašas' anti-Serb policy as a major cause of permanent turmoil in the NDH. Such a policy of letting Italy make enemies of Croats and letting Croats make enemies of Serbs may have seemed a clever ploy to Hitler in April 1941. Ultimately it turned into a major liability for Germany's position in southeast Europe.

---

[1] The scion of a prominent Palatinate family, Weizsäcker ended his career at the Vatican as ambassador. After the war he was tried and sentenced by the Americans for crimes against humanity (1947) and pardoned soon thereafter (1949). See Rolf Lindner, *Freiherr Ernst Heinrich von Weizsäcker: Staatssekretär Ribbentrops von 1938 bis 1943*. ROBE-Verlag, 1997. One of his sons, Richard, was Germany's president at the time of reunification (1984-1994).

Ciano arrived in Vienna on April 20 where he was met by Ribbentrop (below).[1] The following day the *Reichsminister* opened the meeting by saying that the chief objective of the new order in the Balkans was to prevent once and for all the repetition of a betrayal such as Serbia perpetrated in March 1941.[2] He asked Ciano for Mussolini's views on the reorganization of the former Yugoslav lands. Ciano produced a note, written by Mussolini himself, and a map. He said that parts of Slovenia not annexed by Germany would be annexed to Italy but given administrative autonomy. The whole of Dalmatia and the rest of the Adriatic coast from Fiume to Cattaro [Kotor] would also be annexed. Montenegro would be resurrected as a state in personal union with Italy, while parts of northwestern Macedonia and Kosovo would go to Albania. Croatia was likewise to be tied to Italy by a personal and customs union.

Ribbentrop replied that the Führer had already determined the northern border of Croatia with the Reich. As for the rest, he said that "Germany had not talked to the Croats so far, but had merely heard of certain demands raised among the Croatian people." Ribbentrop thereby outlined those demands on a map, which included all of Bosnia and Herzegovina as well as most of the Dalmatian coastline.[3] Ciano responded that Italy's claim was to the *whole* of Dalmatia. According to Ciano, Ribbentrop displayed guarded opposition to the proposed personal union between the two states. To Ribbentrop's mind, he wrote, Croatia is "very near to, even if it is not already actually a part of, the political and economic system of the Reich."

The following day (April 22), after consulting Hitler, Ribbentrop told Ciano that Germany confirmed her political disinterestedness with regard to Croatia, and therefore he had no objection to personal union. Hitler also had no objection to the Italian annexation of Dalmatia and thought that Pavelić should be made to come to Rome immediately to fix with the Duce the

---

[1] DGFP, D, 12, p. 591. Memorandum on Ciano's visit to Hitler.

[2] DGFP, D, 12, No 378. The memorandum of the talks between Ciano and Ribbentrop was prepared by the chief interpreter at the Foreign Ministry, Dr. Paul Otto Schmidt.

[3] Ciano's telegraphic summary to Mussolini of 21 April, in *Ciano's Diplomatic Papers*, Oldham Press Ltd, London 1948.

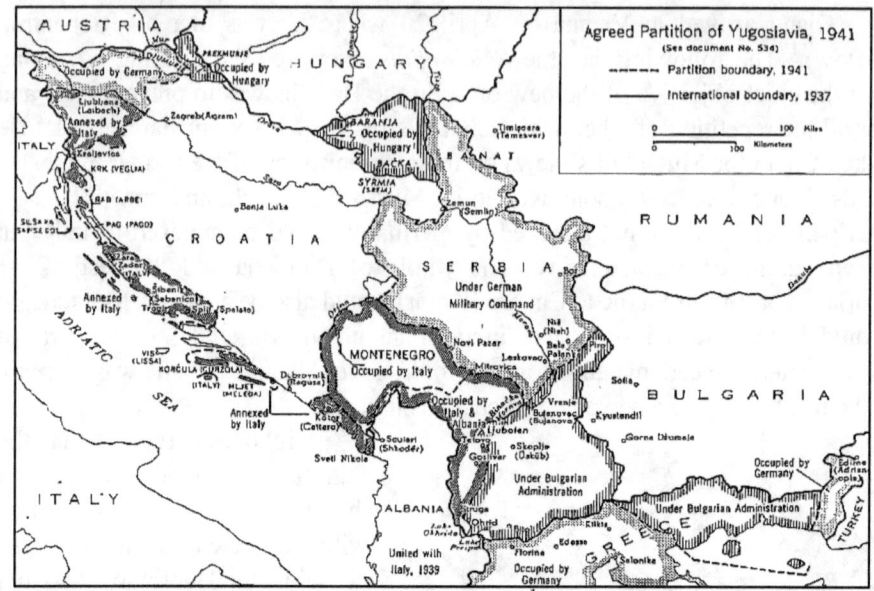

frontiers and political-constitutional issues.[1] Pleased with Ribbentrop's statement, Ciano readily accepted German demands regarding deliveries of bauxite from Dalmatia. But the German foreign minister had another surprise in store for Ciano: he announced that Berlin had decided to maintain an occupation force "in a strip of Croatia running from north-west to south-east in order to safeguard the railroad communication with Serbia." Until that moment the Italians were made to believe that the whole of Croatia was their sphere of interest, from which Hitler would withdraw *all* German troops at the earliest opportunity. The "strip" referred to by Ribbentrop amounted to one-half of the NDH territory, however, with more than two-thirds of its industrial and agricultural potential. It was yet another *fait accompli.*

The talks in Vienna were significant as an illustration of the nature of Germany's relationship with Italy. The topic concerned an area formally in the Italian sphere, but the Germans called all the shots: from the date and venue of the meeting itself to the way in which the agenda was discussed. Disagreements of the first day were resolved thanks to *Hitler's* decision. He gave Italy a free hand in Dalmatia, which he had intended to do anyway. The demand for German control over ore deposits was mentioned almost as an afterthought, although continued deliveries of raw materials were a key German concern all along. Finally, Ciano was simply *informed* of the continued German troop presence in the most productive parts of the NDH.

---

[1] Ciano's telegraphic summary of April 22, ibid. Also: DGFP, D, 12, No 385.

In achieving its objectives the German side was helped by the Italians' gross ineptitude. Unlike Ribbentrop, Ciano went to Vienna with a map but without a political agenda and without a strategy. He appears to have agreed with his friend, journalist Giovanni Ansaldo, that "all of this kaleidoscope of annexations, partitions, divisions, and restorations" would not last: "All this is constructed in sand, fleeting as an unsettling dream, and destined to founder in European chaos. We lack everything to make this system endure: military force, administrative capability, the right, and perhaps the interest."[1]

Poor diplomatic, political and military coordination in Rome led to sloppy, *ad hoc* policy-making. The Vienna talks confirmed the nature of Hitler's strategy in the Balkans. Germany would let Italy enlarge itself on the eastern Adriatic shore; its "lack of political interest in the region" was confirmed. Hitler was going to let Italy fall into the trap of its own making, and he was going to make himself appear magnanimous for doing so.

5. Decision on Dalmatia

Having obtained Germany's *carte blanche* in Vienna Ciano decided to talk to Pavelić immediately and set the meeting for April 25 in Ljubljana. A day earlier he recorded that he was going there "to find out what the Croats thought," and not to conclude anything final. His diary entry outlined two alternatives. The first was annexation of an uninterrupted coastal strip all the way from Fiume to Montenegro. The second entailed annexation of historical Dalmatia only, but in conjunction with a political treaty which would place Croatia under Italian control. The first option corresponded to what Ciano presented to Ribbentrop in Vienna as the scope of Italian aspirations. The second alternative was not discussed with the Germans in Vienna, so on the eve of his departure for Ljubljana Ciano called Mackensen and briefly outlined his and Mussolini's thoughts. The German envoy was given a draft treaty that Ciano intended to present to Pavelić. Designed to last 25 years, it had four key points:

1. Italy guarantees political independence of the Croatian state and inviolability of its territory within mutually agreed frontiers;
2. Croatia will not accept obligations incompatible with the terms of the treaty with Italy, or opposed to the spirit of that treaty;
3. Croatian armed forces will develop in close cooperation with Italy;

---

[1] Bergwyn, op. cit., p. 54

4. Croatia will join the Italian-Albanian customs and monetary union.[1]

Ciano told Mackensen that the proposed treaty would be a substitute for the personal union, which could present "too great a burden for Pavelić's position in the country right now." The Italians did not want to put too much pressure, he said, and the Duce decided to propose the treaty as a means of "making his friend's life easier." Ciano added that the proposed treaty would place Croatia's links with Italy on a footing similar to Slovakia's links to the Reich, albeit "not quite as close." Conveying the news to Berlin Mackensen commented that the Italians had more or less given up the idea of a personal union, and that they were even uncertain whether Pavelić would – or could – accept the proposed treaty.

Ever worried about German sincerity, Ciano took further steps to secure their acquiescence. On 24 April Ambassador Alfieri visited Weizsaecker in Berlin and requested that Ribbentrop should send a "general message" to Pavelić, to the effect that Germany would agree to whatever terms he (Pavelić) agreed with the government of Italy.[2] The Italian envoy stated that Ribbentrop had "promised" to send such message at the meeting in Vienna. An hour later Ciano telephoned Alfieri in order to modify his request: Ribbentrop should not treat his message as an official note but as an informal Italian request that Pavelić be told of "Germany's hope that Croatia and Italy would find a friendly solution that would satisfy both." In fact no "promise" had been made in Vienna by Ribbentrop to send any such message to Pavelić. Weizsäcker wrote in his note for Ribbentrop that Ciano wanted them "to pull the Italian cart" because he was unsure if he could get what he wanted from Pavelić. The Germans decided to stay aloof: they sent a message to Pavelić merely stating that they would not get involved in any Italian-Croatian talks.[3]

Ciano's conduct on 24 April indicates that the Italians were mistrustful of Germany in spite of the assurances they were given in Vienna. In addition, they were uncertain of the position of their presumed client Pavelić and therefore wanted German pressure to be added to their own. Finally, they were not certain – even at that late moment – which option to pursue with regard to the final form of relationship between Italy and Croatia. Especially puzzling is Ciano's apparent readiness to give up – lightly, as it appears – the idea of a personal union, the mainstay of previous Italian combinations with

---

[1] PA, Büro Staatssekretär, Italien, Bd 4, No 895 of 24 April. Mackensen to Ribbentrop, 24 April 1941.

[2] ADAP, 12-2, pp 520-521. Minute on Alfieri's visit to Ribbentrop, 24 April 1941.

[3] Kasche gave Ribbentrop's message to Pavelić on 24 April in the evening, and found him "ready to prevaricate, rather than accept large territorial losses."

Croatian separatists. Admittedly, the political treaty outlined by Ciano to Mackensen would have established such degree of Italian predominance in Croatia that personal union would be unnecessary. Its value as an additional guarantee of the link with Italy would pale in comparison to the customs union, the tutelage over armed forces, and 25 years' duration of the treaty.

Ciano went to Ljubljana with an open mind as to the final form of links between Croatia and Italy. On the territorial issue he was unwilling to pursue annexationist policy along the eastern Adriatic advocated by the Dalmatian lobby in Rome ("usual agitators," he dismissed them in his diary; "to be pro-Dalmatian is a profession for many"). His note on the meeting in Ljubljana was brief and reflected, *en passant*, his view of the new regime in Zagreb:

> I see Pavelić, surrounded by his band of cutthroats. He declares that the solution proposed by us would have him thrown out of his job. He makes a counter-proposal: Dalmatia of the London Pact, with Trau added, goes to us. Spalato and Ragusa, in addition to some islands, would remain Croatian. His followers are more radical than he. They invoke statistics to prove that in Dalmatia only the stones are Italian. On the contrary, Pavelić is favorable to the political pact. He doesn't even exclude the eventuality of a union under one head, or a monarchy under an Italian prince.[1]

According to Pavelić, Ciano put two proposals to him.[2] The first would have given the entire coastline to Italy. The second proposal placed the frontier further west, but entailed a military alliance. Pavelić supposedly asked Ciano if the Italians valued Dalmatia more than the Croats' friendship, to which Ciano invited Pavelić's own solution: "I replied that I was not in a position to make territorial demands and therefore could not ask for the return of Zadar, but I was only prepared to cede a little territory around that city and Trogir."[3] Pavelić claimed that Ciano agreed with this proposal, but could not accept it without consulting Mussolini.[4]

---

[1] *Diary*, 25 April 1941.

[2] "Još nešto o rimskim ugovorima," *Hrvatska revija*, Buenos Aires, Vol. 2 (June 1953). Pavelić's account, written eight years after the event, was composed in response to a series of articles by Eugen Kvaternik questioning his integrity during negotiations with the Italians.

[3] Compare: *Hrvatska*, Buenos Aires, 10 April 1953.

[4] Ibid. Eugen Kvaternik (*Hrvatska revija*, op. cit.) says that during the first session (10:30-12:30) Pavelić was alone with the Italians, while his aides had to wait in the anteroom of the Ban's palace. Pavelić then gave them a five-minute account of the talks, and mentioned that he had even threatened an Italian general with war over Dalmatia. Edo Bulat's account is essentially the same: after waiting in an anteroom while Pavelić was in conference with the Italians, the Croats were ushered in and shown a map with the entire coastal zone marked as Italian territory. Pavelić briefed them on Ciano's demands and they were taken out again.

When Ciano spoke to him by telephone Mussolini was supposed to have answered *Io non posso essere rinunciatore* – "I cannot be the one who gives up" – alluding to the advocates of the controversial Rapallo Treaty between Belgrade and Rome of 1920. Pavelić was told of Mussolini's answer and told Ciano that in that case they could not talk any further.

Kasche reported from Zagreb on April 26 what he was told by Pavelić: that the meeting in Ljubljana was inconclusive, that Pavelić stood firm, and that "government consultations" in Zagreb were continuing.[1] Alfieri's account of the Ljubljana meeting, given to Weizsäcker, was rather different in spirit: the meeting was described as cordial. Pavelić displayed "good will" towards Ciano's demands, but stressed that because of his great responsibility he needed to consult his closest aides.[2] Finally, Mackensen reported from Rome (also on April 26) that in Ciano's opinion the talks went well. Although no final agreement had been reached as yet, negotiations would be continued through diplomatic channels, i.e. between Pavelić and the Italian envoy in Zagreb, Casertano.[3]

The only direct participants who left accounts of the meeting were Ciano and Pavelić. The latter's was written as a polemical defense against serious charges from within the émigré community, from his former followers and aides. Ciano's diary, on the other hand, has the advantage of being free from such pressures; it also has an immediacy that comes with the recording of events as they occur. On balance, the probable course of the meeting was much less dramatic than Pavelić's description would suggest. Ciano described Pavelić as "favorable to the political pact." This is in line with all the previous negotiations between the *Poglavnik* and the Italians (with Anfuso in Karlovac, with Mussolini and Ciano in Rome). It is remarkable that Ciano, the only credible witness, attributed to Pavelić the proposal of "Dalmatia of the London Pact" and "a monarchy under an Italian prince." According to Ciano's diary, Pavelić was the one to suggest the possibility of "union under one head" (personal union), even though Mussolini had previously decided not to press him on that point.

In the end Italy was given Dalmatia more or less in the same boundaries as those offered by the Allies in 1915 and one of its royal princes became Croatia's "King who never was." This outcome, far from being an Italian *Diktat* reluctantly accepted by Pavelić, was the solution *he* suggested in

---

[1] PA, Büro Staatssekretär, Kroatien, Bd 1, No 126. Kasche to the Ministry, 26 April 1941.

[2] PA, Büro Staatssekretär, Italien, Bd 4. Weizsäcker to Ribbentrop of 26 April 1941.

[3] PA, Büro Staatssekretär, Italien, Bd 4, No 933. Mackensen's report, 26 April 1941.

Ljubljana in preference to Ciano's proposals on customs union and military links. This is confirmed by Ciano's diary entry for April 26: "*Except for Spalato*, Mussolini is in agreement with Pavelić." [Emphasis added]

Pavelić did not offer just "a little territory around Zara and Trogir." If so, the rift between him and Mussolini (who could not be a *rinunciatore*!) would have been much greater than just "Spalato." Besides, from Zara to Trogir there is sixty miles; creating a single Italian belt of territory to link the two would have necessarily included the major Dalmatian city of Šibenik, which Pavelić omits in his recollection. A defiant Pavelić, who talks of war over Dalmatia and refuses to negotiate, would have caused greater consternation than is apparent in either Italian or German sources. Ciano finds "his followers more radical than he" and "Mussolini is in agreement with Pavelić." Not for the first time, Pavelić's concern was the effect that Italian demands would have on his followers and not the nature of those demands as such.

The meeting in Ljubljana was followed by ten days of negotiations between Pavelić and the Italian envoy in Zagreb, Raffaello Casertano (on Pavelić's left, above).[1] Casertano's job was not all that difficult, considering that Pavelić had already agreed to the boundaries of "Dalmatia of the London Pact." On 28 April Ciano noted in his diary that Casertano had telephoned to inform him of "significant progress" with the Croats in regard to Dalmatia and the offer of the crown to a Savoy prince. To the Germans, however, Pavelić presented this as an "either-or" choice: "He wants a solution that would avoid the loss of Dalmatia by offering the crown of Croatia to an Italian prince, who would have no political rights."[2] The following day (April 23) Mackensen reported from Rome on Ciano's

---

[1] He signed his name as "Raffaello" rather than the more common "Raffaele" as is mistakenly spelled in various sources. Casertano arrived in Zagreb as a special plenipotentiary of the Italian government on 23 April. He was subsequently appointed *chargé d'affairs* and finally minister, following his success in negotiations with Pavelić. Casertano was one of the few top career diplomats to remain in the service of Salò, as minister in Budapest, 1943-1944.

[2] PA, Büro RAM, Kroatien, No 128. Kasche to the Ministry, 28 April 1941.

statement that the idea of a personal union was no longer in the forefront, but the project of "an independent monarchy with a Savoy prince at its helm."[1]

Casertano arrived in Rome on April 29 to report to Mussolini. Ciano's diary entry on that day indicates that the question of Split remained the only stumbling block: "Pavelić declares that if he were to relent on Spalato he would have to resign, and with him would collapse all his pro-Italian policy." To Ciano's chagrin, Mussolini remained stubborn on this point, although Roatta and the General Staff "warmly" advocated a political solution and considered as dangerous any "extremist" step regarding Dalmatia.

On April 30 Ciano visited the King to inform him of Pavelić's offer of the crown to a Savoy prince. The news pleased the monarch, but he was blunt on Dalmatia: were it not for certain *understandable sentimentality*, he told Ciano, he would be in favor of giving it all up, and even relinquishing the city of Zara! Faced with such lack of enthusiasm of Ciano, the King, Roatta and the general staff, Mussolini softene his instructions to Casertano. Mussolini told him to *press on Spalato, but not to the point of creating a break*.[2]

In the ensuing days the news from Casertano grew encouraging. Ciano recorded on May 2 that *Casertano telephones that all hope for Spalato is not lost*. Two days later, "Casertano reports that Spalato might also be given to us with some reservations on the administration of the city. The Duce is satisfied." The Italians had more or less given up Split, but Casertano managed to wrestle it back. In view of Mussolini's instructions of April 30, Casertano did not need to go to "the breaking point." His success was indicative of Pavelić's lack of determined resistance, rather than the Italian diplomat's negotiating skill.[3] Instead of confronting Casertano with a threat of resignation if Split were annexed by Italy – an option at which he had hinted earlier but which he never seriously entertained – Pavelić made an attempt to soften Italian demands with German help. He did this initially on May 3, when he asked Kasche for support in resisting Italian demands for customs union. On the same day Pavelić told Veesenmayer (who was still in Zagreb) that he could not make any further territorial concessions. Pavelić's requests were transmitted to Berlin and filed without any action being taken.[4] Also on May 3 the newly appointed Croatian minister in Berlin, Branko Benzon, made

---

[1] PA, Büro Staatssekretär, Italien, Bd 4, No 946 of 29 April 1941.

[2] *Ciano's Diplomatic Papers*, p. 439.

[3] ADAP, 12, 2, pp. 566-568. Mackensen to the Foreign Ministry.

[4] PA, Büro Staatssekretär, Kroatien, Bd 1, Nos 140 (Kasche to the Ministry) and 141 (Veesenmayer to the Ministry) of 3 May 1941.

a heavy handed attempt to enlist German support.[1] He unexpectedly called on Weizsäcker at 11 p.m., having previously attempted to talk to Ribbentrop himself.[2] He justified such a late call by a message he had just received from Pavelić about an "ultimatum" presented by Italy, to which the NDH had to reply the following day (Sunday, May 4). Benzon painted in dramatic terms the effect of Italian demands for Croatia and for Pavelić's position and added "all the hopes of the Croats were placed on the Führer." He had to inform Pavelić by 10 a.m. the following day of the position Berlin was taking regarding this communication. Non-plussed, Weizsäcker tried to calm Benzon and questioned the propriety of the term "ultimatum" and reiterated Germany's position that Italy and Croatia should negotiate directly and in a friendly manner a settlement advantageous to both. Filing his minutes of the episode Weizsäcker calmly wrote: "Perhaps the matter was after all not so acute as the Minister had represented to me."

While Benzon was trying to create the impression of an emergency to Weizsäcker in Berlin, further messages from Kasche and Veesenmayer in Zagreb indicated that there was a deadlock in Pavelić's negotiations with the Italians.[3] The signals from Rome were quite the opposite, however. The German embassy in Rome (Bismarck) reported the following day, May 4, that a deal between the NDH and Italy was practically ready and that Mussolini and Ciano were on the point of leaving for a meeting with Pavelić.[4]

---

[1] Born in Split in 1903 and politically inactive prior to 1940, Benzon suddenly went into exile in that year, first to Slovakia and then to Berlin. As an émigré advocate of Croatian independence, he was reputed to have established good connections in the capital of the Reich. After 10 April 1941 Benzon returned to Zagreb. Pavelić told him that "the fate of Croatia was being decided in Berlin" and sent him there as envoy. Cf. Luka Fertilio, "Poslanici NDH u Trećem Reichu: Branko Benzon." *Hrvatska revija*, Vol. XXV, No. 1, March 1975, pp. 48-54.

[2] DGFP, D, 12, No 440. Weizsäcker's note on Benzon's visit dated 4 May.

[3] PA, Büro Staatssekretär, Kroatien, Bd 1, No 149 of 4 May 1941; No 300 of 4 May 1941. The second document states that Benzon was due to fly to Zagreb early on 5 May, since by 12 noon on that day Pavelić had to give his reply to Casertano. However, Benzon only arrived in Zagreb on 9 May (i.e. after Pavelić's meeting with Mussolini), as reported by *Hrvatski narod* on 10 May 1941. Either the Germans had prevented Benzon from getting to Zagreb in time and thus let Pavelić go ahead with the talks on his own, or else Pavelić had decided that it was no longer necessary for Benzon to come, in view of his unsuccessful approach to Weizsäcker.

[4] PA, Büro Staatssekretaer, Kroatien, Band 1, No 1007. Bismarck to the Ministry, 6 May 1941. The meeting was incorrectly placed "in the vicinity of Ljubljana" by Bismarck.

6. The Rome Agreements

German aloofness to Croat requests for help in softening Italian demands was comparable to the aloofness to an earlier Italian attempt to enlist German support in putting pressure on Pavelić. On April 23 Weizsäcker told Alfieri that it was not the business of the German government to force Croatia into a personal union with Italy; exactly ten days later he poured cold water on Benzon's appeals. Germany's position was true to the *letter* of the talks in Vienna between Ribbentrop and Ciano. It also tallied with the *spirit* of Hitler's admission to Glaise that he aimed to prevent long-term stabilization of Croatia as an Italian client state by letting Italy follow its annexationist course along the eastern shore of the Adriatic.

In view of Mussolini's political experience he should not have fallen into the trap of territorial expansion across the Adriatic. He allowed emotions to prevail over prudence; as Ciano noted on 1 May in his diary: "The Duce is aware of our real interest, but is stubborn about yielding on the question of Spalato." Mussolini's insistence may have been due to the pressure of events in Africa, which were catastrophic for the Italians. In the spring of 1941 Italy lost its entire East African "empire." In Libya it suffered a series of heavy defeats at  Bardia (where 40,000 Italians surrendered, opp. p. l.) and Tobruk, losing Cyrenaica to the British. Less than a year earlier its aspirations against France (Nice, Savoy, Corsica and Tunisia) were frustrated by Hitler, who also upstaged Italy in Greece. The morale-boosting effect of gains in Dalmatia was negligible.

A generation earlier this may have worked: Italy went to war in 1915 in order to obtain borders which included Dalmatia. In the nineteenth century Dalmatia was regarded as a legitimate national aspiration, and as late as 1920 it was a hot issue that could bring tens of thousands into the streets. In 1941, however, the public at large seems to have been singularly indifferent to the Dalmatian question. The facts of geography and demography seemed well nigh irreversible: less than one in twenty inhabitants of Dalmatia regarded himself as Italian, and the province was divided from Italy by three hundred miles of the Adriatic Sea. In his diary Ciano mentions "the Dalmatian lobby" with contempt. Imbued with a healthy common sense in the matters of politics, in the spring of 1941 most Italians were more worried about the shortage of basic foods, or by the surrender of the Croatian King-designate's brother the Duke of Aosta to the British at Amba Aladji in northern Ethiopia.

The final treaties between the NDH and Italy were finally agreed upon by Mussolini and Pavelić on May 7 in Monfalcone, in northwest Italy. The talks were supposed to proceed on the basis of Ciano's draft treaty from Ljubljana and subsequent talks between Pavelić and Casertano in Zagreb. Pavelić tried to alter two clauses of the draft treaty – on customs union and on military cooperation – by his "appeals to the generosity of the Duce," as Ciano put it in his diary. On both points a less binding formulation was adopted, as Veesenmayer pointed out to Ribbentrop.[1] Both Ciano and Casertano were dismayed by this outcome. Casertano gave a detailed account of the episode.[2] He was an advocate of "a firm customs union" in preference to territorial gains "of some barren islands which have no economic value to us." At the beginning of the meeting, at the local railway station, Pavelić asked Mussolini for a private talk. According to Casertano's record,

> [A]fter twenty minutes, Ciano, who was growing impatient, went to the lounge. A little later he got out, angry, and said to me: 'All will be spoilt, Casertano!' He took me to the lounge where I found Mussolini lecturing Pavelić, which he enjoyed doing. He started talking about the customs union, but then got entangled in some of his theorizing and ended up saying that customs union was actually an invention of plutocratic democracies. It could never be the basis of relations between two essentially Fascist countries. My idea was thus ruined.

Casertano's chronicle seems credible. Until the meeting itself Pavelić's direct resistance to the Italians was not very strong, and mainly concerned territory. His attempts to obtain German support for the softening of Italian demands proved fruitless. Ciano and Casertano had both thought they had everything more or less wrapped up, but Mussolini's ad hoc improvisation produced a very different outcome. Mussolini would have served his own cause better had he not gone to Monfalcone at all. He could have sent Ciano

---

[1] PA, Buero RAM, Kroatien, No 170. Veesenmayer to Ribbentrop, 8 May 1941. Also PA, Büro Staatssekretaer, Kroatien, Band 1, No 1007. Bismarck to the Ministry, 6 May 1941. The meeting was incorrectly placed "in the vicinity of Ljubljana" by Bismarck.

[2] Casertano interviewed by Vjeko Dobrinčić, "Tko je sve htio 'hrvatskog kralja'?" *Fokus* (Zagreb weekly), No 11, 31 October 1973, p. 21.

with clear-cut instructions to come back with the initialed treaty that included the original clauses on a customs union and military cooperation. Mussolini missed the opportunity in Monfalcone to penetrate Croatia by economic and fiscal means, settling for the proposed dynastic link and vague statements about future cooperation instead. At the same time, the territorial concessions which he obtained from Pavelić guaranteed that the reaction in Croatia to the treaty would be hostile to Italy. The only benefactor was again Hitler.

Pavelić expressed some satisfaction to the Germans with the outcome of his talks with Mussolini in Monfalcone. To Glaise he confided that he did not take the royal issue seriously since the monarch would be just a figurehead.[1] He briefed Kasche in some detail about the territorial arrangements.[2] To his own closest aides, however, even at this late stage he concealed the extent of territorial concessions. To his secretary of state for foreign affairs and future foreign minister Lorković – who had been waiting in the station hall during the meeting in Monfalcone – Pavelić boasted about the concessions made by Mussolini, but said nothing about the final frontier. Even on the train that took the Croatian delegation to Rome for the formal signing of the agreement with Italy there had been a lot of guessing about the final boundary.[3]

Pavelić went to Rome at the head of a large delegation on 17 May 1941, and arrived there the following morning.[4] At the Quirinal Palace "the Crown of King Zvonimir" of Croatia was formally offered to King Victor Emmanuel who presented the king-designate, Prince Aimone (above). The agreements initialed in Monfalcone were signed by Mussolini and Pavelić at noon. In the

---

[1] AJ, T-501, roll 264.

[2] Eugen Kvaternik, "Još ponešto o rimskim ugovorima" (op. cit.) p. 229. Some of Pavelić's followers suspected that his surrender of Dalmatia reflected his regionalist bias against the supposedly over-excitable Dalmatians, softened by climate and corrupted by Yugoslavism, and in favor of the "best Croats" of the Dinaric hinterland of Lika, Zagora, and above all Pavelić's the "heartland province" of Pavelić's birth and childhood, Bosnia-Herzegovina.

[3] PA, Büro RAM, No 170, 8 May 1941.

[4] A detailed account of the ceremonies on 18 May is given in *Hrvatski narod* of 19 and 20 May 1941. See also Vrančić, *Branili smo državu* (op. cit.), Vol 1, pp. 314-322.

evening Pavelić and his entourage were received in a private audience by the pope above). Careful not to create the impression of implicit recognition of the NDH, the Vatican agreed to the Italian demand that both Pavelić and the king-designate be received by the Pontiff, but only in private and separate audiences. Accordingly the Duke of Spoleto was received the previous day (May 17) as an Italian royal prince, not as the king-designate of Croatia.[1]

A state dinner for all two hundred guests followed; that same evening the NDH delegation left Rome. In contrast to the enthusiastic tone of the official Italian press and the formal speeches, there prevailed visible coolness between Italian hosts and their Croat guests. The prevailing mood in Rome was accurately captured by Ciano in his *Diary* on May 18, when he wondered "if what we have built will be lasting. Maybe I am mistaken in my personal impression, but there is a feeling in the air that Italian domination in Croatia is to be temporary, which is why the public is indifferent."

Four documents known as the Rome Agreements. They contained a treaty on the fixing of frontiers, an agreement on military issues related to the

---

[1] The Duke hinted at the possibility of going native and seeking return of Dalmatia to Croatia after taking the throne. Pavlowitch (1978), p. 469.

Adriatic coast, and a "treaty of cooperation and guarantee."[1] The territorial treaty was the most important part of the agreement in terms of political consequences.[2] The military agreement had three parts. The first was related to the demilitarization of the coastal area left to the NDH. The Croatian side undertook not to construct or maintain any fortifications or installations, bases or military factories in a wide area between the coast and approximately 50 miles inland. The second part contained Pavelić's undertaking not to have a navy. The final, third part made provisions for the transport of Italian military units across the NDH territory.

The four key points in the Treaty of Guarantee and Cooperation reflected concessions which Pavelić had obtained from Mussolini in Monfalcone:
1. Italy guarantees independence and territorial integrity of the NDH;
2. Zagreb will not accept deals contrary to the spirit of the Treaty;
3. Military links are limited to the advisory role of the Italian army;
4. Establishment of comprehensive customs and monetary links.

The agreements (commemorated by a special edition of Italian postage stamps, r.) did not provide Italy with the means of establishing effective control over its nominal client-state. The most important clause of the military agreement was *negative*, in that Croatia agreed not to maintain a navy and to keep the coastal zone demilitarized. Had Italy obtained control over Croatia's armed forces and economy as originally envisaged – by means of military cooperation that would go well beyond the "advisory role" of the Italian army, and through

---

[1] Full Croat text of the Agreements: Ministarstvo vanjskih poslova NDH, *Medjunarodni ugovori 1941*, Zagreb: Hrvatska državna tiskara, XXIX, p. 49 on. Also: *Hrvatski narod*, 19 May 1941. In addition, Mussolini and Pavelić exchanged letters expressing agreement on the Croat local administration for the city of Split and the island of Korčula.

[2] Italy gained Sušak with the surrounding boroughs; northern Adriatic islands of St Marco, Krk, Rab and others to the line of Jablanac; all islands in the region of Zara; mainland cities of Šibenik, Trogir and Split and hinterland on average 60 miles deep; mid-Dalmatian islands of Čiovo, Drvenik, Šolta, Vis, Biševo, Sveti Andrija, Jabuka and a few smaller ones; southern Dalmatian islands of Korčula and Mljet; and the Bay of Kotor. The annexed area of some six thousand square kilometers had a population of 400,000, fewer than 5 percent of them Italians. In its final boundaries the NDH had a total of 38,600 square miles (100,000 sq km) and a population of 6.4 million, of whom approximately 3.3 million were Catholic Croats, 2 million Orthodox Serbs, 700,000 Muslims, 170,000 Germans, 75,000 Hungarians, 40,000 Jews, 30,000 Gypsies, and 90,000 members of other minorities.

customs and monetary *union*, instead of the ill-defined "links" – demilitarization of the Adriatic would not have been necessary.

To draw a parallel with another client state, Germany had no need for such provisions in its dealings with Slovakia. Mussolini the Fascist was unable to grasp that physical control is the least effective means of controlling a country. By letting Pavelić off the hook on what should have been two central means of control, military "cooperation" and customs union, and simultaneously by annexing most of Dalmatia, Mussolini got the worst of all worlds. By failing to secure control, he left open the possibility that the NDH could turn to Germany, or become more truly independent at some future date. By alienating Croatia's public opinion, including the Ustašas which he had sponsored for so long, the Duce promoted the shift to Germany and made the desire for independence from Italy more likely. Another result was an erosion of Pavelić's domestic position; yet the Duce was fully aware that the Ustaša leader was his "only pawn on the Balkan board."[1]

Mussolini told the Grand Council in 1939 that Italy had no territorial interests in Europe besides Albania. His subsequent diversion to the policy of territorial expansion in Dalmatia was an aberration of the central policy. Worse still, it was a self-defeating substitute for coherent policy at a time

---

[1] Anfuso, op. cit. p. 191.

when Italy's original objectives were increasingly at odds with the means of achieving them.

The problem of Italy's relations with Croatia was formally solved but it was really just beginning. The Rome Agreements, far from being the solution, were a major part of the problem. With their signing the marriage of convenience between Italian irredentism and Croat ultra-chauvinism was finally consummated. The two could not be permanently reconciled, but they needed each other in order to achieve their separate objectives.

Mussolini exacted his protégé's lump-sum payment in the form of an economically depressed and demographically alien territory. He forfeited a permanent deed in the form of personal union, customs union and military control. Pavelić kept his side of the bargain, in line with the one consistent motive of all his actions: to take power and to stay in power. After that, there was nothing to keep the two parties together. The Ustaša regime turned increasingly to Berlin (as evidenced in the two flags, German and Croatian, previous page, without the Italian tricolor on display, prev. p.) for guidance, support, and hoped-for frustration of Italian designs.

VII
The Ustaša Holocaust

1. Ustašism Unleashed

The twentieth century had witnessed a departure in the conduct of many European states away from the concept of natural morality that provided a salutary restraint on their behavior before 1914. The rise of totalitarian ideologies marked the end of an era that sought, over the previous century, to break away from the traumatic memory of the Terror in France, and insisted that physical elimination of an adversary is not a legitimate way of resolving a conflict. The decline of the religious impulse among Europeans created a gaping hole that was filled by ideologies uninhibited by religious restraints and motivated by the will to power. Before Lenin it was not some mere 'expediency' which had prevented states from resorting to mass extermination as a means to an end. The limitations on the behavior of states derived from an underlying consensus that *raison d'etat* entailed continued membership of the community of civilized nations.

The final break came after the collapse of the Madagascar Plan and in the midst of the ideological mobilization for Hitler's attack on the Soviet Union, with which the decision to embark on the Final Solution broadly coincided.[1] From September 1939 until June 1941 Germany arguably was waging a traditional European war (*ein europäisches Normalkrieg*) against Britain and France that only turned exterminationist with the *Barbarossa*. Until June 1941 the Wehrmacht swept across Europe like a well oiled machine, but the principles of warfare and the treatment of the vanquished did not appear to be fundamentally different from previous attempts at Continental hegemony by Napoleon or the Kaiserreich. Against the Soviets, both ideological and racial enemies, no laws applied, however: the war "aimed at destroying not simply the Soviet government and its ability to wage war but the rule of law."[2]

There was a corner of Europe, however, where the war had stopped being "normal" well before the struggle in the East reached its existential climax. Pavelić's Croatia was the first member of the New European Order to

---

[1] The broad intent was contained in Hitler's famous speech of January 30, 1939. For conflicting views on the exact timing of the decision see Michael R. Marrus. *The Holocaust in History*. University Press of New England, 1987.

[2] Tandy McConnell, "Nazi Criminality." *History in Dispute*, Vol. 11: The Holocaust, St. James Press, 2003, p. 169.

abandon the remnants of traditional restraints. As early as 17 April, a week after coming to Zagreb, Pavelić enacted a fiat, the *Law on the Protection of the People and the State*. It was an all-embracing piece of pseudo-legislation that literally made it "legal" to kill anyone the Ustaša regime wanted killed. Capital punishment was made mandatory for all those who "offended the honor and vital interests of the Croat people" and who "in whatever way" threatened the NDH. There was no appeal and each sentence had to be carried out *within two hours*. The "law," furthermore, had retroactive powers, so that a person could be found guilty of having "offended" the state even before it came into being. "Special popular courts" and mobile court-martials were immediately established.

The following day, April 18, Pavelić signed the first racial law, on "the Aryanization of Jewish property." The NDH accomplished in the ensuing two weeks weeks what it had taken the Nazi regime seven years to achieve in Germany. On April 30 he signed two ordinances – more stringent than the Nuremberg Laws – defining who is Jewish and who is Aryan. The issue was henceforth handled by a Commission for Racial and Political Matters at the Ministry of Internal Affairs.[1] The *Decree on Racial Affiliation* and the *Decree on the Protection of the Aryan Blood and Honor of the Croatian Nation* remained in force until May 5, 1945, four days before the downfall. By the first week of May all Serbs were ordered to wear blue sleeve bands with the

letter P (*Pravoslavni*, Orthodox), and Jews the Star of David and the letter Ž or the word *Židov*, Jew (r.). The Jews were thus made visible in Croatia three months before they were forced to wear the star in Germany. Signs in public places warned that "no Serbs, Jews, Gypsies or dogs" were allowed.

The Ustaša zeal was impressive but not all that

---

[1] The 40,000 Jews of Croatia lived mainly in four cities: Zagreb (11,000), Sarajevo (10,000), Osijek (3,000), and Bjelovar (3,000). Two-thirds were Ashkenazim and the rest Sephardim, mainly descendents of Spanish Jews settled in the Ottoman Empire in the 16th century. Most were middle class: civil servants, merchants, and professionals, e.g. doctors and lawyers.

surprising.[1] The Independent State of Croatia differed from other Nazi satellites in two important respects. The NDH was less confident of itself on the key issue of identity and rootedness than any other German ally (save perhaps Slovakia). The insistence on the "holy Croatian name" which cannot be replaced by any other was strange to the uninitiated. It was indicative of a deep neurosis no less than the claim that the Croats were one of the oldest nations in Europe, fully developed centuries before the Frankish extended family underwent differentiation. The endeavor to make the Croatian language as different from Serbian as possible, desperate in methods, often pathetic and sometimes funny in its results, reflected the same fixation. The challenge of explaining why an undeniably Slavonic language was spoken by the Nordic-Dinaric descendents of Iranians, Goths, Avars and Illyrians was yet another vexing hurdle. It produced different answers from the same Ustaša circle – a dozen names in all – of autodidactic multidisciplinarians. They were sometimes in turns and mostly at the same time political theorists, racial biologists, geostrategists, cultural historians, linguists and social anthropologists. Loath to allow mere data to stand in the way of their creativity, these people turned the Ustaša version of Croatian ethnogenesis into a heroic saga of state-building Aryan warriors defending the West against barbarity and racial pollution.

Pavelić's Croatia was straining to convince itself, no less than to explain to foreigners, that it was worthy of that status among Europe's old nations which those nations had long taken for granted. It was a *Volksgemeinschaft* supposedly characterized by the virtues of pride, struggle for rights, idealism, optimism, selflessness, self-sacrifice and morality. It was civilized yet nobly barbarian ("wild wolves and enraged lions"), long-suffering yet furious, young and vigorous yet old and wise. It was the most complex, the most perfect... and the most underrated nation in the world.

Of no lesser importance, in practical terms, was the fact that the Ustaša regime – alone among the satellites – did not have to suffer the presence of an even more zealously pro-Nazi force waiting in the wings to replace Pavelić if he proved insufficiently enthusiastic or reliable. All other German allies in central and southeastern Europe were headed by individuals and regimes less than totally committed to the increasingly scary Nazi project. Admiral Horthy, Marshal Antonescu, King Boris and Monsignor Tiso were willing to stake

---

[1] As early as May 3, 1941, *Hrvatski narod* explained the racial law decrees by stressing that the NDH was a nation-state in which only Aryans had the right to occupy positions of responsibility and to direct its destiny. Preserving essential hereditary traits of the race is the precondition for maintaining the integrity of the nation.

their own and their regimes' future on the success of Hitler's gamble. They were uncomfortable, however, with his utopian vision; and sooner or later they all proved reluctant to become his fully-fledged partners in the Final Solution. The deportations in Hungary started in earnest only after Horthy's neutralization in the spring of 1944; in "Old Rumania" they did not happen at all. The Arrow Cross, the Legion, the *Ratnitsi*, the Hlinka Guard, had all claimed that *they* would have been more genuinely committed to Hitler's project than their establishmentarian foes. In Pavelić's Croatia the potential opposition came solely from the softer side of the spectrum.[1]

Pavelić alone, among the Quislings, had no qualms and no reservations. For as long as he could have a free hand to destroy the Serbs – the primary *raison d'etre* of his movement and his state – he would deal with the Jews in the same manner (cf. an anti-Jewish poster, r.). This was also the way to prove his preference for the Reich over Italy, which was lukewarm in its anti-Jewish measures. (The most rabid anti-Semites among his followers included a *Mischling*, Eugen-Dido Kvaternik).

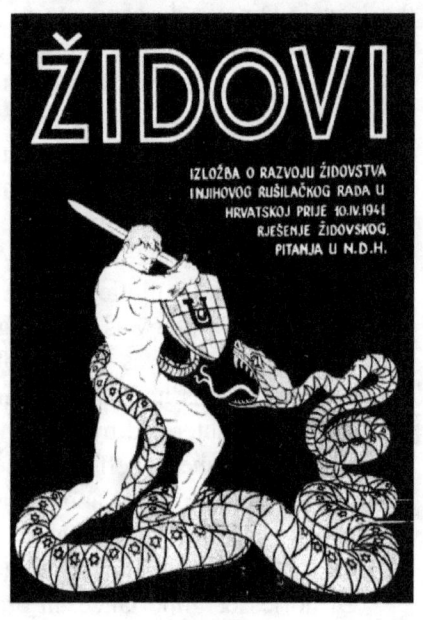

For most rank-and-file Ustašas the Jews were but the collateral damage in the real war – the war against the Serbs. The Ustaša rank-and-file, coming mainly from the economically depressed rural regions in the Dinaric mountain range, had only a vague idea of "the Jew," while a demonized image of "the Serb" was fully formed.[2] In terms of the decision-making calculus, the slaughter of Croatia's Jews was politically motivated whereas with the Serbs the motive had no rational basis beyond raw hatred. Formally packaged as ideological anti-Semitism, anti-Jewish

---

[1] It remained merely potential until the end. Maček the meek half-Slovene Slav was no match for Pavelić the Nordic-Dinaric warrior.

[2] The rank-and-file would have been bemused by the assertion by one of Pavelić's chief propagandists, Julije Makanec, that 'fighting today for Croatia and Europe, we fight for the values that are represented by the names such as Sophocles, Plato, Dante, Bošković, Pascal, Goethe...and against the world whose representatives are Rotschild, Morgenthau, La Guardi [sic!], Apfelbaum and Bela Kun' (quoted by Bartulin, op. cit., p. 399).

measures combined the regime's desire to demonstrate its ideological bona fides to Hitler, to assert an area of independence vis-à-vis the Italians, and to confiscate the Jewish property:

> Aryan trustees were appointed to take over Jewish businesses... Collective fines, which had to be paid in gold or its equivalent, were imposed on the Jewish communities. Overnight, a pseudolegal expropriation drive was launched, which before long turned into an unbridled countrywide campaign of plunder and pillage in which everyone who stood to profit took part – trade unions, youth organizations, sports clubs, the armed forces, and government officials of all ranks. Ordinary citizens also took part in this campaign wherever they could; indeed, the share of "private" elements in the plunder was enormous – at least half of the property of which the Jews were robbed apparently never reached the state treasury but remained in the hands of individual Croatians.[1]

By January 1942, some two-thirds of Croatian Jewry – about 26,000 persons – had been taken to Ustaša camps and killed on arrival or soon thereafter. In "permanently solving the Jewish question" the NDH was ahead not only of other satellites but of the Reich itself. In an interview with a German paper at the end of the summer of 1941, Pavelić could pledge that "the Jews will be liquidated within a very short time."[2]

The destruction of some 15,000 non-Muslim Roma was peripheral to the project, but it was proportionately more thorough than that of the Jews or Serbs. Group exemptions were made only for the Muslim Gypsies of Bosnia-Herzegovina, who were protected by the Islamic clergy:

> The Ustasha regime, always anxious to court the Muslim political and religious elite, decided to exempt the so-called 'White Gypsies' (i.e. Gypsies assimilated into Muslim culture) and most of them did in fact survive the war. The Ustashe justified the exemptions by arguing that the 'White Gypsies' had intermarried with Muslim Croats, had long lost use of their 'Gypsy language' and 'lived with their families completely equally as other Muslims of these areas.'[3]

---

[1] "Croatia," by Menachem Shelah. *Encyclopedia of the Holocaust*. Jerusalem: Yad Vashem, 1990, p. 323-4.

[2] Ibid, p. 324. Several hundred Jews, about one percent, were exempt as "Honorary Arians" for their past services to the Croatian nation and the Ustaša movement. Some were at least temporarily safe because they were considered indispensable to the Croatian economy or because of their professional expertise (notably doctors). The non-religious *Mischlingen* married to non-Jews were exempt, like in Germany. Several thousand Jews were able to flee to the Italian zone, where they were protected by the Italian Army until September 1943.

[3] Bartulin, op. cit., p. 409.

2. "The Last Bullet for the Last Serb"

The notion of resolving the Serb question in Croatia by radical violence had its roots in the relentless hostility of the Croatian estates, of the nobility and the Roman Catholic Church hierarchy, to their special status and privileges obtained from the Crown in the 17th and 18th centuries.[1] In the 1860's that hostility was given an exterminationist articulation by Ante Starčević and was subsequently "democratized" through his Party of Rights. In the early 20th century the Rightist legacy was recomposed as an ideology of unadulterated Serbophobia by Josip Frank, rehearsed in the *Kristallnacht*-like anti-Serb demonstrations in 1902, and tested in the aftermath of the assassination in Sarajevo.[2] In July 1914 Frankist-led rioters took control of the streets of Zagreb with the assistance of the police.[3] The pogrom was recalled four years later by a deputy in the Austrian parliament in Vienna: thousands of Serbs were arrested, hundreds deported, dozens summarily executed.[4] A prominent Croatian politician recalled "the horrible scene at the end of the first day of mobilization," three weeks after Sarajevo, with a mob burning furniture looted from the shops and homes of the Serbs of Zagreb and chanting the rhyme *Hang the Serb from a willow tree*.[5] All over Zagreb, thousands of people poured into the streets clamoring for Serb blood.[6] "Serb houses were ransacked and demolished and Serbs massacred and hanged without judge or judgment."[7] An officer in Karlovac noted in July 1914 that "the entire city was filled with enthusiasm and joy: now was the moment to exterminate the *Vlachs*!"[8] "Some secret force," he went on, "intoxicated even the otherwise moderate Croats."

---

[1] Cf. the suggestion by the Zagreb diocesan official, Ambroz Kuzmić (November 13, 1700), that the "Vlachs" should be "slaughtered, rather than allowed to settle down" (p. 21 above).

[2] Because of his Jewish roots, however, Frank was ignored by the Ustaša propaganda. His daughter Olga committed suicide in August 1941 finding Jewish origins incompatible with the senior posts her husband Slavko and son Eugen were given by Pavelić. Pavelić's wife Mara, Jewish on her mother's side, had no such dilemmas, however. She was rabidly anti-Semitic.

[3] *Obzor*, Zagreb, August 11, 1918.

[4] Speech by Dalmatian deputy Ante Tresid-Pavičić in the parliament in Vienna, as quoted in *Novosti* (Zagreb), October 25, 1918.

[5] Dr. Ivan Ribar, *Iz moje političke suradnje, 1901-1965*. Zagreb: Naprijed, 1965, p. 133. 'Srbe na vrbe' was a common chant, yet again, in the spring of 1941.

[6] Isidor Kršnjavi in *Oesterreichische Rundschau*, October 1, 1914.

[7] S. Budisavljević in the Croatian *Sabor*, August 1, 1918. *Novosti* (Zagreb), August 2, 1918.

[8] Vasa Kazimirović, *Srpsko nasledje*, No. 10 (October 1998).

Those "otherwise moderate Croats" were in the majority in 1941. Many were dissatisfied with the Kingdom of Yugoslavia, but the fruits of quiet persistence pursued by the HSS resulted in the *Sporazum* of 1939 and the creation of the autonomous Banovina Croatia. Had Maček accepted German advances in early April 1941, there could have been anti-Serb and anti-Jewish administrative measures and occasional excesses. It is hardly imaginable, however, that there would have been state-sponsored bloodbath. This is not to say that Pavelić alone, or in conjunction with his handful of returning émigrés, was to blame for the Croatian Holocaust. The older Zagreb elites, the Roman Catholic hierarchy, the *Banovina* bureaucracy incorporated into the new state structure, and the silent majority of "otherwise moderate Croats" well aware of what was going on. (The new regime was barely a week old when the Serbian Bank, Српска банка, was taken over and its Cyrillic sign smashed up, l.).

One fanatical man and his two hundred faithful henchmen would not have imposed their will on the rest of the society had there existed a collective will not to act as his accessories, and had there not existed a tradition of animosity and intolerance upon which he was able to build. That tradition was not dominant in Croatia's body-politic before April 1941, but over the ensuing fout years it proved sufficiently strong for the regime to achieve a disturbing degree of domestic acquiescence for its radically exterminationist policies.

Back in 1914-18 the Serbs suffered persecution but survived. The Habsburg Monarchy was a *Rechtstaat*, after all, in spite of its many lapses under the extreme strain of events following Sarajevo. In the spring of 1941, shocked by the rapid collapse of Yugoslavia, the Serbs also displayed passivity and mute acceptance of the new order. The unspoken assumption was that the NDH was a somewhat less attractive re-enactment of Austria-Hungary and that the initial storm would pass. As they were to learn to their peril, however, in Pavelić's state there was no rational correlation between a Serb's thoughts or deeds, and the state's attitude to him:

The Ustašas refused to acknowledge that having a Serbian national consciousness was not a political act or in any sense something one [did not] intentionally choose. Such an admission would have made their anti-Serbian policies look like a campaign against innocent people. They therefore insisted that being a Serb was in itself a political act and that those who 'wanted to be Serbs' and who 'insisted on being Serbs' could be justly punished for that.[1]

"There were no innocents" at Jasenovac, its commander, Vjekoslav "Max" Luburić, declared two decades after the war.[2] They were guilty of who they were. While enthusiastically participating in the continent-wide Holocaust against Jews and Gypsies, "Croatia's collaborationist government conducted its own genocide against the Serbs within its territories"; but this phenomenon remained largely unknown outside Yugoslavia until the 1990s for a variety of political reasons:

> Of the principal external actors, post-war German attention focused on the Holocaust. Italy still resists fully confronting its less than pristine role in the Balkans... The Vatican, meanwhile, has yet to release its documents on the subject. Within Yugoslavia itself, Ustaša perpetrators strove to conceal their crimes once it became clear that Tito's Partisans would win the Yugoslav Civil War... Tito encouraged all ethnicities to bury their war memories so that Yugoslavia could build a new nation based on brotherhood and unity.[3]

There is no debate between "intentionalists" and "functionalists" when it comes to the Holocaust in the NDH. Pavelić and his émigrés returned from Italy on April 13 determined to kill as many Serbs as possible, as quickly as possible. Exactly two weeks later "Pavelić's onslaught against the Orthodox Serbs... one of the most appalling civilian massacres known to history"[4] started on the outskirts of the city of Bjelovar. On the night of 27-28 April 1941, 190 unarmed civilians were rounded up and shot. Similar ad-hoc mass executions were repeated in different areas throughout the month of May.[5] It is noteworthy, in the photographs from this early period, that there were relatively few victims compared to the numerous and obviously proud

---

[1] Aleksa Djilas, unpublished PhD thesis, p. 245.
[2] Ivan Mužić (ed.), *Maček u Luburićevu zatočeništvu*. Split : Laus, 1999, pp. 71-72.
[3] Michele Frucht Levy: *"The Last Bullet for the Last Serb:* The Ustaša Genocide against Serbs, 1941–1945." *Nationalities Papers*, Vol. 37, No. 6, November 2009.
[4] John Cornwell. *Hitler's Pope. The Secret History of Pius XII.* New York and London: Viking, 1999, p. 249.
[5] See Fikreta Jelić-Butić: *HSS*. Zagreb 1983, p. 47.

perpetrators (l.). By the summer the initiation and training of the novices would be over and the ratios reversed.

Before the bloodbath started in earnest in June and July, the ground was prepared with dozens of speeches by Ustaša officials at public meetings all over the NDH and in countless press articles advocating systemic violence. A German observer on the scene noted the wide circulation, as soon as the new regime took over, of time-tested slogans such as "Hang the Serbs on willow trees" (*Srbe na vrbe*), "there will be blood up to the knee," or "we shall tear their babies out of their mothers' wombs!"[1] The imagery of Pavelić's men was crude: the *so-called Serbs*, subhuman Balkan scum, were culturally and socially unassimilable aliens inherently hostile to the Croatian people, to which they are inherently inferior, and to the Croatian state which they hate. Neither the state nor the people which embodies it could survive, let alone prosper, for as long as this alien thorn remained in the healthy flesh. The concluding message was frank: "Destroy them wherever you see them, and our Poglavnik's blessing is certain," declared Viktor Gutić, district Ustaša chief in Banja Luka.[2] Pavelić's minister of justice was equally clear:

> This State, our country, is only for the Croats, and for noone else. There are no means which we will not be ready to use in order to make our country truly ours, and to cleanse it of all Serbs. All those who came into our country 300 years ago must disappear. We do not hide this as our intention. It is the policy of our State. In the course of its execution we shall simply follow the Ustaša principles.[3]

Mladen Lorković, a supposedly moderate Ustaša mistrusted by the returning émigré *ras* circle as a bourgeois intellectual, added the Jews to the equation. The Croatian nation has to cleanse itself from all elements that are its misfortune, foreign and alien to it, Lorković declared, "our Serbs and our

---

[1] Dr. Josef Matl in *Iskra* (Munich), March 20, 1959.

[2] Gutić also declared that the Serbs should not be treated with any scruples because they are 'a criminal breed.' *Hrvatski narod*, July 11, 1941.

[3] From a speech by Dr. Milovan Žanić. *Novi list* (Zagreb daily), 3 June 1941.

Jews."[1] The blending of Serbian and Jewish negative stereotypes (with Gypsies mainly used as an auxilliary term of anti-Serb abuse) was associated, soon after the Barbarossa was launched, with "Asiatic Bolshevism":

> By conflating the three groups together, the Ustashe produced a racial counter-type that provided an easily identifiable enemy. They identified Serbs as partially non-Aryan due to centuries of miscegenation with dark Balkan elements and various 'Near-Eastern' immigrants during the period of Turkish rule... [D]ue to the mixing with the 'Romanized aboriginals of the Balkan peninsula', the predominant physical features of the Serbs were dark skin, eyes and hair. In 1942, Milivoj Karamarko claimed that a sizeable 15% of Serbs possessed 'non-Aryan Near Eastern and very conspicuous Gypsy' racial features. Furthermore, only a minority of Serbs were Dinaric (25%), while the relative majority (35%) belonged to the Armenoid race, which was characterized by a dark complexion and a personality prone to trickery, fawning and cheating. The Serbs had... 'received a considerable admixture of Gypsy, nomadic and Semitic blood and are therefore clever, cunning, envious and selfish...'[2]

In his famous speech in the town of Gospić, Mile Budak, Pavelić's minister of education, announced: "We have three million bullets for Serbs, Jews and Gypsies. We shall kill one third of all Serbs. We shall deport another third, and the rest of them will be forced to become Catholic." The *so-called Serbs*, Budak added, are not any *Serbs* at all, but people brought by the Turks "as the plunderers and refuse of the Balkans... They should know, and heed, our motto: *either submit, or get out!*"[3] Such an act of submission was not an option for most of the victims, however. The program heralded by Budak (on r., above) and others meant that – as Ernest Nolte has put it – "Croatia became during the war a giant slaughterhouse." Close to two hundred thousand Serbs who were deported to Serbia under the auspices of the the Ustaša State Directorate for

---

[1] *Hrvatski narod*, July 28, 1941.

[2] Bartulin, op. cit. p. 365.

[3] Neither option was in fact made available, in subsequent months and years, to the hundreds of thousands of Serbs affected by Ustaša *cleansing operations*.

Renewal, and unknown numbers of others who simply escaped, could consider themselves lucky. The program itself evolved beyond ethnicity, religion, and violence,[1] to include the peculiar Ustaša concept of *race*. In public statements, in the tradition of Starčević, the Serbs' identity was denied and the term *Vlachs* used instead. It implied their uncertain origins from a mélange, the rabble that came uninvited to Bosnia and Croatia five centuries earlier as plundering Turkish auxiliaries and scavenging camp followers.[2] By religion they were 'Greek-Easterners' (*Grko-iztočnjaci*), the very term *Serbian Orthodox* being formally banned together with the Cyrillic script. At the same time, in line with the parallel Ustaša claim that many of those "so-called Serbs" were originally Catholic Croats converted to Orthodoxy under the Ottomans, the rhetoric of the regime depicted them as apostates and traitors – implicitly not of alien racial stock after all – who had betrayed Croatia to foreign, i.e. Serbian interests.[3] That these people were "actually" Serb was not an option. In practice, whether they were the offspring of uninvited mongrel aliens or former Catholic Croats who had accepted the Serb name by default, made little difference to the peasants of Lika, Kordun, Banija, northern Dalmatia, eastern Herzegovina... Either way, in the summer of 1941, they were deemed deserving of death.[4]

3. Pavelić at the Berghof

The Rome Agreements formally solved the problem of Dalmatia and of Croatia's relationship with Italy. At the same time their signing contributed to the estrangement between the Italians and Pavelić's government. Although ostensibly (and after 18 May 1941 even formally) belonging to the Italian sphere of interest, Croatia increasingly resembled Slovakia. German soldiers walked the streets of its capital, German companies enjoyed concessions to

---

[1] Jonathan Gumz, "German Counterinsurgency Policy in Independent Croatia, 1941-1944." *The Historian*, Vol. 61 (1998), pp. 33-51.

[2] E.g. Mile Budak, as quoted by *Hrvatski narod*, May 27, 1941.

[3] Those interests were identified in propaganda statements with the defunct Yugoslav state, while the parallel economic oppression between the wars was identified with the Jews. The scheming Serb Gypsy-Tsintsars and the exploiting Jews had forged a symbiotic mechanism for the oppression of honest, heroic, toiling Croats. Such seamless blending of Serbophobia and anti-Semitism reflected Pavelić's claim, in his 1936 memorandum to the German Foreign Ministry, that "Yugoslavia was a veritable El Dorado for the Jews."

[4] In early 1942, the notion of *converted Catholic Croats* gained greater prominence because it did not contradict the Ustaša racial theory at a time when half-hearted assimilationist attempts were briefly in vogue.

exploit its mineral wealth, German-speaking Habsburg officers were in command of its budding regular army, and the German minority was granted special privileges by the regime.

The system of occupation in the former Yugoslavia, hastily created in April 1941 and presumably temporary in nature, was weakened from the outset by intra-Axis differences and by the consequences of their decision to install the Ustašas in power. In addition Hitler wanted to impose a Carthaginian peace on the Serbs: he singled them out for special punishment after the Belgrade coup of March 27, but without allocating sufficient resources to the maintenance of such a harsh order. The apparent willingness of Mussolini's reluctant clients, the Ustašas, to be drawn closer to Berlin was a poor substitute for the inherent instability of the area the Wehrmacht was preparing to leave for the East.

Pavelić expressed his desire to visit Hitler in a meeting with Kasche on May 9.[1] The Ustaša leader said that he did not want to make any "political demands" but simply to express his personal gratitude and his country's strong links with the Reich. Kasche thought that such a visit would be useful because of its domestic political objective: Pavelić was due to sign his agreements with Italy, and an endorsement from Hitler could help avert the anticipated popular backlash against the pact that entailed considerable territorial concessions.

The predictions of a negative reaction to the Rome Agreements were correct, as Glaise reported to the OKW on May 19. The effect in Croatia was shattering, he wrote, and many people put all their hope in Germany and Hitler. Three days later Pavelić attempted to rectify this effect by delivering a major speech [see Appendix] in which he sought to explain away the loss of Dalmatia by the need "to make some sacrifices, and a nation unable to make sacrifices is unable to live."[2] Pavelić concluded the address with fresh grave threats against the Serbs, in an attempt to shift the focus away from the Rome Agreements onto the "enemy within":

> We shall not allow enemies of the Croat people to work against it, to poison it from within.[...] The times when the Croat people was but an object are over. The Croat nation is the master now, and everything else will be *its* object. These are clear indications of our intentions, which are being applied and will be carried out. I shall carry them out!

---

[1] PA, Büro Staatssekretär, Kroatien, Bd. 1, No. 192. Kasche to Ribbentrop, 9 May 1941.

[2] As reported by *Hrvatski narod*, Zagreb, 22 May 1941 (Vol. 3, No. 99).

On June 2 Ribbentrop informed Kasche that Hitler would receive Pavelić on the sixth at the Berghof.[1] On the same day Hitler and Mussolini met at the Brenner. Their foreign ministers conferred separately, and Ciano received the usual assurances that Germany approved of everything done so far in Croatia, which in any event belonged to the Italian sphere.[2] To stress that point Ribbentrop said that as far as he was concerned Croatia should sign the Tripartite Pact in Italy, and not in Germany, as Pavelić had signaled he hoped to do during his proposed visit. The latter eventually signed it in Venice on December 15, 1941.

On Pavelić's arrival in Salzburg on June 6 he was first taken to Ribbentrop's estate at Fuschl. Ribbentrop expressed concern about the remaining "conspiratorial cliques" in Serbia which had always spread unrest from that country.[3] Pavelić eagerly responded that the Croats could offer valuable help in uprooting such "cliques," since he had "experts" familiar with the conditions in Serbia and in possession of certain relevant documents. Ribbentrop continued to dwell on the Serb question and asked Pavelić about his plans for the large Serb minority in the NDH (which even according to Ustaša sources came to two million or just under one third of the population).[4] Pavelić replied that "there had been no Serb question" in Croatia until sixty or seventy years earlier, when the influence of the Orthodox Church imbued those people with the "mistaken" feeling of Serb identity. He added that they would be expelled anyway, and that the Slovenes from the Reich would be settled instead.

Pavelić also pledged to deal resolutely with the Jewish question and pointed out that comprehensive anti-Jewish legislation already had been enacted. Asked by Ribbentrop about the internal order of the NDH, Pavelić said the Ustašas would be the only party; as for the religious circles, the Muslims would not present a problem, and the lower Catholic clergy was solidly behind him. On cooperation with the Italian armed forces Pavelić said that it existed at the level of general staffs only; since "the Croats are good soldiers" there was no need for any Italian instructors. He then told Ribbentrop that the NDH hoped to get the Sanjak of Novi Pazar dividing Serbia and Montenegro which had a sizeable Muslim population; this request he repeated to Hitler later.

---

[1] PA, Büro RAM, Kroatien, No. 400. Ribbentrop to Kasche, 2 June 1941.

[2] Minutes of meeting between Ciano and Ribbentrop, 2 June 1941.

[3] PA, Büro RAM, Handakten Schmidt, Aufzeichnungen: 1941 (Teil II).

[4] *Hrvatski narod*, Zagreb, 19 May 1941 (Vol. 3, No. 96).

From Fuschl Pavelić proceeded to the Berghof (above).[1] Responding to Pavelić's expressions of gratitude for his people's independence, Hitler remarked that the course of events had made him "an unwilling instrument of Croatia's liberation": he had not intended to act against Yugoslavia, but the Serbs forced his hand. The key part of the conversation concerned national policy. Picking up the theme already mentioned by Ribbentrop, Hitler described plans to transfer Serbs from the NDH to Serbia and Slovenes from the Reich into Croatia as a "momentarily painful" operation that was nevertheless preferable to "permanent suffering." Then Hitler added the key sentence: "After all, if the Croat state wishes to be strong, a nationally intolerant policy must be pursued for fifty years, because too much tolerance on such issues can only do harm."

With this statement Hitler explicitly endorsed the mass persecution of the Serb minority which had already started, but which reached its climax in subsequent months. Hitler's encouragement to Pavelić to pursue "intolerance" was in line with his intention, stated to Glaise on April 17, to encourage internal Serb-Croat conflict as "the guarantee of a permanent schism between nations which had been within one state until now." Hitler let the Italians make enemies of Croats; and he was going to let the Croats make enemies of Serbs. In the event both Mussolini and Pavelić performed on cue, albeit with varying degrees of enthusiasm. Mussolini was a reluctant irredentist, fearful of being a *renunciator*. Pavelić was an enthusiastic exterminationist.

---

[1] DGFP, D, 12, Minutes of Hitler's talks with Pavelić, 6 June 1941.

4. "Intolerance" at Work

Hitler's advocacy of "fifty years of intolerance" did not make any difference to the thousands of Serbs already slaughtered in the NDH before 6 June. It is nevertheless inconceivable that the wave of bloody terror which engulfed the Ustaša state in the summer of 1941 would have been possible had Hitler wanted to put a stop to it. His encouragement to Pavelić had major long-term impact not because it induced the Poglavnik to do something he had not intended to do in any event, but because it gave him *carte blanche* to go all the way. In Berchtesgaden Hitler made Pavelić *feel authorized* to proceed with his attempted genocide of the Serb population.[1]

The NDH needed no "legislation" for the prosecution to begin. With total power in the hands of Pavelić and his cohorts, and a growing body of Ustaša volunteers (l.) – 30,000 by the summer – willing to prove their worth, they could do literally as they pleased: pick up a Serb village, have it surrounded, order all inhabitants to gather in the local Orthodox church, tie them two by two, and either kill them on the spot, or throw them down a nearby karst pit, or send them to a camp. By June 1941 such atrocities were taking place on a daily basis. The method of killing was savage: a slit throat, or a blow with a heavy club in the back of the head, were the most common. Tens of thousands of Serbs were taken to one of the newly established camps and killed there. The lucky ones saved their lives by converting to Roman Catholicism – a hundred thousand in all, mainly in the northern Pannonian regions – or by escaping to Serbia with no belongings (an estimated 180,000 individuals).

From April to August 1941 a dozen major camps were established to handle huge numbers of deportees.[2] The system of hastily constructed and

---

[1] Hory and Broszat, op. cit. p. 15.

[2] Among the prominent ones, Danica near Zagreb was established in April 1941 and disbanded at the end of the year. Most of the inmates were political prisoners. A camp on Pag Island in the Adriatic was established in June 1941 and dismantled two months later. In the few weeks of its

rudimentally organized facilities, of which the one at Jasenovac was the most prominent, turned the NDH into "a land of concentration camps."[1] One major difference between Ustaša and Nazi terror emerges from countless accounts of savage, sadistic murders of prisoners.[2] Jadovno on Mt. Velebit was a death camp *par excellence*. With no accommodation facilities, no rations, no workshop, and no chance of survival for the condemned – who were thrown by the hundreds down a nearby mountain pit every day – Jadovno was a primitive precursor of the *Vernichtungslager* concept, perfected a year later at Treblinka, Sobibor and Birkenau. Some thirty thousand victims took the one-way trip to Jadovno, tied two-by-two with wire before leaving the transit jail at Gospić. Most inmates of other camps were moved on for extermination to the main camp system at Jasenovac. It became the hub of Croatia's final solution of the Serb and Jewish problem on the basis of one-on-one sadistic violence, with the knife and the club the tools of choice (below.).

The commitment to genocide as a good-in-itself distinguishes Hitler's and Pavelić's bloodbaths from other despotic regimes in history. Some Ustaša leaders acknowledged their priorities. In late 1942, shortly before he was removed from his post as the head of *Ravsigur*, Eugen-Dido Kvaternik told his old classmate, HSS activist Branko Pešelj, that he allowed for the possibility that Germany could lose the war and conceded the danger that in that case the Croatian state would cease to exist. However, he added in the course of a chance meeting, "regardless of the outcome of the war there will be no more Serbs in Croatia."

---

existence, hundreds of people were murdered in this camp. An inquiry commission set up by the Italian army when it took control of the area in August 1941 reported that "shocking acts" had been committed there. Djakovo (in Slavonia), established in December 1941 and disbanded in June 1942, was used mainly to imprison women and children. Most of its inmates either died of typhus or were transferred to Jasenovac to be killed on arrival.

[1] Cf. Croatian historian Antun Miletić in *Koncentracioni logor Jasenovac 1941-1945*. Beograd: Narodna knjiga, 1986.

[2] *Izveštaj Državne komisije za utvrđivanje ratnih zločina okupatora i njihovih pomagača* (1948). Arhiv Jugoslavije (AJ), 110-1.

This "reality of any post-war situation," Kvaternik said, would be a *fait accompli* for whoever turned out to be the victor.[1] He regarded anti-Serbdom as "the quintessence of the Ustaša doctrine, its *raison d'être*."[2]

During the summer of 1941 most killings were taking place in the field by Ustaša flying squads, in towns and villages where the victims lived.[3] Italian Zone II in the Adriatic hinterland northeast of Split and east of Zara was particularly badly hit. The commander of the (Italian) Sassari division reported that "population in some places was completely exterminated, after having been tortured and tormented":

> The horrors that the Ustasi have committed against the Serbian small girls is beyond all words. There are hundreds of photographs confirming these deeds ... pulling of tongues and teeth, nails and breast tips (all this being done after they were raped). The few survivors were taken in by our officers and transported to Italian hospitals where these documents and facts were gathered."[4]

A notorious massacre took place on July 30, 1941, in the town of Glina, in the region of Kordun, just north of the Demarcation Line. It was the second massacre in that town in two months, and one of the largest single acts of mass murder to occur in Croatia in the blood-soaked summer of 1941. In the weeks preceding this event some 500 Serbs were murdered in sporadic Ustaša attacks in the district of Glina, prompting many local Serbs to go into hiding in the surrounding forests.[5] The Ustaša district command responded by announcing a general "amnesty" and a guarantee of safety to those Serbs who returned to their homes, registered with the authorities, and agreed to be converted to Roman Catholicism. Several hundred Serbs, mainly elderly and families with small children unable to endure the privations of life in the wilderness, accepted the offer and turned up at the local Serbian Orthodox church as instructed for the conversion ceremony. The exact numbers are disputed, ranging from at least 300 (cited at Nuremberg in 1946) to 1,200.[6]

---

[1] Branko Pešelj to the author, Washington D.C., May 12, 1988.

[2] Quoted by Michele Frucht Levy, "The Last Bullet..." (2009), p. 811.

[3] Some communities were totally eradicated, such as the Serbian village Prkos, where all 434 victims are known by name. One half (216) were below the age of 18. See Damir Mirković. "Victims and Perpetrators in the Yugoslav Genocide 1941-1945: Some Preliminary Observations." *Holocaust and Genocide Studies*. Vol. 7, No. 3, winter 1993, pp 317-332.

[4] *Il Tempo*, Turin, September 10, 1953.

[5] On May 11, 1941, 373 Serb men were rounded up and murdered the following night.

[6] The latter figure is quoted by Tim Judah in *The Serbs: History, Myth and the Destruction of Yugoslavia*. Yale University Press, 2000, p. 127.

The Serbs were herded into the church (below), the doors were locked shut after the last had entered. Only one of the victims, a man named Ljubo Jadnak, survived after playing dead and later described what had happened:

> They started with one huge husky peasant who began singing an old Serb epic song. They put his head on the table and, as he continued to sing, they slit his throat; then the next squad moved in to smash his skull. I was paralyzed. "This is what you are all getting," an Ustaša screamed. They surrounded us. There was absolutely no escape. Then the slaughter began. One group stabbed with knives, then the other followed, smashing heads to make certain everyone was dead. Within minutes there was a lake of blood. Screams and wails, bodies dropping right and left.[1]

The bodies were taken by trucks to a large pit, prepared in advance, from where Jadnak was later able to make his escape. The church was destroyed by the Ustaše shortly after the massacre.[2] One of the killers, Hilmija Berberović (a Muslim from Bosnia), later testified that the killing was carried out by flashlight in seven or eight shifts, with about a hundred victims liquidated in each.[3]

Jasenovac was selected as the location of the largest camp for three main reasons. It is near the Zagreb-Belgrade main railway line, which facilitated the transport of the prisoners. The complex was surrounded by the rivers Sava, Una and Velika Struga, in the middle of the swampy Lonjsko Polje area, which made escape extremely difficult. Last but not least, on the southern, Bosnian bank of the Sava, the inaccessible and uninhabited Gradina location provided an ideal location for mass executions and for the concealment of the bodies.

---

[1] Gerhard Falk, *Murder: An Analysis of Its Forms, Conditions, Causes*, McFarland, 1990, p. 67.

[2] Fred Singleton, *A Short History of the Yugoslav Peoples*, Cambridge University Press, 1985, p. 177. It was never rebuilt, and some of the construction material was used after the Second World War to make a nearby hydroelectric dam.

[3] *Vjesnik*, Zagreb, 29 July 1969.

In July 1941 transports of prisoners started arriving in Jasenovac in railroad cars, in trucks, and some on foot. Some would be taken to the killing grounds on the banks of the Sava immediately. Most passed through the main gate of the "Collection Camp No. III of the Ustaša Defense Labor Service" (l.). They halted in front of the Camp Administration, where guards escorting the transports delivered them to the commander or one of his deputies. Already starved and tortured during transport, the prisoners were subjected to an inspection which was often performed in person by Vjekoslav-Max Luburić, Ljubo Miloš, or Matijević, the chief commandants in the camp. The guards would then proceed to rob them of their belongings, strip them naked and clothe them in dirty and blood-stained rags. Prisoners who were brought to Jasenovac merely to be killed were kept apart, naked and barefoot, for hours and sometimes for days, either in the main warehouse or out in the open. Most would be taken to the Gradina to be executed by knife or club.[1]

The Jasenovac guards designed a special handle-less knife, the 'Serb-cutter' or *kukičar* ('hooker,' below) for speedier slitting of throats. Epidemics ravaged the camp, especially typhus. Few prisoners who contracted the disease survived. The food was inedible and grotesquely insufficient. The quarters were cold, infested by bugs and lice, and dirty. The inmates were

forced to build barracks and dikes to protect the camp from floods. While they were working, the Ustaše beat them with truncheons and rifle butts, forced them to dig faster, and made them run rather than walk at all times, even after several hours' exhausting labor. If an individual collapsed from exhaustion, he would be finished off on the spot.

---

[1] There were exceptions to this rule, however. According to a survivor testimony at the 1999 trial in Zagreb of the former Jasenovac camp commander Dinko Šakic, "After the 'Kozara (mountain in Bosnia) offensive' in 1942, the Ustashi executed a 'mass of women and children' at Gradina, a site near the Jasenovac camp... while men fit for labour were taken to the camp and assigned to labour groups. Because of the large number of women and children, the Ustashi did not kill them as usual, with mallets, knives and cudgels, but by machine-gun fire,' Šaric said." HINA (Croatian news agency) in English, April 15, 1999.

Whenever the camp was full, the Ustaše would carry out mass executions of prisoners to release capacity. To that end they would occasionally stage 'public performances.' Assembled prisoners would be invited to sign up to go to work in Germany, or asked if they needed to be admitted to a hospital, or if they wished to be transferred to some other camp. They would be killed that same evening. Large groups of prisoners were executed at the Granik or near the villages of Gradina and Uštica, on the Bosnian side of the Sava, and their bodies thrown into the river (above). A rare survivor described the killings at the Granik:

> Sometimes it lasted all night. Victims would wait in the Main Warehouse, or some other building, or out in the open. Before leaving the Ustaše would strip them naked, tie their hands behind their backs, and herd them one by one to the Granik. A victim would be forced to his knees. They would hit him with a mallet, a sledgehammer, or with the dull side of an axe on the head. They would often rip their stomachs open and dump them into the Sava.[1]

Some prisoners had to dig long and deep pits first. The Ustaše would strip them naked and kick out the gold fillings with knives. Witness Egon Berger described the results:[2]

> We buried about 200 to 300 victims daily. Pits were three to eight square meters in size. While we were digging graves, Ustaše headed by Lieutenant Mujica were killing victims tied up with wire. They were hitting them on the temple, or killing them by an axe blow across the neck, or by driving wooden stakes into victim's mouths with axes; the stake would surface at the top of the head. Sometimes they asked victims if they had any relatives, and when they established that they did, they would force them to kill each other. ... They would look over every victim, and when they saw that a victim had gold fillings in his teeth, they would pry them out with their knives.

---

[1] *Izveštaj Državne komisije ...* (1948). Arhiv Jugoslavije (AJ), 110-1.
[2] Ibid.

Torture and death by starvation were commonplace. Repeatedly the inmates of Camp III-C were literally starved to death.¹ The "Bell Warehouse" was a torture chamber specifically designed for that purpose. It was a small barrack without windows but with a glass door, so that from outside it was possible to view the spectacle. The Ustaše locked victims inside, keeping them there without food or water for days on end. From the barracks desperate screams resounded: "Take us out! Kill us!"

  During the tenure of Miroslav Filipović, a former Franciscan (shown in the cassock in 1941 and in his Ustaša uniform a year later, l.) as acting commander at Jasenovac, the killings reached orgiastic proportions even by Jasenovac standards.² Filipović had earned his spurs on February 7, 1942, when as an Ustaša chaplain he set out of Petrićevac (a monastery just outside Banja Luka) and led elements of his Ustaša battalion in slaughtering all Serb inhabitants of the township of Drakulić, northwest of the city, and two neighbouring villages. Over 2,300 Serb civilians were brutally murdered, without a single bullet being fired in the process. German military authorities were dismayed by the massacre, to which they were alerted only after the bloodbath was over.³ The Wehrmacht authorities in Banja Luka arrested Filipović on the orders of General Glaise von Horstenau. Filipović was court-

---

¹ "The witness also described camp section III C, closed down in late 1942. The inmates there were left to starve to death. 'There were cases of cannibalism at the time,' Šarić said." Report from the Šakic trial, HINA (Croatian news agency) in English, April 15, 1999.

² On the night of August 29, 1942, Filipovic ordered a mass execution of prisoners. Bets were made as to who could kill the largest number of inmates. One guard, Lt. Petar Brzica – before the war a seminarian at the Franciscan College at Široki Brijeg – cut the throats of 1,360 Serb inmates with a specially designed knife. A gold watch, a roasted pig, and a jug of wine were his rewards. For the list of sources see *Jasenovac and the Holocaust in Yugoslavia.* New York: Jasenovac Research Institute, 2006. Some sources put Brzica's actual score at "only" 670, e.g. Nikola Nikolić, *Taborišče smrti – Jasenovac.* Ljubljana, 1969, p. 293. One of the guards, Lt. Zrinusic, told an inmate "he had competed in slaughtering, but lost to Ustashi Lt. Brzica. For him, the genuine Ustashi was the one who had bloodied his hands." Report from the Šakic trial, HINA (Croatian news agency) in English, April 15, 1999.

³ Reports sent to Eugen-Dido Kvaternik by the Banja Luka office of the state internal security service on 9 and 11 February 1942 noted that the victims at Šargovac included 52 children killed at the village primary school. The second report established the death toll at 2,302.

martialed by the Germans, sentenced to a term in jail, and transferred to the Croatian authorities for imprisonment.[1] Soon thereafter, however, he was pardoned and elevated to a senior position in the Jasenovac camp command.

5. The Roman Catholic Church and the Ustaša regime

Filipović was one of several dozen Croatian priests who had taken an active and direct part in the campaign of terror. Following the proclamation of the NDH a major segment of the Roman Catholic establishment in Croatia became *de facto* accomplices of the regime.[2] Such designation was applicable even to the very top of the hierarchy:

> Alojzije Stepinac, the Catholic archbishop of Zagreb and a vocal nationalist Croat, conferred respectability on the Ustaša regime by his immediate approval of the new government... Without the urging of prelates and priests, many Croats, who otherwise would have turned their backs on the Ustaša atrocities,, allowed themselves to be co-opted by Pavelić's regime.[3]

The Croatian Catholic establishment, thoroughly aligned with the Habsburg order until the debacle of 1918, looked upon the creation of Yugoslavia as an unwelcome and – as many hierarchs had hoped – temporary episode in the long-term struggle for the souls and territories of the "schismatics." This position was not merely a reflection of an excess of zeal by a peripheral "national" Church, however. After the Concordat with Italy (1929) the Vatican was tacitly supportive of Mussolini's Danubian strategy because it alone could produce a reenactment of Austria-Hungary in the form of a confederation of Central European Catholic states.[4] After the *Sporazum* of 1939 the Roman Catholic hierarchy in Croatia – predominantly steeped in the Frankist tradition – threw its weight behind the separatist wing of the HSS. The connections of the clergy with the "home Ustaša" group was evident in a stream of articles in religious publications calling for complete separation from Belgrade and praising Slovakia's proclamation of independence by Mgr. Tiso:

---

[1] István Deák: *Essays on Hitler's Europe*. University of Nebraska Press, 2002, p. 203n.

[2] See Carlo Falconi. *The Silence of Pius XII*. Boston: Little, Brown and Co., 1970. In his estimate, by July 1941 350,000 people had been killed in the NDH (p. 291).

[3] H. James Burgwyn. *Empire on the Adriatic: Mussolini's Conquest of Yugoslavia, 1941-1943*. New York: Enigma Books, 2005, pp. 52-53.

[4] Cf. Mark Aarons and John Loftus. *The Unholy Trinity*. New York: St. Martins, 1991.

In accordance with the teachings of Christ, the Church in Slovakia had already exerted itself to arrange a new life for the Slovakian people... In the National-Socialist Slovakia, the Church will not be persecuted. Persecutions will be used against the opponents of National-Socialism.[1]

The chief Catholic daily, *Hrvatska Straža* (Croatian Guard, l.), consistently praised Hitler's successes in domestic and foreign policy. The *Katolički Tjednik* (Catholic Weekly), the official organ of the Catholic Action published under the direction of the Archbishop of Sarajevo, called for "a new order" along Nazi lines months before Hitler attacked Yugoslavia. In 1940 and early 1941 official Catholic publications had no qualms about praising *Mein Kampf* for its lucid political vision and asserting that there was no moral or canonical conflict between being a good, observing Catholic and a follower of the National Socialist ideology.[2]

The clerical press compared the proclamation of the Independent State of Croatia with the Risen Savior: "This spring the Croatian people experienced their resurrection at the time of Christ's resurrection. The great son of the Croatian people returned and gave them their liberty and ancient rights."[3] "Holy is this year of the resurrection of the independent Croatian state! The gallant image of our Leader appeared in the heavens. It can and must be said of him that his is a man of Providence."[4] His work is also "the work of God and Providence."[5] The Ustaša were also endowed with divine blessings:

> From the first day of its existence the Ustaša movement has been fighting for the victory of Christ's principles, for the victory of justice, freedom, and truth. Our Holy Saviour will help us in the future as he has done until now, that is why the new Ustaša Croatia will be Christ's, ours, and no one else's.[6]

---

[1] "Catholicism and Slovakian National Socialism," in *Katolički List* (official paper of the Archbishopric of Zagreb), January 1940.

[2] Falconi, p. 409, ff. 13.

[3] *Vjesnik počasne straže Srca Isusova* (The Herald of the Honorable Guard of the Heart of Christ), No. 5, 1941.

[4] *Glasnik biskupije bosanske i srijemske*, No. 13, July 15, 1941.

[5] *Glasnik sv. Ante*, December 12, 1941.

[6] "Christ and Croatia," in *Nedelja* (organ of the Crusader Fraternity), June 6, 1941.

On April 28, 1941, Archbishop Stepinac issued a pastoral letter in which he called on the clergy to take part in the "exalted work of defending and improving the Independent State of Croatia," the birth of which "fulfilled the long-dreamed-of and desired ideal of our people."[1] The pastoral letter  was read in every Croatian parish and over the radio. The clergy hardly needed encouragement, however. From the outset Pavelić enjoyed near-unanimous support of the lower clergy. This phenomenon was duly noted by various Axis officials in the field. The German Security Service (SD) expert for the Southeast, Dr. Wilhelm Hoettl, noted that forced conversions from Orthodoxy to Catholicism – while applicable only to the presumably more docile Serbs of the Pannonian plain north of the Sava (above) and not to the Serbs of Lika, Dalmatia, Bosnia and Herzegovina who were slated for death – figured prominently in the clearical agenda from the outset:

> Since being Croat was equivalent to confessing to the Catholic faith, and being Serb followed the profession of Orthodoxy, they now began to convert the Orthodox to Roman Catholicism under duress. Forced conversions were actually a method of Croatization."[2]

The hierarchy was arguably obliged to take part in state ceremonies, but the priesthood and clerical laity was overwhelmingly pro-Ustaša. Prominent clerical journalists immediately after the proclamation of independence on April 10 joined the emerging press and propaganda apparatus of the NDH, notably Franjo Dujmović and Dušan Žanko. Some of them soon advanced to senior government posts (Ivo Bogdan, Ivo Oršanić). Clerical lay groups and chapters joined the Ustaša movement *en masse*, especially the members of the "Crusaders" (*Križari: Veliko križarsko bratstvo, sestrinstvo*). Their chief Feliks Niedzielsky was appointed supreme commander of the Ustaša Youth, which was modeled on the *Hitler Jugend*.

---

[1] *Katolički List,* April 28, 1941

[2] Walter Hagen. *The Secret Front: the Story of Nazi Political Espionage.* London: Weidenfeld and Nicholson, 1953, p. 238. 'Hagen' was Hoettl.

The role of Stepinac (far right, above) remains contentious. "A devout and austere man... distressed by the deportations and mass killing around him, Stepinac was no admirer of the Nazi and Fascist creeds beyond their authoritarian ideas and anti-Communism," but for over two years "he refrained from open criticism of Pavelić's blood-soaked rule and kept silent over the Ustaša murders of the Orthodox."[1] In what is cited by his apologists as a bold move, on May 24, 1942, Stepinac declared from pulpit that "all men and races are children of God," specifically mentioning "Gypsies, Black, European, or Aryan" – but no Serbs.[2] He did not mention the main victims by name – not even once – for the rest of the war.

After more than two years of Ustaša rule, on October 31, 1943, Stepinac stated in a sermon that "there are people who accuse us of not having taken action against the crimes committed in different regions of our country. Our reply is... we cannot sound the alarm, for every man is endowed with his own free will and alone is responsible for his acts. It is for this reason that we cannot be held responsible for some in the ecclesiastical ranks." Theologically correct in abstract principle, under the circumstances this view amounted to an abdication of moral responsibility. No less contentiously, Stepinac stated at

---

[1] Burgwyn, op. cit. p. 53.

[2] "The Catholic Church had always condemned, and continues to condemn, all injustice and all violence committed in the name of theories of class, race, or nationality. It is not permissible to persecute Gypsies or Jews because they are thought to be an inferior race."

the Council of Croatian Bishops that a "psychological basis should be created among the Orthodox followers" for the mass conversions to Catholicism: "They should be guaranteed, upon conversion, not only life and civil rights, but in particular the right of personal freedom and also the right to hold property." He did not say, or appear to think, that those rights were due to the unconverted Serbs.[1] Stepinac lacked the qualities required of a spiritual and moral leader at a time when countless atrocities were committed in the name of his church. He was not a direct accomplice, but he did not vigorously oppose them either. He may have sinned more by omission than by commission, but he sinned nevertheless. Stepinac's primary fault was in his failure to take an open stand against the bloodbath and terror. By not doing so he has betrayed not only his universal duty to the victims, but also his pastoral duty to his own people. His silence had facilitated the descent into mortal sin of many of his flock. Stepinac's failing was also in his timid and reluctant attitude to those members of the Croatian clergy who openly identified with the Ustaša regime, or even became supporters of and active participants in the genocide. When the anti-Serb and anti-Jewish racial laws of April and May 1941 were enacted the Catholic press welcomed them as vital for "the survival and development of the Croatian nation":

> Defense from Judaism, from that destructive worm, was started by the Fuehrer.... Our Poglavnik has also announced a regulation on the protection of our honor and blood, and we would add, on the protection of the survival and development of the Croatian nation. With it the Poglavnik wants to prevent the dangerous worm from eating away at the tree of our Croatian national life.[2]

On the subject of those laws, the Archbishop of Sarajevo Ivan Šarić declared that "there exist limits to love." While Archbishop Stepinac was careful not to align himself openly with Ustaša policies, Šarić was less circumspect. Stepinac was prepared to try and spare the lives of converts to Catholicism, Jewish ones at any rate; but Šarić ridiculed those who did not have the stomach for genocide, declaring it "stupid and unworthy of Christ's disciples to think that the struggle against evil could be waged in a noble way and with gloves on." He personally expropriated property belonging to many Jews in Bosnia.[3] The Bishops of Banja Luka and Djakovo made public

---

[1] Over a year before Yugoslavia's collapse, on January 17, 1940, Stepinac wrote in his diary: "The most ideal thing would be if the Orthodox Serbs were... to bend their heads before Christ's Vicar, our Holy Father [the Pope]."

[2] *Hrvatska Straža*, May 11, 1941

[3] Falconi, op. cit. pp. 272-273.

statements in the same vein. The Croatian Academic Catholic Society, in a 1941 brochure entitled *Why Do They Persecute Jews in Germany?*, argued that Hitler was to be praised for eliminating the Jews. The leading NDH racial "theorist" was a Roman Catholic clergyman, Dr. Ivo Guberina, whose writings sought to reconcile religious "purification" with "racial hygiene" and give a "scientific" veneer to Ustaša propaganda. He readily acceded that Croatia had to be "cleansed of foreign elements" by means of physical elimination. His teachings were endorsed by the chairman of Ustaša Central Propaganda Office, also a Roman Catholic priest, Fr. Grga Peinović.

Those were the early days of the Ustaša regime, however, before the slaughter started in earnest. The attitude of the Catholic Church in Croatia in the ensuing months and years inevitably depended on whether Pius XII knew of the slaughters, whether he would express his open disapproval and intervene to have them stopped. This did not happen: "When the Ustaša launched their massacres, the Holy See took no overt measures to bring them to a halt."[1] Until the end of the war the Vatican never denounced them:

> Pius and his advisors were willing to ignore Croatian concentration camps and murders because Pavelić's state was a fledgling concern that needed time to develop into a bulwark of Catholicism in the Balkans. His eyes remained fixed on the establishment of a Catholic state in the Balkans, blind to the heinous massacres perpetrated by the Ustaše. Because Pavelić so eagerly sought Vatican diplomatic recognition and led a movement of zealous Catholics, Pius had the leverage to force Pavelić and the Ustaše to stop murdering Serbs and Jews.[2] The Vatican never attempted to use this leverage to prevent this genocide. Pius XII never condemned the destruction of the Serbian and Jewish population in Croatia, even though he held great sway over Pavelić and his followers.[3]

Encouraged by the hierarchs' passivity that appeared tantamount to tacit approval, some priests abandoned all pretense of restraint. Fr. Dragutin Kamber, SJ, as the Ustaša trustee in the city of Doboj, in central Bosnia, personally ordered the execution of hundreds of Serbs. Fr. Perić of the Gorica monastery instigated and participated in the massacre of 5,600 Serbs in Livno and the surrounding villages. He encouraged the local Ustaša bands to start

---

[1] Bergwyn, op. cit. p. 54.

[2] Pavelić requested recognition immediately after arriving in Zagreb: "I fervently ask Your Holiness with Your highest apostolic authority to recognize our state, and deign as soon as possible to send Your representative, who will help me with Your fatherly advice..."

[3] Robert McCormick, entry on Pius XII in *History in Dispute*, Volume 11: *The Holocaust, 1933-1945*. St. James Press, 2003, p. 193.

the slaughter with his own sister who was married to a Serb. All over Croatia and Bosnia-Herzegovina the Franciscan monks (with Pavelić, above), parish priests and lay activists joined Ustaša ranks *en masse*. Some members of Catholic clergy in Croatia allowed themselves to be metamorphosed "into thorough-going butcher-leaders."[1] The military exploits of some, such as Fr. Ilija Tomas of Klepac, were hailed in the press.[2] Another widely praised role-model was Dr. Radoslav Glavaš, "a young and energetic Franciscan" who organized an active Ustaša cell at the monastery at Široki Brijeg.[3]

By making their terror public in wide areas, especially south of the Sava, the Ustašas also sought to instill such fear among the remaining Serb population that their flight to Serbia or conversion to Catholicism would be facilitated. The Croatian Catholic press wrote gloatingly about what was in store for the "schismatics" and enemies of the New Order:

> When in the past God spoke through papal encyclicals, they closed their ears. Now God has decided to use other means. He will set up missions: European missions, world missions. They will be upheld not by priests, but by army commanders, led by Hitler. The sermons will be echoed by cannon, tanks and bombers. The language of these sermons will be international.[4]

The Croatian Holocaust depended on a host of middlemen comprising the social and intellectual establishment. They helped create the *Stimmung* which mediated and legitimized the Ustaša variety of the Final Solution.

---

[1] Falconi, p. 298.

[2] *Hrvatski Narod*, 25 July 1941.

[3] *Hrvatski Narod,* July 4, 1941. Another *young and energetic* priest was Vjekoslav Filipović-Majstorović After losing his clerical rank, he served as a commander of the Jasenovac camp.

[4] *Katolički tjednik*, Zagreb, 31 August 1941.

The contribution of Croatia's Roman Catholic clergy to the process was substantial, probably essential. The devastating moral consequences of that contribution are illustrated by Vladko Maček's personal encounter with a mass murderer. The HSS leader, interned at the Jasenovac camp headquarters building in 1941-42, recalled hearing from the other side of the barbed wire "the screams and wails of despair and extreme suffering, the tortured outcries of the victims, broken by intermittent shooting." They "accompanied all my waking hours and followed me into sleep at night." He noticed that one of the guards assigned to watch him crossed himself each night before going to sleep. Maček was puzzled by the gap between his apparent piety and the monstrosity of his actions, and asked the guard whether he was not afraid of the punishment of God. "Don't talk to me about that," the guard replied, "for I am perfectly aware what is in store for me. For my past present and future deeds I shall burn in hell, but at least I shall burn for Croatia."[1]

The exceptions were few. Three names are recorded for posterity: Bishop Alojzije Mišić of Mostar (l.), Mgr. Svetozar Rittig, who joined the partisans, and Canon Dr. Josip Lončar of the Kaptol Church in Zagreb, who was sentenced to death in August 1941 for anti-state activity (commuted to 20 years' imprisonment and later annulled on the intervention of the papal legate Marconi).[2] "It is not the Jews to whom the Roman Catholic Church owes the biggest apology over World War II, but Serbs," concludes a Jewish-American commentator. "If by not speaking out about Europe's Jews Pius hoped to avoid endangering millions of Catholics, what could have been the reason for not speaking out about Croatia, which itself horrified the Nazis to the point that German and Italian soldiers started shielding Serbs from Ustashas? And what would have been the risk to the faithful inside Croatia?"[3]

---

[1] Vlatko Macek, *In the Struggle for Freedom,* University Park, PA: Pennsylvania University Press, 1957, p. 234.

[2] *Vrhbosna*, 1941, No. 7-8, p. 168.

[3] Julia Gorin in *The Jerusalem Post*, February 22, 2010.

6. The Ustaša and the Holocaust

The Holocaust, understood as the unprecedented program of mass murder in German-controlled Europe of entire populations defined by 'race,' ethnicity and religion, was the product of Nazism but it was launched in Croatia and Bosnia in the late spring and early summer of 1941. Pavelić's Ustaša regime was the first to apply the concept of genocidal terror and extermination; the *Einsatzgruppen* came later. The fundamental similarity between the Ustašas and the Nazis was their destructive nihilism. Just as the military goals of Barbarossa were incidental to the objective of exterminating Jews, enslaving Slavs and creating the *Lebnsraum*, so the formal enlistment of Croatia into the ranks of Axis-sponsored New Europe was incidental to the Ustašas' central purpose of eliminating all Serbs from the Greater Croatia.

Nazi totalitarianism was based on a fluid definition of the state, whose borders could expand eastward, at least, practically without limits, while the NDH ended on the Drina. There were also major differences in methods and conceptual approaches to killing. The Nazi Holocaust adopted the style and methods of a developed industrial state. A complex administrative network was developed, which connected different agencies and levels of responsibility. 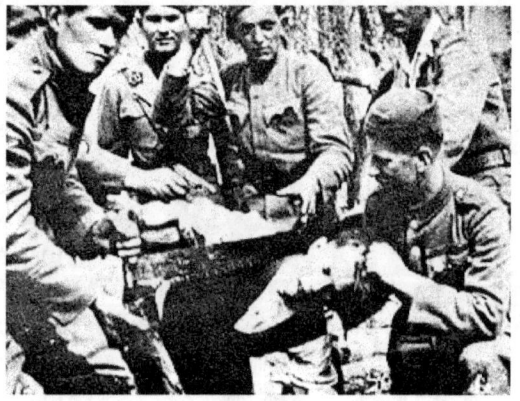 Complex killing equipment was designed, tested, and either discarded (gassing vans) or applied (gas chambers, crematoria).

Ustaša terror was mostly traditional in its tools of execution, with the "Serb-cutter" handle-less knife a rare technological innovation. Nazi system included plans, reports, lists of victims, statistics. Ustaša orders were mostly oral and the apparatus of terror functioned in an arbitrary manner, with a random selection of targets and methods of killing. Nazi terror was for the most part depersonalized, bureaucratic. It was cold and abstract, and "excesses" and "sadism" were frowned upon. The Ustašas were *direct and personal,* and extreme sadism was the norm (e.g. decapitation with a saw, above). Some aspects of Nazi terror – with its somber discipline and bureaucratic pedantry – were "puritanical," whereas the Ustašas engaged in orgies of slaughter and had no qualms about recording the results (opp.p.).

The German "final solution" started far away in the East, in the summer of 1941, by a small number of *Einsatzgruppen*. The Ustaša terror started earlier and was open, explicit. It was happening by broad daylight, in the middle of towns and villages.[1] It was calculated to involve as many Croat and Muslim civilians as possible, through the distribution of Serb land and property. Fr. Mate Moguš, the Roman Catholic parish priest in Udbina, thus told his congregation "These brave Ustašas have 16,000 bullets to kill 16,000 Serbs, after which we shall divide their fields among us in a brotherly manner."[2] Protests were rare.[3]

While many Germans could plausibly claim ignorance of what was being done to the deported Jews in Poland, few Croats or Muslims could have harbored such doubt as entire Serb communities were brutally slaughtered. Moreover, the Croats had lived in a non-totalitarian society until April 1941. The Jewish Question in Germany – however alleged, debated and defined before 1941 – was a far smaller concern for ordinary Germans than the 'Serbian Question' for ordinary Croats. By making their terror public in wide

areas, and especially in the Dinaric regions of the Krajina and Bosnia-Herzegovina, the Ustašas sought to make inter-communal breach irreversible. Their goal was to eliminate *all Serbs*; their inability to do it on a truly industrial scale was a key factor hindering its achievement. The Ustašas also expected to create the feeling of irreversibility in Serb-Croat relations, which would make a revived Yugoslavia unthinkable.

Far from contributing to the Axis war effort, the terror unleashed by the Ustaša regime helped the enemies of both the NDH and the Third Reich. Extermination of *the Serb* was to be pursued even if this endangered vital state interests and played into the hands of real enemies, by causing mass

---

[1] For instance in Glina. Judah, op. cit. p. 127.

[2] Moguš was quoted by the Zagreb *Novi List* on July 24, 1941, as saying, "Until now we have worked for the Catholic faith with the prayer book and with the cross. Now the time has come to work with rifle and revolver."

[3] An exception was a petition sent by prominent Muslims of Banja Luka to two Muslims in Pavelić's government (Džafer Kulenović and Hamdija Bešlagić) on November 12, 1941, protesting the treatment of their 'Serb neighbors.' A-VII, no number, 12 November 1941.

uprisings and by creating conditions for the rise of insurgency, under whatever banner. This disregard for their own rationally understood interests indicated that the Ustaša and Nazi leaders considered genocide a fundamental duty that transcended the importance of victory itself.[1] Such fundamentalist commitment to genocide distinguishes Nazism and Ustašism from other despotic regimes in history. Ustaša racism differed considerably from Nazi racism, however, in that the former was based primarily on the principle that state and nationality should correspond, while "German racism was based on an imperialist expansionism, which sought *Lebensraum* for the German *Herrenvolk*, as well as the enslavement of the Russian *Untermenschen*, in the expanses of the East."[2]

Most Ustaša leaders acted on this assumption that Germany would win the war, but at least one freely acknowledged that the order of priorities functioned independently of the strategic outcome. In late 1942, shortly before he was removed from his post as the head of *Ravsigur*, Eugen-Dido Kvaternik (r.) told his high school classmate Branko Pešelj that he allowed for the possibility that Germany could lose the war and the NDH could cease to exist because it was fatally linked to the fortunes of the Reich. However, he added, "regardless of the outcome of the war there will be no more Serbs in Croatia." This "reality of any post-war situation" would have to be taken into account by whoever turned out to be the victor.[3]

There had been several episodes of ethnic cleansing in the Balkans before 1941, notably in the aftermath of the anti-Ottoman uprisings in the 1800s and following the Greco-Turkish war of 1919-22. The Ustaša terror was without precedent, however, in that it blended local nation-building with

---

[1] The SS insisted on killing, in the 'second wave' (1942-43), even those Jews whose skills were indispensible to the functioning of manufacturing plants and workshops in the General Gouvernement, Ukraine and Ostland which were working for the Wehrmacht.

[2] Bartulin, op. cit. p. 10.

[3] Branko Pešelj to the author, Washington D.C., 1988.

the pan-continental campaign of racial cleansing unleashed by Hitler. The result was a series of genocidal massacres of Serbs, Jews and Roma. It was the first attempt at a *final solution* in the Second World War.

One of the first reports on "the increasing anti-Serb terror by the Ustašas" reached Berlin on July 2, 1941. It was a report by Veesenmayer, who was still the special representative of the German Foreign Ministry in Zagreb. He stated that "authoritative representatives of the regime" looked on the Serbs in Croatia as a problem "which is under the exclusive competence of Ustaša police and court-martials."[1] Glaise von Horstenau was the first high-ranking German official in Croatia who realized that Pavelić wanted to kill or otherwise physically eliminate *all Serbs*.

From his earliest days in Zagreb Glaise started establishing an efficient and reliable intelligence network. It provided him with detailed information on all aspects of life in the NDH, including Ustaša atrocities. Glaise's chief information gatherer was Captain Haeffner, his assistant, who had lived in Zagreb for many years, spoke the language, and had good contacts throughout Croatia. Haeffner's reports contained graphic eyewitness accounts and evidence collected by the Germans (l.). According to his pedantic computations, the number of Serbs "who have fallen as victims of animal instincts fanned by Ustaša leaders" exceeded 200,000 by the beginning of August 1941.[2] As the terror grew, so did Haeffner's disdain for its perpetrators. He wrote of "the strong inferiority complex of Ustaša leaders and their flock vis-à-vis the Serbs, who are more numerous and superior in terms of life energy."

Haeffner's numbers would be regarded as too low by most Serbs and too high by most Croats. The issue of actual numbers of Serb victims in the NDH is still a matter of political and scholarly controversy. Methodologically sound and politically least motivated sources indicate that neither "a million dead

---

[1] PA, Büro Staatssekretär, Kroatien, Bd. 1, No. 290. Veesenmayer to Berlin, 2 July 1941.
[2] Kazimirović, op. cit. pp. 112-117.

Serbs" nor "a hundred thousand, all said" are true. Approximately one in five Serbs in the NDH were killed by the end of the war.

Glaise collected reports of atrocities in a separate file and missed no opportunity to raise the issue with Pavelić, Kvaternik and other NDH officials. Typically he would hit a brick wall, or get promises that were never to be carried out. As an essentially decent officer of the old school Glaise was horrified with what was going on. He was additionally alarmed when he realized that many people blamed the Germans for Ustaša crimes. In his report dated July 18 Haeffner warned Glaise that German troops are seen as "being here to support the Ustaša regime":

> The Ustašas promote the impression that they are acting not only *in agreement* with German instances, but actually *on their orders*. [...] There is a deep mistrust of Germany, because it is supporting a regime that has no moral or political right to exist, which is regarded as the greatest calamity that could have happened to the Croat people. That regime is based entirely on the recognition by the Axis powers; it has no popular roots, and depends on the bayonets of robbers who do more evil in one day than the Serbian regime had done in twenty years.[1]

In early July Glaise decided to take advantage of the temporary absence from Zagreb of the pro-Ustaša German minister, Kasche, and raise alarm in Berlin. Glaise found an ally in Heribert Troll-Obergfell, a former Austrian diplomat and counselor at the German legation in Zagreb. They agreed to raise the issue of Ustaša atrocities in Berlin on two fronts. On July 10 Troll-Obergfell sent a report to the Foreign Ministry about anti-Serb terror. He accurately predicted that Ustaša crimes would create "an explosive situation wherever Serbs lived," a situation that could soon erupt into hotbeds of unrest which would be hard to quell.[2] On the same day Glaise sent his report to the OKW. Its tone was similar to Troll-Obergfell's, and it sounded an alarm about the effect of Ustaša atrocities on German units in Croatia and the future possible challenges those units would have to face:

> Our troops have to be mute witnesses of such events; it does not reflect well on their otherwise high reputation... I am frequently told by [our] army, as well as by some Croat circles, that German troops would have to intervene against Ustaša crimes. This may happen eventually. Right now, with the available forces, I could not ask for such action. Even if we overlook the fact that Croatia is an independent state, also that it is in the Italian sphere, [our] occupation

---

[1] Häffner's report dated 18 July 1941, ibid. p. 113.
[2] PA, Büro Staatssekretär, Kroatien, Bd.1, No.307. Troll-Obergfell to Berlin, 10 July 1941

forces - only six infantry battalions - are too weak to assume adequate police control. Ad hoc intervention in individual cases could make the German Army look responsible for countless crimes which it could not prevent in the past.[1]

These two reports, together with Veesenmayer's report of July 2, were the first official information to reach Berlin about the seriousness of Ustaša crimes. In this first phase those reports tended to express concern about the effect such crimes would have on "the reputation of the German army and the Reich." Security concerns would come later, with the uprising.

Glaise raised the issue of atrocities with Slavko Kvaternik (shown inspecting the volunteers, l.) during the month of July. As a colleague of Glaise's from the Habsburg army, Kvaternik was apparently amenable to open and frank discussion. On one occasion Glaise told Kvaternik that "the Croat revolution was by far the bloodiest and most awful among all I have seen first hand or from afar in Europe since 1917" and warned that not only Serbs, but also Croats did not feel secure any longer.[2]

Kvaternik tried to justify the measures by saying that "they have saved Croatia from a Serb revolution," but Glaise countered by warning him of exactly the opposite effect of such policy. On one occasion Glaise convinced Kvaternik – or so he had hoped - that they should go to Pavelić together and press on him the need to stop the slaughter of Serbs. Kvaternik had promised to support his call for moderation. Once they were with Pavelić, however, Kvaternik changed his tune completely and "talked in such radical tones" that Glaise grew irritated and commented "Dear Slavko, I am happy that you are at least letting me stay alive!" Pavelić listened politely to Glaise's arguments; nothing had changed: the terror grew worse by the day. His appeals for moderation were ignored.[3]

---

[1] BA/MAF, No. 178/41 (*Deutscher General*). Glaise to OKW/Ausland, 10 July 1941.

[2] BA/MAF, No. 207/41. Glaise's report to the OKW, 19 July 1941

[3] BA/MAF, No. 192/41. Glaise's telex to the OKW, 12 July 1941.

With Kasche still absent, Troll-Obergfell spoke to the newly appointed NDH foreign minister Mladen Lorković on July 11 and warned him of the many reports of Ustaša excesses. His words were supported by graphic photographs of massacred victims, taken by German soldiers in the aftermath of Ustaša cleansing actions.[1] Troll asked Lorković to warn Pavelić personally of the problem. He also requested resolute measures to stop any "tendentious rumors" that anti-Serb actions were instigated by the German government.

Requests for intervention to stop Ustaša massacres started pouring in from different German quarters in the second half of 1941: from the Military Commander South-East, General-Field Marshal Wilhelm List (r.), as well as from the leaders of the *Volksdeutsche* in the NDH, notably in the Srem region.[2] Until August 1941 such requests were formally justified by the desire to preserve "the reputation of the German army" and avoid any suggestion that the atrocities were German-inspired. With the outbreak of the Serb uprising came the important acknowledgement that Ustaša crimes were their cause.

By early 1942 the nature of the project was no longer in doubt. The commander of the 7th SS division Prinz Eugen, *Obergruppenführer* Arthur Phleps, declared that "from the start the main Ustaša objective was to annihilate the Orthodox [Serbs], to butcher hundreds of thousands of persons, women and children."[3] Dr. Hermann Neubacher, Hitler's foremost political expert for the Balkans and perennial trouble-shooter in the region, agreed. "The prescription for the Orthodox Serbs issued by the leader and Führer of Croatia, Ante Pavelić, was reminiscent of the religious wars of the bloodiest memory," Neubacher wrote. "One third must be converted to Catholicism, another third must be expelled, and the final third must die. The last part of the program has been carried out".[4]

---

[1] PA, Büro Staatssekretär, Kroatien, Bd. 1, No. 726. Troll-Obergfell to the Foreign Ministry, 11 July 1941.

[2] Gert Fricke, op. cit. pp. 39-40.

[3] OKW *Tagesbuch*. Nr. Ia/545, 44 J.G.

[4] Hermann Neubacher. *Sonderaufrag Südost 1940-1945. Bericht eines fliegenden Diplomaten.* Goettingen: Muster-Schmidt-Verlag, 1957, p. 18.

General Paul Bader (l.), commanding German forces in in Serbia, saw this annihilation as the goal not limited to the Ustaša regime: "There is no doubt at all that the Croats are endeavoring to destroy the entire Serb population."[1] Even the hardened Nazis were shocked: "The Ustašas committed their bestial crimes not only against males of military age," said a Gestapo report prepared for Himmler, "but especially against helpless old people, women and children."[2] Some were concerned that the Ustaša were so focused on exterminating Serbs that they were neglecting the killing of the Jews, which should be a priority.[3]

German demands went unheeded by the Ustašas: in the matter of their way of "solving the Serb question" Pavelić and his followers displayed remarkable determination to preserve their autonomy of action. In any event Pavelić realized that he could afford to ignore such appeals for as long as there was no pressure from the top, from Berlin, to do otherwise. Estimates of the number of Serbs killed, made by German and Italian officials during the war, were staggering. Frequent overestimates reflected their impression of an insane mayhem. In a report to Himmler, SS General Ernst Frick estimated that "600 to 700,000 victims were butchered in the Balkan fashion."[4] General Lothar Rendulic, commanding German forces in the western Balkans in 1943-1944, estimated the number of Ustaša victims to be 500,000:

> When I noted to a high official close to Pavelic that, in spite of the accumulated hatred, I failed to comprehend the murder of half a million Orthodox, the answer I received was characteristic of the mentality that prevailed there: "Half a million, that's too much – there weren't more than 200,000!"[5]

---

[1] Karl Hlinicka. *Das Ende auf dem Balkan 1944/45: Die Militärische Räumung Jugoslawiens durch die Deutsche Wehrmacht.* Goettingen: Musterscheudt, 1970, p. 187.

[2] PA, Büro RAM, Kroatien, 1941-42, 442-449. IV/D/4.

[3] Cf. Menachem Shelach (ed.), Yossef Lewinger & Alexander Matkovski, *History of the Holocaust: Yugoslavia.*

[4] Hlinicka, op. cit. p. 292.

[5] Lothar Rendulic. *Gekaempft, gesiegt, geschlagen.* Welsermühl Verlag, Wels und Heidelberg, 1952, p.161.

We will never know the true figures, "in part because so many perpetrators worked to destroy the evidence, in part because so many of the events took place spontaneously and without the rigorous record keeping that marked the Nazi administered Holocaust."[1] Non-native scholars place the number of Serb victims at between one-third and one-half of a million[2]. Four hundred thousand Serb victims is at the lower end of a reliable estimate.[3]

In 1941 the Greater German Reich was a superpower with 80 million Germans, 12 million of them in uniform and eight million in the Nazi Party. It killed an estimated 18 million European civilians between June 1941 and May 1945, just over one-half of them Slavs and about one-third Jews.[4] In 1941, by contrast, the Independent State of Croatia was an underdeveloped and unconsolidated state with just over three million Catholic Croats and some 30,000 men in Ustaša uniform (like this platoon of the Black Legion, opp. p.), growing to 100,000 – albeit no longer an all-volunteer force – by 1944. Between April 1941 and May 1945 it killed half a million civilians, four-fifths of them Serbs. Between 75 and 80 percent of all Croatian and Bosnian Jews were dead by the end of the war and over 90 percent of Gypsies. Its many weaknesses notwithstanding, the Ustaša state made a disproportionate contribution to the Holocaust. Among the satellites it provided an unsurpassed example of state criminality, on a par only with the criminality of the Third Reich itself. In the end the victims of the Ustaša, no less than the victims of

---

[1] Michele Frucht Levy. *"For We Are Neither One Thing Nor The Other*: Passing for Croat in Vedrana Rudan's *Night. Cultural Logic*, 2009 <http://clogic.eserver.org/2009/Levy.pdf>

[2] Michele Frucht Levy: *"The Last Bullet for the Last Serb:* The Ustaša Genocide against Serbs, 1941–1945." *Nationalities Papers*, Vol. 37, No. 6, November 2009. She notes that "the concentration camp Jasenovac, notorious for the particularly grisly nature of its one-on-one tortures and murders, has come to symbolize the frustration of Jewish and especially Serb victims. Designated as an official memorial for all Yugoslav war victims, it thus buried the enormity of Serb suffering there and throughout the chain of concentration and holding camps in the NDH."

[3] According to Yad Vashem's Shoah Resource Center, "More than 500,000 Serbs were murdered in horribly sadistic ways (mostly in the summer of 1941), 250,000 were expelled, and another 200,000 were forced to convert to Catholicism." Sabrina P. Ramet has the figure of 487,000 murdered Serbs, as well as 27,000 Gypsies and 30,000 Jews (*Eastern Europe – Politics, Culture, and Society since 1939*. Indianapolis: Indiana University Press, 1998, p. 161). The United States Holocaust Memorial Museum's recent estimate of "up to 400,000 Serb civilian victims of Ustaša genocide, roughly one-half of them women, children, and old people" broadly corresponds to the "scholarly consensus" of statistical researchers whose work provides empirically valid guidance in the absence of useful extermination records.

[4] R.J. Rummel. *Democide: Nazi Genocide and Mass Murder*. Rutgers, New Jersey: Transaction Publishers, 1992.

the Nazis, were all of humanity, for it was the value of humanity that both were out to annihilate.

There is an important final difference between Germany and Croatia, however. Germany has been confronting the darkest episode in its history for over six decades now. Only an insignificant fringe still holds that the episode did not happen, or that it was not all that dark, or both. Croatia, by contrast, has yet to confront squarely the darkest episode in its own history. The Ustaša *Weltanschauung*, even when formally disowned, remains internalized by a significant segment of Croatia's society in general and by its political, academic, media and ecclesiastical establishments in particular.

The Ustaša criminality is measured not only by the numbers of dead Serbs, Jews and Gypsies, but also by the impact of their crimes on the society at large. That impact remains enormous, seven decades after the deed.

VIII
The Uprising

1. Causes and Characteristics

The Ustaša terror caused a series of Serb uprisings during the summer of 1941 in different parts of the NDH. The initial form of rudimentary self-defense in many Serb villages was to create village guards and observation posts on the surrounding roads. Their task was to warn the inhabitants if an Ustaša column was approaching. When alerted people escaped into the surrounding countryside. Improvised sanctuaries (*zbegovi*) were organized in remote spots, such as caves and hidden crevices, to accommodate women, children and the infirm. Village committees organizing such evacuations were usually led by men with some prior military experience, typically reserve officers or gendarmes. The next task was to provide these emerging groups with weapons. They were for the most part hunting rifles and farm tools; a military rifle was a highly prized rarity in the early days.

In eastern Herzegovina there was a spontaneous Serb uprising as early as June 1941, in response to a wave of savage slaughters the Ustašas carried out throughout the area.

The first organized resistance is commonly associated with an attack on the Ustaša garrison in the city of Drvar, in northwestern Bosnia, on July 26, 1941. Three months had passed since the first mass muder of Serb civilians in Bjelovar. Resistance soon spread to the neighboring areas of Lika to the west and northern Dalmatia to the southwest. Thinly spread platoon and company-sized local Ustaša outposts quickly lost control of the situation. They were unable to cope with lightly armed but desperate Serb peasants (above) fighting for survival.[1]

---

[1] Unable to stem the tide, retreating Ustaša units went looking for the mountain sanctuaries in which Serb non-combatants were hiding. After a clash at Divoselo in Lika on August 5, 1941,

The occurrence and intensity of insurgent activity was directly correlated to the intensity of anti-Serb terror in a given area. The regions of Bosanska Krajina, Lika, Kordun, Banija and northern Dalmatia, which were also the scene of mass slaughters, were up in arms by late July and early August. (The Serb inhabitants of these regions were specifically excluded by the Ustaša authorities from potential conversion to Roman Catholicism.) At the same time, several areas with a Serb majority or plurality (Srem, Posavina, Semberija, eastern Bosnia, parts of Slavonia) remained quiet for as long as they were little affected by terror. In Srem, for instance, the security situation rapidly deteriorated only after an unprovoked and particularly bloody Ustaša "cleansing action" in 1942.

The *Einsatzgruppen* massacres leading to the extermination of Soviet Jews were routinely justified by the claim that their actions were a necessary part of anti-partisan operations.[1] The Ustašas made the same claim, but the Germans knew better. As Troll-Obergfell reported to Berlin on August 10, the uprising was caused entirely by the Ustaša terror:

> Croatians will say they are repelling rebels, but contrary to Croatian assertions that the fault for unrest lies exclusively with the Serbs, the German military commands and sober Croatian circles are of the opinion that the uprising was essentially attributable to the wild and bloody Ustaša conduct.[2]

This view was endorsed by the Nazi Party *Auslandsorganisation* chief in the NDH, Rudolf Epting. In a report to Hitler he named the Ustašas as the culprits.[3] Walter Schellenberg of the Reich Security Service (RSHA) foreign department, concurred.[4] Even local NDH military officers and civilian officials acknowledged that much, complaining that the "cleansing" affected primarily those least able to resist, while the young and strong escaped to the woods. "The cleansing work of the Ustašas was almost public," reported the First Gendarmerie Regiment command on August 16, "which was one of the main reasons for the exodus of the people into the woods":

---

the Ustaša withdrew into the nearby Velebit Mountain. They stumbled upon, and killed, all 565 women and children hiding there.

[1] See Andreas Hillgruber, "War in the East and the Extermination of the Jews," in *The Nazi Holocaust*. Mecler: Westpoint, CT, 1989, p. 103.

[2] PA, Büro Staatssekretär, Kroatien, Bd. 2, No. 24. Troll-Obergfell to the Foreign Ministry, Zagreb, 10 August 1941.

[3] Hory and Broszat, op. cit. pp. 129-131.

[4] Ibid. p. 132.

The cleansing was carried out in houses and yards, on the road, in the presence of parents and children. There was competition over who will be the first to go into a more prosperous household... there was drunkenness and barbarous scenes of cleansing babies in cribs, old people, entire families, and sadistic joy in bestial torture before the final cleansing. Such acts coused honest and reliable Croats to whisper, ' This is a shame for the Croat people, their culture, and the Catholic faith... The gendarmes were completely powerless to stop all this.[1]

The Ustašas' attempt to exterminate the Serbian peasant and small town "establishment" – with teachers, priests, merchants and educated people always the first target – created a political vacuum. This opened the way for the Communists to gain an early foothold, and eventually to reestablish themselves in a new area after the defeats of the winter 1941-42 forced them out of Serbia and Montenegro. In the upheaval that followed the first wave of pogroms there was no ideological background to Serb resistance, which was in the early phase purely a struggle to preserve bare life. This was to change soon, however. The attack on the Soviet Union suddenly enabled the Communist Party of Yugoslavia to present itself as a legitimate national force, able and willing to appeal to the latent Russophile sentiment of the Serbs on both sides of the Drina. Its invoking the image of "Mother Russia" was a cynical ploy, of course, but it worked wonders for the small band of Party cadres hard pressed to deliver a convincing pitch to their would-be recruits.

The CPY had followed an uneven path both before and after the collapse of Yugoslavia. In the spring of 1941 the position of some leading Croatian Communists, such as Andrija Hebrang (above), was ambiguous. They were ready to accept the new order, and even contemplated seeking legalization as the "Communist Party of the Independent State of Croatia." The separatist wing of the Croatian CP finally lost ground only in the wake of *Barbarossa*, when the Comintern's injunction declared in favor of reestablishing independence and territorial integrity of the Yugoslav state.

In the months of June, July and August 1941 the Serbs in the NDH desperately looked east for deliverance. Atavistic trust in "Mother Russia" transcended all ideological reservations and offered a ray of hope in the veritable nightmare of Pavelić's *Endloesung*. This almost religious veneration

---

[1] V.I.I. Zbornik, V-1, 341, 343.

of the great Slav ally was common both to those Serbs who were traditionalists, free from ideological prejudice, and to the minority of activists who loved Russia first and foremost as "the first country of Socialism." Initially the two groups were able to form a common front, united as they were by the pressing business of fighting the Ustašas. Such distinctions did not matter at first to the uprooted mass of Serb peasantry, blinded with grief, that took to the hills in many parts of the Ustaša state in the early summer of 1941 (below). The red-blue-white Serbian tricolor and the Communist red banner often flew side by side, and the five-pointed red star could be seen alongside the traditional cockade on caps and hats, in June and July.

In the initial stage the uprising was a purely Serb affair. Croats and Muslims were extremely rare among the insurgents; almost all of them belonged to the small but disciplined core of Party cadres sent by the CPY into the field after the Soviet Union was attacked. Those activists were in an awkward position, however. For years they had been indoctrinated in the spirit of extreme antagonism to "greater Serbian hegemony," and took the Party rhetoric for reality. Croatian-inspired "anti-greater-Serbianism," embraced by CPY propagandists, had developed into anti-Serbianism *per se*. The outlook was imposed not only on the non-Serbs in Party ranks but also on the Serb "proletarians" whose class-conscious credentials needed to be proven by their adherence to the Croatian variety "anti-greater-Serbianism" that had been adopted by the CPY.

In the 1930's communist recruiters paid particular attention to the lean and hungry students of Belgrade University from the provinces, long on ambition and short on everything else. Those from the periphery of the Serb nation proved especially prone to the Comintern slogans against "greater-Serbianism" that were adopted in the name – and on behalf of – the socialist ideology of "mother-Russia." Marxist utopianism was skillfully wedded to Slavic romanticism, but detached from any recognizably "Serbian" tradition. Montenegrin and Macedonian "revolutionaries" had to prove the sincerity of their commitment by distancing themselves from the Serb name and identity. Accordingly, from the depths of their history they were searching for any trace of a distinct identity – anything that would differentiate them, first from the proscribed "greater-Serbs," and ultimately from *all* Serbs.

Until the mid-1930s Yugoslav communist party opposed the very existence of the Yugoslav state, to the point of expressing verbal support for the Ustaša movement and trying to woo its members into the Party fold. An example is provided by an editorial published in the Party official organ on the "Lika uprising" of 1932: "The Communist Party salutes the Ustaša movement of the peasants of Lika and fully backs them. It is the duty of all Communist organizations and of every Communist to help this movement, to organize it and to lead it."[1] Just as the CPY hoped "to organize and to lead" the Ustašas in the early 1930s, it sought "to organize and to lead" the leaderless victims of those same Ustašas a decade later. In this latter venture the Party had scored considerably greater success. The peasant masses were not to know that CPY was instructed only belatedly to turn "pro-Yugoslav." Even the despised "Versailles creation" was deemed preferable – from the viewpoint of Soviet interests – to the peril of triumphant Nazi-Fascism. Such somersaults finally became credible after 22 June 1941. The Russian factor – the claim that the Russian *Rodina* (r.) was every Serb's second motherland – enabled CPY activists to preach the mantra of "brotherhood and unity" of Serbs and Croats in freshly burnt Serb villages, or to advocate incessant struggle against *all* occupiers, which entailed explicit rejection of pragmatism conducive to survival.

The Communist Party sought to exploit for its revolutionary ends the Calvary of the Serb population of Croatia and Bosnia-Herzegovina, by imposing itself on the leaderless peasantry and manipulating it. The Ustaša atrocities were formally condemned by the Party for tactical reasons. Its top brass knew better, and cynically observed that the Ustašas had "done the job" for the Communists by liquidating the Serbian establishment. By destroying the pillars of the old order Pavelić's *Einsatzgruppen* were clearing the ground for the agents of the Comintern. Left without traditional leaders and long before 1941 devoid of clear national goals – let alone a strategy for their fulfillment – the Serbs were going to pay an exorbitant price for their own

---

[1] "Ustaški pokret u hrvatskim zemljama." *Proleter*, No. 28, December 1932.

incoherence. Within the insurgent movement the *revolutionary realism* of the Communist Party of Yugoslavia inevitably clashed with the *existential realism* of the "nationalists." By the end of 1941 various local non-Communist resistance groups, which came to be collectively known as Četniks, realized that co-existence with the Communists was no longer possible, since it demanded endless Serb sacrifices on behalf of distant masters and revolutionary objectives.[1] The ensuing three-cornered civil war rounded out the Hobbesian drama that had no precedent even in the collective tragedy of Europe in 1941.

2. Italian Response

Italian military commanders in the NDH were aware of the tension between different nationalities in the area well before the flare-up of insurrection. In early May deputations of Muslims from western Bosnia were already asking the Italians to extend their occupation zone, and Serb community leaders made similar approaches to the *Sassari* division.[2] As the Ustaša terror flared, resulting in the Serb uprising, the Italians faced a dilemma. They could either help their Croat "allies," or act in some other way to restore order. In some areas, notably eastern Herzegovina, from very early days, armed Serb groups made it clear to the Italians that they did not have a quarrel with them but only with the Ustašas. On several occasions in June 1941 Serb village heads approached Italian garrisons to request food and protection.[3] As Italian units moved into the area of unrest to secure the lines of communication between Dubrovnik and its hinterland they encountered no opposition from the insurgents. The insurgents and Italian military commands had a common goal: restoration of order. If this objective demanded the removal of the cause of unrest, the Ustaša armed bands and Pavelić's administration, the Italians had no qualms about acting accordingly.

With considerable political and diplomatic skill Italian commanders proceeded to achieve their primary objective, pacification. General Dalmazzo, the commander of the Sixth Army Corps in the region of Dubrovnik which included the rebellious eastern Herzegovina, concluded that the Ustašas and local pro-Ustaša Muslims were guilty of causing the uprising. He supplied the

---

[1] See Veselin Djuretić, op. cit. (1985), for an elaboration of the two concepts of "realism."

[2] T-821, roll 232, frame 6: 6th Corps Command to the Second Army Command, 10 May 1941; frames 8-9: 11 May 1941; frame 27: 17 May 1941.

[3] See e.g. three reports by the Sixth Corps to the Second Army Command: T-821, roll 232, frame 78 (31 May 1941); frame 116 (9 June 1941) and frame 120 (11 June 1941).

Second Army headquarters with detailed reports to that effect, and was given a free hand in restoring order.[1] Dalmazzo did not seem too keen to observe the niceties of NDH "sovereignty" if it clashed with his task. The Italians promptly disarmed the remaining sixty Ustašas in Trebinje, and armed Serb rebels entered the city on 1 August 1941 without incident.[2] The Serbs undertook not to attack Italian troop movements by road or rail provided that such transports carried no Croat soldiers or officials. The victims of recent Ustaša massacres were exhumed from mass graves and buried with proper Orthodox Church rites, which were allowed once again by the Italians (r.). Normality had returned, at least temporarily, to that part of the NDH, at no cost in lives or treasure to the Italians. The situation was even more complex in southern Lika, where on numerous occasions local Italian units had to use the threat of arms to protect the surviving Serbs.[3] In northern Dalmatia the Italian commander, General Monticelli, told the NDH prefect, David Sinčić, that the Ustašas' murderous acts were entirely to blame for the uprising.

As such episodes illustrate, in the summer of 1941 Italian commanding officers in the NDH had to cope with tasks totally different from their colleagues in other theaters of war. Both politically and militarily they faced a challenge more complex than their German counterparts. The early slaughters on their side of the Demarcation Line were more bestial, the Serbs' reaction to them more violent, and the overall ethnic balance more even. The Dalmatian issue made a significant segment of the Croat population hostile to the occupying forces, a problem the Germans had rarely encountered in their zone. While Glaise was agonizing over the dilemma posed by the Ustaša-instigated uprising, and worrying about the "reputation of the German Army" and its inability to prevent the massacres, Italian officers enjoyed much greater autonomy of action in matters where the boundary between military and political issues was blurred.

---

[1] T-821. roll 232, frame 163. Sixth Corps to the Second Army Command, 19 June 1941. Same roll, frame 279: Sixth Corps to the Second Army Command, 10 July 1941.

[2] There are numerous reports to that effect from the Sixth Corps to the Second Army Command, eg. of 3, 10 and 18 August 1941. T-821, roll 232, frames 414, 454, 502.

[3] V.I.I. Zbornik, XIII-1, 293-4; 285, 295-6.

By acting in a conciliatory manner with non-Communist Serb insurgents, the Italians made it more difficult for the Communists agitators to advocate total war against "all enemies," as instructed by their center in Moscow.

A politically sophisticated approach adopted by key Italian generals caused differentiation within the Serb insurgent ranks in the second half of 1941, most notably in Lika and northern Dalmatia. This enabled local Italian commanders to have a clear picture of where they stood with the local insurgent leaders. The latter often approached Italian military commanders and stated that they were only fighting against the Ustašas, insisting that they had no links with the Communists. Especially in Northern Dalmatia the process of intra-Serb differentiation resulted in the permanent expulsion of the radical, pro-Communist minority from the area. The commander of an Italian division reported that "the entire population in some places was exterminated, after being tortured and tormented":

> The horrors that the Ustasi have inflicted on Serbian girls are beyond all words. There are hundreds of photographs confirming these deeds ... pulling of tongues and teeth, nails and breast tips (all this having been done after they were raped). The few survivors were taken in by our officers and transported to Italian hospitals where these documents and facts were gathered."[1]

As early as May 21 the commander of the Sassari division learnt of the Ustaša long-term plans, when three Croat dignitaries visited him, led by the Franciscan friar Vjekoslav Simić. According to the Italian record, they declared that they had been designated by the Zagreb government to take over the civil administration in the Knin region.

> The Italian general asked them what the intent of their policy was. Fr. Simić replied, "To kill all the Serbs as soon as possible." The division commander did not believe his own ears. He made him repeat the statement, which Simić did: "To kill all the Serbs, that is our program." "I am aghast," the Italian commander replied, "that such a heinious project is promoted by a man of the cloth, a Franciscan at that!"[2]

The Italian army chief of general staff, General Mario Roatta (described by Count Ciano as "the most intelligent general I know"), decided that his troops would not assist what he saw as the Ustaša campaign of "wholesale extermination of the Serbian Orthodox populace." He found the Ustaša acts

---

[1] *Il Tempo*, Turin, September 10, 1953.

[2] *Il Tempo*, No. 250, September 9, 1953.

deplorable: "Their campaign was characterized by the slaughter of tens of thousands of persons, including the aged, women, and children, while other tens of thousands, confined in so-called concentration camps (consisting of stretches of desolate land, bereft of shelter, surrounded by barbed wire and cordons of guards) were left to perish of exhaustion or torture."[1] The Italian troops could not remain indifferent to such excesses, Roatta (below) went on, and therefore "they immediately intervened wherever they were located... and thus saved the lives of much of the Serbian-Orthodox population," earning the "grateful recognition and gratitude of the Serbian Orthodox people of Croatia." He continued the same policy when he became senior Italian commander in the former Yugoslavia in 1942-43.

In September 1941 the Italian 2. Army commander, General Vittorio Ambrosio (opp. p. r.) decided to expel all Ustašas from the Italian zone and thus to "undo the legacy of four months of Ustaša misrule."[2] The head of the Italian military mission in Zagreb, General Oxilia, supported Ambrosio's decision.[3]

Eventually non-Communist resistance groups would become known as *Četniks* (irregulars, guerrillas), but many differences existed between them. Those in Serbia, under Draža Mihailović's more or less direct control, had to fight both Germans and Communists. In Montenegro local leaders sought understanding with the Italians without giving up long-term national objectives. Local Serb groups in the NDH were left to their own devices and had no contact with Mihailović until well into 1942. The most prominent of those groups, led by Momčilo Djujić in the area of Knin and *Tromedja* ("Tri-Boundary" of Lika, Dalmatia and Bosnia) established a strong and effective fighting force that enabled the local Serb population to feel secure from Ustaša incursions and shielded from communist attempts to push the Serbs into a self-defeating conflict with the Italians.

---

[1] Mario Roatta's *The Battle of the Balkans and Its Consequences* (Ch. 8, p. 170). See Lazo M. Kostich, *Holocaust in the Independent State of Croatia*. Chicago: Liberty, 1981, p. 155.

[2] VI.I., *Zbornik*, 13/1, No. 130, pp. 345-353. Also T-821, roll 474, frame 535. 2. Army, "Occupazione zona demilitarizzata," 30 August 1941.

[3] V.I.I. *Zbornik*, 13/1, No. 128, pp. 335-342. Oxilia to Comando Supremo, 23 August 1941.

During the summer of 1941, while Italian commanders were bringing some semblance of normality back to Herzegovina, northern Dalmatia and parts of Lika, in many parts of Zones II and III the Ustaša terror was continuing unabated. Mostar, Gospić, Livno and Duvno were but some of the locations south of the demarcation line where thousands of Serb civilians were killed in July and August. Italian commanders concluded that a determined effort to eliminate *all Ustaša presence* throughout the area of their nominal responsibility, and a concomitant willingness to expand the Second Army's occupation zone, were necessary to pacify the Serb rebel movement. An extension of the occupation zone would serve the additional purpose of consolidating the Italian strategic position in the heart of the Balkans, and provide a springboard for further expansion into the Danubian basin, should such an opportunity arise while the Germans were preoccupied in the East. To the Italians, who were growing increasingly disenchanted with their nominal protégés in Zagreb, this was an attractive option.

By the middle of August of 1941 the disdain and contempt of Italian officers and common soldiers for the Ustašas turned into an articulate anti-Ustaša stand of the Italian Army establishment as a whole. It was indicative of the relative independence of the Italian army from Fascist ideology and politics. Mussolini had never brought his officer corps to heel as thoroughly as Hitler had done in the late 1930s. Much more than its German counterpart, the Italian army was a political factor in its own right, and on the issue of Croatia it acted as an autonomous pressure group with considerable decision-making power. The army exercised its influence on Mussolini to such an extent that by mid-August he decided to remove the Ustašas, politically and militarily, from the entire coastal area of the NDH (Zone II). It was decided that Italian units would reoccupy the area, and take control of its civil administration in addition to the military control.

Without any prior consultation or warning, Pavelić was merely informed of this decision by Casertano on August 16.[1] Mussolini's instructions to Casertano did not allow for any consultations, let alone negotiations, between the Italians and Pavelić on the issue. The Italian High Command (*Comando*

---

[1] V.I.I., *Zbornik*, 12/1, No. 118, p. 312. Roatta to the Second Army, 15 August 1941.

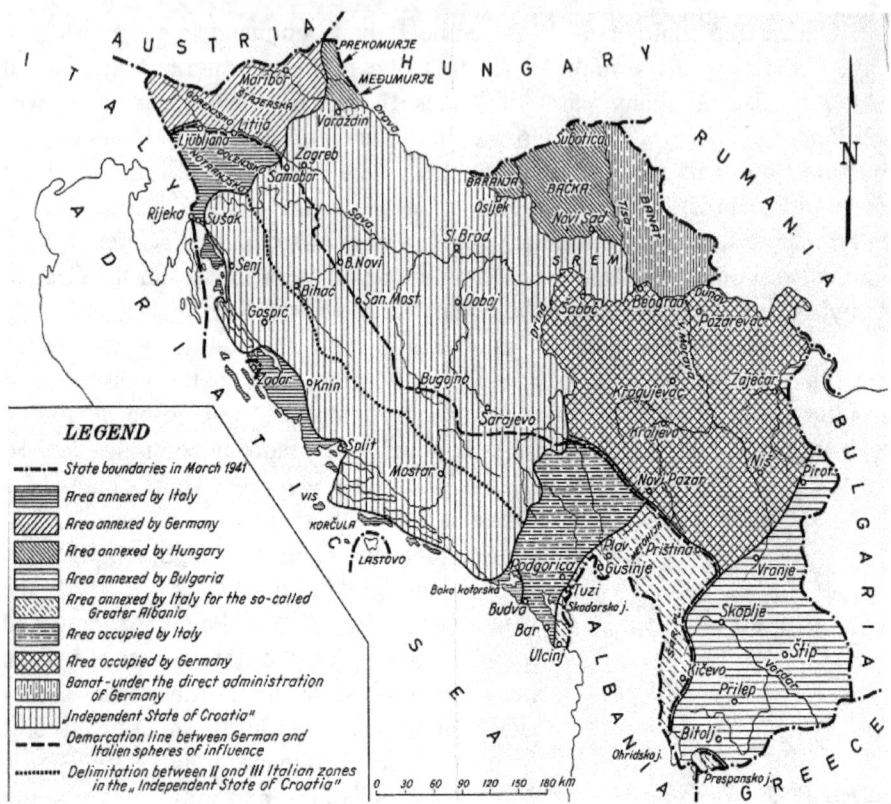

Supremo) had already issued its orders to the Second Army to reoccupy *immediately* the "Demilitarized Zone" on August 15, one day *before* Pavelić was to be given the news.[1] Casertano said that it was in the interests of the successful conduct of the war in general, and of the security of Croatia in particular, to extend Italian protection of the coastal area against any surprise. It was therefore necessary that the NDH civilian and military authorities transfer full responsibility to the Italians. Zone II, accounting for approximately one-third of the NDH territory (map above), was about to be excluded from its authority.

Casertano's communication caused great excitement in Zagreb. Pavelić at first stated that he could see "no need" for such a move. He asserted that Croatian forces were able to deal with the situation, and expressed fear that Italian action would actually contribute to further spreading of unrest. Within

---

[1] As a prelude the Italians decided on 5 August to take control of the railroad connecting Knin with Gospić. The measure was explained to the Croats by the need "to secure the coastal area against a sudden British attack" and to prevent further influx of insurgents into the area.

hours, Pavelić, Lorković and Kvaternik-senior met with Kasche and Glaise, urging them to seek help and intervention from Berlin. This they did, but for different reasons. Kasche was pro-Pavelić from conviction – the only high-ranking German official in the Balkans supportive of the Ustaša regime – and believed in the "state-building strength" of the Ustaša movement. Glaise, on the other hand, was anti-Italian to his Austrian bone and distressed at the spectacle of Italy's increasing control over old Habsburg lands.

The Ustaša leadership attempted, somewhat clumsily, to enlist German support. On August 18 the NDH *charge d'affairs* in Berlin visited State Under-Secretary Woermann at the Foreign Ministry and informed him of the Italian note to Pavelić. He said that the *Poglavnik* was determined to reject it, and needed German help in doing so. He added that the Croatian minister, Benzon, was on his way back from Bratislava to Berlin.[1] The following day Benzon spoke to Weizsäcker. He advocated the "condominium" formula in Zone II, with the Croatian civilian authorities retaining their presence. He said that even this watered-down formula was "painful" to accept yet the NDH would do it, not out of any fear of Italy but because it respected the overall strategic interests of the Reich. Pavelić's appeals for German intervention prior to the signing of the Rome Agreements in May 1941 were discreet, and (with the exception of Benzon's unauthorized approach to Weizsäcker) restrained in scope. At that time Pavelić was still in the process of consolidating his position and he could not feel secure until his debt to Italy had been repaid. He sought German assistance in reducing the payment but he could not hope to avoid it altogether. In August 1941, however, the pretense of a lasting community of interest with the Italians was gone. In their appeals to the Germans some Ustašas even suggested that their Italian partners would eventually stab them in the back, since "the strategic position which the Italians intend to acquire in Croatia may under given circumstances serve goals which are not in the spirit of Axis policy."[2]

Kasche tried to elicit support for Pavelić in Berlin and sent a series of telegrams criticizing the Italians. Ribbentrop responded by reminding Kasche, once again, of the "principled instruction that the *alpha* and *omega* of German policy in the entire Mediterranean area was its alliance with Italy."[3] Germany must avoid the role of arbiter that the Croats may try to impose on it. Kasche was told not to accept any such appeals and to advise Croats to resolve all

---

[1] T-120, roll 208. Büro Unterstaatssekretär, Pol. No. 786 of 18 August 1941.
[2] T-501, roll 264. Glaise's report to the OKW, 17 August 1941.
[3] T-120, roll 208, frame 875. Ribbentrop to Kasche, 21 August 1941.

issues in direct friendly dialogue with Italy.¹ Similar warnings were sent to Kasche by Ribbentrop on August 21 and September 1, 1941.² The official Croatian reply was given in a long verbal note by Lorković to Casertano on 18 August.³ Unable to reject Italian demands regarding the forthcoming reoccupation of Zone II, the NDH government stated that it could not "accept responsibility" for their consequences. Sensing defeat – and possibly recalling his successful personal appeal to Mussolini in Monfalcone three months earlier – Pavelić tried to approach the Duce. On 19 August he sent him a telegram requesting that General Ambrosio, the commander of the Second Army, should not assume civilian authority in the demilitarized zone. Pavelić suggested an Italian-Croatian condominium instead: the creation of a Croatian "General Administrative Mission" (*Obće upravno povjereništvo*), attached to the Second Army headquarters, which would "coordinate" the civilian activities with the Italians.⁴

In his reply Mussolini agreed to the proposal but stressed that it would be "up to the Italian Army to determine the precise forms of any such cooperation."⁵ General Ambrosio would have a free hand. On 26 August Ambrosio went to Zagreb and received Ustaša official representatives in the Italian legation to discuss reoccupation.⁶ The head of the Italian military mission in Zagreb, General Giovanni Battista Oxilia (r.), suggested to the Supreme Command on 23 August that Pavelić ought to be put in his place:

> It is possible that Pavelić and those around him have sympathies and admiration for Germany. It is also possible that, pressured by his ministers, he intends to maneuver between two great powers, thus securing greater independence for Croatia. It certainly seems to me that this is the most suitable moment for pressure on the Croatian government, so that it fulfils its treaty obligations with

---

¹ Also on 21 August 1941 Ribbentrop instructed Weizsäcker to tell Benzon that there was no need for the German government to take any position on "an issue which concerned bilateral relations between Italy and Croatia." Weizsäcker did so on 22 August.

² T-120, roll 208, frame 877. Ribbentrop to Kasche, 21 August 1941.

³ T-120, roll 208, frame 1008. Kasche to the Foreign Ministry, 18 August 1941. Also: T-501, roll 263, Glaise to the OKW, 18 August 1941.

⁴ VI.I.. *Zbornik*, 13/1, p. 333. Pavelić to Mussolini, 19 August 1941.

⁵ As quoted in Krizman (1983), pp. 164-165.

⁶ VI.I., *Zbornik*, 13/1, No. 130, pp. 345-353. T-821, roll 474, frame 535. Second Army Command, Operations Department, "Occupazione zona demilitarizzata," 30 August 1941.

greater loyalty and sincerity... [and] that the powerful trump card which we are holding, will induce individuals and the government to act accordingly.[1]

All "irregular" Ustaša units – often local bands guilty of many atrocities against the Serbs – were promptomly disarmed and disbanded. The "regular" Ustaša militia was given the deadline of September 1, 1941 to leave the Second Zone. The NDH government was informed that the Second Army would take over all administrative responsibilities a week later. Only a few scattered units of *Domobrani*, without heavy weapons and under operational control of the Second Army, were left as a token of Croatian military presence in Mostar and a few other locations.[2]

All Italian orders and public pronouncements referred to *occupazione* or *rioccupazione* of Zone II.[3] The meaning of Ambrosio's measures was clear from his proclamation to the people of the Second Zone on September 7, which stated that he was "assuming military and civilian authority in the area." Having made sure that no Ustašas would get in the way of their new course, the Italians promulgated a series of administrative measures aimed at restoring Serbs' rights. In areas with a Serb majority they were reinstated to local administrative posts, while Serb property confiscated by the NDH was returned to its original owners. Following the example of Trebinje, Orthodox churches were reopened and contact established with local leaders of insurgent groups. If one of Ambrosio's objectives had been to isolate the extremist wing of the insurgent movement, his strategy soon appeared to be working in northern Dalmatia and in Herzegovina. Although in a few places (notably around Drvar) Communist-dominated groups strengthened their position at the expense of the vacillating "nationalists," this was an exception, rather than the rule, in the Italian-controlled area.[4] As the Italian army started its advance into the western Bosnian and Herzegovinian towns armed Serb groups were mostly friendly. For many the dominant sentiment was to exact revenge on the Ustašas and their supporters. In some cases local Croats reversed the pattern by seeking Italian military protection against the vengeful

---

[1] V.I.I. *Zbornik*, 13/1, No. 128, pp. 335-342. Oxilia to the Supreme Command, 23 Aug. 1941.

[2] Vrančić, op. cit. (1985), Vol. 2, p. 122.

[3] Some Ustašas confused propaganda and reality. Vjekoslav Vrančić (*Branili smo državu*) asserted that, far from being an "occupation," this was "an agreement that Italian troops, which were in Croatia as an allied army, should take over the security of an area and perform some state functions within it... Surrender of those functions and the resulting limitations are based on the state's own will, they have the meaning of self-limitation of authority, and therefore do not reduce its sovereignty."

[4] T-821, roll 232, fr. 691, 735. 6th Corps reports to 2. Army Command, 16 and 22 Sept. 1941.

Serbs.[1] In addition, in several locations the Ustašas were still active in spite of the order to leave the Second Zone, and staged sporadic anti-Serb actions in the first half of September.[2] Even a hint of Ustaša comeback was sufficient to convince most Serbs that they should stick to their guns. If the Italian solution was to be complete and permanent, therefore, it was necessary to rid the area under occupation of *all* Partisans and Ustašas. It was also necessary to fill the vacuum between Zone Two and the demarcation line, which was turning into a haven both for Partisans and Ustašas expelled from the reoccupied area. Ambrosio's design, approvingly executed by his field commanders (below), thus had to be completed by *the reoccupation of Zone Three* – another huge chunk of NDH territory, including some of the wildest mountain landscape in the Balkans.

By mid-October 1941 the Italian occupation was extended all the way to the demarcation line with the Germans, and covered about one half of NDH territory. This was done with the usual disregard for the government in Zagreb, which fatalistically accepted the inevitable. It had had to field off another crisis only a fortnight earlier, when on September 26 Ambrosio unilaterally proclaimed the inclusion of the reoccupied territory into the Italian customs zone. Only urgent appeals by Lorković, who was in Venice discussing various aspects of economic cooperation with Italy, resulted in the formal withdrawal of Ambrosio's proclamation.[3] In practice all customs barriers between Italy and the Italian zone were nevertheless removed. The NDH was in effect divided into two separate economic, administrative, military and political halves. Only the merest pretense of its sovereignty remained in the Italian-occupied half.

In the longer run it turned out that, far from solving the problem of insurgency, the extended occupation area became a part of the problem. It was an area where topography and climate sometimes represented obstacles to successful performance of tasks comparable in magnitude to enemy action. This compelled Italian commanders to confine their units to the fortified

---

[1] T-821, roll 232, frames 635-639. 6th Corps to 2. Army Command, 8 September 1941.
[2] T-821, roll 232, frame 684. 6th Corps to 2. Army Command, 15 September 1941.
[3] For an Ustaša view of this episode, see Vrančić, op. cit. (1985), Vol. 2, pp. 140-142.

towns, and to expend great effort just to keep their lines of communication open. The insurmountable internal divisions, Orthodox-Muslim, Orthodox-Catholic, Četnik-Partisan, Partisan-Ustaša and Četnik-Ustaša, set the stage for the multi-cornered conflict which was at its worst in the newly-enlarged Italian zone. Initially the Italians believed they could manipulate different parties, and early results were encouraging. By the end of 1941 and in early 1942, however, they found themselves drawn into a tangled web of temporary alliances with local Serb leaders, who put their regional interests first, and who were easily swayed by the mood of their men:

At this point the Četniks (l.) had no tight organization and their political objectives were ambiguous; the Italians had no faith in their Balkan mission and barely had policy. Mussolini had intervened in early November to restrain the Second Army's openly pro-Serb posture, informing Ambrosio that all measures were to be carried out in conjunction with the Croatian civil authorities and that the Italians were at all costs to avoid creating the impression that they favored the Orthodox population. Frustrated by continuing disorders, Cavallero wavered between giving Ambrosio full powers to suppress the revolt militarily by declaring the whole area a zone of war, and the defensive strategy of pulling the Italian troops to the cities and along the major lines of communication.[1]

With the situation in North Africa deteriorating yet again, no fresh troops could be allocated to the Balkans. At the same time, in the winter of 1941-1942 many Communist units, having been routed in Serbia and Montenegro, infiltrated the Italian zone of the NDH and challenged Ambrosio's precarious balance. The Germans were facing a major crisis of their own in Russia; the Ustašas were the cause of disorder in the first place; and the Četniks volatile and unreliable from the Italian viewpoint. The failures of the occupation system in Yugoslavia were becoming increasingly obvious. The only party profiting from the murky times ahead were Tito's Communists.

---

[1] Milazzo, op. cit. p. 60.

3. German Reaction to Uprising

German representatives in the NDH reacted to the first wave of anti-Serb atrocities primarily out of concern for their "reputation." In their early reports they focused less on the acts themselves than on the political problems that could follow if the Germans were perceived as the willing underwriters of Pavelić's genocidal course. In the course of the summer of 1941, with unrest erupting in various parts of the NDH, the focus of their concern shifted to the military and strategic consequences of the slaughters. With the exception of Kasche's, German reports invariably singled out the Ustaša policy as the chief cause of unrest. As before, Kasche's independent-thinking deputy Troll-Obergfell used occasional absences of his boss from Zagreb to send messages to Berlin which were highly critical of Pavelić's regime.

The RSHA had an extensive network in the NDH and was thorough in reporting Ustaša atrocities and the effect they had on the unrest. On the basis of dozens of field reports it reached the conclusion that the Ustašas were to blame for the resistance. The same overall view was presented in early 1942 to the *Reichsfuehrer* SS, Heinrich Himmler, in a detailed report:

> As the chief cause of increased activity of the bands one must name atrocities carried out by Ustaša units in Croatia against the Orthodox population. The Ustašas committed their deeds in a bestial manner not only against males of conscript age, but especially against helpless old people, women and children. The number of the Orthodox that the Croats have massacred and sadistically tortured to death is about three hundred thousand.[1]

The same report mentioned forced conversions to Roman Catholicism as major contributory factor to unrest, "especially as they are accompanied by terror. The Catholic Church has instigated Ustaša crimes even by the very use it has made of them in its conversion drive." The report recommended a radical change of course in the NDH, where the Ustaša regime "should no

---

[1] PA, Büro RAM, Kroatien, 1941-42, 442-449. IV/D/4 RSHA to Himmler, 17 February 1942. It is somewhat ironic that the same behavior traits and motivation which various German instances saw in Pavelić's followers, his own propagandists ascribed to their enemies. In 1941 Lorković thus described the Četniks to a German paper as "lawless subhumans," while Ivo Bogdan asserted in 1942 that "Partisan characteristics were marked by the 'appalling atrocities perpetrated on the peaceful population', which [he] remarked, could not have been committed 'by beings that deserve the name of humans.' In explaining these Partisan atrocities, one must take into account, Bogdan continued, 'the centuries old alluvium of impure Balkan blood, the sediment of which has risen to the surface'..." (Quoted by Bartulin, op. cit., p.368)

longer be allowed full freedom of action, especially in rebel areas." German foreign ministry plenipotentiary representative in Belgrade Felix Benzler joined the chorus of disapproval by reporting to Ribbentrop:

> From the founding [of the NDH] until now the persecution of Serbs has not stopped, and even cautious estimates indicate that at least several hundred thousand people have been killed. The irresponsible elements have committed such atrocities that could be expected only from a rabid Bolshevik horde.[1]

Lower-ranking German officers were well aware by that time that harmless civilians were subject to Ustaša slaughter because they were *Serbs*, and not because they were rebels; the insurgency was a consequence, not the cause, of the terror: "Captain Konopatzki [714th Division intelligence officer] maintained that 'Serbs,' not Partisans, not Četniks, not enemies, were the object  of Ustaša attacks. Major C. Geim, General Bader's intelligence officer, argued that the Ustaša attacked Serbs with the objective of 'exterminating the Serbian portion of the population in Croatia."[2] By the end of 1941, urgent demands for intervention to stop Ustaša massacres started pouring in from many German quarters.[3] Rudolf Epting, the Nazi Party foreign branch (*Auslandsorganisation*) chief in Croatia, in a report to Hitler, named the Ustašas the main culprits for the unrest.[4] Walter Schellenberg of the Reich Security Service (RSHA) foreign department (l.) also held that the slaughters caused the rebellion: "Without recruits from the Serb population which was terrorized by the Ustašas, this Četnik warfare would have been nipped in the bud."[5] Wehrmacht eyewitnesses noted the Ustaša 'slaughtered' the villagers and 'plundered' their property in acts of pure terror.[6] Yet the most consistent and thorough German critic of Pavelić's regime was Glaise von Horstenau.

---

[1] PA, Büro Staatssekretär, Jugoslawien, Bd. 4. Benzler to Ribbentrop, 16 February 1942.

[2] Jonathan Gumz, op. cit.

[3] Gert Fricke, op. cit. pp. 39-40.

[4] Hory and Broszat, op. cit. pp. 129-130.

[5] Ibid, p. 151.

[6] 714. Division, Operations Staff, "Activity Report: Recent Fighting," NA, T-315, Records of German Field Commands. Translated and quoted by Jonathan Gumz, op. cit.

He was the first among high-ranking Germans to express doubts about the viability of the regime, to publicize its atrocities, and to stress the Ustaša course as the root cause of unrest. His views on the subject fully coincided with a host of his military colleagues (notably Löhr, Rendulic, and Weichs), professional soldiers with a direct experience of conditions in the southeast.

Faced with a barrage of attacks on the Ustaša regime and with a major increase of insurgent activity in the NDH in the final quarter of 1941, Hitler had three options. One was to wash his hands of Croatia altogether, and let the Italians sort out the mess in the country – which was, after all, in their "sphere" anyway. The other was to try and replace Pavelić with a more credible political force, or with a politically neutral civil servants' government. Finally, he could try to muddle through with Pavelić, but seek to place him and all his resources under tighter German control.

In the autumn of 1941 two full-strength German divisions cleared Serbia of most rebels, carrying out drastic reprisals in the process: a hundred civilians were to be shot, in principle, for a dead German soldier, fifty for a wounded one. The ratio was applied in the cities of Kragujevac (r.) and Kraljevo in the final week of October, where over 5,000 Serb civilians were summarily executed. For the OKW and Hitler, the Partisans and Četniks, regardless of their evident ideological antipathy, represented but two sides of the same coin: the "Serbian conspiratorial clique" was raising its head again, and had to be smashed. While Mihailović went more or less underground, Tito withdrew to the NDH. This was a move dictated by necessity, but eventually it proved advantageous: the Ustaša state, by its anti-Serb policies, continued to provide a reliable pool of potential recruits, which could no longer be found in Serbia and Montenegro. By killing the leaders, Pavelić's men enabled the Communist Party to impose itself with far greater ease than if it had had to contend with Serbian teachers, priests, and other pillars of the traditional village society.

The first German option – to pass the hot potato completely to the Italians – temporarily prevailed at the end of 1941, with the military crisis in the East concentrating Hitler's mind. The OKW wanted to withdraw German forces from Serbia and the NDH.[1] When told of this idea, General List suggested that only one German division should remain in Croatia, and Glaise be retained at his post, while Italy would secure the railroad between Zagreb and Belgrade.[2] The OKW directed List on 16 December to free forces in both Serbia and Croatia for the East Front, replacing them with Bulgarian, Italian, and possibly Hungarian and Romanian troops. The Italians promptly declared their readiness to move the Second Army even further north.[3]

The news produced panic in Zagreb. Both Kasche and Glaise were indignant, the former because he was supportive of "his" Ustašas, the latter because he saw every German retreat to the Italians as a personal insult. In addition, both were upset because they had not been consulted. Kasche claimed that the continued presence of German troops was essential for the maintenance of order because the Italians were not able to control the situation in their zone as it was, let alone in an area twice its size.[4] Kasche warned that an Italian occupation of the whole of Croatia would cause the unrest to spread to the Croat population. Glaise noted that some Croats felt a total surrender of the whole of Croatia to the Italians would be preferable to the disappointment caused by the Reich's disinterest in the country's destiny.[5] The new course, Glaise opined, would cause more difficulties for the Ustaša regime, "considering the avarice which is characteristic of our allies and which will affect our economic interests in the country."

Pavelić kept the news secret from anyone but Slavko Kvaternik and his deputy Laxa.[6] Their reaction was predictable: Kvaternik-senior called it "a catastrophe." He said that he would "resign and go to the front." He warned Glaise that German prestige and interests would suffer.[7] On December 24 Glaise reiterated the deep impression of the new OKW directive on the Croat military and their renewed suspicion of the Italians who, "contrary to all

---

[1] AJ, T-120, roll 208, quoted in Krizman (1983).

[2] Paul Hehn (ed.). *The German Struggle against Yugoslav Guerrillas in World War II*. Boulder, Colorado: East European Monographs, 1979, pp. 77-78.

[3] T-821, roll 64, frame 993. Unsigned account of the meeting in Rome (*Riunione giorno 30 dicembre*) with Ciano, Roatta, Ambrosio, Casertano and Magli in attendance. For Ciano's views on extending Italian occupation zone see *Diary*, entry for 17 December 1941.

[4] T-120, roll 208, No. 1634. Kasche to the foreign ministry, Zagreb, 16 December 1941.

[5] Gert Fricke. *Kroatien 1941-1944: Die "Unbehaengige Staat" in der Sicht des Deutschen Bevollmaechtigen Generals in Agram, Glaise v. Horstenau*. Freiburg/i. Breisgau: Rombach Verlag, 1972, p. 62.

[6] Pavelić's deputy foreign minister Vrančić first heard of the plan only after 1945.

[7] T-501, roll 264. Glaise to the OKW, Zagreb, 22 December 1941. Krizman (1983), p. 232.

custom, had not informed the Croatian army of their new task."[1] The gloomy mood in Zagreb was reinforced by Hungary's sudden annexation of Medjimurje and by increased anti-Croatian agitation in Budapest. There were rumors that the Sava would be the final demarcation line between Italy and Hungary and that Germany would give up any role in Croatia in order to concentrate on the key task of fighting the Russians.

The feeling of abandonment by Germany – which refused to intervene in the dispute over Medjimurje – coincided with the bad news from the Russian front. By the end of November the Barbarossa gamble had ran out of steam.[2] On 6 December the Russians counter-attacked. Pavelić was helpless to prevent the intended German pullout, and in any event when the crisis broke he was in Venice (r.) meeting Ciano to sign the Tripartite Pact on behalf of Croatia. Ciano noted in his diary on December 14 that Pavelić would "ask for many things, all of which would have to be rejected." Indeed, he did ask for a gradual return of Croatian authority in the Italian zone, but to no avail.[3] He also paid a courtesy visit  to the king-designate, but this, too, was an empty gesture: as Ciano had told Mussolini, the issue of the monarchy had been put aside "for the time being."

On December 24 Hitler reversed his decision and scrapped plans for entry of Italian troops into the German occupation zone. The crisis in Russia was under control and his directive of December 16 was abrogated.[4] He may have realized that one infantry division and a few additional local defense battalions – unlikely to tip the scales either way in the snows of Russia – was an acceptable price for the continuity of his Balkan policy. One option in Croatia, to pass the troubled creation to Mussolini altogether, was thus discarded for good.

---

[1] Hehn, op. cit. p. 82.

[2] General Halder held that "we have reached the end of our human and material forces."

[3] On Pavelić's visit, see Krizman (1983) pp. 246-247.

[4] In contrast to the Germans, the Italian posture was entirely reactive. The news of Hitler's change of heart, Ciano's recorded on 28 December, did not elicit any comment from Mussolini.

4. The Dangić Affair

The second alternative was to seek a political solution to the Ustaša problem. Kasche kept saying that Pavelić was the only trustworthy German ally in the area, but his was an isolated voice. Closer to the mood of most German representatives in the Balkans was Glaise's opinion that "aversion against the Ustaša movement is felt by everyone who did not directly profit from it," that the NDH was "scarcely able to function in its present hybrid composition" with the "attack and resistance capacity of the Croatian soldier declining from week to week." Glaise added that "all this reflected weariness and lack of training, but also the refusal to engage in a struggle regarded, in wide circles of the Croatian people, as a civil war, whose outbreak and expansion was blamed on the hated Ustaša."[1]

Glaise and other German officers realized that the guerrilla problem was not only military, or primarily military, but political. Such conclusions were similar to those reached by their Italian colleagues. An opportunity to test their political acumen and to exercise pragmatism on the ground was offered to the Germans in early 1942 in eastern Bosnia, where they carried out an extensive mopping-up operation following the successful anti-insurgent drive in Serbia. This was an area along the eastern border of the NDH with a slight Serb majority over Muslims. Early slaughters in the summer of 1941 plunged the area into chaos and armed resistance. A strong personality soon emerged to lead the insurgents in the person of a gendarme major, Jezdimir Dangić (above). He was in his prime at 45, a law school graduate and – as a native of Bosnia – well acquainted with local conditions. His case provides an example of the restraints which German military commanders on the ground faced from their political masters.

Dangić realized as early as September 1941 that his primary objective, to preserve as many Serb lives as possible, inevitably clashed with the Communists' strategy, *the worse - the better*. Unlike Mihailović in Serbia, Dangić did not cherish any illusions about and therefore did not seek any

---

[1] T-501, Roll 264, miscellaneous reports from Glaise to the OKW.

accommodation with the Communists.¹ Always ready to fight the Ustašas, he avoided conflict with the Germans, whose local presence was weak in mid-1941. In early September, having established primacy over various local Četnik leaders in eastern Bosnia, Dangić issued proclamations which advocated the creation of a "united national Serb front" against the Partisans.² Most local Serbs were suspicious of the Party's slogans of "brotherhood-and-unity" anyway, for as long as their presumed Croat and Muslim "brothers" were out to kill them. Dangić recognized Mihailović's nominal authority but acted on his own and established contact with the Nedić administration.

Had Dangić been active in the Italian zone he would have been a prime candidate to reach an arrangement with someone like General Ambrosio to have the Serbs' rights to life and property restored, in return for an undertaking against Partisans. His men had no problem making deals with the Italians.³ He had to deal with the Germans instead, who took a dimmer view of *all* "bands." His initial approach went through General Milan Nedić (r.), at the end of 1941, when the Serbian chief administrator informed the Wehrmacht command in Belgrade that Četnik leaders in eastern Bosnia were willing to "arrive at an understanding with the German authorities."⁴ Wehrmacht field commanders confirmed that during operations in eastern Bosnia "it was apparent that Dangić's Četniks avoided combat with German troops and did not fire on them." As the official OKW record prepared some months later explained, this paved the way for subsequent negotiations in Belgrade with Dangić "in an effort to save German blood."⁵  On January 30, 1942, Chief of Staff to the Commander in Serbia, Colonel Kewisch, met with Dangić who declared that his sole objective was to keep Ustašas and Communists out of East Bosnia, and to maintain order.

---

¹ His prewar experience as a gendarmerie officer and district administrator (*sreski načelnik*) was more helpful in understanding the Communist mindset than that of a regular army officer background would have been.

² T-314, Roll 1457, frames 702-703. Wehrmachtverbidungsstelle Belgrad to Befehlshaber Serbien, Belgrade, 29 September 1941.

³ Milazzo, op. cit. pp. 70-71.

⁴ T-501, roll 251, fr. 1138-1139. Colonel Kewisch, *Aktenvermerk*, Belgrade, 19 January 1942.

⁵ T-501, roll 256, frame 1098. Bevoll. Kdr. Gen. in Serbien/Ia to Wehrmachtbefehlshaber Südost. Belgrade, 4 February 1942.

On January 31 and February 1 further discussions took place between Dangić, Nedić and the Wehrmacht Commander in Serbia, General Bader.[1] What Dangić wanted was similar to what his counterparts in Herzegovina and northern Dalmatia had obtained from the Italians: local autonomy for the Serbs, expulsion of Ustaša civil and military apparatus, complete truce with Axis forces, coupled with the commitment to resolute anti-Communist action in return. The Germans were tempted.

Croatian representatives attached to the Wehrmacht in eastern Bosnia soon learnt of Dangić's attempts.[2] They alerted Pavelić to the intentions of German military commanders, but he seemed prepared to go along with these plans at first. On January 23 the Wehrmacht commander in Serbia, General Bader, signed a provisional agreement with Pavelić in Zagreb, whereby the area between the Drina, Sava and Bosna rivers in eastern Bosnia would come "until further notice" under direct German military authority. A Croatian civilian commissioner would be attached to the German military command; he would also act as liaison officer, similar to the post created at the Italian Second Army headquarters. Dangić would control large parts of this area, but he would be subordinated to the Germans.

It was on this basis that German military representatives negotiated with Dangić, in Nedić's presence, on the night of January 31-February 1. Dangić was told that the separation of eastern Bosnia and its inclusion into Serbia – which he had requested - was not possible, since this was an issue beyond Bader's competence. However, while purely nominal Croatian sovereignty would remain, all real power (*Entscheidungsgewalt*) would be in the hands of the Wehrmacht.[3]

General Bader believed that the only possibility of pacification in eastern Bosnia was to reach an understanding with Dangić that would entail his acceptance of German authority. He therefore arranged for fresh talks with Dangić on February 2 in the presence of Benzler, who represented the foreign ministry in Belgrade. At the meeting the only sticking point was that of formal NDH authority, with Dangić rejecting any possibility of cooperation with the Ustaša government. At that point Bader invited Kasche, Glaise and NDH delegates to Belgrade to find a solution.

---

[1] T-501, roll 250, frames 1089-1090. Bevoll. Kdr. Gen. in Serbien/Ia to Wehrmachtbefehlshaber Südost, Belgrade, 5 February 1942.

[2] Vrančić, op. cit. (1985), Vol. 2, pp. 197-198.

[3] For a full stenogram of the talks with Dangić, see Karl Hlinicka, *Das Ende auf dem Balkan 1944/45*. Goettingen: Musterscheudt, 1970, pp. 174-198.

In discussions with Kasche and Glaise on February 2 General Bader obtained their agreement to the transfer of local authority in eastern Bosnia to Dangić, with only the formal retention of NDH sovereignty. Kasche expressed doubts if such a solution would be acceptable to Pavelić, however. When Ustaša representative Vrančić was invited later in the day to sign the formal agreement, General Bader attempted to present the Croatian side with a done deal. According to Vrančić (r.), he spread a map in front of him and other German and Croatian officials, pointed at a shaded area of eastern Bosnia and declared that his command had decided to hand over military and civilian authority in those districts to Dangić.[1] He requested the NDH government to withdraw its military units and civilian officials.

Unaware of the agreement already reached among the Germans, Vrančić initially expected Kasche or Glaise to object. Encountering silence, he said that such a decision was unacceptable to the NDH government as it would create a dangerous precedent which other rebels would seek to emulate, "from Caribrod to Ljubljana." He pointedly added that General Bader would have difficulty in justifying his decision in Berlin. Vrančić correctly sensed that the general lacked authorization from the top. Indeed, faced with the problem of obtaining approval from diverse political and military instances in Berlin, Bader soon gave up his idea.

The first attempt by German military commanders to seek political solutions to eminently political problems of the NDH thus ended in failure. The cause of that failure was in the fact that General Bader did not enjoy the necessary political support of his superiors.[2] His was an imaginative action undertaken on his personal initiative. In early 1942, however, it was too early for the German high command to accept the necessity of political solutions to military problems in the Balkans. The Ustaša government had only limited

---

[1] Vrančić, op. cit. (1985), Vol. 2, p. 203.

[2] Dangić's end was tragic. He was taken prisoner by the Germans, escaped from the POW camp and made his way to Poland, where he fought heroically in the Warsaw uprising and was decorated by the Polish AK. However, the advancing Russians arrested him and extradited him to Tito, who duly had him shot in Sarajevo in 1945.

ability to influence German decisions, but it correctly sensed the relative powerlessness of the Wehrmacht field commanders to act against the official thinking in Berlin. Such thinking was evident in Keitel's letter to Roatta of February 2 in which he rejected Italian methods in seeking *modus vivendi* with the Serbs. Keitel stated that "everything must be accomplished, both militarily and politically, in order to strengthen the Croatian government to support its measures against the insurgents."[1]

5. German-Italian Military Discord

On political orders from Hitler the OKW persisted in its view of the insurgency in the NDH as an uprising (*Aufstand*), and insisted on the designation of the insurgents as "rebels" and "bandits." While Italian and even German field officers quickly perceived the schism between the Četniks and the Partisans, the Dangić affair made it plain that only Italians were free to exploit the possibilities. They stopped fighting the Četniks throughout their occupation zone. Italian general disenchantment with the insistence of Berlin on a strictly military solution to the war in the Balkans was reflected in the scant support offered by the Second Army to the Germans during operations in eastern Bosnia in early 1942. Latent intra-Axis rivalry and growing jealousies over influence in the NDH acted as additional impediments to the creation of an effective united front, and threatened to compromise the entire Axis war effort in the area.

The need to devise a common Axis anti-insurgent strategy in the NDH seemed obvious to German field commanders. On the one hand, they were prevented from applying political solutions to political problems, and specifically making allies of Četniks. On the other, they had to contend with the Ustaša regime, which they grew to detest and regard as the cause of their problems. Besides, the OKW assigned far lower priority to the Balkans than to other war theatres (Russia, Africa), and German forces in the NDH were weak – no more than one full division at a time. If the Italians were to sabotage operations, the task of the German Commander South-East and his subordinates would be impossible. Therefore, on January 21 List asked the OKW to exercise "suitable political influence" on the Italians; significantly, he also requested "the appointment of a leader in Croatia who would be made responsible for the maintenance of ordered conditions."[2]

---

[1] Keitel to Roatta, in Hehn, op. cit. p. 141.

[2] Keitel to Cavallero, Berlin, 4 February 1942, in Hehn, op. cit., p. 99.

On February 4 Keitel wrote to his Italian counterpart, chief of the general staff Ugo Cavallero (r.) and suggested "unified and energetic measures" in the former Yugoslavia in order "finally to break the backbone" of the insurgent movement.[1] Stressing the need for coordinated political and police action in conjunction with military operations, Keitel came to the point: "The military-political methods that have been applied until now in Croatia are in need of scrutiny. In my opinion the prerequisites for arriving at an amicable agreement with the enemy do not exist. The continuation of the present uncertain situation prevents any consolidation of the Croatian state and must in the long run lead to its dissolution."

The Germans may have thought that the change of command at the Italian Second Army, which occurred at this time, was a good omen. General Ambrosio, who was seen as a chief advocate of the pro-Četnik policy, was replaced, but only to be moved to the more influential position of army chief of staff. The new appointee, General Mario Roatta, soon dispelled all hopes that his thinking would be more in line with German plans. On January 26 Roatta told the chief German liaison officer with his army, Colonel Rohrbach, that he favored a joint and simultaneous action to destroy the centers of revolt by concentrated attacks.[2] This sounded like the OKW line.

More worryingly for the Germans, however, Roatta also hinted at the possibility of withdrawing most Italian units to a line closer to the Adriatic coast and leaving behind only a few strongly fortified garrisons, with mobile defenses limited to the main roads.[3]

As he expanded on his plans Roatta sounded more and more like his predecessor. He calmly mentioned "a further possibility" of an *even more*

---

[1] Report of the German Liaison Staff with the Italian Second Army No. 153/42 of 26 January 1942. Hehn, op. cit. pp. 100-101.

[2] Milazzo, op. cit. pp. 70-72.

[3] He further told the German that he had no scruples about influencing the peoples concerned with generous promises which one did not need to keep. He casually said that, "for example, one could easily have promised Graz and Klagenfurt to Croatia, or hired gangsters to carry out political assassinations of Italians in France, if it was deemed expedient."

extensive cooperation with the Serbs, if necessary at the expense of the Croatian state. He thought that only in this way had it been possible – especially in Herzegovina – to maintain peace and to keep isolated and exposed Italian garrisons without fighting. The Croatian government would naturally seek to obstruct such policy, added Roatta, which only went to prove that it had been a mistake to create an independent Croatia, "a state basically hostile towards Italy." It would have been better to regard the whole of the Balkans as enemy territory for the duration of the war, Roatta concluded, and act accordingly.

Roatta's statements, made so soon after he had assumed command at Sušak, indicated that by the beginning of 1942 a distinct Italian army view of the Croatian problem, a view independent of Rome, was firmly in place. That view boded ill for German plans. German apprehensions were to grow in subsequent weeks, with reports reaching Salonika and Berlin of the unwillingness of the Second Army to fight the rebels. The news of fresh deals between Italian officers and Četniks kept coming throughout February. Hitler's about-face in December (when he decided against allowing Italian troops to occupy the whole of the NDH) caused Mussolini to renew his suspicions of German-Croatian intrigues. Such misgivings coupled with the Italian generals' view that political problems required political solutions, resulted in almost total lack of Italian support during German operations in eastern Bosnia in early 1942.

In the meantime Cavallero replied to Keitel's letter of 4 February. He expressed agreement with the proposed joint mopping-up operation, but - reflecting both Mussolini's suspicions and hurt pride - asked that the action should be carried out under Italian overall command. He proposed further discussions at the headquarters of the Second Army in Sušak. In his reply Keitel said he was ready to accept "a temporary Italian high command... provided that the guarantee exists for an energetic military operation, previously agreed upon in detail."[1] On the same day (February 23) he sent directives to List: "The talks are to be limited to the discussion of military measures and political questions are to be avoided. The imperative is to bring the military directives of the Italian Second Army into agreement with those of the Wehrmacht Commander Southeast."[2]

The Germans proceeded with characteristic thoroughness to prepare for the talks. On February 27 the acting Wehrmacht Commander South-East,

---

[1] Hehn, op. cit. p. 102.
[2] Teletype of the OKW/W F St Ops No. 00732/42 to Wehrmachtbefehlshaber Südost, 23 February 1942. Hehn, op. cit. p. 103.

General Walter Kuntze (r.), conferred in Zagreb with Glaise, Kasche, Bader, Benzler and Veesenmayer.¹ The following day the Croats were also included in the talks (Slavko Kvaternik and General Laxa). The Germans suggested common approach to the military aspects of mopping up operation. Their forces around Sarajevo were to occupy the mountain passes around Sarajevo and Tarčin. The Italians were to be asked to reach those passes simultaneously from their zone. For this operation the support of 10-12 Croatian battalions was needed. In addition to the Sarajevo operation, the insurgent area in the region of Banja Luka was  also to be "mopped up" of insurgents at the same time. The Italians were to be asked for support in the same manner as in the Sarajevo operation.²

The first round of talks in Abbazia (the final venue, rather than Sušak) took place on March 2. It included only Germans and Italians. Kuntze elaborated on his proposed plan of operations along the lines agreed in Zagreb two days earlier. General Ambrosio, however – in his new role of the army chief of staff – had different ideas. Symptomatically, he started by saying that "only Croatia will be considered" – whereby he meant by "Croatia" only the German zone of occupation, to the north of the demarcation line. To an even greater surprise of Kuntze and other Germans he added that, supposedly in accordance with the agreement between Keitel and Cavallero, the Italian Second Army would have command of the joint operation. This was not how the Germans had understood the agreement on the question of command. Ambrosio then suggested that the focus of operations should be on eastern Bosnia, around Sarajevo at first, so that Axis forces should not be split; western Bosnia would be dealt with later. He then came to the crucial part:

> After the operation it will be necessary to leave large and smaller Italian garrisons as police in the insurgent territory until Croatia can provide sufficient police forces. Because of this the demarcation line will be discontinued. An eventual shifting of the demarcation line must, if the occasion arises, remain reserved for a later ruling.³

---

[1] T-120, roll 208, No. 366. Kasche to Ribbentrop, Zagreb, 28 February 1942.
[2] Hehn, op. cit. p. 109; also on T-501, roll 267.
[3] ibid. p. 110.

Kuntze avoided a direct answer but insisted on the need for simultaneous operations in both east and west Bosnia. He thought this possible if the Italians could secure three or four divisions. The following day, March 3, Croatian General Laxa joined the talks.[1] The Italians stuck to the position that sufficient forces were not available for simultaneous operations both east of Sarajevo and west of Banja Luka, and suggested that they should be taken in succession (hence designations *Trio I* and *Trio II*). The Germans reluctantly accepted this model. The starting points and allocated forces for the east Bosnian operation were also agreed. (The protocol assigned the Croatian forces a secondary role: unlike German and Italian units they were not listed by name, but merely mentioned as the reserve of the German 718 division.) But while the Germans wanted an early start, the Italians said they could not be ready until April 15, "after the snows melt." The final agreement reflected this demand.[2]

The key political issue in this protocol (point 8) concerned the authority in the pacified areas: "After the pacification of the individual zones the Croatian civilian authorities will be appointed for administration according to the decision of the Commander in Chief of the Italian Army." The potential significance of this provision went unnoticed by the politically less-than-astute General Laxa, who signed the Protocol without complaint. However, State Secretary Vrančić spotted the problem on the train back to Zagreb and alerted Lorković and Slavko Kvaternik immediately on his return there.[3]

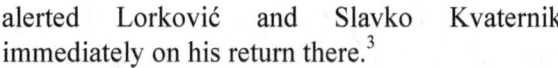

Point 8 gave rise to the Ustaša fears that if Italians move into east Bosnia they would not leave the area, including the key city of Sarajevo. Slavko Kvaternik (in his 1942 "Marshal's" uniform, l.) addressed a letter to Keitel expressing Croatian anxieties and asked that they be brought to Hitler's notice. Kvaternik asked that the demarcation line remain unmoved, and that administrative authority stay with the NDH organs. Among German officials in Zagreb these objections caused some

---

[1] Full German minutes of the Abbazia discussions are on T-120, roll 208. Also in ADAP, E, I, Goettingen 1972, pp. 33-35.

[2] Full Protocol is in Hehn, op. cit. pp. 112-113.

[3] Vrančić, op. cit. Vol. 2, pp. 232-236.

rethinking. In his report to Weizsäcker in Berlin on 6 March Veesenmayer warned that the Italians' operations could extend a long way beyond the demarcation line, with the affected territory coming under Italian permanent administration.[1] Kasche suggested a supplement to the Abbazia Protocol, which would guarantee return of NDH administration "as soon as possible."[2] Glaise was also worried about Italian intentions, which in his case was a permanent state of mind.

In the end Weizsäcker suggested to Ribbentrop a diplomatic solution. Since Germany should not be seen as an advocate of the NDH in its relations with Italy, the Croats should be asked to present their proposal on administration of the zone of operations to the German and Italian high commands. This proposal would then be subject to further discussions between Rome and Berlin. Weizsäcker also noted – appropriately enough – that Croat representatives were in Abbazia and could have suggested changes to the Protocol if they so desired. He concluded that Germany should not ask for additional clauses suggested by Kasche.

On March 14 Troll-Obergfell was given a verbal note by the NDH foreign ministry which formally restated all of the earlier objections to the Abbazia Protocol.[3] The Germans decided against taking any diplomatic steps. Instead, both the OKW and the Italian Supreme Command approved the Protocol in its original form on March 17, whereby it became final.[4]

When Bader, Roatta and Laxa met in Ljubljana for final talks on 28 March, the Italians once again brought up the moot question of passage through Sarajevo, Croatian administration of the occupied zone, and the "disturbing question" of negotiations with the rebels.[5] At the very beginning of the conference Roatta startled all by saying that Vrančić had informed him that the NDH government intended to provide the Četniks in Herzegovina with weapons, in exchange for which they would fight against Communists and secure the border with Montenegro. Laxa, somewhat confused, admitted that some talks with insurgents had indeed taken place. Roatta eagerly added that he therefore considered that the German and Italian authorities were also authorized to negotiate with them. As far as he was concerned, Article 10 of the Abbazia Protocol, which prohibited such negotiations, was void.

---

[1] PA, Büro RAM 13, Kroatien, No. 570. Weizsäcker to Ribbentrop, Berlin, 6 March 1942.
[2] T-120, roll 208. Weizsaecker to Ribbentrop, 7 March 1942. Also: ADAP, E, II, pp. 27-29.
[3] ADAP, E, II, No. 448, of 14 March 1942.
[4] V.I.I. Zbornik, XII/2, p. 108, No. 25, # 18. Comando Supremo to 2. Armata, 17 March 1942.
[5] Combat Group Bader Ia No. 101/42 of 29 March 1942, in Hehn, p. 119-120.

 The Ustašas were be embarrassed by the wily Roatta, who had arranged the meeting between Četnik representatives and Vrančić. A few days earlier Vrančić was appointed administrative commissioner with the Second Army. While still in Zagreb he unexpectedly received an invitation to talk with Dobroslav Jevdjević (l.), a prominent Četnik political leader from eastern Bosnia-Herzegovina. Since Jevdjević's close relationship with the Italians was common knowledge, Vrančić went to Sušak and informed Roatta of the invitation. The latter apparently expected this and offered to arrange a meeting the following day in Split. Roatta even provided his hydroplane to Vrančić and the meeting took place at General Dalmazzo's headquarters. The meeting was not productive but Roatta dramatized its implications in order to discredit the Croats and justify continuation of his Četnik policy.[1]

The whole German strategy appeared in shambles again, just a little over two weeks before the planned beginning of "Trio": instead of unity of purpose and policy there was disagreement; instead of a division of military tasks from political issues the two were more intertwined than ever. On 30 March, obviously in some despair, Kuntze telegraphed Rintelen in Rome, asking his intervention with Cavallero to stop Roatta's plans, "to avoid endangering the success of the joint operation."[2] Addressing the OKW three days later, Kuntze changed his pitch. Instead of seeking the means to enforce the ban on Roatta's negotiations with the non-Communist rebels, Kuntze asked to be allowed to conduct such negotiations himself:

"Should General Roatta adhere to his decision, which he considers tactically absolutely necessary," Kuntze wrote, "then Combat Group Bader must also be empowered to negotiate with the national Serb bands, otherwise Roatta's plan would be endangered."[3] This was an attempt by Kuntze to obtain clearance from Berlin for an approach he regarded as advisable and reasonable, but could not be pursued without prior clearance, in view of the

---

[1] Cf. Vrančić, op. cit. Vol. 2, pp. 265-270. For Kasche's report on Vrančić's mission, see T-120, roll 208, frame 603. Kasche to the Foreign Ministry, 6 April 1942.
[2] *Wehrmachtbefehlshaber Südost* Ia, No. 845/42 of 30 March 1942, in Hehn, p. 121
[3] Wehrmachtbefehlshaber Südost Ia, No. 869/42 of 3 April 1942.

way the attempt with Dangić had ended. The reply from Berlin, however, was predictable: no negotiations with "the bands" were allowed, regardless of their coloring.[1] Similar instructions were passed on from the Comando Supremo in Rome to the Second Army.[2] In the event Roatta never regarded them as binding, while his German colleagues hardly expected that he would.

In the end, there was no "Trio"; at best, there was a "Duo." Roatta kept postponing the planned commencement date, finding a series of ingenious excuses. He complained of transport difficulties ("the threat of British submarines in the Adriatic"), of climate ("deep snow in several regions of north Herzegovina"), of the inadequacy of roads and railroads to the take-off area.[3] Exasperated, Bader decided to go it alone. He exploited an advance by two *Black Legion* Ustaša battalions under Lt. Col. Jure Francetić (below) in the area of Rogatica and Srebrenica (April 8-11) and ordered 718th German division into action on April 14 without waiting for the Italians. A week later he reported: "Joint German-Italian operation miscarried due to the absence of Italians. [...] No subsequent fitting in of Italian forces is possible."[4]

By the time his "Combat Group Bader" was dissolved on May 28 its combing operations had been completed with a mixed success. It was possible for German-Croatian units to penetrate eastern Bosnia, with the notorious Ustaša "Black Legion" indulging in the customary orgy of slaughter of Serb civilians in the process. Most Partisan units managed to escape south, however, towards Sanjak and the area of the Italian zone where Bosnia, Herzegovina and Montenegro meet. Dangić and most of his men were taken prisoner and deported to Germany.

The ensuing anti-Partisan operation in western Bosnia, in the region west of Banja Luka (Kozara mountain, June-July 1942) was also a purely German

---

[1] German Liaison Officer with the Italian Second Army, No. 0785/42 of 7 April 1942, in Hehn, op. cit., p. 127.

[2] Hehn, op. cit., p. 125.

[3] Ibid. p. 124.

[4] Ibid. p. 127.

 affair with some Croatian support. It was notable for a new round of atrocities against the Serb civilians all over the Kozara region (l.). This time they were perpetrated without much German opposition since the victims were presumed to be guilty by association, having found themselves in the insurgent-held territory. Ustaša units were not allowed to engage in anti-Serb hunts on their own, however, or of their own volition, if the Germans could help it. On June 12, 1942, *Feldgendarmerie* disarmed an Ustaša company after they murdered several Serb civilians in Sokolac, in eastern Bosnia.[1] In late October, another Ustaša company was disarmed in the vicinity of Sarajevo and ten of its members arrested by the Wehrmacht.[2]

The absence of Italian troops from operations in either eastern or western Bosnia indicated that Roatta was not interested in shedding the blood of the Second Army unless he could be assured of tangible *political* gains. With their confidence in their chief ally badly shaken, the Germans were in for a new surprise in June and July 1942: general Roatta suddenly withdrew Italian forces from most of Zone 3 and parts of Zone 2. He did so hastily and thus created a power vacuum in a large corridor from Bosanska Krajina in the northwest to Sanjak in the southeast. With the war in Russia and North Africa entering the decisive phase, Ambrosio's motives for reoccupation of this area a year earlier no longer applied. Roatta wanted to save his forces and have them at hand near the coast, rather than continue the seemingly endless game of bloody hide-and-seek in the Dinaric wilderness.

The Ustaša government was delighted by Roatta's sudden readiness to give them a foothold south of the demarcation line.[3] On June 19 an agreement was signed in Zagreb by Pavelić and Roatta providing for the return of NDH civilian administration, although limitations still applied in places where the

---

[1] BA/MA,RH 31 III/2 Der Deutsche General in Agram an das OKW, 16 Juni.1942.

[2] BA/MA, RH 26-114/14 Lagebericht des Kdr.Gen. fuer die Zeit 8 November 1942.

[3] On Roatta's visit to Zagreb see T-120, roll 208, No. 1470. Kasche to the Foreign Ministry, 20 June 1942.

Italians retained their garrisons.[1] In return Pavelić was prepared to swallow the bitter pill of legalizing Četniks under Italian patronage, under the label of "anti-Communist armed groups."

There was a key limitation of the Ustašas' freedom of action, however: local Italian commands could veto all actions by the NDH security forces. It is evident that neither Pavelić nor his aides were involved in preparing the agreement. Both economics minister Vladko Košak and envoy to Supersloda Vrančić suspected that the deal was simply too good to be true. They did not bear in mind, it appears, that the NDH forces were hardly able to cope with the insurgency north of the German-Italian demarcation line, where they could rely on the Germans who did not shun action against the "bandits." Garrisoning large additional areas would have been a challenge even under peaceful conditions. While ostensibly presenting Pavelić with a "gift," Roatta was contributing to further destabilization of the NDH.

The danger was not lost on the Germans; the OKW was first alerted to the risks inherent in Roatta's plan only three days after the signing of the agreement in Zagreb.[2] On July 2 a new warning came from Salonika that it would be difficult to establish raport between national Serb bands and Croats. Since the Croats were equal neither to the "national Serbs" nor to the Communists, the area evacuated by the Italians would become "a continuous insurgent center."[3] Kuntze expressed concern for the crucial bauxite mines near Mostar, and some hope that, after the suppression of insurgents in eastern Bosnia, there was not going to be yet another flare-up, now in the Italian-evacuated area. That this was an idle hope was confirmed already on July 4, when strong Partisan forces attacked several points on the key railroad connecting Sarajevo with Mostar. Besides, in many places (e.g. Bihać, Ključ, Bosanski Petrovac, Drvar, Glamoč, Kupres, Livno, Prozor) the Italian withdrawal occurred without prior notification, enabling the Partisans to take advantage of the situation. This prompted some Germans to suspect deliberate Italian policy of creating problems for Pavelić's government.[4] With increasing alarm the Germans registered the steady advance of Tito's "proletarian brigades," battle-hardened shock units, along the newly vacated corridor just south of the demarcation line.[5]

---

[1] For full text of the agreement see: V.I.I. Zbornik, V/32, pp. 303-310, No. 116.

[2] Hehn, op. cit., p. 131,

[3] T-120, roll 380, No. 1864. SD to Luther, 8 July 1942.

[4] Cf. Krizman (1983), p. 348.

[5] E.g. T-120, roll 380, No. 1864. Police Attaché Helm to SD, Zagreb, 23 July 1942.

The long march into the geographic heart of the Croatian state gave a new impetus to the Partisan activity throughout the area evacuated by the Italians. It enabled Tito in the second half of 1942 to establish a large territory under his control, to recruit new men, and to recover from the crisis of the previous winter and spring. By November he felt emboldened enough to create a quasi-legislative body, AVNOJ (Anti-Fascist Council of the National Liberation of Yugoslavia) which announced the abolition of monarchy as its formal rogram.

The main benefactors of Roatta's partial retreat to the coastal belt were the Partisans. Pressured from all sides, they surged in the direction of least resistance. Had Italian garrisons remained, it is doubtful that Tito's penetration of the corridor to western Bosnia would have been accomplished so successfully and swiftly. Being outside German reach had become an obvious prerequisite for Tito's survival, but avoiding combat with entrenched Italian garrisons was also a necessity. Italian soldiers were disinclined to carry out offensive operations in the Balkans but they were tenacious defenders of solidly fortified positions.[1] Many cases of Partisan atrocities over Italian prisoners, notably in Montenegro but also in Dalmatia, provided additional motivation to fight rather than surrender.

The fighting qualities of the Italian soldier (l.) were regarded as inferior by the Germans, Ustašas and Partisans alike. It is a matter of record, however, that the Italian Army was able to retain control over areas it deemed essential until the collapse in September 1943. All key points in the Italian-held area, all key urban centres – Ljubljana, Karlovac, Knin, Šibenik, Split, Dubrovnik, Mostar, Kotor, Podgorica and Cetinje... – remained under firm control until September 1943. The coastal road along the Adriatic and key railroads (Rijeka-Ogulin-Split and Mostar-Dubrovnik-Zelenika) remained operative in Italian hands throughout the period.

---

[1] For a detailed study of the Italian Army performance from an official Italian viewpoint, see the official history: Salvatore Loi. *Le Operazioni Delle Unita Italiane in Jugoslavia (1941-1943)*. Ministero della Difesa, Stato Maggiore dell'Escrito, Ufficio Storico, Rome 1978.

6. The Četnik Dilemma

A salient feature of Italian occupation policy was its support of the local Serb population in its attempts to resist Ustaša onslaughts, and its tolerance - gradually turning into patronage - of their armed groups, commonly known as Četniks. General Dalmazzo was an early promoter of such policy in his area (Dubrovnik and Herzegovina) which would split the insurgents and turn Četniks into part of the solution, rather than part of the problem of occupation.

Increasingly hostile to the Ustaša regime and jealous of the Germans, and yet unable to devise a truce with the intransigent Communists, Italian commanders were prone to read too much into the Serb nationalist movement, seeing sometimes more strength, discipline and leadership than was justified. They also expected that by establishing a relationship based on their protégés' dependence for arms and supplies they could contain the Četniks' anti-Croat revanchism, and turn them primarily into an effective anti-Communist force. In the summer of 1941 the goal of the Italian army was to reassure Serb insurgents, to make them lay down their arms and go home. A year later the aim was to strengthen them for deployment against Tito's men. By building up the credibility of local Četnik leaders in their zone of occupation, the Italians also hoped to prevent any attempt by General Mihailović (r.) to bring them to heel. For his part Mihailović avoided direct contact with the Italians, although the British were  encouraging him to maintain contact with them and to take advantage of their possible withdrawal, collapse, or surrender.[1] Both sides wanted to avoid clashes, and in any event Mihailović operated mainly outside the Italian zone in 1941-42.

The departure of Italian troops from large areas of their zone in the summer of 1942 was accompanied by Pavelić's undertaking to recognize those very Četnik units which had been vilified by the Ustašas for a year as the source of all evil in the NDH. While most observers regarded any NDH-Četnik détente as impossible, in the summer of 1942, in some areas at least, it was in both sides' interest to try and reach a modus vivendi. The first high-

---

[1] See statement by Peter E. Boughey of the wartime Yugoslav Section, S.O.E. London, quoted in Nora Beloff (1985), p. 78.

ranking NDH official to establish direct contact with Četnik representatives was the Croatian delegate to the Second Army, Vjekoslav Vrančić, but his meeting with Jevdjević and Grdjić in Split was unsuccessful. The encounter was probably set up by Roatta to embarrass the Croats on the eve of final discussions in Ljubljana about "Trio." Vrančić's posture at least indicated the willingness of certain more pragmatic circles in Zagreb to restore some religious and property rights of the Serbs.

At the end of April 1942 a local Serb commander in western Bosnia, Uroš Drenović established contact with the Domobrans in the area of Varcar Vakuf. Drenović's men were under attack by superior Partisan forces from Drvar and the Croatian garrison was also hard pressed. The result was a rare agreement between the perennial adversaries, signed on April 27. This agreement was sanctioned by the NDH Armed Forces Ministry, and approvingly referred to by Glaise.[1] In several locations all over Bosnia local Četnik commanders and *Domobran* officers and municipal officials rather than Ustašas, signed agreements similar to the one reached by Drenović.[2] To both sides it was clearly a temporary expedient. In the multi-cornered war all kinds of temporary alliances are possible, however, as the Partisans were to prove a year later. With the proletarian brigades' "long march" in full swing, both Domobran units and Četnik detachments in their path were in a similar predicament. The two sides preferred to get out of each other's way and take advantage of even just a few weeks' respite. The fragility of the armistice was only emphasized by the news of fresh Ustaša atrocities in other parts of the NDH. In the summer of 1942 Glaise sent to the OKW a series of new reports of anti-Serb outrages. He knew that to the Ustaša leadership the notion of a *loyal Serb* was a contradiction in terms. The treaties with their armed groups they saw as an insult that could be tolerated only temporarily.

By the end of 1942 the occupation system established in Yugoslavia after April 1941 was in tatters. Most of the NDH was in a state of chaos, with effective Ustaša authority reduced to less than half its territory. German attempts to devise a common military strategy had failed, owing to Italian

---

[1] V.I.I. Zbornik, IV/4, No. 136. Croatian Armed Forces Ministry daily report No. 120 of 30 April 1942. T-501, roll 264, frame 1056. Glaise to OKW, Zagreb, 1 May 1942.

[2] Similar agreements were signed by Lazar Tešanović, commander of Četnik battalion "Mrkonjić" on 23 May 1942; commander of Četnik units of the Ozren and Trebava mountains, on 28 May; Radoslav Račić, commander of Četnik detachment "Borja," on 9 June in Banja Luka; Borivoje Keserović, commander of the Majevica mountain, on 15 June; and by Radivoje Kosorić, for eastern Bosnia, on 16 January 1943. The last of the above managed to carry on his lonely struggle in the mountains around Pljevlja well into the 1950's. He was eventually killed by a booby-trapped radio. (Kosorić's niece Danojla to the author, 1983)

unwillingness to fight a war on German terms for the sake of the Ustašas who had caused trouble in the first place. Italian attempts to maintain peace in their occupation zone had also failed, as became obvious with the push of Tito's brigades from the southeast. The myriad of Četnik units throughout the NDH, while composed of capable men and sometimes ably led – notably by the Dinara Division commander Djujić (below) who combined military ability and political skill. To their misfortune they were not unified and lacked centralized command and control structure. Mihailović was recognized as their leader only nominally: Local commanders went on coping as best they could, and hoping for a British landing.

After almost two years in power the Ustašas had failed to exterminate the Serbs, and they were unable to quell the unrest – even locally – without German support. They had failed to consolidate the Independent State of Croatia, which was growing less *independent*, less of a *state*, and less *Croatian* by the day. The symbolism was but the substance was ebbing away. This failure was not merely military. It went to the roots of the Ustašas' political purpose. They were not interested merely in gaining power in an "independent" Greater Croatia, and consolidating the state. Its attainment was linked to the major project in social  engineering that entailed eliminating one-third of the population – some two million Serbs – by means of physical extermination, expulsion, or conversion. The two objectives, while inseparable in the minds of Pavelić and his cohorts, were incompatible. Just as Hitler contributed to his own defeat by openly presenting the Barbarossa as a war of conquest over the Slavic *Untermensch* and thus leaving the Russians no alternative but to fight for sheer survival, Pavelić's core vision precluded the possibility of "stabilization" of the NDH by making its existence contingent upon the destruction of the Serbs.

On the eve of Stalingrad and El Alamein the role of the Ustašas in Hitler's New Europe was marginal but nevertheless disproportionate. With their stunning bloodlust they helped create a minor nuisance for Hitler and a focus of some interest for the British and the Soviets, in the form of Tito's Partisans. Of all the groups in the Hobbesian Yugoslav nightmare, by the fall of 1942 the Partisans were the only ones who could say that they were not doing too badly under the circumstances.

IX
Germany Takes the Initiative

1. German Economic Dominance

Hitler and his aides constantly reiterated to their Roman allies that Italy enjoyed precedence in Croatia. However, by the second half of 1942, Germany was beginning to play an ever increasing role in Croatian military and political affairs. Two factors contributed to this. One was the rise of insurgent activity, which occasionally threatened key military and economic interests, such as the railroad from Belgrade to Zagreb and the mining of strategic minerals in Bosnia-Herzegovina. The other factor, potentially more serious, was the external threat to the Balkan peninsula. For the first time, German commanders had to consider the possibility of an Allied landing on the Adriatic coast. In order to deal with both threats, the Germans had to disregard old Italian claims to precedence in the Independent State of Croatia. At first, it seems, this did not happen due to an elaborate design, but more or less incrementally and spontaneously – just as most German arrangements in occupied Europe tended to proceed.

In 1942 there was no German master plan, in the Balkans or beyond, for the European "New Order." Contrary to the prevailing post-war wisdom, which tended to read in all of Hitler's actions a systematic premeditated quest for hegemony in Europe, or even world domination, his notions of "global power" and "eastern empire" should be taken as metaphors or "utopian figures of speech."[1] Post-war planning was a major theme in various elements of the Nazi power structure; but all they had in common was a vague notion of the "rings" of control, radiating from the centre and mainly extending east- and southeastwards. Typically for an unsystematic mind, piecemeal projects sometimes caught Hitler's imagination. One such was to turn Belgrade and the area around it into a "Reich fortress," from which all Serbs would be removed and German settlers brought in.[2]

No such plan, on a macro- or micro-level, had ever attained the status of official policy. Competing ideas and designs for a New Order only had to fit

---

[1] See Martin Broszat, 'Soziale Motivation und Fuehrerbindung,' in *Vierteljahrshefte für Zeitgeschichte*, IV (Oct. 1970), 392-409.

[2] On the 'Reich Fortress Belgrade,' see Hans-Ulrich Wehler, 'Reichsfestung Belgrad,' in *Vierteljahrshefte für Zeitgeschichte*, No. 11, 1963.

into the Führer's overall framework. However, except for his anti-Jewish obsession, there was little guidance or consistency in Hitler's 'vision' of the new Europe. Therefore, in various sections of the Nazi bureaucracy one could even encounter moderate and relatively sensible ideas, which allowed for a degree of 'partnership' with the states which fought on the side of Germany.[1] Admittedly, the primacy of Germany was always implicitly taken for granted, even in relation to its 'partner,' Italy.

More common were some brutally frank ravings about the *Herrenvolk* and *Untermensch,* the kind of talk that emanated from the circles of Rosenberg's foreign department of the party and Himmler's SS. The first Croatian minister in Berlin, Branko Benzon, was fascinated by such talk. He counted among his friends in Berlin a group of "SS intellectuals," among whom the most prominent figure was *Brigadeführer* Walter Stahlecker (r.), who openly talked of conquering the whole world.[2] He and his circle reveled in "half a billion Germans by the year 2000." In a matter-of-fact manner they spoke of Germanizing smaller nations – Croats, as self-styled "Goths," naturally included.

At times the tension between different visions of the future held by different German agencies could not be concealed. The Slovak minister in Berlin recalled a characteristic episode which occurred at a dinner hosted by him.[3] A young German officer, rather drunk, delivered an impromptu oration about his exploits on the Russian front from which he had just returned. He enthused about the destruction of the "Slav Untermensch" and the re-enactment by the German Reich of the "holy and eternal laws of Life, desecrated by Christians, Jews and Slavs." He was cut short by a fellow guest, a high-ranking official from the ministry of propaganda. He took the officer away from the table and then proceeded to assure the horrified Slovak minister and other guests that the Reich was going to create a New Order in which each European nation would have its function and its place according to merit. In 1942, at the peak of Germany's conquests (map, opp p..), post-war planning started in earnest.

---

[1] One such 'sane' view was advocated in 'Vorschlage fur eine neue deutsche Kapitalpolitik,' *Mitteleuropaeischer Wirtschafitag* (Berlin, I 940).

[2] Luka Fertilio, "Poslanici NDH u Trećem Reichu." *Hrvatska* revija, XXV, 1 (March 1975), 50.

[3] Ibid. p. 53.

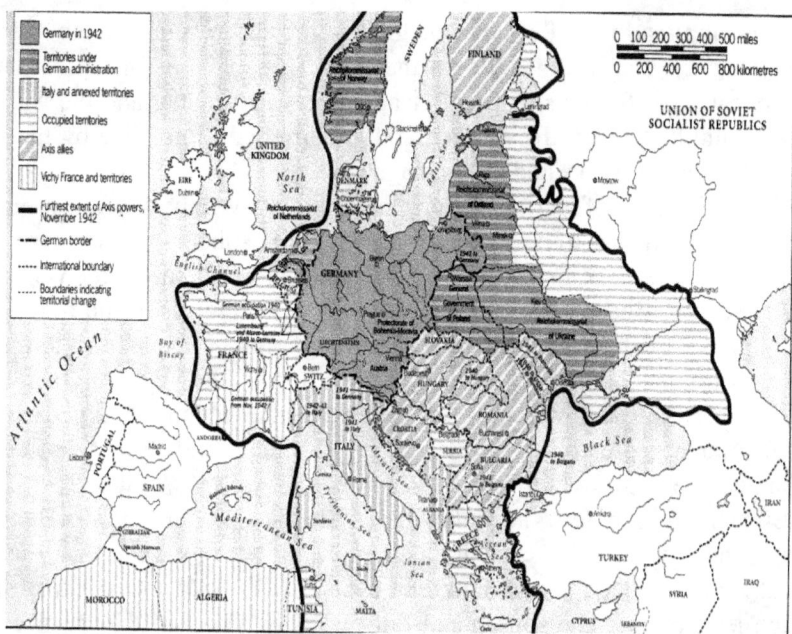

As far as can be deduced from Hitler's ad hoc and fragmentary comments, Croatia was not to be included in the 'first ring' of German power. Only later in the war Hitler started talking of the need to abolish the small states of Europe altogether, just as his power to do so diminished.[1] Until 1943 this core area, under direct German administration, supposedly comprised the Reich, the annexed and acquired areas, the entire Danube valley (with the status of Hungary a moot point) and "the eastern territories."[2] Beyond this sphere of immediate and unconcealed German control were the loosely defined second and third rings of dominance. This huge and diverse *Militittärgrenze* would feel German control less directly than the *Grossraum*, but its resources would be at the disposal of the Reich. This allowed for an Italian "zone of interest," but not in any way Mussolini would have found agreeable. Hitler may have been sincere in his protestations to his only "friend" that Croatia belonged to the *spazio vitale* of the new Roman Empire. Nevertheless, the logic of the distribution of power within the Axis camp dictated that an Italian sphere would exist only at the sufferance of the Reich.[3]

---

[1] *The Goebbels diaries*. Garden City, NY, 1948, p. 357; entry for 8 May 1943..

[2] Adolf Hitler, *Secret conversations, 1941-1944*. New York, 1953; entries for: 13 Oct. 1941; 26 Feb. 1942; 13 May 1942; 29 June 1942.

[3] Dietrich Orlow, *The Nazis in the Balkans: a case study of totalitarian politics*. Pittsburgh, 1968,, pp. 108-9.

The implications of such strategic realities were not lost on German military and civilian officials down the line. This explains the gap between often-repeated professions of Italy's leading role in Croatia, and the way this role was simultaneously disregarded and undermined in practice by the wide array of German military and civilian agencies.

The eariy signs of German determination to deny Italy its lomg-promised primacy in Croatia are to be found in the economic sphere. German economic domination in the Balkans, largely well-established even before the war broke out, was seen in Berlin as *conditio sine qua non*, regardless of the final shape of the "New Order." Italian zone of interest or not, in economic terms the NDH was treated as an integral part of "the South-East" by everybody who mattered in Berlin and Vienna. This applied to the economic experts of the foreign ministry, to the ministry of economics, and to its influential specialized agencies (notably the *Südosteuropa-Gesellschaft*, SOEG).

Eight months before Yugoslavia was attacked, in July 1940, Hermann Goering announced, in his capacity as the head of the four-year plan, the goal of establishing a continental economic system (*Grossraumwirtschaft*) under German leadership.[1] The subsequent fall of Yugoslavia and the creation of a Croatian state changed nothing in the applicability of these principles to the south-east. Such principles were well established by early 1941.[2] Each country's economic policy was to be shaped in line with German interests, Croatia's no less than Romania's or Bulgaria's. The economic development of each state in the area was to be restricted to the sectors in which Germany had a particular interest, such as agriculture, exploitation of mineral wealth and energy potential. Gearing these countries' primary and semi-processed goods to the German market would also make them irreversibly dependent upon Germany for most manufactured and finished goods.

On May 16, 1941, less than a week after the Ustaša state came into being, the Germans signed a "confidential protocol" on economic co-operation with the Croatian government. This document was in line with the above principles.[3] Bilateral committees were to be established, with two clear sets of guidelines: economic interests of the Reich would be taken into special account, and Germany was to enjoy the right of unlimited exploitation of industrial raw materials, above all ores. It was also promised preference if

---

[1] DGFP, ser. D, X, no. 103, p. 115. State Secretary and Deputy to the Commissioner for the Four Year Plan to the Foreign Ministry, the Deputy Führer *et al.,* 3 July 1940.

[2] Orlow (1968), p. 101.

[3] ADAP, D, XII, no. 526, p. 831. Confidential Croatian-German Economic Protocol, Zagreb, 16 May 1941.

new concessions were granted. Even before the Rome Agreements were signed later that month, formally regulating Croatia's status as a client state of Italy, the NDH was becoming an economic satellite of Germany. This was happening without Italian knowledge, let alone approval. In carrying out their plans for economic domination of Croatia so swiftly, the Germans enjoyed two advantages. First of all, Italy had failed to tie Croatia to itself in the economic sphere, even when it could devise formal mechanisms for doing so. During the improvised conference with Pavelić in Monfalcone, in the first week of May 1941, Mussolini had clumsily spoiled Ciano's plan to link Croatia to Italy through a customs union. Pavelić was allowed to get away with the vaguest of promises regarding future economic co-operation.

Furthermore, German economic interests were already granted extraordinary rights by the Italians themselves, at the foreign ministers' meeting in Vienna in April 1941. On that occasion, Ciano – apparently preoccupied with the territorial enlargement in Dalmatia – failed to take due notice of Ribbentrop's demand that the Reich be given special economic concessions in Croatia. He agreed to this without ado, guaranteeing German presence in the Italian-occupied zone, such as the bauxite mines in Herzegovina. Such demands were not limited to the Croat state. Italy also agreed in Vienna not to incorporate into its 'greater Albania' those parts of the Serbian province of Kosovo which were rich in lead and zinc: formally, Trepča and Mitrovica thus remained part of Nedić's rump-Serbia, under direct German control. Such instances were indicative of the fundamental Italian problem: lack of policy.

The Germans lacked a detailed master plan, but at least their individual agencies had an idea what overall direction they were taking. What was envisaged in Rome, however, was not one all-continental Grossraum, but two separate albeit allied spheres, supposedly self-contained, each with its own financial centres and currencies.[1] When it came to execution, however, the lack of coherence became obvious. The culture of power in its theatrical sense had left Mussolini oblivious to the importance of more mundane but deeper-penetrating devices. It is unlikely that Italy's claims to parity in the shaping of the New Order would have been accepted by Germany in the long run; at best, an Italian sub-sphere in a Reich-dominated Europe could have fitted into Hitler's broad picture. In either case, already in April 1941 the Germans regarded Croatia as a "second ring" nation for economic purposes, regardless of Italian aspirations.

---

[1] For a statement of Italian economic ambitions see: T- 120, cont. 1095, frames 4501 34-137, 148-9, 155-6. A memorandum by the Italian minister of trade Ricardi.

In June 1941 the Italians established a permanent Italian-Croatian economic commission on the basis of Article 4 of the Rome Agreements. It was headed on the Italian side by the former finance minister, Count Giuseppe Volpi di Misurata. His Croatian counterpart was Vladko Košak, an economic expert who was regarded (together with the foreign minister, Mladen Lorković) as one of the more capable men in Pavelić's largely mediocre team.

In 1941 the commission held three plenary meetings. At the first meeting the Croats preempted any Italian pressure for closer customs and monetary links, knowing that they could count on German support in their resistance to Italian demands. A trade and payments agreement was signed, but its validity was only three months.[1] It was not renewed: the subsequent two sessions were deliberately used by the Croatian side to present any meaningful economic cooperation as impossible, allegedly because of the Italian Army policy in the extended occupation zone.[2] Košak repeatedly claimed that the *de facto* removal of the customs frontier made further talks and agreements meaningless. His defiant posture was again underwritten by the discreet German encouragement to the Croats, through Kasche in Zagreb.

Subsequently, economic penetration of Croatia by Italy occurred only in the zone held by the Second Italian Army, in an area vastly less developed than the other, German-held half. The key industries in the *Ustaša* state were in Zagreb itself, in the central Bosnian basin Sarajevo-Zenica-Tuzla and in the Sava river valley – all of them in the German zone. The most important resource in the Italian zone – bauxite – was also in German hands, in accordance with the Vienna agreement between Ribbentrop and Ciano. Even what "exploitation" there was in the Italian zone was a crude and unsystematic affair. It consisted mainly of exporting timber, tobacco and foodstuffs across the non-existent customs boundary into Italy. The chief beneficiaries were some corrupt local Italian officials such as the prefect of Fiume, Temistocle Testa, who had allegedly made a fortune on Croatian timber deals.[3] On the whole, by the spring of 1942 the Italians realized that their nominal "zone of predominance" in Croatia was bringing them few tangible economic benefits. This led to renewed pressure on the Croats, and a demand that they agree to a customs union.[4] Particularly irritating to the Italians were several German-Croatian joint monopolies, founded in the

---

[1] *Hrvatski narod*, Zagreb, 17 and 24 June 1941.

[2] For the proceedings see: Vjekoslav Vrančić (1985), II, 145-9.

[3] Ibid. p. 149.

[4] ADAP, E, 2, pp. 300-2. Kasche to the Foreign Ministry, 1 May 1942.

preceding months, most importantly for the manufacture of chemicals and explosives. The Croats were reminded that the NDH belonged to the "Italian greater economic zone." The meaning of this term was left vague, and Italian rhetoric was not accompanied by a concrete set of specific proposals. In the end, all came down to a demand that Zagreb should not sign any new far-reaching economic agreement without informing Rome first. Once again, the Italians applied verbal pressure which was not followed by any tangible gains.

Things looked more serious in July 1942, when a Croatian delegation came to Venice for talks on 'fundamental issues' with a top-level Italian trade and economic team. At the same time a press campaign got under way in Italy, led by Virginio Gayda who was regarded as the voice of officialdom. He argued that the interests of "the dominant power" (Italy) in its Balkan sphere of influence had to be given priority.[1] *Giornale d'Italia* complained that the government of Croatia was not taking into account the fundamental economic interests of Italy.[2] The Croats were worried and asked German minister Kasche for help.[3] They even suggested giving up the German-Croatian monopoly in chemicals, if this could stave off renewed Italian demands regarding customs union and currency reform.[4] A week later Zagreb repeated its request for German advice and support.[5]

Whereas in political matters Germany was careful not to be drawn into the role of an arbiter, and especially not to be seen as supportive of Croatian demands, in economic issues such inhibitions were absent. This enabled the Croatian team to return to Rome in the second week of August determined to resist Italian pressure, secure in the knowledge that quiet German encouragement enabled them to do so.[6] In the event, Italian demands fell short of the customs union, and everything continued as before. After August 1942 there followed further tensions between Italy and Pavelić's government in the political and military sphere. In the key field of economy, however, the Italians lacked the strategy and effective means of ensuring a strong presence in Croatia, let alone domination. German precedence in all areas of the NDH economy continued unchallenged until the end.

---

[1] T-120, roll 208, No. 1894. Troll-Obergfell to the Foreign Ministry, 25 July 1942.

[2] Bogdan Krizman, *Ustaše i Treći Reich* (Zagreb, 1983), p. 357.

[3] T-120, roll 208, No. 1894. Troll-Obergfell to the Foreign Ministry, 25 July 1942.

[4] T-120, roll 208, No. 1902 of 25 July 1942.

[5] T-120, roll 208, No. 1948. Kasche to the Foreign Ministry, 31 July 1942.

[6] T-120, roll 208, No. 2089. Kasche to the Foreign Ministry, 12 Aug. 1942.

2. German Generals vs. Pavelić

By the early autumn of 1942 the Balkans had become a regular topic of discussion at the OKW. The growth of Tito's Partisans in the NDH was the chief cause of increased concern for an area which was regarded as peripheral to the war effort until that time. The existence of a hundred thousand armed men under Communist command within speedy reach of the possible Allied landing points on the Adriatic was understandably regarded as intolerable.

Events in Russia and in northern Africa precluded any engagement of sizeable German forces; even with some reinforcements in 1942 they only amounted to two and a half weak divisions in the whole of the NDH. Croatian conscript home guards, the *Domobranstvo,* were unreliable and undisciplined. Imposition of German operational command over Croatian units north of the demarcation line was seen as necessary by an increasing number of German officials. This was the clear message from the commanders in the field, and it was repeatedly echoed in Zagreb by Glaise. He wanted all Croatian units from the size of battalion upwards brought under German control.[1] This, of course, would imply a further erosion of Italy's position, and a further step towards turning Croatia into a *Reichsprotektorat* in fact, if not in name.

An episode in the Bosnian town of Livno, in the Italian zone, contributed to the view that direct German control over Croatian units was necessary. A group of about a dozen German civilians working for the company *Hansa-Leichtmetall* organized strong resistance when the Partisans attacked Livno in August 1942. They were eventually overwhelmed and captured, but engineer Hans Ott – the leader of the group – eventually arranged the first successful exchange of prisoners between the two sides.[2] In his subsequent report, Ott stated that most Croat soldiers ran

---

[1] T-501, roll 264. Glaise to Lohr, 11 Sept. 1942.

[2] Cf. Slavko Odić, *Neostvareni planovi* (Zagreb, 1961), p. 245f; Krizman (1983), pp. 375-88.

away as soon as the attack had started. Some were forced back to their positions, literally at gunpoint, by the handful of Germans. Subsequently they were "quite useful" defenders and a few received German medals and battle badges (opp. p.); but German determination and guidance was needed to make them so.[1] Left to their own devices they were unreliable. During the Kozara operation against Tito's forces in the spring of 1942, Brigadier General Stahl, who commanded the West Bosnian Combat Group, constantly had to intervene to prop up "the unsteady Croats." They were often "seized by panic," he reported to the OKW, to the point where "two Croatian battalions lost all their ammunition, machine guns, and entire equipment."[2]

The problem of the Home Guard reliability was chronic to the NDH. To an untrained eye they looked like German soldiers (below) but they rarely fought like Landsers. The failure of the *Domobranstvo* to become an effective fighting force was due to several factors. It suffered from chronic shortages of artillery and other heavy weapons, despite repeated promises to remedy the situation by Germany and Italy. Its officer corps was inadequate to the task of fighting a counter-insurgency war. Large numbers of Croat officers on active duty in the Royal Yugoslav army initially joined the Home Guard, but they were mistrusted by the returning Ustaša émigrés. The senior ranks were filled by presumably more reliable former Austro-Hungarian officers. They were men in their late fifties or older, however, long retired and ill-versed in modern warfare.[3] Pavelić's attempts to remedy this with hastily designed officer training courses produced a number of competent younger professionals by the end of the war, but too late to affect the outcome.

---

[1] T- 120, roll 1141, No. 2485/42. Helm to Himmler, Sarajevo 21 Sept. 1942.

[2] Paul N. Hehn (ed.), *The German struggle against Yugoslav guerrillas in World War II: German counter-insurgency in Yugoslavia 1941-1943* (New York, I 975) , p. 129.

[3] Their younger colleagues called them *Mirogojci*, after Zagreb's Mirogoj cemetery.

A significant problem was the rivalry between the Home Guard and the Ustaša militia, which despised the former for its lask of fighting spirit and its unwillingness to engage in murderous sprees against the Serbs. The two were never fully integrated, the program initiated in December 1944 to do so notwithstanding, and as the war progressed the Ustaša were taking ever more dwindling resources from the Domobrans. The lack of combat effectiveness of the Home Guard reflected the chronic problem of morale. Overwhelmingly, the conscripts were neither enthusiastic "new Croats" in Pavelić's mould of fierce lions and wolves nor fervent revolutionaries in Tito's image of self-sacrificing proletarian shock-troops. They were peasants keen to go home and shying away from a fight they did not feel as their own. To most of them neither the prospect of slitting "Vlach" throats nor the prospect of fighting under the red star for a communist "New Yugoslavia" proved appealing. When the war started going badly for the Axis, the problem became acute for the NDH authorities. (In Petrovaradin, across the Danube from Novi Sad, in Septemberr 1944 the local Domobran garrison went over to the Partisans en masse, including the regimental band.). Integrated units were effective in preventing further en masse desertions to the Partisans. Shootings of would-be deserters *pour encourager les autres* were an additional feature of the attempt to rekindle some fighting spirit among the conscripts.

Faced with the spreading insurgency, the inability of the Domobran units to deal with the situation, and the growing hostility of Glaise in Zagreb and German officers in the field, Pavelić dismissed Slavko Kvaternik as commander of the Home Guard and his son Eugen-Dido as head of the principal security service (RAVSIGUR). He also allowed temporary truces with local Četnik units, mainly in Bosnia, provided that they focused their energies on fighting the Partisans.

Last but not least, he made an attempt to diversify the methods of solving the Serb question by creating the "Croatian Orthodox Church" in April 1942. This was a half-hearted attempt at nominal Croatization of the surviving Serbs, following the lackluster results of conversion to Roman Catholicism.[1] Neither option was taken seriously by the hard-line Ustaša – led by Pavelić himself – who preferred extermination plain and simple.

---

[1] The hierarchy, led by Archbishop Stepinac, was unenthusiastic about what was obviously conversion under duress. Contrary to earlier estimates, no more than 100,000 Serbs – some 6 percent of the total – were converted in 1942-43. Even this option was closed to Jews and Gypsies, and to 'Greek-Eastern school teachers, priests, tradesmen, artisans, rich peasants and the intelligentsia.' The Serbs in the old Military Border region south of the Sava River, regardless of social or educational status, were also not allowed to convert.

After September 1941 further expulsions to Serbia were halted by the Germans in Belgrade for reasons of internal security. Even the head of the new "Church" was a Russian émigré monk, Germogen (with Pavelić, below), rather than one of the fifty or so "Croat Orthodox" clerics who were drafted into its ranks. The schizophrenic nature of the experiment doomed it to failure. Traumatized by the experience of the preceding twelve months of

terror, most Serbs saw the self-designated *Croatian Orthodox Church* as a tactical ploy rather than as a viable means of finding personal or group security through the acceptance of the Croat designation.

Their suspicions were well founded: the slaughters of civilians continued in early 1942. On February 7 the Ustašas killed over two thousand unarmed Serbs in the villages of Drakulić and Šargovac just outside of Banja Luka, and at a nearby mine, well away from the areas of insurgent activity; 343 victims were children under the age of 14.[1] In March a punitive Ustaša expedition was sent to Kordun, already "cleansed" in the summer of 1941. In March and April the Ustaša *Black Legion* operations in eastern Bosnia took the lives of some 3,000 Serb civilians in the municipalities of Sokolac, Han Pijesak, Milići, Vlasenica and Bratunac. For none of them was the acceptance of "Croatian Orthodoxy" an option. For the perpetrators, any attempt at Croatizing the despised "Vlachs" was an unwelcome distraction from the task at hand.

---

[1] One of the leaders of the killing party was an Ustaša chaplain, Fr. Miroslav Filipović from the nearby Prebićevac Monastery. A schoolteacher at the Šargovac school, who survived because she was a Croat, recalled that she had no reason to be alarmed when Filipović arrived at the school because on previous occasions his manner had been friendly. When Filipović and some Ustaše entered her classroom, the children looked on with curiosity but no fear. But Filipović then took a child, Vasilija Glamočanin, and slit her throat in front of the class. He then urged the Ustaša who accompanied him to deal similarly with the other children, and assured them that he would take the sin upon himself. Similar atrocities occurred on 12 February 1942 at two more villages in the area, Piskavica and Ivanjska. At Glaise's insistence Filipović was court-martialed and handed over to the Ustaša for internment. He was subsequently appointed a top commander at Jasenovac, where he became known as "Fr. Satan."

Glaise and German commanders were incensed by the Ustašas' continuing murderous zeal. In the spring of 1942 German units were ordered into action to disarm an unruly Black Legion unit (four of its brigade HQ officers, r.) which was caught literally red-handed in a Serb village northeast of Sarajevo. Other Wehrmacht field reports from that period described Ustaša violence as "uncontrolled and transgressing all boundaries":

> The same terms, 'plundering,' 'excesses' and 'atrocities,' also described acts which Wehrmacht commanders explicitly prohibited their troops from participating in and therefore further reinforced the terms' criminal connotations when used in reference to Ustaša violence... as "in defiance of all the laws of civilization ... Lt.Col. von Wedel, who commanded a regiment in *Kampfgruppe Westbosnien*, complained to Glaise-Horstenau of an Ustaša's company massacre of Serb women and children. According to von Wedel, the Ustaša killed them "like cattle" in a series of "bestial executions."[1]

General Walter Kuntze, commander of Wehrmacht forces in the Southeast until August 1942, characterized the NDH as the "problem child" of the region. By that time this view was replicated down the German command chain: Ustaša violence produced the "general insecurity" and the "renewal of bands" in areas of the country the Wehrmacht had "mopped up."[2] The intelligence staff of the commanding general in Serbia warned that the "boundless and undisciplined efforts of the Ustaša are the main reasons for the further development of anarchic conditions."[3]

Illustrative of the tone of Glaise's reports from that period is the description of a camp near Slavonska Požega commanded by a former Roman Catholic priest, one Klajić:

---

[1] Hehn, op. cit.

[2] 714 Division, Operations Staff, T-315/2258/887.

[3] Kommandierender General und Befehlshaber in Serbien, Intelligence Staff, "Situation Report" quoted by J. Gumz (op. cit.)

On 27 August [1942] 378 Serbs from Bosnia were brought and put into a barrack. They were tortured en route and covered in blood. From some higher authority an order came to kill 20 among them each day. [...] The others were beaten by the Ustašas every day for no reason with rifle butts. Each day twenty men were taken out. Ten were killed with clubs, while the other ten had to dig graves, throw bodies into them, and lay down themselves, to be shot. During a regular round of torture, one prisoner tried to grab the torturer's rifle. When Klajić was told of this, he ordered that all prisoners be machine-gunned with dum-dum bullets. Firing went on for an hour. The spectacle afterwards cannot be described. The walls were covered with blood and pieces of flesh and spilt brains hanged from them, with mutilated bodies on the floor.[1]

Senior German military officers in the Southeast saw such behavior not only as reprehensible in itself, but – more importantly still – as detrimental to pacification and therefore likely to cost German blood. They agreed that a rational solution to the Serb problem was the political prerequisite without which no military answer was possible.[2] This was a rare point on which Glaise, in particular, agreed with his Italian colleagues who had adopted a similar stand already in the summer of 1941. It was shared by General Alexander Löhr (l.), who was unexpectedly appointed *Wehrmacht* Commander South-East in August 1942.

Born in the Banat, Romanian on his mother's side and Orthodox by religion, Löhr knew enough about the situation in the Balkans to be unhappy with his assignment.[3] Soon after assuming command, Löhr invited Glaise's views on the Croatian problem and agreed with them wholeheartedly. As a result, on 7 September Glaise presented Pavelić with Löhr's demand that, on top of their military prerogatives, German commanders in Croatia should also be able to exercise their authority over Croatian civilian authorities.[4] Löhr had not obtained prior political clearance from Berlin for such action, however. Pavelić immediately

---

[1] BA/MAF, RH 31/iii/7 O.U. Glaise to OKW, Zagreb, 20 September 1942.

[2] See e.g. Glaise's conversation with Löhr in Sofia on 17 Sept. 1942: T-501, roll 264 (also quoted by Krizman (1983), p. 399.

[3] KAW (Kriegsarchiv Wien – Vienna War Archives), B/521, Nr. 1484. Löhr's personal letter to Diakow, no date.

[4] T-501, roll 264. Glaise to Löhr, 11 Sept. 1942.

alerted Kasche. He and the foreign ministry raised alarm at the top, told Kasche to stand firm, and Pavelić rejected Löhr's dernand.[1] Ribbentrop did not respect or like his envoy in Zagreb but he needed to maintain the fiction of Croatian sovereignty, in order to preserve at least some role for himself.

By the second half of 1942, the difference between the OKW and the Wilhelmstrasse in the treatment of Croatia had turned into a chronic dispute. Kasche out of conviction, and the foreign ministry out of bureaucratic self-interest, kept maintaining that Croatia was 'capable of life' and the Ustašas were a 'state-creating' movement. Even when he was forced to admonish Kasche for excessive pro-Ustaša bias in his reporting, which was often, Ribbentrop remained determined to prevent military encroachment on what he regarded as his ministry's domain.

Löhr did not give up. Six weeks after taking his post, he reported to Hitler and vented his views about the Ustašas. He said that "Croatian troops are disintegrating," that their officers were "reluctant to conduct joint operations with the Wehrmacht," while "the Ustaša government itself is on the verge of chaos."[2] Löhr then came to the point, and expressed the view that the entire German attitude to the Ustašas and Pavelić needed re-examination, especially since their crimes enabled the Partisans to grow strong. All of this Hitler dismissed with a wave of the hand: the Ustašas should be allowed "to let their steam off" with the Serbs, Pavelić was faithful to him, and he (Hitler) did not want to be in the way of his none-too-numerous friends.

Told by Löhr of what had happened, Glaise was gloomy. But when he heard of Hitler's invitation to Pavelić to visit him in the second half of September 1942 he promptly drew up a list of issues that needed to be raised.[3] Above all, Glaise sought establishment of decisive German influence in Croatia's armed forces, "if necessary without the Croats' own general staff." Ustaša militia was to be reorganized and brought to heel, with an obligatory German participation at all levels. Glaise's performance at the forthcoming meeting was especially important since Löhr's staff had informed him that he would be appointed commanding general of all German troops and services in Croatia, as well as all Croatian units in the German-held area.[4]

---

[1] T-120, roll 208, NO. 2623. Kasche to the Foreign Ministry, 19 Sept. 1942.

[2] See: Vasa Kazimirović, *NDH u svetlu nemačkih dokumenata i dnevnika Gleza fon Horstenau 1941-1944* (Belgrade: Nova knjiga-Narodna knjiga), p. 237.

[3] T-501, roll 264, Glaise's note of 22 Sept. 1942. Also see Krizman (1983), p. 403.

[4] BA MAF (Federal Archives, Military Archives, Freiburg), RH 31/III/11. Foertsch to Glaise, 25 Aug. 1942.

By the early fall of 1942 Löhr and Glaise reflected an articulate Wehmatacht line in Croatia, overwhelmingly supported by the lower ranks. They sought to extend the control and influence of the German army in the NDH for pragmatic reasons, dictated by the military necessity. Pavelić's regime and the foreign ministry of the Reich both had reasons of their own for resisting such a course. The decision ultimately rested with Hitler.

On September 23 Pavelić flew to Vinica, in the Ukraine, and visited Hitler at his operational headquarters there.[1] As a sign of special favor he brought along the Black Legion Commander, Ustaša Col. Jure Francetic (next p. top), who was seen as Kvaternik's designated successor but who was killed by the Partisans three months later. Pavelić also paid a visit to the Croatian Legion fighting alongside the Wehrmacht on the Eastern Front (below).

Hitler started the meeting with his customary remarks about his "political disinterestedness" in Croatia. He emphasized the strategic importance of the  lines of communication to Greece and added that Germany had a general interest in stabilizing the Croatian regime. In his view, it was the best guarantee against the resurgence of Yugoslav programs by "young Serb fanatics," which would threaten to block – yet again – Germany's passage to the south-east. He also mentioned the significant economic interest of the Reich in Croatia, "which does not affect Italian interests at all." Hitler concluded his introductory remarks by saying that he would gladly withdraw "the last German soldier" from the NDH if only the safety of key communications could be guaranteed.

Pavelić could feel encouraged by such statements: for as long as Hitler talked of the need to support his regime, he could afford to overlook pressures from other German quarters. Pavelić took the opportunity to paint a rosy picture of successful pacification in areas under his control, while the remaining trouble spots, he alleged, were in the Italian zone. Well aware of Hitler's soft spot, he boasted that the Ustašas had "evacuated" all Jews from

---

[1] ADAP, E, III, pp. 530-8. Schmidt's minutes of the talks between Hitler and Pavelić, 23 Sept. 1942.

the area under their control, but in the Italian zone they could not do so. Then came a bombshell: Hitler said that the Germans would take into their hands complete control over Croatian troops. This was mentioned at the end of the conversation, almost like an afterthought.

This was a step in the right direction for the Wehrmacht, but not a victory. There was no discussion of the fundamental political issues previously raised by Löhr, and contained in the notes prepared by Glaise. For his part, Glaise had to remain mute throughout: to question the role of the Ustašas in Vinica would have been tantamount to contradicting the Fiihrer. Glaise was unhappy with such an outcome. However, it soon appeared he would be given a chance to even the score somewhat. Only days after the meeting Hitler asked Glaise to prepare a memorandum on the situation in Croatia, which – the Führer said almost threateningly – had to be "one hundred percent reliable." True to form, on hearing this Ribbentrop immediately intervened, fearing that his ministry was being left out. Thus in the end the memorandum for Hitler was written by the German minister in Zagreb, Pavelić's friend Kasche, with Glaise in the role of a consultant.[1]

Far from being reliable, the end-product embodied the Kasche view of Croatian affairs. Its key line was that in the interest of the successful conduct of the war the NDH government should be supported and "everything should be done to secure that the population follow and respect it."[2] A touch of Glaise's influence was detectable only in the acknowledgement that the Ustašas "are filled with a blind destructive will against real and imagined enemies of the state, above all Serbs, and have carried out excesses which, due to their unruliness and lack of any restraint, have seriously shaken the development of the state and the confidence of the people."

---

[1] T-120, roll 208, NO. 2753. Kasche to Ribbentrop, 28 Sept. 1942.

[2] ADAP, E, 4, pp. 1-8. Memorandum for the Führer, signed by Kasche, Glaise and Löhr, Zagreb, 1 Oct. 1942.

Kasche was missing the point. In the autumn of 1942 he still could not perceive Pavelić and his movement as a major part of the German problem, rather than its solution. This he would not do until the bitter end. Hitler's demand for 'one hundred percent objectivity' was defeated by a victory – in this particular round, anyway – of the *Auswärtiges Amt* over the Wehrmacht. It is significant that in one respect at least both sides were in agreement: Italian influence in Croatia needed to be curtailed even further, especially in the strategically important zone of bauxite mines in Herzegovina. The catalogue of Italian "misdeeds" quoted by Kasche was so extensive and sharply worded that Ribbentrop felt compelled, in his reply, to stress that the German-Italian alliance remained the basis of German foreign policy, and that in no circumstances could the Croatian interest be allowed to bring the Axis allies into dispute.

Even in its watered-down version, the memorandum for Hitler soon resulted in an unusual note from the German legation in Zagreb to Pavelić. Such a move, most unlikely to have been made with the approval of Kasche (below), would not have been possible without prior approval from the highest authority.[1] The Germans complained that "the Ustaša militia is partly unusable for planned military operations because of the lack of military rearing and discipline." It was also stated that "the struggle against insurgent bands has to be not only unsuccessful, but even conducive to a further spread of insurgency, due to the methods of Croatian, primary Ustaša units." Finally, the Germans noted "with indignation" numerous reports that "Ustaša instances which carry out violent measures in the field often claim that their action was ordered or requested by Germany." This was the only official German government statement to Pavelić about "Ustaša excesses" until that time. The Ustaša practice did not change much as its result, but the discrepancy between Kasche and other German instances in the Balkans was to grow sharper.

Another consequence of the memorandum was Göring's intervention in Rome, where he visited Mussolini on October 23 (top, opp. p.). Göring admitted that the Germans were concerned about the situation in Croatia and

---

[1] T-501, roll 265, The Reich Foreign Ministry to the Foreign Ministry of the Independent State of Croatia, 12 Nov. 1942. On this note also see Krizman (1983), pp. 428-9.

he mentioned the efforts being made to play Germans and Italians off against one another. He stressed that continued bauxite deliveries from the Italian zone of the NDH were essential to the German war effort. There was a veiled reproach to the Italians in Goering's statement that "in Serbia, where Bulgaria and Germany kept order, there was peace. Only in Croatia was the situation uncertain."[1] The tone and substance of Göring's  remarks left no doubt who was calling the shots in Croatia, regardless of Italian pretensions or Ribbentrop's hope to maintain his position within the Nazi hierarchy by keeping up the fiction of an equal partnership with the Italians.

After the meeting at Vinica and the subsequent memorandum fiasco, German military commanders in the Balkans gathered to lick their wounds on October 31 at Löhr's headquarters.[2] Glaise's introductory remarks were derogatory of Pavelić in the extreme: he was insincere to the Germans and no longer on top of the situation. Löhr said gloomily that the Führer "for the time being" was not contemplating Pavelić's removal. Therefore, something had to be done to improve the situation under the existing, Ustaša government.

Unperturbed by Löhr's resigned remark about Hitler's pro-Ustaša course, General Bader reiterated the standard view of the generals: that military means alone were inadequate for the task, and that a change of course in Zagreb was required. It was agreed that their goal should remain to subject Croatian military units to an ever stricter German control. It was further agreed to prevent the Croats' autonomous action, to place their units under German command when such action was approved, and eventually even to inspect their combat readiness at the barracks.

In the event the generals proceeded to secure not only greater control over Croatian units but also to increase the drafting of Croats into the *Wehrmacht* Legionnaire regiments. Their success was a measure of Germany's growing weaknesses as 1942 drew to a close.

---

[1] ADAP, E, IV, 98. Minutes of Goering's talks in Rome, 23 Oct. 1942.
[2] V.I.I., *Zbornik*, XII/2, 840-5.

3. The Wehrmacht Takes Command

The new course became apparent on several fronts at once. On January 17, 1943, Pavelić's finance minister Košak went to Berlin to ask for fresh deliveries of arms and for lines of credit to finance such purchases. Ribbentrop supported the request but the OKW informed the foreign ministry that no such deliveries were possible. At the same time the military expressed readiness to equip and supply 40,000 Croat soldiers, but only provided that they were drafted into German ranks. The outcome unsurprisingly "caused disappointment in Zagreb."[1]

On February 2 Glaise presented Pavelić with the new OKW regulations on the recruitment of Croats into three new German legionnaire divisions. Pavelić requested that the men at least wear Croatian uniforms.[2] This was not accepted: the Legionnaires were outfitted in the standard-issue feldgrau with a Croatian shoulder patch (l.) and a checkered-shield right-side helmet badge (opp. p. top). Furthermore, even those new units which would nominally remain part of the Domobran order-of-battle were to be subordinated to the Germans for training and deployment. By early 1943 Croatia's armed forces were rapidly becoming an auxiliary arm of the German Wehrmacht.

Another victory for Glaise's views was reorganization of the NDH armed forces' administrative and command structure. The ministry of the home guard (*Ministarstvo domobranstva*) was abolished, and on January 23 the armed forces ministry (*Ministarstvo oružanih snaga*, MINORS) was created in its stead.[3] This diminished the Ustaša militia's autonomy of action, thus fulfilling a key objective of the Wehrmacht ever since the summer of 1941.

---

[1] ADAP, E, 5, pp. 116-17. A note by the Trade Department of the Foreign Ministry for Ribbentrop on talks with Košak, 18 Jan. 1943. For reaction in Zagreb see: T-77, roll 895. Glaise to the OKW, 24 Jan. 1943.

[2] ADAP, E, 5, pp. 171-2. Kasche to the Foreign Ministry, 3 Feb. 1943.

[3] Krizman (1983), p. 491f.

The success for the OKW was evident in the *Führer's Instruction No. 47* of December 28, 1942, for the conduct of war in the South-east.[1] It prepared the ground for the biggest anti-Partisan action of the whole war. The Instruction stated that the situation in the Mediterranean increased the danger of an attack on Crete, on German strongholds in the Aegean and on the Balkan Peninsula. It had to be expected that in such a case the attack would be supported by insurgents in "western Balkan states." Hitler therefore instructed the armed forces commander South-East, who had under his command Army Group E, to pacify the rear and to destroy guerilla bands of all kinds. That this was to be done 'in co-operation with the Italian Second Army' sounded almost like an afterthought, if not a mere formality. For Glaise, Löhr and their colleagues, the key was in the fourth paragraph of Hitler's instruction. It gave Löhr all the authority of a territorial commander in the parts of Croatia, Serbia and Greece possessed by German units; those were the areas of operations, and Löhr was to exercise 'executive authority' in them, through subordinate commanders. Significantly, "[t]he parts of Croatia held by German units, or in which German units operate, are also to be treated as areas of operations."

The OKW promptly informed Ambassador Ritter, Ribbentrop's liaison officer at the high command, that for the duration of military operations in Croatia all authority would pass to the German forces' commander.[2] Ritter

---

[1] Cf. V.I.I., *Zbornik*, XII/2, pp. 961-5, for Serbian/Croatian translation of Instruction No. 47.
[2] T-120, roll 212, no number. OKW to Ritter, 3 Jan. 1943.

was asked to convey the news "cautiously" to the Croats. He briefed Kasche the following day.¹ The telegram offered some sugar coating for Pavelić: Löhr would "always inform the military leadership of the NDH in good time about the area of planned operations and the time of their execution."

Glaise also received the good news from the OKW at the same time, and wasted no time in going to Pavelić with it.² His probably jubilant mood must have been in sharp contrast to that of Kasche. The latter, apparently unaware that the source of the instruction was Hitler himself, once again took it upon himself to defend Pavelić. In a long telegram Kasche presented in rosy terms past co-operation between German units on the ground and NDH civilian representatives attached to them. He advised greater German support to the NDH civilian authorities: "If one were to deny cooperation to the Croatian civilian authorities, that would mean the Germans were denying their past contribution and releasing Croats from political responsibility. That would confirm enemy propaganda and justify Italian political demands."

Ten days later Kasche was reduced to pleading for the acceptance of Pavelić's somewhat desperate suggestions "which would create the ostensible impression that the NDH is an equal partner in cooperation with the Germans and the bearer of sovereignty"³ He concluded his long telegram with a plea for the continuation of the old system of Croatian (civilian) administrative authority in the zone of operations, in conjunction with German military commanders who would have NDH liaison commissars attached to their staffs. But this time Kasche's remained a lonely voice. The generals had won the day: they could get on with anti-insurgency preparations assured that their work – at least for the duration of operations – would not be undermined by the meddling Ustašas following in their wake. By having their armed forces finally brought under formal as well as real German control, and their territory under German commanders' jurisdiction, by the end of 1942 the Ustašas had lost most of the few remaining vestiges of NDH sovereignty. But even if the resistance of Pavelić and Kasche could be overcome, the problem of the Italian role remained. Glaise's view was that "Croatia was primarily a political question to which it was difficult to provide an answer without clearing up the 'condominium' with Italy." The full extent of the burden this "condominium" presented to the Wehrmacht became apparent as the two Axis allies prepared plans to deal with Partisans and Četniks in the NDH.

---

[1] ADAP, E, 5, pp. 19-20. Ritter to Kasche, 4 Jan. 1943.

[2] T-120, roll 212, No. 98. Kasche to the Foreign Ministry, 7 Jan. 1943.

[3] ADAP, E, 5, pp. 114-15. Kasche to Ribbentrop, 17 Jan. 1943.

4. "Weiss" and "Schwarz"

The combined operation against Tito's Partisans in the NDH, known as *Plan Weiss*, was the most determined anti-insurgency drive in the former Yugoslavia during the Second World War. It was carried out on Hitler's initiative in response to the new strategic realities in the Mediterranean. The guiding principles for the action were supposedly agreed between Germany and Italy during Hitler's meetings with Ciano and Cavallero on 18-20 December 1942.[1] In the preliminary round of talks with Ciano, Goering stated that Pavelić was weak, but he was "still a man of the Axis," and therefore had to be helped, although no concessions were due to him. The following day, talking to Ciano, Ribbentrop said that the Croats occasionally tried to play the Germans against the Italians. He would have none of it, however; personally he always advised them to resolve their problems directly with Ciano. Turning to the insurgency within the NDH, Ribbentrop spoke as if the Četniks and Mihailović were the main threat. The real enemies, to Ribbentrop, were *the Serbs* – with whom the Italian commander in Croatia, general Roatta was making deals! They were more dangerous than the communists, Ribbentrop concluded, against whom Roatta wanted to use those Serb nationalists.

During the second session with Ciano, to which two chiefs of general staffs, Keitel and Cavallero, were also invited, Ribbentrop made renewed anti-Serb and anti-Četnik statements.[2] He said that the Italians' co-operation with them had to stop, and named Roatta as a culprit. Pressed for an answer, Cavallero agreed in principle but added that the German commander of the operation, Löhr, would need to come to Rome for a joint planning session.[3]

At the final session Hitler reiterated that he had "no political interest in Croatia": he had met Pavelić but twice and had purely formal talks with him. But Pavelić's regime had to opt for Germany and Italy if it wished to survive, and therefore it was a lesser evil than the rising tide of Yugoslavism. He expressed satisfaction with the agreement reached on the forthcoming actions.

Hitler's assumptions about the 'agreement' were too optimistic. Ciano was not impressed with Hitler's plan.[4] Although Cavallero half-heartedly

---

[1] The minutes of all four rounds of talks are in ADAP, E, 4, pp. 538-55, 562-4 and 582-5.

[2] Kazimirović (1988), p. 153.

[3] T-821, roll 21, frame 975. Comando Supremo, Argomenti militari speciali trattati nei colloqui presso il Quartiere Generale germanico nei giorni 18, 19 dicembre 1942.

[4] Ciano, *Diary*; entry for 6 Jan. 1943.

accepted it, the commander of Italian troops in Croatia, General Roatta, opened his heart to him. There was no alternative for the Italian army in the Croat state but to continue co-operation with non-communist Serbs. German demands to disarm them would not be openly rejected, but simply not applied. Even as Löhr was about to begin the talks in Rome with Italian generals, Roatta frankly told his high command chief that the Četniks were his only trump card in the area, and should not be discarded.

Unaware of Roatta's position, Löhr demanded redeployment of Italian units to occupy the areas held by the Četniks, and to prepare for their eventual diaarmament.[1] Although familiar with the Italians' evasive techniques by that time, he seems to have thought that the authority of Mussolini and Cavallero would compel Italian commanders in Croatia to act against the Četniks. At the same time, Roatta was telling his subordinates to do just the opposite. On 11 January 1943, nine days before the operation was due to begin, Roatta issued his final instructions to those *Supersloda* units which were due to take part in operations in Croatia.[2] He did not make any reference to Cavallero's undertaking to Keitel and Ribbentrop that all Italian arms deliveries to the Četniks would be halted. On the contrary, Roatta gave orders which

were, it seems, deliberately vague on this point, and allowed for the possibility that M.V.A.C. units ("Voluntary Anti-Communist Militia," above, Italian-supported Četniks) be actively used against Tito. While the arrangements with the Germans obviously made it difficult for Roatta to plan openly any large-scale involvement of Četnik forces against Tito, he was certainly not going to disarm them, even less to fight them.

Löhr himself could not escape doubts about the forthcoming operation. He looked at "Weiss" as "an experiment with several question marks." The tempo and scope of operations came from above, he told Glaise, and he was

---

[1] Ugo Cavallero, *Comando Supremo: Diario 1940-1943 del Capo di S.M.G.* (Bologna, 1948), entry for 3 Jan. 1943.

[2] V.I.I., *Zbornik*, IV/9, No. 211. Roatta to V Corps Commander, 11 Jan. 1943.

only allowed to fill in the preconceived framework.[1] Oblivious of Roatta's schemes, Lohr outlined his plan to the Italians. The action would consist of three phases. *Weiss I* called for the encirclement and destruction of Partisan units in western Bosnia and Lika. *Weiss II* would push those Partisan forces which managed to escape encirclement into the trap further south, where they would be destroyed. Simultaneously, *Weiss III* was to take place in the Italian zone, and had for its objective the complete disarmament of *all* Četniks. While four German divisions and assorted NDH units were to advance from the north, three Italian divisions were supposed to block Tito's retreat south.

In contradiction to what Cavallero ostensibly had agreed with Hitler in Berlin in December, and with Löhr in Rome in January, in the days just before *Weiss* the Italians speeded up their deliveries of arms and equipment to various groups of Četniks in their occupation zone. Roatta was determined to play his "white ball" in full. Cavallero was aware of this, and approved. In spite of his reputation for subservience to the Germans, he even authorized the inclusion of Četnik "volunteers" from Montenegro in the NDH.[2]

At the same time, both Roatta's commanders and Četnik officers were forced to improvise at the last moment. They were supposed to manoeuvre often unruly groups, inexperienced in major combined operations, into place on the anticipated route of retreating Partisan brigades. Only very late in the day did it dawn upon Četnik leaders that Roatta's support for them was not merely an act of altruistic sympathy for the Serbs: they were assigned the crucial role of stopping the main body of Tito's battle-hardened shock troops. Roatta expected those Četnik units to bear the brunt of the fighting, which would save his own men, and have the added benefit of widening the gulf between Tito and Mihailović.[3] However, major difficulties remained. Besides tactical ones, both Roatta and the Četniks had to keep an eye on the Germans and Pavelić. The Italians in particular were weary of the possible political and military fallout resulting from such blatant breach of their 'agreement' with Hitler. Montenegrin Četniks in particular were a problem, because of their known propensity to engage in acts of anti-Ustaša revenge against civilians (e.g. in Foča during winter 1941-2). At the same time, seen as good fighters, they were regarded as indispensable by Roatta.[4] They were therefore given orders by the Italians to refrain from any excesses and to avoid contact with

---

[1] BA MAF RH 31/III, 12. Löhr's handwritten letter to Glaise, 11 Jan. 1943.

[2] V.I.I. *Zbornik*, IV/9, No. 218. Comando Supremo to Comando 2. Armata, 15 Jan. 1943.

[3] V.I.I. *Zbornik*, IV/9, No. 217. Supersloda Operazioni to Comando Supremo, 12 Jan. 1943.

[4] T-821, roll 298, frames 114-16. VI Army Corps to Division Murge, 22 Jan. 1943.

German or Italian troops. In the end, the outnumbered Četniks were beaten by Tito's forces in the winter of 1943. Due to greater manoeuvrability, the Partisans almost invariably managed to enjoy local superiority. Their forces were more experienced, and desperate to break through Četnik lines. As was expected by the Germans, the Partisans were overwhelmed by German forces and suffered huge losses in the north (Lika, Bosnia), after some of the heaviest fighting seen in the Balkans up to that point in the war.[1] However, instead of three Italian divisions blocking Tito's way south, to Löhr's chagrin there were only parts of one (Murge at Prozor) and some thousands of uncoordinated Četniks. By the beginning of February the Partisans were in full

retreat, battered, but not destroyed. They threatened to break out of the pocket across the Neretva River. If they did, the entire German plan would be compromised, the core of Tito's forces would get away, the Četnik heartland in eastern Herzegovina would be threatened, while most Italian forces remained inactive. The Germans complained bitterly about Italian scheming.[2] As Löhr's staff gathered further evidence of Italian *combinazioni*, the OKW asked Rome for an explanation.[3] But by that time the pliant Cavallero was gone, and General Ambrosio, anything but pro-German, headed the Comando Supremo instead. This boded ill for Hitler's plans.

Ambrosio was the very embodiment of the Italian army 'line' in the Balkans, and he proceeded to frustrate yet again the German strategy of dogged pursuit of all guerrillas. Ambrosio replied to the OKW that 'if' the disarming of Četniks was to be carried out, it had to be done 'with caution, not in haste.'[4] Even the transfer of Roatta from his command at Sušak in the first week of February did not help from the German standpoint: just as Roatta had continued Ambrosio's policies a year earlier, the new Supersloda commander, General Mario Robotti (with Pavelić, above), continued Roatta's.

---

[1] *Das Kriegstagebuch des Oberkommandos der Wehrmacht* (KTB/OKW - War Diary, German High Command), III/5, entries for 25, 29 and 30 Jan. 1943.

[2] T-501, 1-011 264, frame 899. Glaise to Löhr, 28 Jan. 1943.

[3] KTB/OKW, Vol. 3, 31 Jan. 1943.

[4] Ibid. 7 Feb. 1943.

On February 8, 1943, at a meeting in Belgrade, Robotti flatly refused any continuation of joint action. This was due to commence on February 15, and was designated *Weiss II* and *III* by Löhr.[1] Robotti was acting on Roatta's advice, whose goal had been to keep the Germans out of Herzegovina.

The renewed intra-Axis dispute over Četniks had little to do with the actual strength of Serb nationalist forces. Its root cause was the unwillingness of Italian commanders to fight a war in the Balkans on German terms, under German command, and – ultimately – for German objectives. Besides keeping German forces out of the Italian zone, Ambrosio, Roatta and Robotti were primarily interested in keeping their forces intact in the aftermath of Germany's debacle at Stalingrad. The fight with Tito (r.) was secondary in the context of wider developments that could be anticipated.

In spite of Hitler's and Ribbentrop's efforts, *Weiss* was turning into yet another episode of the civil war in Yugoslavia which the Partisans were able to survive. One of Löhr's commanders, General Lüters, admitted in his final report on *Weiss* that Tito's forces were well organized, skilfully led and possessed of a high combat morale. They compensated for the lack of heavy arms by exploiting dark, fog and rain and imposing close-range combat "when they showed themselves to be fanatical… and tough fighters."[2]

Nevertheless, in Berlin the Četniks' apparent weakness was regarded as immaterial. The Germans saw the whole problem as a function of an expected Allied operation in the Balkans which would revive the Četniks, "giving the officers a clear advantage over Tito [r.], or what was worse, would bring Tito and Mihailović together."[3] Unwilling as ever to seek a political solution of the Croatian problem, which amounted to the replacement of Pavelić and his Ustaša cohorts, Hitler and Ribbentrop were again missing the mark. At the same time, they had little means to enforce their will on the Italians. Frustrated by the situation in the Balkans and upset by the policy of Italian

---

[1] V.I.I., *Zbornik*, IV/10, No. 197. Robotti's notes on the Belgrade meeting, 8 Feb. 1943.

[2] Ladislaus Hory and Martin Broszat, *Der kroatische Ustascha-Staat, 1941-1945* (Stuttgart, 1964), pp. 149-50.

[3] Matteo J. Milazzo, *The Chetnik movement and the Yugoslav resistance* (Baltimore and London, 1975), p. 121.

officers there, Hitler sent a lengthy letter to Mussolini. It was delivered to Rome by Ribbentrop on 25 February 1943. Hitler pleaded for Italian support in the continuation of *Weiss*.[1] He stressed, yet again, the presumed danger presented by the Četniks and asked that all supplies to them be halted:

> If we do not succeed to disarm the Communists and Četniks in the same measure, and to pacify the land completely, then at the moment of invasion disorder will break out, all links with Peloponnesus cut off or interrupted, the few German divisions will be busy fighting the Communists and Četniks, and Italian troops will no longer be able to halt the invasion...

Hitler was essentially right, from the viewpoint of a joint Axis war effort. The Četniks were unreliable. Their partnership with the Italians was one of necessity, not choice, and it would have ended with the landing of the first British company in Dalmatia. Some Četnik commanders openly admitted that much to the Italians, as if the latter had not suspected it anyway.

There was more than met Hitler's eye, however. The remarkably persistent policy of support for the Četniks, pursued by the Italian army even to the point of defying Mussolini's orders, by 1943 had a different motivation than in 1941 or 1942. In the past one could cite among the Italians' motives their sympathy with the persecuted Serbs, the general disillusionment with the Ustašas, the need to have local allies, the wish to drive a wedge between Communists and 'nationalists,' or the desire to preserve Italian forces by fighting Tito to the last Četnik. In early 1943 new elements came into play. After Stalingrad and El Alamein, Mihailović's assumed links with the British could have been a source of attraction, rather than repugnance, to Ambrosio, Roatta, Robotti *et al*. The Italian generals thought politically, unlike their German colleagues. If Italy was to get off Hitler's crippled bandwagon, then it had to cultivate those who could (or so the generals hoped) facilitate such a transition. There are strong indications that an active policy to that effect existed both among some Italian diplomats and in the Army. Just as protecting Jews made sense for those Italian officials who sought to extricate Italy from the Axis, so the Četnik connection – apart from its military value – was attractive to those Italian generals who by that time realized that Germany was doomed.[2] According to the testimony of Guido Lucich-Rocchi, an Italian officer who spoke Serbian fluently and served in the Dalmatian cities of Knin

---

[1] ADAP, E, 5, pp. 171-2. Hitler to Mussolini, 16 Feb. 1943.

[2] For the Italians' obstruction of Hitler's *Endlösung*, see Jonathan Steinberg, *All or nothing: the Axis and the Holocaust 1941-1943* (London and New York, 1990).

and Split during the war, the command of the Second Army was distinctly Anglophile, and hoped for a link with Mihailović and the British through their Serb 'nationalists.'[1] The same impression was shared by General Umberto Salvatores who, then still a colonel, commanded 6. Bersaglieri Regiment in Lika and Bosnia.[2] The atmosphere indicated that the British would not have been seriously resisted, had they landed in Dalmatia.

The Italian military governor of Montenegro, General Alessandro Pirzio-Biroli, probably went further than any other Italian commander in the Balkans when he sent a message to Mihailović already in late 1942, to the effect that he wanted a separate peace with the British. General Mihailović duly passed the message on to London, but Eden – possibly suspecting a provocation – subsequently wrote, 'I have decided against pursuing any of these contacts.'[3]

Steeped in the tradition a priori inimical to what both Mussolini and Hitler stood for, the Italian officer corps remained motivated by its traditional values: by its loyalty to the crown, and by the legacy of the *Risorgimento*, with its liberal-nationalist connotations. There was also a deeply rooted sense of decency and propriety, so well manifested in the Italians' efforts to save Jews in their zone. Having preserved their autonomy vis-à-vis Mussolini's pseudo-totalitarian regime, Italian officers fully exercised it in the Balkans in the winter of 1943.

Determined to clarify Italian ambiguities, Hitler instructed Ribbentrop-and General Warlimont (r.), chief of army staff, to go to Rome and get Mussolini's explicit assurances on the Četnik issue. Ribbentrop reiterated the standard line of Hitler and of the foreign ministry: the issue of Mihailović, and of the pacification of Croatia, was not a political, but a purely military question; this he repeated the following day to Mussolini and Ambrosio.[4] Mussolini somewhat meekly responded that Italian commands in the Balkans certainly were not getting instructions from Rome to aid and abet the Četniks, thus implying that they were disregarding his orders. Ambrosio inserted an ambiguous note with his statement that it was

---

[1] Lucich-Rocchi to Stevan Pavlowitch, 25-26 Mar. 1974. See also Luigi Pietromarchi's statement to Bogdan Radica in *Hrvatska 1945* (Munich-Barcelona: Naklada Hrvatske Revije, 1975), pp. 283-4.

[2] Salvatores to Stevan Pavlowitch, 24 Feb. 1973.

[3] P.R.O., F.O. 371, R 8802/3700/22, minute from Eden to Churchill, 2 Dec. 1942.

[4] ADAP, E, 5, pp. 314-21. Minutes of German-Italian talks in Rome.

not possible to defeat both sides, Četniks and Partisans, at once; the Partisans had to be beaten first. Encouraged by Ambrosio's intervention, Mussolini went on to blame the Pavelić government for the rise of insurgency, which the Ustašas caused, he thought, by their policy of extermination of the Orthodox minority. This, he added, was amply documented. Ambrosio rounded up the Italian reply to Hitler's and Ribbentrop's points by saying that the fear of an Allied landing in Dalmatia was exaggerated, because the passage of a large invasion fleet through the Gate of Otranto into the Adriatic would be risky, and the Dinaric Alps along the coast hard to break through.

Warlimont tried to concentrate on practical issues, and suggested that the ensuing tasks be joint German-Italian action to destroy Communist forces north of the Neretva, followed by a thorough pacification of the area and the breaking up of Mihailović's movement. Ambrosio expressed renewed scepticism, primarily because – he thought – the problem in Croatia was political, rather than military. This was sharply contradicted again by Ribbentrop, who said that it would be easy to solve political issues once the war was won. Mussolini, reluctant as ever to contradict his German interlocutors, cut the argument by agreeing with the broad outline of the German plan: he asked Ambrosio to work out the details with Warlimont.

The result was a letter from the Comando Supremo addressed to the German high command, which was supposed to confirm the agreement. To Ribbentrop's chagrin, however, this letter contained major discrepancies from what the Germans thought had been agreed. Above all, there was no mention of Mihailović at all. This induced a visibly upset Ribbentrop to comment to Alfieri, who visited him at his Rome residence on February 28, that "in the Italian high command there were at work certain forces which could not be called Fascist."[1] For once the former champagne salesman displayed a modicum of lucidity. Alfieri promised to sort out the problem, and returned two hours later with Mussolini's

---

[1] For a record of Ribbentrop's conversation with Alfieri see ADAP, E, 5, pp. 321-3.

handwritten instructions to Comando Supremo on how to reply to the German high command. The letter, written in French for the Germans' benefit, promised resolute action against Mihailović.

Simultaneously, Warlirnont reported back to the OKW the problems he was encountering with his Italian colleagues. Jodl instructed Warlimont to tell the Comando Supremo that Hitler himself had ordered German troops, under German command, to press their attack on the bauxite area around Mostar until those bands – Četniks and Partisans alike – were destroyed.[1] The combination of Ribbentrop's pressure through Alfieri, and of the OKW conveying Hitler's personal orders, finally swayed Mussolini. During the final talks, on February 29, Mussolini and Ribbentrop (above) agreed on all issues because the Duce finally adopted Hitler's train of thought. He said that Mihailović was a dangerous foe and once again promised that Ambrosio would act resolutely. Ribbentrop departed from Rome ostensibly reassured.

Mussolini did not have his heart in the German plan to disarm all Četniks. As soon as the Germans' pressure eased with Ribbentrop's departure from Rome, he wrote to Hitler that he had ordered Generals Robotti and Pirzio-Biroli to halt further arms deliveries to the Četniks 'as soon as the Partisans ceased to be a dangerous armed movement.' Almost gleefully, Mussolini added that he had just received the news that the German forces had established contact with the Četniks in the upper Neretva area, and avoided fighting them.[2]

German units led by the 7th SS mountain division *Prinz Eugen* [commanded by Artur "Papa" Phleps, pictured atop his command APC in Herzegovina, r.] had entered the Italian zone of occupation for the first time. They soon realized that it was not possible to carry out Hitler's orders on the disarming of Četnik units. Italian commanders warned their Četnik protégés of the Germans' advance in time and sometimes evacuated them under the Germans' noses. When Tito's shock troops broke out of their pocket north of the Neretva, it was through Četnik lines south of the river that they attacked in

---

[1] KTB/III, pp. 172-3.

[2] ADAP, E, 5, No. 192. Mussolini's letter to Hitler, 9 Mar. 1943.

force. In the ensuing chaos the Partisans gained superiority over their chief domestic rivals. Yet Bound by Hitler's instructions, the OKW did not alter its overall plan. Tito was not captured, but his loss of manpower and territory was deemed irreparable by the Germans. Mihailović was seen as the chief remaining enemy. The Germans therefore decided to pursue their attack primarily against the *Yugoslav Army in the Fatherland*. The German High Command instructed its forces in Croatia to prepare for the new action codenamed *Schwarz*, and do it on their own. Furthermore, it was decided even to conceal any such plans from the Italians:

> In view of the close links between Mihailović and the Italians, the Führer attaches great importance to the strictest concealment of both the intention and the preparations. The Commander Southeast should report where and when preliminary arrangements [with the Italians] are unavoidable, while the right to authorise such contacts remains with the OKW.[1]

Unknown to the Germans, however, the Partisans had entered the area of north-west Montenegro and southeast Herzegovina where the brunt of the German attack was to take place. To both sides' surprise, they were to receive the heaviest blow of German assault, meant for Mihailović's forces. What followed was a full month of some of the most desperate fighting of the entire war in Yugoslavia, known in Titoist historiography as the battle of the Sutjeska. In the end, the Germans (on march near Glamoc, above) failed to deal a decisive blow to either Tito or Mihailović. After five months of strenuous operations, costly in blood and material, the relations with their Italian ally in the Balkans were at low ebb. The entire Axis occupation system in the area was in disarray. The Italians avoided fighting, the Croatian field officers (opp. p. top) were in charge of troops either prone to desertion or to bloody excesses, and the Germans were thinly spread. Tito was the only benefactor.

---

[1] KTB/III, p. 255.

Weiss and *Schwarz* were keyt landmarks in the shifting military and political situation in the Balkans. German troops for the first time started operating in the Italian zone, at times even without giving prior notice to their allies, let alone seeking their agreement. They started operations without expectation of Italian support, and in the end tried to avoid any Italian involvement. The first half of 1943 was thus marked by the final German predominance in the military-operational sphere in the entire area of the NDH. This had occurred even before the fall of Mussolini. Italy had no resources, no strategy and no policy capable of preventing such an outcome. By early 1943 she also had no will to prevent it.

The rivalry between Germany and Italy in the Balkans, always latent and sometimes blatant, was a salient feature of the Axis occupation policy in the Western Balkans. Its roots are to be found in the fundamental, and ultimately fatal, contradiction in Italy's foreign policy in the 1930's. Hitler's categorical and repeated renunciation of South Tyrol demanded Italy's acceptance of the *Anschluss*. But even if Alto Adige was safe for Italy, the Danubian area and the eastern Adriatic were not. For all his anti-Habsburg sentiment, after 1938 Hitler could not avoid inheriting the strategic interests of the old Monarchy. German-Italian rivalry in the Croatian puppet state in 1941-3 initially could be described as the result of Hitler's twin desire to preserve the alliance with Italy, while eliminating Italian influence from the Danubian basin. Alas for Mussolini, Hitler's 'Danubia' was a flexible term, ultimately expanded to include the northeastern Adriatic.

The uncertainty regarding the community of interests between Germany and Italy, unclarified throughout the late 1930's, became manifest in Croatia in 1942-3. Their long-term objectives remained very different, although this difference was not spelt out. Mussolini was prepared to fight a battle in his *mare nostro* to secure a resurrected Roman Empire and gain access to the oceans. His objectives, while immodest, were nevertheless limited. What Mussolini failed to perceive in time was that Hitler's goals were ultimately unlimited. Although Hitler was more 'irrational' than Mussolini, he displayed skill and 'rationality' in the application of policy. The clash of two concepts in the Quisling state of Croatia provides an illustration. Rationally applied policy at the micro-level enabled the Germans gradually to establish control over NDH economy, over its armed forces and its key communications, and yet to continue paying lip service to the supposed primacy of Italian interests in the area.

Even in those areas where Italians proved resistant to German demands, over the treatment of Jews sheltering in Dalmatia and over the Italian Army's cooperation with Serb irregulars, this resistance was inconsequential to the broad picture. Key Italian shortcomings – lack of policy and lack of resources – were rooted in the frivolity of Mussolini's regime. He told the Grand Council of Fascism in 1939 that Italy had no territorial interest in Europe besides Albania. His subsequent diversion to the annexation of Dalmatia and the creation of a Balkan zone of influence was an aberration of the central principle, a substitute for coherent policy. Italy's Balkan policy was bankrupt, and accurately reflected the bankruptcy of Mussolini's strategic design.

X
Accomplices in Coat-Tails

1. Pavelić's Foreign Ministry

By the time the Second World War broke out European diplomacy was in decline. With the advent of Ciano, Ribbentrop and Molotov, the traditional diplomat – treacherous if necessary, civilized always – retreated before the relentless and brutal ideologue. Diplomatic discourse became a temporary expedient, not the normal and permanent way of carrying on relations with other states. For the members of Hitler's "New Europe" diplomacy was reduced to symbolic representation devoid of substance. By December 1941 Russia had turned the war in Europe from *ein Normalkrieg* into *Totalkrieg*. Hitler had the satellites fully under control. He decreed that they should declare war on Britain and the United States. They followed suit, Croatia included.

The Independent State of Croatia was a paradigmatic product of the New Order. It was clear to its supporters and to its foes alike that it stood or fell depending on Hitler's fortunes. It was considered to be an illegal entity not only by Britain, Germany's only enemy still fighting in the spring of 1941, but also by the neutrals. President Roosevelt denounced the invasion of Yugoslavia. On May 18 Acting Secretary of State Sumner Welles specifically condemned the creation of the Croatian "protectorate." Pavelić's police closed and sealed the U.S. Consulate in Zagreb and the American consul left the city in June 1941. For the rest of the war U.S. policy avoided any action that might be understood as acknowledging the existence of the NDH.[1] Allen Dulles' OSS (Office of Strategic Services) mission in Berne merely monitored the activities of the NDH government, with special emphasis on its policy of extermination of the Serbs and Jews.

Pavelić acknowledged the link between the Axis war effort and his state's existence from the outset. In April 1941 he told Veesenmayer that "he did not intend to conduct any foreign policy at all – Adolf Hitler was doing that."[2] There was an element of sycophancy in his statement, understandable at a time when he was still uncertain of his standing in Berlin. His words, which pleased Veesenmayer, nevertheless manifested the reality that Germany's "allies" were not partners but vassals.

---

[1] FRUS, 1941, vol. II, pp. 979-984. In 1954 the U.S.

[2] DGFP, D, 12, No. 341. Veesenmayer to the Foreign Ministry, 14 April 1941.

Reflecting the *Führerprinzip* pervading all its institutions, the formal diplomatic arm of the new state – its foreign ministry and its foreign service – was a simple extension of its power structure. This goal was opposed for various reasons by the myriad of mutually non-aligned forces, from Ambrosio or Roatta in Sušak and Dalmazzo in Dubrovnik to Glaise in Zagreb, Djujić in Knin, Tito in Drvar, Himmler in Berlin, or Mihailović in eastern Bosnia. Indirectly it was also opposed by every nation at war with the Axis. Therefore, the two restraints of rigid internal structure and hostile external environment left little room for diplomacy from the outset. An option for the Croats, as some German sources approvingly noted, was to abdicate any role in foreign affairs altogether:

> The Poglavnik's state has given up taking part in grand politics. Foreign policy must reflect in a healthy manner the actual power of the state. Taking part in grand politics had been a sick phenomenon and a madness of the Versailles era, it is emphasized in authoritative places in Zagreb... [Croatia's foreign policy] is no longer entrusted to an incidental play of Cabinet members, it is no longer based on personal talent and relations of a foreign minister; now it represents an organic part of the entire order of the state. Its foreign policy, to put it aptly, is shaped by natural-legal, geopolitical, biological and ideological conditions.[1]

The Ministry for Foreign Affairs of the Independent State of Croatia was created by a decree issued by Pavelić on April 16, 1941, when he appointed the first Ustaša government. Pavelić kept the foreign ministry portfolio for himself, and on April 18 appointed Dr. Mladen Lorković as secretary of state in charge of day-to-day running of the new ministry.

With the signing of the Rome Agreements Pavelić's outstanding foreign obligations were settled and he could delegate more of his authority to Lorković, who became foreign minister. Lorković had to start from scratch. Most Ustaša ministries could at least initially rely on the existing administrative structure of the Banovina of Croatia (jurisprudence, health, forestry and mining, education etc). The only other ministry which had not had an equivalent in the Banovina was that of defense, but Pavelić and Slavko Kvaternik could rely on a large number of former Habsburg officers untainted by "Yugoslavism" to provide the initial backbone of the newly established regular army, *Domobranstvo*. In subsequent weeks hundreds of Croats who had been regular officers in the Yugoslav army requested and obtained transfer to the *Domobranstvo*.

---

[1] *Donauzeitung*, German-language Belgrade daily, 26 October 1941, article by Oberacher.

There were few Croats in the Yugoslav diplomatic service before 1939. They were loyal to the Yugoslav state and its dynasty, the minister to the Holy See, Niko Mirošević-Sorgo, being a good example. The number of Croat diplomats and foreign ministry officials was increased after the *Sporazum*. The newcomers were mainly political appointees and moderate Mačekists, such as Ilija Jukić, deputy foreign minister under Cincar-Marković. Others were politically unaffiliated but odious to the Ustašas, like the late historian Bogdan Krizman who came from a family of liberal Croatian "Yugoslavs." In addition, the *esprit de corps* of the Yugoslav foreign service had a strong pro-Western slant. This was manifested in the desire of Yugoslav diplomats – regardless of ethnic origin – to leave Axis-controlled territories whenever they could after April 1941, and to offer their services to the Yugoslav government in exile. Pavelić could not and did not count on the Croats in the Yugoslav foreign service to develop his diplomacy. Only three offered their services to him; all were rejected.[1]

Mladen Lorković (r.) was an educated and energetic Germanophile. He spent over ten years in Germany prior to April 1941, first as a student and then as an émigré and Ustaša activist and the author of a book that summarized the key tenets of Ustaša ideology[2]. His first task was to create a skeleton staff of officials who possessed the necessary skills to draft the order of battle of the newly created ministry. They were mostly lawyers, and with a few exceptions they were not sworn Ustašas before April 1941. To Lorković it was more important to gather efficient bureaucrats than politically committed zealots. This proved to be the right approach: most permanent officials appointed in 1941 remained at their posts throughout the ensuing four years, and – unlike most politically appointed diplomats – did at least a fair job of ticking over within the narrow limits prescribed by Pavelić.

By appointing and promoting bureaucrats without an Ustaša pedigree Lorković could also count on their initial dependence on him personally. For instance, Vjekoslav Vrančić was unknown in Ustaša circles and observed the events of 10 April from the sidelines. He was made head of the political department of the foreign ministry on the basis of his previous business

---

[1] ASSIP, Izbeglička vlada, Ministarstvo inostranih poslova, F-4, No. 318. Višacki to Ninčić, Madrid, 12 June 1942.

[2] *Narod i zemlja Hrvata*. Zagreb: Matica hrvatska, 1939.

career. (In the early 1930s, while in Argentina, Vrančić was on the payroll of the Yugoslav ministry of social welfare). Already by August 1941 Vrančić was promoted to state secretary and deputy foreign minister. He was routinely engaged in various missions involving Germans, Italians, Četniks and at the very end Western Allies, but he always remained excluded from substantial decision making. Eventually, although hand-picked and promoted by Lorković, Vrančić accepted his boss's fall from grace with perfect *sang froid*. A good bureaucrat, he remained a loyal servant of Pavelić to the bitter end.

Lorković's pragmatic approach caused dissatisfaction among some Ustašas who expected the foreign ministry to provide sinecure, and perhaps some glamour, to the deserving veterans of the movement. A letter was sent to Lorković by Pavelić's private office inquiring why the head of the foreign ministry's personnel department, Vlaho Buško - apparently not a sworn Ustaša at that time – "had not been replaced by Ustaša Juraj Položnjak in accordance with the Poglavnik's instructions."[1] In reply, Lorković wrote that he had already explained to Pavelić that Buško should remain because of his expertise and personal qualities, to which Pavelić agreed, and that Položnjak had been given a clerk's post. Even when forced to take "a good Ustaša" on board, Lorković gave him lower position than the one originally demanded.

The appointment of heads of legations was politically colored: Ustaša background was a must for mission chiefs, especially in Rome and Berlin. Although movement affiliation counted elsewhere too, several ministers and consuls without any Ustaša record were appointed apparently on the strength of their aristocratic pedigree, presumably in an attempt to raise the tone of the service. By the end of July 1941 a group under Vrančić had completed its task of preparing organizational blueprints.[2] The foreign ministry of the NDH was divided into five departments.[3] In its first six months it had opened a total of eight legations, three consulates-general, six consulates, one consular agency (Belgrade), one "cultural delegation" (Vichy) and one trade delegation (Zurich). A total of sixty people were employed at the foreign ministry in Zagreb, and a hundred diplomats and support staff at twenty posts abroad.

The upper crust of the NDH foreign service was a mix of penniless but titled gentlemen like the envoy in Madrid Pejacsevich and the consul in Prague Vuchetich, Germanophiles without political clout or diplomatic skill

---

[1] ASSIP, MVP NDH, VT I/41, No.297/41. *Ured Poglavnika* ministru, 1 December 1941.

[2] Vrančić (1985), Vol. II, ch apter 1.

[3] The departments were: 1) general; 2) political; 3) legal; 4) press, publications, and cultural relations; and 5) consular and economic affairs.

(Benzon), self-serving eccentrics (Židovec), and trusted Pavelić loyalists (Perić, Bulat). Subsequently, unlike the ministry in Zagreb which included a core of adequate bureaucrats, the NDH foreign service was a mixed bag of political appointees, excitable diplomatic dilettantes, and pauperized descendants of the Croatian-Hungarian nobility. They were supported by an auxiliary *demi-monde* staff which routinely engaged in petty smuggling and black marketeering.[1]

The result was an uneven and indifferent performance. Reports were sent by chiefs of missions without any apparent schedule, frequently by some (Židovec in Sofia was a veritable scribomaniac), almost never by others (Pejacsevich, Bulat). The quality of those reports was embarrassingly low. They consisted mainly of trivial dinner party gossip, press summaries and records of bland conversations with various officials and private individuals. The form and tone of reports by ministers, consuls and other officials suggests that they were not merely unwilling, but unable to engage in analysis. There were no strategic evaluations of the developments in their country of residence. Rare "situation reports" radiated undue optimism, e.g. on the "negligible" effects of the bombing in Germany, or on Italy's "determination to continue the war" on the side of Germany in the summer of 1943. Of course Pavelić had never intended his foreign ministry to be more than a technical support service. Even at that level it performed poorly, and many difficulties emerged due to the inexperience of his diplomats and fierce personal rivalries among them.

2. The Gaffes

Considerable embarrassment to the nascent NDH diplomacy in its early months was caused by the minister in Berlin, Branko Benzon. Haughty and brimming with self-confidence, he was not a popular figure either as a schoolboy or in later life.[2] Barely a fortnight after his arrival in Berlin, Benzon attempted to raise the alarm with Weizsäcker about Casertano's supposed ultimatum to Pavelić.[3] Weizsäcker indicated in his subsequent note for Ribbentrop that Benzon should not be taken seriously. Then came the rowdy party at one of Berlin's premier hotels, the *Adlon*, hosted by Benzon,

---

[1] See correspondence regarding personal integrity and reliability of two security guards employed by the Consular Agency in Belgrade: ASSIP, MVP NDH, VT I/41, No. 91/41.

[2] See L. Fertilio on Benzon in *Hrvatska Revija*, Vol. 25, No. 1, March 1975, pp. 48-54.

[3] See Chapter V for Benzon's activity just prior to the signing of the Rome Agreements.

which resulted in several thousands of dollars' worth of damage in broken mirrors, furniture and crockery. The Wilhelmstrasse reluctantly agreed to foot the bill, but Benzon's star was fading both in Berlin and in Zagreb. Then came Benzon's single-handed attempt to sow seeds of doubt in the reliability of no less a personality than their chief ally, Mussolini.

Benzon repeatedly tried to act, in his contacts with German officials, as their unacknowledged but tacitly accepted confidante, an ally who was aware of their secret disdain for the Italians, and who felt that – since he shared such disdain – there was no need for pretenses. In this approach he was frequently rebuked, but persisted to the point of telling Weizsäcker, in the aftermath of Pavelić's trip to Rome to sign the Agreements, that Mussolini had expressed doubts about the prospects for an Axis victory in the war. Weizsäcker carefully intervened by saying that Pavelić must have misheard Mussolini.[1] This indiscretion caused great interest and went all the way up to Hitler.

Weizsäcker (l.) was asked to provide a more detailed account of Benzon's story three days later.[2]

Benzon repeated his version of events to Ribbentrop's aide Walter Stahlecker.[3] According to Benzon's account, Pavelić – on his return from Rome – suddenly asked Benzon in private whether he really believed in the victory of the Reich. When Benzon queried how he could even ask something like that, Pavelić first evaded the answer, but then told him confidentially that Mussolini had said he did not believe in ultimate German victory. For this reason – Benzon went on – Pavelić had decided to accept a Savoy prince to be king of Croatia, since "the defeat of Italy would not necessarily mean the defeat of the House of Savoy."

Stahlecker listened to all this politely, but then asked bluntly whether Pavelić may have invented the statement attributed to the Duce. Benzon, apparently nonplussed at the German's implication that his head of state was a liar, simply replied that he thought that "improbable." Stahlecker excluded any possibility that Mussolini had really said anything of the kind, but he did not disbelieve Benzon's claim that Pavelić had conveyed the story in that form. He concluded that it must have been a "misrepresentation" by Pavelić.

---

[1] ADAP, D, XII/2, No. 709. Weizsäcker's note to Ribbentrop, 20 May 1941.

[2] PA, Büro RAM, Kroatien, Fuschl-Nr 1626. Weizsäcker to Ribbentrop, 23 May 1941.

[3] ADAP, D, XII/2, pp. 777-778. A note by Walter Stahlecker dated 31 May 1941.

It is difficult to establish the facts of Benzon's story. It is highly unlikely that Mussolini – who was by no means free of doubts about the prospects for an ultimate victory – would have confided such thoughts in Pavelić. It is possible that Pavelić "planted" the story on Benzon expecting him to tell it to the Germans. It is more probable that Benzon had embellished the story not only because of his spite for Italy but mostly because of his desire to present himself as a valuable source of confidential information to the Germans. The Germans had their agents in the NDH foreign ministry anyway, in the person of Ernest Bauer who worked until April 1941 for a bogus German news bureau in Zagreb. In the diplomatic service their man was Theodor Albert, counsellor at the NDH legation in Bratislava. While Bauer provided information about the ministry on an impromptu basis, Albert was a true agent: he supplied formal written reports to the German minister in Bratislava, Ludin.[1] Eventually Albert grew disenchanted with the Ustaša regime and filed reports to Berlin supportive of the replacement of Pavelić. He was found out, due to Kasche's indiscretion, and fired; he was told that, had he not been a German, he would have been shot.

The story of Mussolini's alleged defeatist statement to Pavelić was a first class indiscretion on Benzon's part. He had no authority from Pavelić to disclose the contents of their confidential conversation. As Croatia's representative in the Reich he not only implied that Pavelić had shared Mussolini's alleged doubts about the outcome of the war, but that such doubts explained why he had offered the crown of Croatia to the Duke of Spoleto. In the end Benzon was told by Stahlecker that *someone* was not telling the truth, and that – as far as the German side was concerned – *it was not Mussolini*. Benzon's attempt to act as a voluntary informant on his own boss and on the third most powerful dictator on Earth was roundly scorned by the Germans. Benzon's position in Berlin became untenable.

Shortly thereafter Benzon complained to Lorković that he was a victim of "slanderous and malicious gossip" about his lifestyle and his qualifications for the post.[2] He realized that his credibility in Berlin and Zagreb was irretrievably gone and asked to be relieved of his duties. Pavelić did not allow this, possibly because Benzon's withdrawal after only two months would have reflected poorly on his regime's shaky reputation in Berlin. Pavelić may have

---

[1] See e.g. Albert's report to Ludin, dated 11 December 1942, on the conflict between Pavelić and S. Kvaternik: T-120, roll 212, No. 2210. On Albert's status as regular informer see PA, Nachlass S. Kasche, Pol. 2, No. 436950. On his subsequent dismissal see S. Kvaternik's statement: A-VII, NDH, I.O. 9 6/9 1-104.

[2] ASSIP, MVP NDH, VT I-41, F-1, No. 7/41. Benzon to Lorković of 19 June 1941.

also wanted to give Benzon a little more rope to hang himself, in order to demolish completely the credibility of the man who had entertained very high ambitions in the early days of the NDH. After Benzon's scandalous party at the *Adlon* had become public knowledge in Zagreb and the subject of ironic gossip among diplomats all over Europe, his troubles were compounded by an investigation of the financial improprieties of his trade attaché, Marko Jurinić.[1] In the end Benzon was reduced to writing a whining personal letter to Lorković in which he openly admitted his incompetence:

> I ask you again, begging and praying that this does not remain a voice in the wilderness, to allow me to return to Zagreb and be released of duty here in Berlin. Otherwise I shall be forced to do so without your leave, even if this means that the most severe punishment awaits me in Zagreb. This situation cannot go on. I do not understand why I – by all accounts very capable in my own profession – must continue to perform another duty with which I am unfamiliar, and which I perform so poorly as to cause chagrin of those to whom I am accountable for my actions.[2]

Benzon's letter indicated that he was a spent force. He remained at his post for another three humiliating months, during which he managed to draw German scorn and ridicule with two more gaffes. In September he complained to the under-secretary of state at the German foreign ministry, Ernst Woermann, that his legation's negotiations with the German ministry of labor on the status of Croatian workers in the Reich were stalled.[3] Woermann calmly replied that it would have been far better had the NDH legation communicated with the foreign ministry on this issue from the beginning, rather than attempting to initiate direct negotiations with the ministry of labor, "on its own." Benzon changed the subject and said he wanted to talk to Woermann "at some length" about the status of the Zemun area – between the Danube and the Sava, opposite Belgrade – which the Croats wanted to bring under their control from the authority of the German military commander in Serbia. Woermann replied to Benzon that he was "out of touch" on that issue, since an agreement on the status of the Zemun Triangle had been reached some days previously. To Benzon this news came as complete surprise.

Just a few weeks before Benzon's departure from Berlin, the Consul-General in Vienna, one Dr. Jurak, informed Lorković that he had severed all

---

[1] ASSIP, MVP NDH, VT I-41, F-1, No. 1/41. Ministry to Benzon, no date (July 1941).

[2] ASSIP, MVP NDH, VT I-41, F-1, No. 14/41. Benzon to Lorković, Berlin, 3 July 1941.

[3] T-120, roll 208, U.St.Saek. Pol. No. 874. A note by Woermann of 19 June 1941.

contact with Benzon, at that time still his nominal superior. He only added: "you, Mr. Minister, know why."[1] Lorković did not even reply to what would be an urgent issue in a normal bureaucratic setup. Perhaps he did not want to make Jurak's life any more difficult than it was, since that man had problems of his own. He had already threatened to resign his post because of a personal clash with Vjekoslav Vrančić.[2] In view of Vrančić's strong position at the ministry it is unlikely that Lorković had given Jurak much comfort in that dispute.[3] The complaints about the performance of the important Consulate-General in Vienna were commonplace. An internal foreign ministry memorandum on a tour of the Reich by a group of Croatian journalists contained specific reference to their poor impression of the work done by the Consulate. The report singled it out for criticism because it maintained "weak contact with German institutions" and was held in low esteem among the local Croatian colony in Vienna.[4]

Temperamentally different to Benzon but in his wy even more eccentric was Vladimir Židovec, the NDH minister in Sofia. A lawyer with prewar Ustaša affiliations, he was a compulsive writer of reports on every detail of his daily existence in the Bulgarian capital. Trivial aspects of everyday life were worthy of page upon typewritten page marked "Top Secret" and addressed to "the Minister's eyes only." Lunches with Slovak press attaches and Finnish lumber salesmen were described in excruciating detail, from uninspiring menus to verbatim accounts of mind-numbing "confidential conversations." Visits to Bulgarian historical sites by German journalists were equally worthy of a report, as well as the Minister's chance meetings with back-bench *Sobranie* (Assembly) deputies. Some of them seem to have been attracted to Židovec by his willingness to foot restaurant bills, which atoned for his lack of personal panache. When Židovec was succeeded by Stijepo Perić in 1943, the latter noted his predecessor's irritating habit of talking to people as if he were conducting an interrogation, pen and paper in hand.

---

[1] ASSIP, MVP NDH, VT I-41, F-1, 200/41. Jurak to Lorković, Vienna, 8 November 1941

[2] ASSIP, MVP NDH, VT I-41, F-1, 207/41. Jurak to Lorković, Vienna, 11 November 1941.

[3] A farcical event involving Pavelić's daughters Višnja and Marija could not have helped his career. In a separate letter to Lorković, Jurek described an incident at the Vienna railway station, where he and his consulate staff waited in vain for the anticipated arrival of Pavelić's daughters. They had apparently arrived at the far end of the platform, left by another exit oblivious of the greeting party, and had to find accommodation on their own. Evidently upset about the incident, he wondered how could they have failed to spot the car with a Croatian flag outside, and remarked dejectedly that "everything would have been right had they only telephoned the Consulate."

[4] ASSIP, MVP NDH, VT F-2, No. 238/42. Unsigned memorandum of 17 March 1942.

Židovec was an obsessive pedant, too: in a didactic letter to Lorković he suggested "the best method" of filing his voluminous reports in a special individually indexed binder. At some length he explained to his minister how they ought be bound into a separate book (to be marked "top secret," of course) and cross-referenced.[1]

The minister in Sofia was notoriously unable to get on with people in general, but most of all with his staff. He was on particularly poor terms with the military attaché, Lt.Col. Adam Petrović. In a letter dated October 30, 1941, Židovec accused him of writing reports "based on unreliable information," and asked that Petrović's reports be submitted to him for approval before being dispatched.[2]

Petrović was only one of Židovec's problems. On the same day, in a separate letter to Lorković, he requested that the legation secretary, Celebrini, be withdrawn and replaced by someone more reliable, if possible "actively linked to our Ustaša movement."[3] Shortly before Christmas 1941, in another "urgent" letter, Židovec complained that Lt.Col. Petrović's assistant – one Sgt. Hajek – had secretly and "craftily" read Židovec's outgoing reports and told the military attache of their contents.[4]

On December 22 Židovec prepared a detailed "end-of-year report on staff performance," which was apparently his own invention, since no such reports were received from any other post abroad or written within the Ministry. He was negative or coldly sarcastic in his estimate of everyone in the legation, with the exception of the press attache, Mosner.[5] Barely a week later, a "personal" letter from Židovec to Lorković followed, with a vicious attack on Vlaho Buško, head of the foreign ministry personnel department. According to Židovec, Buško had informed legation staff in Sofia of his unfavorable comments about their work and personalities, which was "a stab in the back" with grave consequences.[6]

Židovec repeatedly demanded the replacement of another secretary, Milovan Mocnaj. When this was eventually done, the minister soon discovered that the new secretary, Škrobot, was "even worse" than his predecessor. He was allegedly in the habit of "disclosing official secrets to

---

[1] ASSIP, MVP NDH, VT I-41, F-1, No.363/41. Židovec to Lorković, 22 December 1941.

[2] ASSIP, MVP NDH, VT I-41, F-1, No. 145/41. Židovec from Sofia, 30 October 1941.

[3] ASSIP, MVP NDH, VT I-41, F-1, No.170/41. Židovec to Lorković, 19 December 1941.

[4] ASSIP. MVP NDH, VT I-41, F-1, 41, Židovec to Lorković, no date.

[5] ASSIP, MVP NDH, VT I-41, F-1, No. 361/41. Židovec to Lorković, 22 December 1941.

[6] ASSIP, MVP NDH, VT I-41, F-1, No. 384/41. Židovec to Lorković , 30 December 1941.

unauthorized persons," for which reason Židovec had the man "officially interrogated" in the presence of his only reliable staffer, Mosner.[1]

This case becomes clearer in the light of yet another mini-crisis at the NDH legation in Sofia, which occurred a month later. The newly appointed chief clerk (*perovodja*), Ferek, within weeks of his arrival asked the Ministry to be moved to another post because of "an irreparable conflict" with the minister. Apparently Židovec wanted to test Ferek's integrity "by planting supposedly confidential material that should not be there on my office desk, in order to clandestinely observe what I was going to do."[2] The clerk's attempt to read the documents - which he found on his own desk - in order to establish what they were and where they should be filed, was taken by Židovec to prove Ferek's unreliability. Židovec filed his own formal complaint against Ferek and requested that he be relocated "at his own cost."[3]

In addition, Židovec sent a total of four formal requests for the replacement of Lt. Col. Petrović in 1941-1942.[4] He also complained that the Bulgarian minister in Zagreb, Mečkarov (in some documents referred to in French transliteration, Metchkaroff), was able to obtain certain confidential documents directly from the *Domobranstvo* Ministry, supposedly thanks to the pernicious influence of Lt.Col. Petrović.[5] Židovec had had a deep grudge against Mečkarov; he warned Lorković of the Bulgarian minister's alleged Masonic connections and a supposed appetite for malicious gossip. Židovec's almost paranoid attempts to prove his own reliability and credentials may have been linked to the fact that his surname was the Croatian equivalent of "Jewson."

Židovec was eccentric but gloomy. There were more amusing characters in the NDH diplomatic service, like the consul in Prague, Vuko pl. (for *plemeniti*, title of nobility) Vuchetich. His job does not appear to have been demanding, as there are only a few of his reports in NDH foreign ministry files. One of them related that one evening he went drinking with a couple of consulate officials and two female secretaries "in a Dalmatian tavern" in the Old City. Their official car – left outside unattended, since the driver had joined the fun – was stolen and no insurance could be collected.

---

[1] ASSIP, MVP NDH, VT F-2, No. 669/42. Židovec to the Foreign Ministry, 7 September 1942. See also Nos. VT652/42 and VT699/42 on the minutes of the interrogation.

[2] ASSIP, MVP NDH, VT F-2, No. 805/42. Ferek to Lorković, Sofia, 31 October 1942.

[3] ASSIP, MVP NDH, VT F-2, No. 947/42. Židovec to the Foreign Ministry, 27 October 1942.

[4] E.g. Židovec's letter to Lorković of 2 December 1942. MVP NDH, VT F-2, No. 893/42.

[5] ASSIP, MVP NDH, VT F-2, No. 937. Židovec to Lorković, Sofia, 31 December 1942.

Illustrative of the problem of discipline was Lorković's circular of October 14, 1941, forbidding all diplomatic personnel to travel without prior permission from the Ministry, and announcing the establishment of regular courier service, "thus removing the most common excuse for unauthorized travel."[1] On several occasions he had to issue additional individual warnings to diplomats because of unauthorized travel, their own or their staff's.

Petty and not so petty cases of embezzlement and fraud were also a problem. In November 1941, Vuchetich reported that he was taking disciplinary measures against three consulate officials – i.e. all officials except for himself – because of their fraudulent claims for duty-free goods.[2] Even before that incident the consulate in Prague had become a hotbed of gossip and back-stabbing. There are a dozen letters in which staff members revealed each other's wrongdoing, incompetence, and outright criminality to the minister. More serious was the case of a diplomatic courier, Mijo Gavranović, who was caught by the Ustaša police trying to smuggle a large quantity of Reichmarks into the NDH in the diplomatic pouch.[3]

The behavior of the Ustaša Youth Organization's representative in Rome, Mate Šuić, was bizarre. He insisted on having his own office in the legation building and was given one. His work was so undemanding that he would make only occasional, once-weekly appearances. There was no correspondence to be kept, no telephone calls to be answered. But even on those few days when Šuić made his appearance, he behaved "with such insolence and audacity to everyone, including the minister" (Perić) that the latter felt he "had no choice" but to ban Šuić from the building altogether and to cease all contact with him.[4]

3. Areas of Activity

The NDH foreign ministry files contain a lot of trivia but little material relating to the key issues of Croatia's external relations. No visible trace exists of "decision-making" on negotiations with Italy (May 1941), on preparations for Pavelić's meetings with Hitler, on the emergency over the German intention to withdraw from Croatia in December 1941, on the Abbazia talks

---

[1] ASSIP, MVP NDH, VT I-41, No. 90/41. Ministry circular, 14 October 1941.

[2] ASSIP, MVP NDH, VT I-41, F-1, No. 266/41. Vuchetich to the Foreign Ministry, Prague, 26 November 1941.

[3] ASSIP, MVP NDH, VT I-41, F-1, No. 71/41. Ravnateljstvo ustaškog redarstva (Directorate of Ustaša police) to the Foreign Ministry, 10 October 1941.

[4] ASSIP, MVP NDH, VT F-21, No.755/42. Perić to the Foreign ministry, 8 October 1942.

(*Trio*) etc. With most states' diplomatic documents it is possible to reconstruct at least an outline of the path from policy conception, through formulation, to execution. In the Croatian case none of the above steps are discernible. There is no sign of policy planning or review meetings of department heads with the minister. It is also impossible to trace the lines of communication between Pavelić and the ministry. It is likely that they consisted entirely of oral instructions from him to whoever was the minister at a time. In any event and at all times Pavelić reserved substantive diplomatic activity for himself. The areas of activity left to the foreign ministry were in the main twofold: consular work and the maintenance of relations with other Axis satellites.

In consular activities no record exists of any guidelines regarding the issuance of NDH visas to foreigners. Visas were often approved on the spot if accompanied by an official letter from the host country's government; otherwise, requests were referred to Zagreb. To quote one curious example, in April 1942 Židovec informed the ministry from Sofia that a trainload of French refugees from Iran were requesting NDH transit visas in order to return home. Consular activities primarily concerned two groups: Croat prisoners of war in POW camps awaiting repatriation, and tens of thousands of guest workers in Germany from the NDH.

In April 1941 the Wehrmacht was instructed not to round up Croats in the Yugoslav army, but to release them as "friendly nationals." In the general confusion following the capitulation of the Yugoslav armed forces, many Croats were nevertheless taken prisoner and transported to Germany, as it was impossible for German field commanders to check their national origin. They were taken to transit camps (the largest of which was Traiskirchen near Vienna, later used for training of Croatian troops bound for the Russian front), and thence to permanent camps all over Germany. The NDH foreign ministry instructed local authorities to gather data on imprisoned Croats and fill in pre-printed cards on each POW. Those cards were then sent to the NDH legation in Berlin, which passed them on to the OKW. Up to 28 thousand Croats were taken prisoner in April 1941, and by February 1942 the foreign ministry had sent some 20,000 personal cards to Germany. However, the legation in Berlin was instructed to double-check and ensure that "not a single Serb should slip through" (*da se ne provuče po koji Srbin*).[1]

The same discriminatory attitude was applied to thousands of Serbs from the NDH who were drafted to work in Germany. On 14 November 1941 Vrančić sent a circular letter to the legation in Berlin and to the consulates in

---

[1] ASSIP, MVP NDH, I-41, F-1, No. 247/41. Foreign Ministry to the Legation in Berlin, 20 November 1941.

Munich, Vienna, Graz and Maribor, in which he stressed that no Serbs domiciled in the NDH should be issued with proper Croatian passports (*Putnica*, 1.). They were to be issued only with one-way passes to return to the NDH. According to the instructions from the foreign ministry in Zagreb, however, this was to be done in secrecy: "They should be formally treated as Croat citizens in communication with German authorities, but privately urged to convert to Roman Catholicism before being issued with proper documents."[1]

The Germans became aware of what was going on and resolutely opposed such policy. To them it was important to retain every foreign worker at his post, and the idea of one-way tickets to the NDH for Serb workers – while in line with Pavelić's own brand of *Endloesung* – could not have suited Albert Speer's manpower planners. German protests over this issue were mounting by the end of 1942. They were based both on moral indignation and pragmatism inspired by the worsening labor shortage in the Reich. Glaise and other German officials had repeatedly advocated sending Serbs from the NDH to Germany as labour – a prospect which many Serbs also found vastly preferable to the alternative of remaining at the mercy of the Ustašas. German displeasure at the discriminatory Ustaša policy against Serb workers in German factories was evident in a cable, sent by the NDH legation in Berlin, which urged the foreign ministry to ensure – on German request – that *all* workers who went home on leave should be allowed to return to the Reich.[2] When the German legation in Zagreb gave the NDH foreign ministry detailed instructions on granting work and residence permits to workers coming from the NDH, it stressed that no workers of Aryan descent (i.e. Serbs included) were to be discriminated against.[3]

Judging by the names of people who appear in consular records and related correspondence, it seems that after the winter of 1942-1943 the Serbs from the NDH working in Germany were granted access to some consular

---

[1] ASSIP, VT I-41, F-1, No. 225/41. Ministry circular, 14 November 1941.

[2] ASSIP, VT F-2, No. 868/42. Legation in Berlin to the Foreign Ministry, 20 November 1942.

[3] ASSIP, MVP NDH, VT F-2, No. 963/42. Legation to the Ministry, November 1942.

services. A rare instance of this was the case of Dr. Aleksandar Djurić, a Serb from Bosnia, who was a lecturer at the university in Prague. He and his two Czech brothers-in-law were sentenced to death by the Germans in 1944 for subversive activity. The legation in Berlin apparently requested to have the sentence postponed pending appeal.[1] Djurić was in the end executed.

Politically more sensitive was the case of scores of Muslims from Bosnia, former volunteers from the SS *Hanjar* Division, who were sent to labor camps near Berlin in the aftermath of a rebellion at Villefranche-de-Rouergue, in France. Some of them started escaping from the camps and making their way to the NDH legation, seeking assistance and repatriation. At first NDH consular officers attempted to assist them and even presented a verbal note to the Auswärtiges Amt supportive of their complaints. The Germans responded simply by tightening security at the camps and denying access of any Croatian officials to the "deserters."[2]

4. Croatian-Hungarian Dispute

The only area in which the NDH foreign ministry was able to indulge in some conventional diplomacy, in appearance if not substance, was in its relations with other Axis satellites. Ministerial visits, cultural exchange conventions, consular protocols and trade agreements with Slovakia, Hungary, Bulgaria or Romania were performed, or negotiated and signed, undoubtedly with Pavelić's blessing, but without visible supervision or guidance from the Poglavnik's headquarters. These relations soon became reminiscent of the pre-war Little Entente pattern. Until 1938 Belgrade, Bucharest and Prague had been united in their opposition to Hungarian revanchism. In 1941 Croatia, Slovakia and Romania also established close links, united by the problems each of them had had with Hungary.

Slovakia was bitter about the Hungarian annexation of Slovak southern border areas after Munich in 1938. Romania was still shell-shocked after the Vienna arbitration by its Axis "friends" which almost reduced it to its pre-1914 borders. The return of Bukovina and Bessarabia in the east, which eventually cost Romania half a million soldiers lost in the Russian steppes, could not allay fears that Hungary still coveted southern Transylvania and other "lands of the Crown of St. Stephen" that had been left under Romanian sovereignty in 1940. In the case of the NDH the problem concerned an area

---

[1] Milan Blažeković. "Slučaj Dra Aleksandra Gjurića." Hrvatska Revija, No. 2, 1960, p. 292.

[2] Milan Blažeković. "Sjećanja uz temu 'Slavni hrvatski vojnici'...." Hrvatska Revija, No. 4, 1968, pp. 535-538.

between the Mura and Drava rivers inhabited mainly by Croats and known as Medjimurje (Muraköz). It was occupied by Hungarian troops in April 1941, when they also marched into Bačka and southern Baranja.

Horthy (below) was willing to take part in all German ventures starting with Czechoslovakia in the fall of 1938, since they provided Hungary with an opportunity to overturn the legacy of Trianon. By April 1941 he had obtained parts of southern Slovakia, the Carpathian Ruthenia and northern Transylvania. On March 27, 1941 Hitler confidently counted on Hungarian participation in his planned action against Yugoslavia as well, since it included the former Hungarian provinces of Bačka, Baranja, Banat and Medjimurje. Initially he envisaged even for Croatia itself some form of "autonomy in close association with Hungary." Horthy accepted Hitler's offer without consulting his prime minister, Count Teleki, who had signed a pact of

friendship with Yugoslavia only four months previously.[1] Teleki, true to a Hungarian nobleman's form, committed suicide on April 3, saying in his farewell note to Horthy that "we have thrown away the nation's honor", and "we shall become the robbers of corpses! The basest of nations." Horthy gave his troops the order to advance into Yugoslavia only after he had hastily extended his recognition to Pavelić – the first head of state to do so. The proclamation of the NDH was interpreted by the Regent as proof that Yugoslavia had ceased to exist. Hungary was therefore – in his view – no longer bound by its "Pact of Everlasting Friendship" with Belgrade.

The advance of Hungarian troops into Medjimurje alarmed the Croats, who already by mid-April suspected that the Honved's intention was to stay there for good.[2] It was also no secret that Hungarian irredentism coveted an outlet to the Adriatic. Hitler's offer to attack Yugoslavia was conveyed to Horthy by the Hungarian minister in Berlin, Döme Sztojay. In his report to Horthy Sztojay hinted at the implicit promise of an outlet to the sea for Hungary, "yet he [Hitler] knows that your heart draws Your Highness also to the Adriatic, and that Hungary is in need of a free seaport. Although Fiume

---

[1] *The Confidential Papers of Admiral Horthy.* Budapest: Corvina Press, 1965. Document No. 38. Horthy to Hitler, 28 March 1941.

[2] PA, Büro Staatssekretär, Kroatien, Bd. 1, No. 81. Freundt to the Ministry, 17 April 1941.

belongs to Italy, Hitler held out the prospect that he would throw in his influence in this question."[1]

Hungarian ambitions were bound to clash with Croat nationalism, and Medjimurje could be seen as the first step on the road to Sušak. Initially at least, the Hungarians regarded Medjimurje as a bargaining chip, which could be used as a means of obtaining extra-territorial rights on the railway between the Hungarian border and Fiume-Sušak.[2] That solution was also favored by Germany, and Ribbentrop seemed to believe that the Hungarians would evacuate Medjimurje if granted extraterritorial transit rights across Croatia to the Adriatic.[3] Hungary at first hinted that it would demand only formal sovereignty over Medjimurje, while the NDH would be allowed to administer it without claiming sovereign rights (the "Bosnian solution" of 1878). By the end of May, however, negotiations The Croats wanted Medjimurje without preconditions, while Hungary grew unwilling to give it up without major concessions by the NDH.[4]

Croatia "acknowledged" Hungarian historical claims.[5] Only a day later both Lorković and the Hungarian minister in Zagreb, Marossy, told Kasche that the offer was not accepted in Budapest.[6] This was soon confirmed at a higher level. The Hungarian prime minister, Laszlo Bardossy (r.), told the German minister in Budapest, Erdmannsdorff, that he had advocated speedy negotiations with Croatia on Medjimurje, on duty-free transit and on a possible exchange of minorities. The Croats were slow to respond and dragged their feet hoping to enlist support from other Axis powers.[7] In the meantime, numerous delegations from Medjimurje went to Budapest to lobby against giving it to the NDH, and Hungarian public opinion – in Bardossy's words – turned against any territorial concessions.

---

[1] *The Confidential Papers of Admiral Horthy*, p. 173.

[2] PA, Büro RAM 13, Kroatien, No. 109. Kasche to the Foreign Ministry, 23 April 1941.

[3] PA, Büro RAM 13, Kroatien, No. 374. Ribbentrop to Kasche, 26 April 1941.

[4] PA, Büro Staatssekretär, Kroatien, Bd.1, No. 381 Kasche to Foreign Ministry, 29 May 1941

[5] PA, Büro Staatssekretär, Kroatien, Bd. 1, No. 643. Kasche to Foreign Ministry, 2 July 1941.

[6] PA, Büro Staatssekretär, Kroatien, Bd. 1, No. 657. Kasche to Foreign Ministry, 3 July 1941.

[7] PA, Büro Staatssekretär, Kroatien, Bd. 1, No. 752. Erkmannsdorff to the Foreign Ministry, Budapest, 4 July 1941.

Finally, the Hungarian premier said that any return of Medjimurje to Croatia would have to be accompanied by major further concessions – e.g. transfer of close to 200,000 Catholic Slavs from Bačka to the NDH.

Those people, commonly known as *Bunjevci* and *Šokci*, were viewed in Budapest as distinct nationalities, albeit "ethnically akin to Croats." As for the Slav-speaking inhabitants of Medjimurje, it was claimed in Budapest that they were ethnically quite different from Croats, and that they were *Hungarian by blood and culture, if not language.* Hungary also claimed to possess lists, prepared by the Ustaša authorities in Zagreb, of people who would be persecuted for their Hungarophile sympathies if and when the NDH took over.[1] Bardossy's firm stand was confirmed by an even more emphatic "no" to Lorković, which came on 9 July from the Hungarian deputy foreign minister, Vörnle. He told Erdmannsdorff that Hungary regarded Lorković's offer of 2 July as a transparent trap, calculated to get something (i.e. Medjimurje) for nothing.[2] Vörnle added that Hungary did not believe Croatian protestations of friendship because it had reliable information that the NDH favored "a Slovak proposal to create a new Little Entente which would be directed against Hungary, just like the old one."

The Hungarians' anti-Croat agitation was also felt in Berlin. In the capital of the Reich it was Romania, rather than Slovakia, that was presented as the villain of the piece. Minister Sztojay told Weizsäcker on 8 July that the Hungarians had deciphered a document according to which Slavko Kvaternik declared himself in favor of a joint Croatian-Romanian frontier.[3] Sztojay added that for this reason Kasche had allegedly declared in Zagreb his opposition to the return of western (ex-Yugoslav) Banat to Hungary; this Weizsäcker flatly denied, asserting that Kasche must have been misquoted. In fact the Germans had no intention of giving the Yugoslav part of Banat to either Hungary or Romania. While nominally a part of Nedić's Serbia, this rich agricultural province was administered by the local *Volksdeutsche* in conjunction with Himmler's SS.

In an episode typical of the intrigues between Hungary and her nominal allies, Hungarian defense minister Bartha passed a message to Glaise in August 1941 to the effect that Hungary would like good rapport with both Croatia and Slovakia, but Romania was trying to prevent this warming up of

---

[1] Krizman (1983), p. 85.

[2] PA, Büro Staatssekretär, Kroatien, Bd. 1, No. 777. Erkmannsdorff to the Foreign Ministry, 9 July 1941.

[3] T-120, roll 208, note by Weizsäcker No. 502 of 8 July 1941.

relations. "In case of war with Romania, which is certain to take place, Hungary wants to secure its back," he went on, and suggested that Medjimurje could be given to the NDH after all, if it proved cooperative.[1] The foreign ministry in Berlin was duly informed of this, but it warned Kasche that Bartha's protestations should not be taken for granted: they were not at all in line with the news from Budapest, which indicated increasing antipathy to the Croats.[2] Lorković was nevertheless sufficiently impressed by Bartha's message to tell Kasche that "the Hungarian general staff was less annexationist-minded about Medjimurje than the politicians." In early September Bartha repeated to the Germans his view that Medjimurje should be given to Croatia.[3] He claimed that Horthy and the circle around him were chief advocates of keeping the province. (The apparent discrepancy between the views of Bartha and Horthy corresponded to the differences between Italian generals and Mussolini over Dalmatia.)

A month later, on August 19, the ubiquitous Benzon told Weizsäcker that "the Hungarians plotted with Italy against Croatia." He claimed that Bardossy had presented a memorandum to Italy purporting, among other things, that he (Weizsäcker) had told Sztojay that Hungary could count on Germany's support over Medjimurje.[4] Not for the first time the calm but exasperated Weizäecker had to point out to the excitable Croatian envoy that Germany hoped for a solution of the dispute between the NDH and Hungary, but had no intention of taking sides in the dispute. But Ribbentrop's secretary of state grew tired of such intrigues, and for once appeared determined to get to the bottom of the matter. On 20 August he warned Sztojay to refrain from conveying misleading information to Budapest, hinting that he knew about the memorandum sent to Rome.[5] Sztojay denied any knowledge of such a document. Weizsäcker succeeded in getting a copy through Kasche, however, and found out that for once Benzon was right.[6] One of the two Hungarian memoranda on Medjimurje (*"L'isola della Mura"*) addressed to Rome contained the claim that "the Secretary of State at the Reich Foreign Ministry has admitted that the Hungarian side could not have gone any further in its patience and consideration, and said that he had understanding for the position

---

[1] T-120, roll 208, No. 1021. Kasche to the Foreign Ministry, 19 August 1941.
[2] T-120, roll 208, Büro Unterstaatssekretär, Pol. No. 797. Wörmann's note of 20 August 1941.
[3] T-120, roll 208, No. 1103. Kasche to the Foreign Ministry, 2 September 1941.
[4] T-120, roll 208, note by Weizsäcker No. 1021 of 19 August 1941.
[5] T-120, roll 208, No. 540. Note by Weizsaecker, 20 August 1941.
[6] T-120, roll 208, Pol. 2, No. 3-1880/41. Kasche to Weizsäcker, 27 August 1941.

of Hungary." After receiving the memoranda from Kasche Weizsäcker called Sztojay again on 2 September and faced him with the evidence contrary to his previous claims.[1] The Hungarian envoy was embarrassed, and conveyed Bardossy's profuse apologies to Weizsäcker. He claimed that the "misunderstanding" had been caused by the "unauthorized action" of the allegedly misinformed Hungarian minister in Rome, Villanyi, who had retired in the meantime.

Hungary's attempts to solicit Italian support against their mutual Balkan neighbor bore some semblance to the Versailles era. Just as Italy came to regard the NDH as an heir to Yugoslavia and a rival on the eastern Adriatic shore, mutual perceptions of Hungary and its non-Germanic neighbors followed the same pattern. The Budapest press reacted furiously to the mutually supportive speeches given by the NDH minister in Bratislava, Dragutin Toth, and the Slovak president, Mgr. Tiso, on the occasion of Toth's presentation of credentials. It was said that "the tone and the anti-Hungarian slant" of those addresses were hardly different from the atmosphere which had prevailed in the contacts between Belgrade and Prague a decade earlier.[2]

On 9 July 1941, on Horthy's instructions, the Hungarian military commander at Csáktornya (Čakovec, the principal town in Medjimurje) Colonel Timar Zsigmond proclaimed the introduction of full Hungarian administration in the province. He stated that "Muraköz has finally and eternally rejoined Hungary." All Croatian civil servants were summarily dismissed. As far as the Hungarians were concerned the issue was thus finally resolved.[3] This was done without any prior or subsequent formal notification to Zagreb, although the negotiations were still going on.

Lorković reacted the following day, 10 July, with a protest note to the government of Hungary, the first such document drafted by the Ustaša foreign ministry. He asked for an explanation of the military commander's action, implying that he was acting on his own authority, and asserted that the NDH would never accept amputation of Medjimurje.[4] Marossy replied a day later with a personal note to Lorković in which he stated that Medjimurje was "an undoubtedly Hungarian territory."[5] Pavelić told Glaise that he would lodge a

---

[1] T-120, roll 208, No. 571. Weizsäcker's note on talks with Sztojay, 2 September 1941.

[2] T-120, roll 208, No. 473. Information Bureau III to Weizsäcker, 20 August 1941.

[3] Krizman (1983), p. 65.

[4] PA, Büro Staatssekretär, Kroatien, Bd. 1, No. 705. Troll-Obergfell to the Foreign Ministry, 10 July 1941.

[5] A-VII, NDH, Kut. 233, Reg. No. 37/7. Marossy to Lorković, 12 July 1941.

protest with all member countries of the Tripartite Pact. If Hungary persisted, he would close the frontier with Hungary and send its minister packing.[1]

Until that time Germany had remained aloof and preferred to let her two small clients sort out their differences on their own. However, Pavelić's threat of open diplomatic action at a time when the Barbarossa was in full swing could not be tolerated. Therefore the under-secretary of state, Woermann, prepared a memorandum on 11 July 1941 which suggested that the Croatian government should be dissuaded from the measures contemplated by Pavelić.[2] This was conveyed to Zagreb, and Lorković subsequently assured Kasche that the NDH would not break off relations with Hungary.[3] They were only downgraded, and Pavelić's representative in Budapest, Ivo pl. Gaj, initially had the title of chargé d'affaires instead of minister.

In subsequent weeks the cold war between the NDH and Hungary escalated. On 26 July Lorković had a conversation with the Hungarian chargé d'affaires, who threatened that Hungary would seal the entire Hungarian-NDH frontier if the crossing point at Petrovaradin – which the Croats had closed the previous week – was not immediately reopened.[4] Lorković expressed surprise at such over-reaction over what he called a temporary measure, caused by the exodus of Serbs from Bačka across the NDH territory to Belgrade. He then complained that "the treatment of Croats in Medjimurje is similar to the treatment of Serbs in Vojvodina." The Hungarian press started a simultaneous anti-Croatian campaign, led by the pro-government *Magyar Nemzet*, and echoed in various government-sponsored publications.

Lorković's complaint that Hungary's treatment of Serbs in Vojvodina was similar to that extended to Croats in Medjimurje was exaggerated. Hungarian army units and gendarmes killed several thousand Serbs in Novi Sad and southern Bačka in January 1942, while killings of civilians in Medjimurje were extremely rare. The anti-Serb raid (*racija*) in the winter of 1942 was itself an isolated episode, however. It caused considerable controversy and a subsequent investigation in Budapest. On the whole, however, the Hungarians' treatment of the Serb minority was far better than the Ustašas'. Serb civilian losses in the Hungarian occupied areas during the

---

[1] PA, Büro Staatssekretär, Kroatien, Bd. 1, No. 707. Troll-Obergfell to the Foreign Ministry, 10 July 1941.

[2] PA, Büro RAM 13, Kroatien. Note by Wörmann No. 2292 of 11 July 1941.

[3] T-501, roll 264. Glaise to the OKW, 20 July 1941.

[4] ASSIP, MVP NDH, VT I-41, F-1, No. 24/41. Lorković's note, 26 July 1941.

war were lower than the average for Yugoslavia as a whole.¹ This must have been disappointing to Slavko Kvaternik, who in 1941 eagerly advised the Hungarian general staff representative, Kalman Kory: *We'll throw the Serbs into the Sava, and you throw them into the Danube.*²

Far from following Kvaternik's advice, the Hungarians upped the ante in September 1941 by concentrating troops along Croatia's northern border and conducting military exercises in the region.³ In October two prominent Croats in Medjimurje were arrested as hostages following the murder of a pro-Hungarian village mayor, and all local border traffic was ended.⁴ At the same time Hungary extended its publicity to other satellite capitals.⁵ It was effective enough by mid-October for Lorković to instruct all NDH posts abroad to collect information "on any anti-Croatian propaganda by the Hungarians."⁶ The MVP Department Balkans-East reported an escalation of "Hungary's anti-Croatian propaganda in several European capitals."⁷ The agitation was notable in Sofia, which was unsurprising since Bulgaria had its own reasons for unease about any regional grouping that included Romania. The Bulgarians expressed their concern to Židovec about an alleged Romanian offer of a pact to Slovakia and Croatia.⁸ Lorković replied that no such Romanian offer had been made, and that the NDH would never join any anti-Bulgarian combination. Ex-premier Tsankov subsequently urged Lorković to seek improved relations with Hungary, especially in view of the fact that both Croatia and Bulgaria had their problems with Italy.⁹ The Bulgarians had an ongoing dispute with Italy over western Macedonia, which the Italians included in their Greater Albania.

In November 1941 Židovec had a "tense" conversation with the Hungarian minister-councilor in Sofia, Alain de Paikert. To Židovec's horror, the Hungarian drew a parallel between Croatian rights in Medjimurje and Serbian rights in Bosnia, saying that both provinces belonged to their present

---

[1] See Kočović, op. cit., on Yugoslav losses. Comp. Vladimir Žerjavić, in *Gubici stanovništva Jugoslavije u Drugom svjetskom ratu*. Zagreb: Jugoslavensko viktimološko društvo, 1989.

[2] Kazimirović, op. cit., p. 108.

[3] T-120, roll 208, No. 1143. Kasche to the Foreign Ministry, 11 September 1941.

[4] ASSIP, MVP NDH, VT I-41, F-1, No. 124/41. Vrančić to Gaj, 25 October 1941.

[5] ASSIP, MVP NDH, VT I-41, F-1, No. 86/41. Židovec to Lorković, 13 October 1941.

[6] ASSIP, MVP NDH, VT I-41, F-1, No. 95/41. Lorković's circular of 16 October 1941.

[7] ASSIP, MVP NDH, VT I-41, F-1, No. 103/41. *Odsjek Balkan-Iztok* (Department Balkans-East) to Dr Huehn (Culture and Press Department) 18 October 1941.

[8] ASSIP, MVP NDH, VT I-41, F-1, No. 123/41. Židovec to Lorković, 24 October 1941.

[9] ASSIP, MVP NDH, VT I-4, no number.

masters [i.e. to Hungary and the NDH respectively] on the basis of historical, rather than ethnic considerations.[1] (Adding insult to injury, de Paikert denied that there was any "Croatian nobility," pointing out that their peerage charters were all granted by Hungarian kings.) The intransigent attitude of Hungary was equally apparent when Židovec spoke to the Hungarian minister in Sofia, Arnothy.[2] Throughout November he also reported a series of pro-Hungarian articles in the Bulgarian press.[3]

Finally, on 16 December 1941 the Hungarian parliament voted in favor of a government-sponsored bill, which included Medjimurje in "the southern lands" re-annexed to Hungary. Bardossy hailed "the faithful people of Murakoz" on their long awaited return to "the Hungarian motherland."[4] The Hungarian annexation of Medjimurje was followed by another Croatian protest.[5] This was an empty gesture: in December 1941 the crisis peaked in the East and Germany was even less willing than before to intervene. It even contemplated pulling out of the NDH altogether at that very time. Without German intervention there was no way for Pavelić to alter the Hungarian decision. Romanian and Slovak papers published articles supportive of Croatia, but those countries could not and would not go any further. Bulgaria kept quiet, Italy was gleefully expecting to march north of the demarcation line, and Pavelić's modest resources were overstrained by the raging insurgency in that half of the NDH still under his jurisdiction.

The dispute with Hungary indicated the narrow limits of Ustaša foreign policy even in an area where it was allowed some autonomy of action. Those limits were dictated by the perception of the *power* of Croatia by other actors; and Horthy had no doubt that it was negligible. This perception of weakness was coupled with Horthy's contempt for the Croats in general and for the Ustaša regime in particular. In early 1942 he wrote:

> The Croats, who for 800 years as part of Hungary were never exploited, could have lived continually subsidized and with no care; but they wanted to lay the foundations of an independent state. In this endeavor in my opinion they will never succeed, because they are not an element on which a state can be built.[6]

---

[1] ASSIP, MVP NDH, VT I-41, F-1, No. 206/41. Židovec to the MVP, 11 November 1941.

[2] ASSIP, MVP NDH, VT I-41, F-1, No. 292/41. Židovec to the MVP, 1 December 1941.

[3] ASSIP, MVP NDH, VT I-41, F-1, No. 241/41. Židovec to the MVP, 19 November 1941.

[4] ASSIP, VT I-41, F-1, No. 378/41. Gaj to the MVP, Budapest, 29 December 1941.

[5] ASSIP, MVP NDH, VT F-2, No. 46/42. NDH note to Hungary 15 January 1941.

[6] *The Confidential Papers of Admiral Horthy*, p. 192.

Horthy's views on Hungary's southern neighbors predated the war. In 1936 he wrote to Hitler that "the Serbs are those adversaries within the Little Entente to whom one could hold out a hand without blushing. Before the War they were our enemies with a visor held open, and they fought courageously in the War... [T]he Serbs are the best soldiers within the Little Entente."[1]

In a long letter to Hitler on 10 January 1942, Horthy opined that the majority of the population of Croatia is hostile to "the rootless Ustaša regime," with Bolshevik ideology "spreading not only among the Serbs in Croatia, who have every reason to hate the present Croat domination, but also among the Croat population."[2] He then summarized his view of geopolitical conditions in the Danubian basin:

> Now we Hungarians are living, so to speak, with open doors towards the Balkans, surrounded by peoples whose hatred is directed in the first place against us. This hatred manifests itself clearly even today. The reason is mainly that these peoples would not readily forfeit the valuable stretches of Hungarian lands adjudicated to them in Paris. In the form of an alliance and cooperation of Romanians, Croats and Slovaks we are again witnessing the birth of a second Little Entente which does not even try to conceal its hostile intentions.[3]

In subsequent months Pavelić had to come to terms with the Hungarian decision on Medjimurje because he had no alternative. Unconsolidated and on the brink of chaos, externally unsupported except for two other satellites with whom it even did not share a frontier, the NDH had no maneuvering space. Subsequent normalization of relations started with the promotion of Gaj to the rank of minister in early 1942. Trade talks, interrupted in December, were resumed, and although Medjimurje still appeared on Croatian maps as NDH territory, the subject was taken off the agenda. By the middle of 1943 the relations with the NDH were described by the Hungarian foreign ministry as "good-neighborly and normal. The two countries are separated by natural frontiers. Ethnic mixing is insignificant."[4] Hungary's traditional antagonism towards "the profiteers of Trianon" had remained, but Croatia was no longer regarded as negatively as Slovakia and Romania.[5] NDH diplomacy in its dispute with Hungary learned the fundamental lesson of foreign policy

---

[1] *The Confidential Papers of Admiral Horthy*, pp. 83-84.

[2] ibid. p. 188.

[3] ibid. p. 90.

[4] ibid. p. 238.

[5] ibid. p. 240.

making: in order to effect a desired outcome, a state needs to have the resources to alter its environment in accordance with that objective. Devoid of such resources and coherent strategy, the Ustaša state also proved devoid of ability to conduct foreign policy in a substantive sense.[1]

5. Partners in the Holocaust

A hundred-odd middle-class professionals, mostly lawyers and in many cases not formal members of the Ustaša movement, put their services at the disposal of the regime and enabled its foreign ministry to function, however inaptly. This fact invites some comment about the nature of Croatia's body-politic. Croatia's contemporary historiography, when not openly apologetic of the country's record in 1941-1945, often seeks to establish that the four years of Pavelić's rule were an anomaly which temporarily superimposed itself on the Croatian society only due to the distressing legacy of two previous decades of the Kingdom of Yugoslavia. That society's refusal to confront the past, reinforced by the political expediency of the present, brings to mind the lines from Oscar Wilde's *De Profundis*, which Japanese prime minister Konoye left underlined on his deathbed: "Terrible as it was what the world did to me, what I did to myself was far more terrible still."

The scope of moral issues raised by Pavelić's regime is similar to that facing a student of the Third Reich. Without participation of a sizeable segment of the urban middle class, Pavelić's project would not have functioned even in its ramshackle form. If a regime so exceeds the bounds of previously conventional morality as to put one third of its population outside the law, and to devote resources to the brutal murder of some hundreds of thousands of them, then anyone on its payroll cannot avoid being tainted. Vlaho Buško or Count Pejacsevics may not have been personally evil. They, and thousands of people like them in Zagreb, Osijek, Varaždin or Karlovac were "normal" men whose ostensibly harmless work aided and abetted a regime of institutionalized evil and immorality.

The sinister essence of the NDH totalitarianism, surprisingly enough, was not evident in its underdeveloped Ustaša form, in the coarse persons of

---

[1] At his trial in 1946 in Zagreb it was alleged that Archbishop Stepinac had received the NDH Foreign Ministry archives at the end of the War. Vladimir Dedijer's *The Yugoslav Auschwitz and the Vatican: The Croatian Massacre of the Serbs During World War II* (Buffalo, N.Y., 1992), pp. 414-416, includes a copy of a receipt showing that Stepinac received eight sealed boxes from the NDH Foreign Ministry at the end of the War. Dedijer asserted that these boxes were subsequently taken to Rome, presumably to College of San Girolamo.

Pavelić, Boban or Luburić. It was far more tangible in the Ministry of Foreign Affairs of the Independent State of Croatia, among the decent, eminently God-fearing, *Mitteleuropeaisch*-educated bureaucrats. They knew that nasty things went on at the camps, or in the villages south of the Sava, and they would have fainted if forced to view the tangible results of a day's hard work by Luburić's *Obrana* at Jasenovac. Describing one such bureaucrat, one of Pavelić's ex-diplomats – the NDH delegate to the German food directorate in Berlin – wrote in the late 1970s:

> Matko Mašeg was not a 'disappointed Ustaša.' He was a man honest and religious, who – like many others – could not partake in the methods of political struggle prevalent at that time in the Balkans. That is why he asked for another assignment. He remained a supporter of Croatian statehood and he retained respect for Dr Ante Pavelić until his death... He was socially withdrawn, sentimental and given to philosophizing...[1]

It was hardly remarkable that a "religious" and "sentimental" man could not stomach the "methods of political struggle" [sic!] in the NDH. It is more interesting to note that he resolved the problem by making sure that he did not have to see, and therefore to "know." It is possible that there were people in Zagreb who did not know what was happening some fifty miles downstream at Jasenovac, but it was possible only if one willfully chose not to know. Jasenovac was much closer geographically and figuratively than "the East" had been to a Berliner. The difference between an Agramer who had internalized and emotionally accepted Pavelić's *Endloesung* as a welcome thing, and his neighbor who had refused to acknowledge that it was taking place at all, was that of degree rather than kind.

The paradox of the banality of evil is that Matko Mašeg's office work (in procuring foodstuffs for Pavelić's besieged and shrinking domain) probably had more disastrous long-term effects on the fate of the victims of the Ustaša regime than the work of any single murderer leading the Black Legion's flying squads. At its essential level, the control exercised by the center of all real power – Ante Pavelić – depended on the acceptance by all those on the state payroll (from the under-secretaries of state to the notaries-public in local boroughs) of the inviolability of the regime's goals and norms of behavior.

A man could go to Berlin in order "not to know," but even there the reality of those "methods of political struggle" back home occasionally caught

---

[1] Milan Blažeković. "Poslanstvo NDH u Berlinu 1944-1945." *Hrvatska Revija*, Vol. 29, No. 3 (115), September 1978, p. 556.

up with them. A case in point was when they were instructed from Zagreb that the Serb guest-workers in Germany should be given only one-way passes back to the NDH instead of proper passports; nobody could pretend not to know what was the purpose of that order. But it was in connection with the "Jewish question" that Pavelić's diplomats confirmed their status as fully-fledged accomplices *par excellence* in the crime of genocide.

Anti-Jewish legislation was introduced immediately after the proclamation of the NDH, before there could be any pressure in that direction from the Germans. The "Ordinance on the Protection of Aryan Blood and Honor of the Croat People" and the "Ordinance on Racial Origin" were proclaimed already in April 1941.[1] The synagogue in Zagreb (above) was razed to the ground, rather than converted to some other use. Thousands of Jews were killed by the Ustašas in 1941, well before the extermination camps in Poland started operating in earnest. They were murdered with the brutality that surpassed almost anything known in Nazi Europe. Overall,

> The Jews [in Yugoslavia] experienced widely disparate treatment at the hands of the local population. In Serbia, the local populace was friendly and helpful, as were the Italians in the coastal areas. Important elements among the Croat population supported, at first at least, the Fascist government of Ante Pavelić. No succor could be expected for the Jews from the local urban populations of Zagreb and Osijek.[2]

The Ustaša regime was primarily interested interested in killing as many Serbs as possible. Lorković was therefore only too happy to have the remaining Croatian Jews "deported" to the Reich, and signed an agreement

---

[1] *Hrvatski Narod*, Zagreb, 1 May 1941.

[2] Yehuda Bauer. *The Holocaust in Historical Perspective*. London: Sheldon Press, 1978, p. 66.

with the Reich government, agreeing to pay a sum of 30 Marks for each deported Jew, as compensation to the Reich for organizing deportations.[1]

The sore spot for both Croats and Germans was the fact that a third of Croatian Jews had managed to flee into the Italian-held areas, where their lives were at least temporarily safe. This was the subject of repeated German-Croatian consultations and an additional argument for Pavelić in his attempts to obtain greater German support against Italian field commanders.[2] In July 1942 Luther reported to Ribbentrop that in Zagreb there was growing concern about the attitude which the Italian government would take with regard to the preparations for mass deportations:

> So far as the Croatian side is concerned, they are in principle in full agreement with the Jewish deportations. They consider it of special importance to effect the deportation of the four to five thousand Jews in the Second Zone, which is occupied by the Italians (including the important towns of Dubrovnik and Mostar). They constitute politically a great hindrance, and their removal would ease matters generally.[3]

The problem was "the effective resistance of the Italian authorities to the anti-Jewish measures of the Croatian Government." In August Kasche urged intervention in Rome, after Lorković had failed to obtain Casertano's assurances that the Jews under Italian control would be deported.[4]

In a memorandum for Hitler on the situation in Croatia prepared a month later Kasche praised the Croats for applying anti-Jewish measures wherever they were in control. At the same time, the NDH Minister in Rome, Perić (l.), was under Italian pressure to agree to a different formula: the transfer of Croatian Jews to Italy. The Croatian side resisted such demands, arguing that Croatia's agreement with Germany made it impossible for Zagreb to agree to the transfer of the Jews to Italy without the consent of Berlin. If such a transfer

---

[1] Leon Poliakov and Jacques Sabille. *Jews Under the Italian Occupation*. New York: Howard Fertig, 1983, p. 134.

[2] See account of Pavelić's conversation with Hitler at Vinica, above.

[3] Poliakov and Sabille, op. cit., p. 135.

[4] ibid. p. 138.

could nevertheless be arranged, Croatia would ask from Italy the same conditions that had been promised by Germany: "the right to take over the possessions of the transferred Jews."[1] This problem could be resolved to the full satisfaction of both Germans and Croats only after the fall of Italy.

Both before and after that time, the diplomatic efforts towards the final solution of both the "Serb Problem" and the "Jewish Problem" were earnestly made by Pavelić's accomplices at the Foreign Ministry of the Independent State of Croatia. Its "civilized" accomplices would not have willingly shared their dinner table with Luburić's cutthroats from Jasenovac. Yet for all its *Mittel*-European, bourgeois spirit and composition, and for all its ostensible disdain for "Balkan methods," it was an organization well worthy of the Ustaša name.

---

[1] ibid. p. 142.

XI
The Turning Point

1. German-Partisan Contacts

The summer of 1942 was the critical period of the war on all fronts. The fall saw several dramatic reverses of the Axis, and as 1943 began Germany was on the strategic defensive which would continue until the war's end. In January Roosevelt and Churchill met in Casablanca and decided that the focus of their immediate action would be in the Mediterranean area. Aware of the threat to his position in the southeast Hitler engaged in relentless pursuit of insurgents in the NDH in the first half of the year, determined to secure his rear in case of an Allied landing. The shifting military environment also opened possibilities for political realignments in the Balkan area.

On the German side four different projects directly concerned the Ustaša state. One was supportive of Pavelić, three were not:

- Sensing that Mihailović and the Western Allies were a threat to Tito's plans no less than they were to the Germans', the pro-Ustaša German minister in Zagreb, Siegfried Kasche, advocated an understanding with the Partisans.
- Three key German generals in the Balkans (Glaise, Löhr and Lüters), reinforced by the newcomer Lothar Rendulic, continued their attacks on the Ustaša regime hoping to remove it altogether.
- Also opposed to Pavelić, albeit for different reasons, was Heinrich Himmler, who had empire-building ambitions in the Balkans and energetically proceeded to pursue them throughout 1943.
- An unexpected reinforcement to the generals came from the Wilhelmstrasse in the person of Hermann Neubacher, who was given wide powers in the second half of 1943 to organize "national anti-Communist forces" in the Balkans. Neubacher sought to do this by conducting a policy more conciliatory to the Serbs and implacably hostile to the Ustašas.

Hard pressed and in danger of annihilation, the Partisans established contact with the Germans in early March 1943, ostensibly in order to renew the exchanges of prisoners. The first contacts were established in the summer of 1942 through Hans Ott in Livno, and the first exchange of prisoners was completed on 5 September 1942. Such exchanges continued until the end of the year, and included captured Ustašas as well as Germans. Initially, the talks involved a captured German officer, one Major Strecker. They soon evolved into political negotiations which eventually went far beyond the objectives described by Tito shortly before his death.[1]

Five months earlier, in November 1942, Tito put out his first feelers to find out if the Germans would let him concentrate all his forces against the Četniks. In return he offered a truce south of the Sava and an end of all Partisan attacks on the key Zagreb-Belgrade railroad north of the river.[2] Although both Kasche and Glaise supported the idea, it could not be pursued because at that very time Hitler decided to deal a mortal blow to all insurgents with his "Directive 47."

At the height of *Weiss II* three high-ranking Partisans went to the 717 Infantry Division headquarters to negotiate an exchange for Strecker. They were Koča Popović (with Tito, r.), Milovan Djilas and Vladimir Velebit, the first under his own name, the other two under aliases "Marković" and "Petrović." Djilas was the most senior, as a member of the Politbureau of the Communist Party of Yugoslavia. In line with Tito's later account of the event, they initially said that they wanted recognition as belligerents. However, according to German records, they also stated that they did not want to fight against the Croat state, and certainly not against the Germans, but only against the Četniks.[3] According to Colonel  Pfaffenroth, Lüters's chief of staff, they even said that they would also fight the British if they landed on the Adriatic Coast.

On March 11 in the evening Glaise obtained the information from Gornji Vakuf about the Partisans' offer. Just like Lüters earlier in the day, Glaise felt that he did not have the authority to authorize political talks which the

---

[1] "During the battle of the Neretva... we had a number of German and Italian prisoners. Among them was battalion commander Strecker... Of course we did not want to liquidate them, because we adhered to the Geneva Convention on POWs. Three of our comrades went to negotiate on the exchange of prisoners, whereby our forces would be granted the status of a belligerent side in the spirit of the norms of the law of war. We only succeeded in exchanging prisoners..." (Tito's account broadcast on Yugoslav television, 12 November 1978)

[2] The first to publish a full account of negotiations in English was Walter Roberts (1973). See Tomasevich, *The Chetniks*, p. 244; Krizman (1983), p. 540; Pavlowitch (1971).

[3] T-501, roll 267, No. 15. A note on the telephone report by Colonel Pfaffenroth, General Lüters's chief of staff, 11 March 1943.

Partisans were suggesting. He telephoned his friend Wilhelm Hoettl at the RSHA for an opinion.[1] Germany's chain of upward communication was soon in full swing. Hoettl immediately contacted the RSHA chief of foreign intelligence, Walter Schellenberg, who passed the information to Ribbentrop. When Ribbentrop approached Hitler with the news, however, he cut the whole business short by saying that "one does not negotiate with the rebels, one shoots them."

Initially unaware of Hitler's rigid stand, Kasche reported on March 17 that Ott's negotiations with Tito's plenipotentiaries had opened the possibility that the Partisans would halt all combat against Germans, Italians and Croats, and – once this was agreed by the Germans – retreat to the Sanjak to deal with the Četniks.[2] Kasche also indicated the Partisans' stated readiness to accept "pacification" of the NDH and added that both Lorković and Casertano viewed the proposal favorably. A few days later Kasche eagerly reported that,

"in the context of the Partisans' earlier statements," their actions against Četnik forces in Herzegovina were "quite useful" to the Germans.[3]

The Partisans, too, had not realized that Hitler rejected *a priori* their bold schemes. Assuming that the possibilities were still wide open, when Djilas went to Zagreb on March 26, accompanied by Velebit (second from right, l.), he offered the Germans an open-ended truce. In return the Partisans only asked to be left alone by the Axis forces which would enable them to devote all their energies to fighting Draža Mihailović in the area of Sanjak.[4] This offer tallied with Kasche's earlier message of March 17, which suggests that the truce with the Germans and Ustašas, followed by a showdown with Mihailović, was the consistent Partisan line, approved from the top. Glaise and Kasche saw eye to eye on an issue for once. Unhappy about what they regarded as a wasted opportunity, they urged substantive negotiations with the Partisans on their respective

---

[1] See W. Hagen (1953), Ch. 4.

[2] T-120, roll 212, No. 1174. Kasche to the foreign ministry, 17 March 1941; also: ADAP, E, V, pp. 416-417; PA, Büro Staatssekretär, Kroatien, Bd. 4, No. 316. Comp: Hory and Broszat, op. cit., p. 144.

[3] T-120, roll 212, No. 1271. Kasche to the foreign ministry, 23 March 1943.

[4] T-120, roll 212, No. 1303. Kasche to the foreign ministry, 26 March 1943.

fronts, at the foreign ministry and at the OKW. They both asked the Communists to stop, as a token of good will, all attacks on the key railroad connecting Belgrade and Zagreb, thus creating a basis for eventual negotiations.[1] The Partisans immediately accepted this measure and the attacks were unilaterally halted. They were renewed only some months later, when Tito realized that the Germans would not play along.

On March 29, following Hitler's instructions, Ribbentrop poured cold water on Kasche's combinations. He forbade any further contact with the Partisans and sharply asked for Kasche to explain his undue advocacy of unauthorized talks.[2] Kasche (to Pavelic's left, below) justified his attempts by restating his conviction that a political solution was needed to the Partisan problem, "so hard to solve by military means."[3] His argument was essentially the same as that made by the Italian generals, except that he advocated an understanding with the Partisans in order to crush Mihailović, while the Italians worked with the "national" Serbs against Tito. Kasche's approach was preferable from the point of view of the Ustašas, to whom even the Communists were more palatable than the "greater Serbian" Četniks. As for the Italians, by the spring of 1943 they were well disposed to support any combination which promised pacification and allowed them to keep their forces intact, undispersed, and close to the Adriatic coast.

The common ground that the Germans *objectively* had with the Partisans in the spring of 1943 was their opposition to Mihailović. This had given Tito great hopes. Without waiting for the outcome of talks in Zagreb he issued strict orders that all Partisan activity against German, Italian and NDH forces should be stopped; this was reiterated even after Djilas and Velebit returned from Zagreb.[4] He sent couriers (sometimes under German protection) to Partisan units with the message that "the most important task right now is the

---

[1] Krizman (1983), p. 543; Kazimirović, op. cit. p. 182f.

[2] ADAP, E, V, pp. 501-502, Ribbentrop to Kasche, 29 March 1943.

[3] T-120, roll 212, No. 1333. Kasche to Ribbentrop, 30 March 1943.

[4] Djuretić, op. cit., Vol. I, p. 248.

destruction of the Četniks of Draža Mihailović.¹ At odds with Tito's self-professed respect for the laws of warfare was his simultaneous order to shoot all captured Četnik officers "without mercy" and "on the spot," while other ranks were to be secretly liquidated as well if they did not join the Partisans.²

Kasche was not the only one to be rebuked from afar. Moscow, too, reacted with dismay to the news that Tito was negotiating with the Germans.³ At that time the Soviet Union was engaged in the demolition of Mihailović's reputation in the West on the grounds of his alleged collaboration with the enemy. Any leak of what Tito was up to would have been highly embarrassing. In addition, it could not have suited Stalin to give Hitler any respite in the Balkans while the Wehrmacht was recovering after Stalingrad and preparing for the summer round of fighting.

Persistent in lobbying for his pet project, Kasche addressed Ribbentrop one more time on April 17 requesting permission to talk to the Partisans and play them off against Mihailović.⁴ Ribbentrop's renewed *nein* came four days later. He told Kasche that the Germans had at long last succeeded in convincing Mussolini of the need to destroy both insurgent groups simultaneously, and therefore they could not suddenly start advocating a policy vis-a-vis Tito which not very different from the previous Italian position vis-a-vis Mihailović.⁵

In early May 1943 Tito finally realized that the Germans would not change their mind. He sent a message to his units to resume the acts of sabotage, suspended in late March. Once again, however, the Četniks were named as the chief enemy. The lull in fighting in April, coupled with Tito's hopes of a deal with the Germans, slackened his guard and probably contributed to the shock and confusion in his ranks when Operation *Schwarz* suddenly hit his forces in mid-May.

When Italy capitulated four months later, Kasche renewed his pleading for a deal with the Partisans.⁶ He claimed that many Croats had joined Tito's forces for "national reasons," driven to revolt by the Italian behavior. Acting in accord with Pavelić, he added that the NDH would grant them an amnesty.

---

[1] A-V.I.I. *Zbornik* II/8, p. 392. Tito, Ranković, Žujović to Iso Jovanović, 29 April 1943.

[2] A-V.I.I., Box 7, Reg. No. 2-2; Djuretić, Vol. I, p. 249.

[3] The Comintern to Tito, in J.B. Tito, *Sabrana djela*, Vol. XIV, Belgrade 1984, p. 201.

[4] ADAP, E, V, pp. 616-618. Kasche to Ribbentrop, 17 April 1943.

[5] T-120, roll 212, No. 502. Ribbentrop to Kasche, 21 April 1943. Same document in: ADAP, E, V, pp. 668-669.

[6] ADAP, E, VI, p. 511. Kasche to Ribbentrop, 9 September 1943.

Kasche's stated objective this time was to "demolish the political and moral base" of the Partisan movement by detaching Croats from Tito and drawing them to the Ustašas. Kasche was encouraged by contacts with a leading Croat Partisan, Marijan Stilinović, through the ubiquitous Ott.[1] Those talks resulted in several agreements. The Germans were able to purchase horses and export timber and chemicals from some Partisan-held territories in Croatia. While falling short of a breakthrough, such contacts kept the door ajar for more agreements if Kasche obtained the green light from Berlin.

Kasche's advocacy of a deal with Tito's Partisans was supported by Glaise, but their motives were different. Glaise took a broader view than Kasche and realized that any truce with Tito or victory over Mihailović would be of merely temporary benefit, for as long as the root political cause of insurgency – the inherently chaotic Ustaša regime – remained in power. Kasche, on the other hand, expected that a truce with Tito would improve the position of the Ustaša regime, with which his own career had become closely linked. At that time Löhr energetically demanded not only the removal of Pavelić and the Ustašas from power, but also the replacement of Kasche from the post in Zagreb. A sleight of hand that would consist of allowing Tito to wipe out the Četniks *and* to keep his Partisans quarantined in the middle of nowhere in Sanjak – and all that with no loss of German blood – would have made Kasche's position inviolable, and any further debate about Pavelić's regime superfluous.

Glaise and Löhr scored a partial victory at the end of 1942, but they had never become fully reconciled that in spite of their pleading Hitler decided to keep the Ustašas in power. They had full control over Pavelić's armed forces and administrative authority over the zones of operations. This resulted in a significant reduction of atrocities by the Ustašas after November 1942. (This applied to the two key camps, Jasenovac and Gradiška, only to a limitied extent, where the mass killings had continued, albeit at a reduced rate.) The Wehrmacht top brass wanted a commitment from Hitler to a radical political switch in Croatia. Only such fundamental change, they thought, could remove the political roots of the insurgency.[2]

In February 1943, at the height of *Weiss*, Glaise wrote to General Warlimont, with whom he enjoyed an excellent rapport.[3] "Giving the state to

---

[1] Cf. Kazimirović, op. cit., p. 191, quoting statement by Glaise's interpreter Willibald Nemecek. Compare with statements by Glaise's aide-de-camp Metzger and his accounts clerk Engelbert Teufelhardt, in KAW/B-67.

[2] T-501, roll 267. Glaise to OKW, 27 January 1943.

[3] T-501, roll 264. Glaise to Warlimont, 15 February 1943.

a clique of rootless émigrés" was a flawed experiment, but the solution could still be found, Glaise opined, if Germany took power in Croatia in the form of a military administration, supported by "an auxiliary apparatus of non-Ustaša Croats." Only Maček's people could do that, but Glaise wondered whether its leaders could be won over for cooperation "at this advanced time." When Löhr advocates getting rid of the Ustašas – Glaise added – "he is certainly pointing at the putrid abscess on the state organism of Croatia." He concluded that if it was impossible to remove Pavelić the alternative was to continue merely "scraping along" (*fortwurlsten*) and making the best of a poor deal by increasing German influence at all levels.

A sustained attack on Pavelić by the German military establishment came on March 3, 1943, when Löhr, as the Wehrmacht Commander South-East, presented Jodl with his memorandum addressed to Hitler on "The Necessary Political, Administrative and Economic Reforms in Croatia After Military Operations."[1] It categorically demanded not only the removal of Pavelić and the Ustašas from power, but also an urgent replacement of Minister Kasche, "who, as an ideologue, does not see the reality." The demand by a German general that the head of a diplomatic mission be removed from his post was bold and unprecedented. It was the culmination of a brewing dispute between Löhr and Kasche. The Austrian general could not stand the SA activist-cum-diplomat; he detested Kasche both personally – as the embodiment of an arrogant, yet socially inferior Prussian – or politically, because of his blindly pro-Ustaša zeal. Kasche, for his part, accused Löhr of seeking a conciliatory policy towards the Četniks, which he knew was anathema to Hitler as well as Ribbentrop.[2]

In view of a host of Glaise's similar reports, Löhr's memorandum did not come as a surprise at the OKW. The bluntness of its tone and the scope of changes it advocated were without precedent. Löhr's step was prompted by Pavelić's demand that the areas taken from Tito during *Weiss I* be given to the NDH authorities to administer. Löhr was determined to resist any such hand-over, and stated in his memorandum that the aftermath of *Weiss* demanded radical reforms. He said that the Croats were not able to rule themselves: the government had no credibility and the NDH armed forces were in permanent disarray. German forces of law and order were reduced to being "passive observers of Ustaša terrorism against the Orthodox, which – according to the Ustašas' own count – resulted in the death of 400,000 people."

---

[1] For the full text of Löhr's memorandum, see ADAP, E, VI, pp. 32-36. Hory and Broszat, pp. 146-147.

[2] PA, Staatssekretär Ritter, Pol. 8, No. 1. Kasche to the foreign ministry, 20 January 1943.

Löhr's suggested solution envisaged Pavelić's replacement by a government of "Maček's followers and experts," although Loehr did not anticipate Maček's own participation. Kasche's removal would be followed by Glaise becoming the "special plenipotentiary of the Reich and commander of German troops," empowered to exercise executive authority in the NDH. The Ustaša movement would be disbanded altogether, and the land "purged of unreliable and corrupt elements." A strong propaganda campaign against Tito's Partisans would be developed, and the anti-Serb course abandoned.

2. The SS and the NDH

Löhr's memorandum was prepared just as Hitler decided to entrust Heinrich Himmler (r.), whose power within the Nazi establishment was on the constant rise, with extensive powers to establish order there. On March 10, 1943 Hitler issued an order of great long-term significance for the Ustaša state. It had four key points:
1. All areas affected by Operation *Weiss* to remain German zones of operation until further notice;
2. Himmler is authorized to establish police forces to ensure pacification in those areas and its members would be recruited locally;
3. German commanders would determine the boundaries of the zones;
4. Himmler's plenipotentiary in Croatia would receive instructions only from the *Reichsfuehrer*, and was to report directly to him.[1]

Aware of Hitler's new order, Keitel decided not to send Löhr's memorandum to Hitler but to forward it to Himmler instead. In his covering letter Keitel emphasized that, according to Hitler's wishes, Himmler's task in Croatia had to be camouflaged "to the outside," and above all vis-à-vis the Italians, under the guise of purely military measures for the establishment of peace in operational areas.[2]

Hitler's special assignment to Himmler was the culmination of a long struggle by the *Reichsfuehrer* to turn the Balkans into an SS sphere of interest. This ambition was linked with his attempts to acquire an exclusive authority over the *Volksdeutsche* of southeastern and central Europe. Himmler's

---

[1] ADAP, E, V, No. 194, pp. 385-386. Hitler's order of 10 March 1943.
[2] Comp. Krizman (1983), p. 510, and Kazimirović, op. cit., p. 247. Both quoted Werner Maser. *Nürnberg, Tribunal der Sieger*. Düsseldorf-Wien, 1977.

ambition was linked to the refusal of the Wehrmacht to recognize service in the *Waffen SS* as equal to the performance of the Reich military service. This severely limited the pool of available *Reichsdeutsche* volunteers. To meet the growing need for manpower Himmler started clandestinely recruiting the *Volksdeutsche* from the Balkans and Central Europe even before the war. As German influence over those areas spread, so did the ability of the SS to control the ethnic Germans.[1]

The fall of Yugoslavia – a country with a German minority of over half a million – provided the first opportunity for unbridled SS recruitment, not only in the German-occupied Serbia (Banat) but also in the NDH (Slavonija, Srem). The first to give up some sovereignty over their German citizens were the Slovaks, who within months of independnce in March 1939 granted their 130,000 *Volksdeutsche* full autonomy, approved their direct links with Germany, and created separate German units within the Slovak army. Concessions escalated until in 1944 the Slovaks completely relinquished authority over their *Volksdeutsche* to the Reich and the SS. The Hungarians were forced to follow a similar path, albeit with greater resistance to German demands. In Romania Himmler had never obtained full jurisdiction over local ethnic Germans.

Unlike occupied Serbia – which formally included Banat – the NDH was recognized as a sovereign state by the Reich. This required at least formal negotiations on the status of the *Volksdeutsche*. This was not a problem: the concessions granted to the German minority in the summer of 1941 turned the *Volksgruppe* into a virtual state within the Ustaša state in political, administrative and military affairs. On September 16, 1941, a bilateral treaty allocated ten per cent of each annual levy of *Volksdeutsche* for voluntary enlistment with either the Wehrmacht or the Waffen SS. The rest were organized into separate units, the *Einsatzstaffel*, which grew to four battalions by mid-1942, or in the separate German units in the NDH Home Guard (*Domobranstvo*).

The ten-percent allotment was the first such concession granted to the Reich by another state. "By virtue of this measure Croatia was surrendering authority over a segment of its citizenry in regards to their military service. Furthermore, service in the Reich military would fulfill the Croatian military obligation."[2] The treaty was a source of irritation to the Italians. Kasche

---

[1] Valdis O. Lumans. "The Military Obligation of the Volksdeutsche of Eastern Europe towards the Third Reich." *East European Quarterly*. Vol. 23, No. 3 (1989), p. 309.

[2] Lumans, op. cit., p. 313.

reported from Zagreb that they saw in the *Volksgruppe* legislation an attempt to turn the NDH into a German protectorate.[1]

Himmler's next step was to eliminate the possibility of joining the Wehrmacht, which was still open to those ten percent of recruits. He also wanted to transfer all Germans in the *Domobranstvo* to the SS, and to expand recruitment without restrictions. Uncoordinated resistance to his plans from threee mutually antagonistic quarters – Kasche, Glaise, and the Italians – ensured Himmler's victory. In May 1942 the OKW conceded all military matters related to the *Volksdeutsche* in the Balkans to Himmler. In July Ribbentrop followed suit. He instructed Kasche (who had, as usual, espoused the cause of "Croatian sovereignty" in the matter) to inform Pavelić that the SS would launch an extensive recruitment campaign. Its aim was to enlist *all* NDH Germans in the 17-35 age group. This was "legalized" by an exchange of notes in September and October 1942. It is significant that the SS enlistment was *not* voluntary for the *Volksdeutsche* in the former Yugoslavia: their leaders "offered a collective declaration on behalf of the membership that was binding for all."[2] The leader of the *Volksgruppe* in the NDH Branimir Altgayer (with Kasche, Lorković and Pavelić, r.) set an example. He saw active service in 1943 as an SS *Hauptsturmführer* in Russia.[3]  Hitler's order of March 10, 1943, completed Himmler's triumph in the intra-German struggle for control in the NDH. Himmler appointed *Brigadefuehrer* Konstantin Kammerhofer as his plenipotentiary in Croatia. Kammerhofer arrived in Zagreb at the end of March.

As an old SA trooper Kasche disliked the SS and opposed Himmler's efforts to build an autonomous power base in the NDH. He complained that

---

[1] T-120, roll 208, No. 1435. Kasche to the foreign ministry, 14 September 1941.

[2] ibid. p. 314.

[3] Mario Jareb. "The German Ethnic Group in the Independent State of Croatia from 1941 to 1945." *Review of Croatian History,* Vol. 3, 2007, No. 1, p. 212. Jareb quotes the *Jahrbuch der Deutschen Volksgruppe im Unabhängingen Staate Kroatien 1944* which published a list of 312 SS men from the NDH killed in action in Russia between August 1941 and September 1943.

the Ustašas were faithful to Germany and that Himmler wanted to lure Croat recruits for the SS with bribes, "which is not in accordance with the all-German policy."[1] In a meeting described by Glaise as very difficult, Pavelić complained to Kammerhofer about the open infringement of sovereignty. Encouraged by Kasche, Pavelić tried to solicit Ribbentrop's support. His minister in Berlin, Mile Budak, handed a note to Weizsäcker on 12 April which stated that placing of Croatian gendarmerie under the SS, "even if seen in the most flexible form," was incompatible with Croatia's sovereignty:

> Such subjugation would be welcome to the enemy propaganda. It would see it on the one hand as an end to Croatian independence, while on the other it would hold the German Reich responsible for all measures aimed at the maintenance of the public order and security [and] bring into question yet again the frontiers between Croatia and Italy.[2]

Weizsäcker did nothing: he knew that Himmler's gains were irreversible. Kammerhofer (l.) flaunted his victory in two meetings with Kasche, on March 27 and 31, 1943.[3] The newly appointed *Höherer Polizeifuehrer* in Croatia spoke and acted as if he were a *Reichskommissar*. To Kasche's insistence that Croatia was an "allied sovereign country" Kammerhofer replied that he would extend the territory under his control beyond the zones of operations, and to the entire northern part of the country, and that he would recruit 2,500 *Volksdeutsche*, as well as thousands of Croats, into his gendarmerie.

Glaise and Löhr decided that if they could not beat Himmler they would join him in curtailing Pavelić. On 4 April they decided that the time had come to extend German "executive authority" over all NDH units north of the Sava river.[4] This was a rare instance of the Wehrmacht and the SS acting in political unison. Glaise's confidential telegram to Himmler of 10 April 1943 (the second anniversary of the NDH) informed the SS chief that there was no

---

[1] PA, Büro Staatssekretär, Kroatien, Bd. 4, Kasche to the foreign ministry.

[2] ADAP, E, V, pp. 576-578. Budak to Weizsäcker, 12 April 1943.

[3] T-120, roll 212, No. 1323. Kasche to the foreign ministry, 30 March 1943; T-120, roll 212, No. 1346. Kasche to the foreign ministry, 31 March 1943.

[4] T-501, roll 267. Note on the talks between Glaise and Löhr, 4 April 1943. Also in V.I.I. *Zbornik*, XII/3, pp. 206-208.

obstacle to carrying out "our plans" south of the Sava as well, because it was an area where the Germans had "executive power" anyway. Glaise added that the full control of public security throughout Croatia by the Germans was the final goal: only peripheral issues were open to discussion with the Croats.[1]

The *ad-hoc* coalition between the Wehrmacht and Himmler was impossible to resist. On 24 April Pavelić signed a protocol which formally provided for the establishment of a German gendarmerie in the NDH.[2] The NDH government was given only an advisory role in the arrangement, but at the same time it was obliged to cooperate in the execution of Kammerhofer's decisions. Pavelić also agreed that Kammerhofer would be free to recruit his security forces "by voluntary enlistment, drafting and transfer from other Croatian units."[3] Service with his gendarmerie would be recognized as satisfying NDH military obligation. The members of the new force would swear their allegiance to Adolf Hitler. All areas of engagement were to be determined by the Germans; the Croats would be merely "informed" of any such decision.

Himmler moved immediately to consolidate his gains. He produced another bitter pill for Pavelić: the establishment of an SS division composed exclusively of Muslims from Bosnia-Herzegovina, and officered by Germans.

3. Bosnian Muslims and the SS

The claim that Bosnian Muslims were "Croats of Islamic faith," however tenuous, was a key pillar of Ustaša ideology. It was also a prerequisite of practical politics, as only by asserting those Islamized Slavs' "purest Croatness" Pavelić could lay a viable claim to Bosnia-Herzegovina, in which the Croats accounted for only one-sixth of the population. Most Bosnian Muslims saw themselves as members of a distinct community, however, and avoided commitment. They were under-represented in the top tier of the regime by four members of Pavelić's advisory bodies, Džafer Kulenović (in civilian clothes, l.), Ademaga Mešić and Hakija Hadžić). Large numbers did join the Ustaše and participated in the atrocities, but the majority stayed aloof,

---

[1] T-501, roll 264. Glaise to Himmler, 10 April 1943; quoted by Krizman (1983), p. 532.

[2] T-501, roll 264. *Gedaechtnisaufzeichnung* signed by Glaise and Pavelić, 24 April 1943; also in *Zbornik*, XII/3, pp. 236-237.

[3] Glaise remarked that "the recruitment of volunteers is turning into a farce... From the Poglavnk's own bodyguard a dozen obedient Ustašas have deserted, only to appear that same evening with a mocking sneer, dressed in *ganz*-new SS uniforms, in front of their former superiors... Outside Croatian barracks SS agents are waiting in ambush."

especially in the areas with a large Serb population. A significant minority, furthermore, were self-declared Serbs.[1]

Among the Muslims who were initially prepared to give the new regime a benefit of the doubt, by the end of 1941 cautious support gave way to disillusionment. Discretely at first, some Muslims started advocating autonomy for Bosnia-Herzegovina within the NDH; others contemplated a form of Bosnian self-rule under direct German tutelage, altogether outside the Croat state. The inability of the regime to protect Muslim civilians from Serb reprisals, notably in the Drina River valley in eastern Bosnia, contributed to the mood of disenchantment. Resolutions condemning Ustaša crimes were signed by prominent Muslim citizens and sent to Zagreb.[2] In November 1942 a group of prominent Muslim businessmen, intellectuals and imams sent a memorandum to Hitler in which they accused the NDH of failing to create an ordered state and suggested the establishment of a separate political-administrative Bosnian unit centered in Sarajevo and controlled by Germany:

> They further suggested the establishment of a Bosnian-Muslim legion called the Bosnian Guard, which would also include Muslim personnel in Ustaša and Domobran units. In the territory of the proposed County of Bosnia all activities of the Ustaša movement and its units would be suspended. After the war Bosnia should be included among other European countries under the protection of the Third Reich, and it should enjoy the same degree of independence as its neighbors, the Memorandum stated.[3]

---

[1] Some of the most important names in Bosnian-Herzegovinian literature – Osman Djikić, Avdo Karabegović, Mehmed-Meša Selimović, Skender Kulenović, Ćamil Sijarić – were, as Selimović put it, "of Muslim background, Serbian by nationality." In our own time the Sarajevo-born film director Emir Kusturica – whose father, Murat, had always declared himself as a Serb – put it thus: "OK, maybe we were Muslim for 250 years, but we were Othodox before that and deep down we were always Serbs, religion cannot change that. We only became Muslims to survive the Turks." (*The Guardian*, London, 4 March 2010)

[2] Prominent Muslims of Banja Luka sent a petition to two Muslims in Pavelić's government (Džafer Kulenović and Hamdija Bešlagić) on November 12, 1941, protesting the treatment of their "Serb neighbors."

[3] Hrvoje Matković, *Povijest Nezavisne Države Hrvatske*. Zagreb: Naklada P.I.P. 2002, p. 89.

The authors also envisaged ceding some parts of Bosnia with a Croat majority to the NDH, some predominantly Serb regions to Montenegro, and subsequent population transfers and exchanges to ensure a Muslim majority in the autonomous Bosnian state.[1]

Any German attempt to assert Muslim distinctiveness and encourage expressions of a separate "Bosniak" identity was tantamount to an attack not only on the ideological foundations of the NDH but also on its practical existence. Heinrich Himmler proceeded to do both. The assertion about the "Croatian" character of Bosnian Muslims had never been taken seriously by the Germans. Hitler's remark about "fifty years of intolerance" was primarily anti-Serb, of course, but could have been meant to encourage Croatization of Muslims.[2] Glaise agreed with the assessment of his assistant Metzger:

> Bosnian Muslims would follow the Croats because they have the power... but at all times they would certainly seek to protect their special Muslim interests. Any assimilation of Muslims by Croats is out of the question, because a Muslim remains a Muslim. Just as he was not really a Serb when he passed himself for one, he will not become a Croat now.[3]

The Muslim obsession was a Himmlerian idiosyncrasy. In the SS chief Islam had found its most ardent admirer and promoter in the pre-multicultural Europe. Himmler's hatred of "soft" Christianity was matched by his liking for Islam, which he saw as a masculine, martial religion based on the SS qualities of blind obedience and readiness for self-sacrifice, untainted by compassion for one's enemies. While Hitler did not think much of Himmler's neo-pagan mysticism, he was happy to let Islam become the "SS religion." By creating an SS division composed of Bosnian Muslims he hoped to enhance the links between the SS and the Islamic world. Himmler believed that all Islamic nations were potentially sympathetic to Nazism and that among the Bosnian Muslims this feeling would be enhanced if Germany encouraged "Bosniak" particularism.[4] One of his closest aides, *Obergruppenführer* Gottlob Berger, boasted that "a link is created between Islam and National-Socialism on an open, honest basis. It will be directed in terms of blood and race from the

---

[1] No Muslim autonomist tendencies were present in Herzegovina and parts of Bosnia which were in the Italian zone. Already in September 1942 the Italian Army armed and equipped exclusively Muslim units in its network of the Voluntary Anti-Communist Militia (MVAC).

[2] See Hory and Broszat, op. cit., p. 94.

[3] From Metzger's report on the ethnic composition of the NDH, dated 23 April 1941. All his reports to Glaise are in BA/MAF, boxes 146-170.

[4] Compare with Holm Sundhausen. *Zur Geschichte der Waffen SS in Kroatien*, p. 188.

North," he wrote, "and in the ideological-spiritual sphere from the East." Himmler saw in Bosnian Muslims potentially good soldiers who hate "the common Jewish-English-Bolshevik enemy" and are unreservedly pro-Nazi. His plans had the objective of creating an autonomous and undisputed SS foothold in Bosnia, which he intended to turn into the new SS military frontier.[1] In his drive to recruit Bosnian Muslims Himmler enlisted the support of Haj Mohammed Amin al-Husseini, the Grand Mufti of Jerusalem and the former President of the Supreme Muslim Council of Palestine (with Hitler on November 21, 1941, below).

In May 1941, the Mufti declared jihad against Britain, "the greatest foe of Islam," and made his way to Berlin. To Hitler he declared his readiness to raise support for Germany among the Muslims in the Soviet Union, the Balkans, and the Middle East. He conducted radio propaganda through the network of six stations and set up anti-British espionage and fifth-column networks in the Middle East. In the annual protest against the Balfour Declaration held in 1943 at the Luftwaffe hall in Berlin, the Mufti praised the Germans because they "know how to get rid of the Jews, and that brings us close to the Germans and sets us in their camp."[2] He also pledged to solve the Jewish problem in Palestine "in the same way as the Jewish question in the Axis lands is being solved."

The Muslim spiritual leader visited the NDH in April 1943 under SS auspices. His visit gave a great boost to Muslim autonomist hopes. Pavelić refrained from making any comment about El Husseini's tour, but his aides bitterly complained to Kasche about it.[3] In spite of Ustaša displeasure Himmler's recruitment drive was a resounding success: by the end of 1943 more than twenty thousand Bosnian Muslims had enlisted in the 13. SS Mountain Division, which in May 1944 was given the name *Hanjar* (Turkish

---

[1] See Hory and Broszat, op. cit., p. 157.

[2] B. Schechtman, *The Mufti and the Führer: The Rise and Fall of Haj Amin el-Husseini*. New York, 1965.

[3] T-120, roll 212, Büro Staatssekretär, No. 1575. Kasche to the Ministry, 15 April 1943.

curved sword; the Muslim fez was adopted as its headgear). The total number of Bosnian Muslim volunteers in Himmler's units, including Kammerhofer's police, reached 46,000 by September 1943.[1] This exceeded the number of Bosnian Muslims in all the NDH forces, and was vastly greater than the number of Muslims with Tito's Partisans. Especially irksome to Pavelić and Kasche was Himmler's unwillingness to give his new division the designation "Croatian." By July 1943 the Croats complained to Kasche that the SS prevented them from exercising authority over their own citizens. Aggressive recruitment for Waffen-SS and for Kammerhofer's police was creating havoc in NDH units, insubordination and desertions. In addition Kammerhofer was extending his activity way beyond the areas of operations, with his recruiting centers and offices appearing all over the country.[2] Kasche attempted to help his hosts by intervening directly with the SS through Berger, when he visited Zagreb in July, but to no avail.[3]

By the spring of 1944, when the *Hanjar* Division returned to the Balkans, the area it held under control was excluded from any NDH authority and even local administrative officials could continue in their posts only if they took the SS oath. The new division had its moment of crisis in the early days, when a detachment of its sappers rebelled against mistreatment by German officers at Villefranche de Rouergue in France, where they had been sent for training. Five months later, however, when al-Husseini inspected the division in in Silesia (opp. p. and above), he was well pleased with its appearance and Himmler was satisfied regarding its combat readiness. The creation of an SS state-within-the-state was accompanied by unbridled propaganda favoring Bosnian-Muslim autonomy.

---

[1] Sundhausen, op. cit.; also quoted in Kazimirović, op. cit., p. 201f.

[2] T-120, roll 212, No. 2769. Kasche to Ribbentrop, 8 July 1943.

[3] T-501, roll 265. Kasche to Berger, 12 July 1943; Krizman (1983), p. 591.

The extent of Himmler's plans can be gleaned from a long report on the NDH prepared by *SS-Brigadefuehrer* Ernst Fick and the views of *Standartenfuehrer* Bayer who was in charge of ideological education for both *Hanjar* and *Prinz Eugen* divisions. Recounting the Ustašas' record, including slaughter of hundreds of thousands of Serbs, lack of discipline and unreliability, Fick concluded that Pavelić's authority was reduced to that of "the mayor of Zagreb, but without the suburbs." To bring order to the country and secure the rear in case of an Anglo-American landing, he suggested that all males aged 12 to 70 should be removed from the NDH and sent to the Reich as laborers. This would include the Ustašas and Domobrans; of the former one third could be drafted into the SS, of the latter "not more than 10 percent." Bayer, who was in charge of SS indoctrination of Bosnian Muslim as well as ethnic German novices, went even further. He suggested that Pavelić should be taken to Germany with his entire government for "mental evaluation and reeducation." He thought that the same treatment should be extended toKasche and to the staff of the German legation in Zagreb, who were afflicted by the same malaise.[1]

Himmler's motives in opposing Pavelić were different to those that motivated the opposition of the Wehrmacht. His calculus was primarily linked to the internal power politics of the Nazi hierarchy, rather than optimal combat results. Kammerhofer's police and Waffen SS recruitment among Bosnian Muslims and the *Volksdeutsche* of Croatia had as their objective the creation of an autonomous SS military frontier in the Southeast The project was an example of Himmler's empire-building, which grew more ambitious with each passing year of the war. Even the recruiting posters appealed on "Bosnians" (*Bosanci*), and not on "Croats of Islamic faith," to join his Muslim

---

[1] BA/Koblenz. NS 19/279. Pers. Stab RFSS. Fick's report to Himmler.

SS division (below). Their indoctrination was in an Islamized variety of Nazism (opp. p.). The cumulative effect of Himmler's efforts and those of the Wehrmacht was further reduction of Pavelić's authority. The decline could have been terminal but for the fall of Italy, which suddenly restored his fortunes in Berlin.

In March 1943 Hitler had a series of meetings with his allies Mussolini, Horthy, and Antonescu, who were in need of some morale boosting after the disasters in Russia and North Africa. This especially applied to Mussolini, who urged separate peace with Russia "which nobody can conquer or hold." After three days of Hitler's harangues (7-10 April) he returned to Rome empty handed and far from reassured.

Pavelić was one of those invited and met Hitler on April 27 at Klessheim Castle near Salzburg.[1] Before lunch Pavelić and his entourage were treated to a lengthy monologue by Hitler on the inevitability of an Axis victory, supported by statistics and maps. In the afternoon Hitler stated that there was "no urgent need for the meeting" since the cooperation between Germany and Croatia functioned well. He wanted to see Croatia pacified, which would free German troops for other tasks, secure the supplies of bauxite and lines of communication. Pavelić painted the internal political-military situation in rosy colors: the resistance of most of Tito's "bands" was broken and only some sporadic hotbeds of unrest remained. He claimed that there were "practically no unresolved internal political issues" in the NDH: party-political difficulties existed only among the intelligentsia, while the "masses" were only interested in the victorious conclusion of the war. Pavelić asked for greater autonomy of

---

[1] ADAP, E, V, pp. 713-714. Paul Schmidt's notes of the meeting between Hitler and Pavelić, 27 March 1943.

military units in the NDH from distant command centers. By this he alluded to Löhr, his archenemy, who commanded German troops in Croatia from Salonika. Hitler decided that this issue should be left to Keitel and Glaise.

Responding to Pavelić's remark that all Serbs, regardless of political orientation, were enemies of Croatian statehood, Hitler described the Serbs as "old troublemakers." He said that he had appeased Yugoslavia as much as possible, but to no avail. To Pavelić's remark that Belgrade was "opposed to everything which is not pan-Slav" Hitler retorted that the Serbs would oppose pan-Slavism if it were triumphant, because they were habitual oppositionists and plotters. Pavelić remarked that people in Belgrade cafés had always indulged in excessive discussion of foreign policy, and added that such tendencies were also present in Croatia. Hitler said there were such people in Germany too, "who dwell on world politics over a cup of tea because they have nothing better to do."[1] The only direct effect of Pavelić's visit, to the chagrin of the German field commanders, was an increase in the incidence of Ustaša anti-Serb terror in the aftermath of *Weiss*. The outrages had been

reduced after the imposition of Wehrmacht control over NDH units in November 1942. Hitler's new anti-Serb remarks encouraged Pavelić to try the old methods again in the areas "liberated" from Tito's Partisans.

Immediately prior to the meeting at Klassheim Pavelić had appeared defensive about the issue of anti-Serb persecution and its negative effect on the Axis war effort. What he obtained was a new nudge from Hitler, similar to his remark on "nationally intolerant policy" two years earlier. General Lüters complained in a letter to Glaise of a series of fresh Ustaša outrages, "especially after the Poglavnik's visit to the Führer's Headquarters."[2] Lüters listed several incidents reported by German troops in the field, and added that the Wehrmacht could not sit back and passively observe what was happening. To the contrary, German soldiers were forced in the areas of operations to prevent, even with arms, people of criminal disposition such as Gutić from occupying important posts, and from subverting, consciously and systematically, the action of

---

[1] Schmidt ended his minutes on a perhaps unconsciously funny note: "Tea was served next."
[2] T-501, roll 267. Lüters to Glaise, 6 June 1943.

pacification. Pavelić and Glaise clashed over an incident at Ivanić Grad where a German company, commanded by Captain Holeczek, used threat of arms to stop an Ustaša unit from terrorizing the surrounding villages. When Pavelić complained about "interference," Glaise energetically replied that the German officer was right to stop Ustaša activity detrimental to public order. He added that in any event the Croatian side was obliged to inform him in advance of all its intended police actions.

Glaise gained an ally when General Lothar Rendulic was appointed commander of the Second Panzer Army and thus the senior commander of German forces in Croatia in August 1943. Rendulic soon came to share Glaise's view that Pavelić and the Ustašas were an impediment to pacification in the Balkans. He suggested that the NDH government should be replaced by a German military administration, "with only a pretense of regard for the Ustaša state."[1] This view was also shared by Hermann Neubacher, who was appointed special political envoy in the southeast in August 1943. His task was to "politically organize national forces and guide them in their struggle against Communist bands." No German official in the Balkans enjoyed such wide powers as Neubacher, who quickly joined the ranks of Pavelić's enemies by arguing "against the continued existence of Pavelić's regime." That regime regarded him, in his own words, "as the main Enemy of the State."[2]

4. Italian Armistice

The crisis of Italian morale, obvious by the beginning of 1943, did not escape attention of Ustaša officials. Reports of the possible toppling of Mussolini by Badoglio and the royal family started reaching Zagreb in January.[3] The government reshuffle and Ciano's removal from the foreign ministry in February were interpreted as a sign of Mussolini's greater resolve.[4] But the continuation of pro-Četnik policy in the Italian occupation zone and Casertano's unyieldingly hostile attitude to the Ustaša government indicated that the change in Rome would not affect Italian policy in Croatia.[5]

It affected the Italian army even less. Roatta did not share Ambrosio's appetite for expanding the Italian occupation zone, but both he and his

---

[1] PA, Büro Staatssekretär, Kroatien, Bd. 6, No. 162771.

[2] Neubacher, op. cit. p. 155.

[3] Eg. A-VII, NDH, Kut. 286, No. 12/5. Dujmović to Lorković, Rome, 13 January 1943.

[4] A-VII, NDH, Kut. 256, No. reg. 51/6-1. "Top Secret Circular," 24 February 1943.

[5] Same source. Circular dated 21 April 1943.

successor Robotti continued with the same policy.¹ Based on cooperation with the Četniks in Herzegovina and Dalmatia, it also entailed sheltering thousands of Jews, avoiding large-scale combat against Partisans, , and generally doing all sorts of things which were odious to the regime in Zagreb. Ever unhappy with the role of Italy, Glaise wrote to Löhr (April 20, 1943) that the Germans could not resolve the political riddle in Croatia for as long as the "condominium" with Italy remained.

In March 1943 Pavelić's officials acknowledged for the first time in their reports the possibility of an Allied invasion of Italy and the danger that this could knock out Italy from the war.² By the end of the month Zagreb was echoing rumors from Rome created by the visit of Archbishop Spellman of New York to the Vatican. For the first time a foreign ministry circular spelled

out a theme that was to become an obsession of Pavelić's "analysts" in the last two years of war: the prospect of a separate peace between Germany and the Anglo-Americans in the face of the Soviet juggernaut, and the possibilities it would create for the NDH.³ In April the newly-appointed Croatian administrative commissioner with the Italian army at Sušak, David Sinčić, reported upon returning from Rome that "certain Italian opposition leaders" were negotiating with the British minister at the Vatican, and that some fascists – including Ciano – were joining this conspiracy. He concluded that "changes were indeed imminent in Italy" and that there was going to be British action in the Balkans as well.⁴

The Germans picked up the same signals. In May Glaise reported that "with regard to our allied comrade [Italy] the question is not 'if,' but only 'when'..."⁵ Weizsäcker's successor, Gustav Adolf Baron von Steengracht (above), cautioned Kasche of the need to display "maximum understanding for Italian sensitivities"; Ribbentrop had given him a similar warning five

---

¹ See eg. A-VII, NDH, kut. 25f, No. reg. 43/4-2. Lorković to Perić, 27 February 1943.
² A-VII, NDH, kut. 256, No. reg. 56/6-1. NDH foreign ministry circular, 9 March 1943.
³ A-VII, NDH, kut. 306, No. reg. 8/5-1. NDH foreign ministry circular, 23 March 1943.
⁴ A-VII, NDH, I.O. 9, No. reg. 6/7-1-87. Statement by Sinčić to interrogators, 1946.
⁵ Krizman (1983), p. 569.

weeks previously.[1] Glaise ascribed the Italians' renewed insistence on their "rights" in Croatia to the need to make amends for the loss of Tripoli.[2] He remarked that it had been clear from the outset that the Croatian state and its regime depended on German arms. The Germans knew this, but it was diplomatically necessary to go on pretending otherwise.

In early June the Italians were given – for the last time, as it happened – fresh German assurances of the primacy of their interests in Croatia.[3] The gesture was meaningless, yet Kasche raised his voice against it. On June 22 he complained that the "special position" of Italy in Croatia was incompatible with the Wehrmacht training and developing the NDH armed forces; with the Croatian economy adjusting itself to the German war economy; and with the *Volksdeutsche* maintaining their special status.[4]

Kasche could have added more items to his list. Italian predominance was impossible if the SS was to have its own police network and recruitment centers throughout the NDH; if German troops were to operate freely in the Italian zone; if the Wehrmacht were to control deployment of Croatian troops. Strictly speaking, Kasche's remarks about the impossibility of any real Italian predominance in Croatia were correct, and what he enumerated were also some of the causes of Italian displeasure. However, Kasche alone seems to have been bothered by the formalities, and he was no longer being taken seriously in Berlin.[5] He did not understand that after the collapse in Africa and the Allied landing in Sicily it was necessary, more than ever before, to tell the faltering ally what he wanted to hear. Mussolini's demoralization was evident at his meeting with Hitler on July 19, and empty gestures cost nothing. Even if they had been allowed some scope for increased control and influence, by early summer 1943 the Italians would not have known what to do with it. In 1941-1942, when they had the will and the resources, the

---

[1] T-120, roll 212, No. 560. Ritter to Kasche, 29 April 1943.

[2] T-501, roll 264. Glaise to Schuchard, 26 May 1943.

[3] T-120, roll 212, No. 275. Steengracht's note on the meeting with Alfieri, 7 June 1943.

[4] T-120, roll 212, No. 2551. Kasche to the foreign ministry, 22 June 1943.

[5] Kasche demanded that only Ustaša sources should be used by the authorities in Berlin for assessments of situation in Croatia. He resented the reports of other German officials, which differed fundamentally from his own. To Löhr (25 June 1943) Kasche protested that German intelligence used suspect and unreliable agents (*V-Leute*), including Croats who indulged in "political speculations" and, what was even worse, many "particularly crafty" Serbs. "Do such people have greater weight than those from the state leadership, recognized by us? Are their estimates more reliable, are they more politically trustworthy and agile than those in the Government?" asked Kasche melodramatically, lamenting lack of "trust in and camaraderie" with the Ustašas.

Italians lacked a coherent strategy for achieving real control in Croatia. Two years later both the will and the resources were gone.

The atmosphere in Croatia was hardly better, Glaise reported on 16 July.[1] He expressed some hope, however, that "in case of an undesirable outcome on the other side of the Adriatic" the return of coastal territories to the NDH could raise the faltering Croat morale. Even so, "the Croatian army cannot be counted upon at all seriously." The Ustašas would be happy to see the Italians go, but other people knew that their departure would create scope for increased Partisan activity in the evacuated area.[2]

The news of Mussolini's fall spread through Zagreb like brushfire.[3] In the course of the day on July 26 Pavelić conferred with Kasche twice and said that on the one hand he was glad, because "he expected favorable developments regarding Dalmatia, but that he was afraid, on the other, of a rapid enemy landing and other new dangers."[4] Pavelić expressed concern – which proved justified – that Tito's units could obtain large stocks of weapons from the Italians. By the end of July Glaise had also received news that Italian officers were in contact with Tito with a view to surrendering to his forces their arms and important strategic points such as Split, and "thus lay the ground for the Yugoslav revolutionary army to greet the British."[5] For all his political astuteness, even Glaise seems not to have realized that Tito wanted a British landing on the Yugoslav coast no more than the Germans did.

The Germans did not believe Marshal Pietro Badoglio (l.), who was profuse in his assurances that Italy would fight on. They prepared for every eventuality, both in Italy itself – by infiltrating troops and securing mountain passes – and in the south of France. In the Balkans, as early as July 25 Löhr

---

[1] T-501, roll 264. Glaise to Förtsch (for Löhr), 16 July 1943.

[2] T-120, roll 212, Unterstaatssekretär Pol. No. 395. A note by Undersecretary of State Hencke, 16 July 1943.

[3] T-120, roll 212, No. 3125. Kasche to the foreign ministry, 27 July 1943.

[4] T-120, roll 212, No. 3118. Kasche to the foreign ministry, 26 July 1943.

[5] KTB/III/2, p. 890. Glaise to OKW, 2 August 1943.

sent instructions to Lüters based on the assumption that Italy would drop out of the war.¹ Löhr's swift reaction to the news was followed by formal approval from Berlin, where Hitler signed his *Directive No. 48* on the disposition of German forces in the Balkans.² The Ustašas had to be acquainted with German plans because in view of the insufficient forces at Löhr's disposal Croatian troops were expected to perform extended garrison duties. On July 27 Budak informed Croatian legations abroad that Italy was "certainly on the road to a separate peace."³

The collapse of Mussolini and the imminent breaking up of the Axis should have made Pavelić and his followers worried rather than exultant: the overall prospects of Germany, on which their own survival so surely depended, were increasingly grim. The lure of short-term gain outweighed long-term gloom, however. The likelihood of regaining the coastline created a jubilant mood in the ruling circles. Helm reported only days after Mussolini's fall on the atmosphere in Zagreb:

> Within the Ustaša leadership the view is now prevalent that Italian troops must not be allowed to leave Croatian territory with their arms. [...] The demand 'Trieste to Germany, Rijeka to Croatia' will be put forward as the slogan for demonstrations. The liberation of Dalmatia, in the opinion of Ustaša circles, will provide for the full rehabilitation of the Poglavnik by proving that he was forced to conclude treaties which were in essence contrary to the interests of Croatia. As an internal-political success, the liberation of occupied areas will help create a broad popular base for the Ustaša movement, while in the field of foreign policy the growth of confidence in Germany is emphasized.⁴

Pavelić's leading Dalmatian activist Edo Bulat seconded this assessment when he spoke to Kasche in strongly irredentist terms, taking for granted the pending return of Dalmatia to Croatia.⁵ In the same spirit Lorković asked Kasche to ensure the inclusion of Croatian units in German forces that would be sent to secure the coastal area. Aware of the significance of Croatia in the aftermath of anticipated Italian desertion, Hitler issued an order on "the increase of Croatian fighting strength" on September 7, 1943.⁶ This document

---

¹ See Löhr's order to Lüters of 25 July 1943, in *Zbornik*, XII/3 (*Dokumenti nemačkog rajha*), p. 464 and on.

² Ibid, pp. 472-477.

³ A-VII, NDH, kut. 257, No. re. 19/5-1-2. Budak's circular to all legations, 27 July 1943.

⁴ T-120, roll 212, No. 3168. Kasche to the foreign ministry, 29 July 1943.

⁵ T-120, roll 212, No. 3183. Kasche to the foreign ministry, 30 July 1943.

⁶ KTB, Band III, Zweite Halbband, pp. 1456-1459.

was yet another compromise between the opposite viewpoints of Kasche on one side and the OKW on the other. Hitler's orders reiterated recognition of Croatia as an independent state. It insisted on ensuring the "energetic and positive cooperation" of the Croats, under German guidance, in enhancing the German war effort. Particular emphasis was placed on the role of German-trained and equipped mountain brigades (*Gorski zdrugovi*, in action in Bosnia in 1943, below), nominally in the Home Guard order of battle but operating as independent tactical units under German command.

The Order was preceded by a new controversy between the generals and Kasche. General Rendulic, Glaise's ally, followed his predecessors in concluding that Pavelić and the Ustašas were a major impediment to the fulfillment of his brief from Hitler to pacify and control the area with as few German troops as possible. Obviously ill informed about the sentiments of various players so soon after his arrival, however, on August 19 Rendulic confided his thoughts to none other than Kasche! He suggested to the dismayed diplomat that the NDH government should be replaced by a German military administration, "with only a pretense of regard for the Ustaša state."[1] Following alarm duly raised in Berlin by Kasche, Rendulic was reprimanded.[2] He was dismayed by Kasche's failure to act in a gentlemanly manner and keep confidential conversation private. He severed all contact with Kasche until his departure from the Balkans a year later.

On September 8 at 9:30 p.m. the Italian armistice was confirmed from Berlin. By midnight 500 Italian soldiers in Zagreb were disarmed without a fight.[3] During the night German units were already advancing towards the Adriatic coast. To Pavelić the pressing issue was to advance his territorial claims, not only to the pre-war Yugoslav lands annexed by Italy in May 1941, but if possible also to Fiume and Istria. At a meeting at 11 p.m. on the eighth,

---

[1] PA, Büro Staatssekretär, Kroatien, Bd. 6, No. 162771.

[2] The animosity was mutual, and Kasche often made sarcastic remarks about Rendulic's unwillingness to admit his South Slav background.

[3] T-120, roll 212, No. 3817. Kasche to the foreign ministry, 9 September 1943.

Kasche told Pavelić and his ministers of Hitler's and Ribbentrop's decision that "Croatia has the right to recover all lost areas along the Adriatic."[1] Kasche gave Pavelić a written note to the same effect. At 1 a.m. on September 9 Pavelić read the proclamation about the imminent recovery of the Adriatic littoral on the radio. He also thanked Hitler with a telegram suggesting an agreement on rather more than the Germans had promised:

> Fuehrer! It is two and a half years now since the Croat people, at the victorious advance of your gallant units, saw its hard struggle for freedom crowned by the creation of the Independent State of Croatia. Today once again the Croat people expresses its gratitude to you, deeply moved by the recovery of its passionately loved coastal lands and by your generous recognition of the right of the Croat people to recover lost Croatian territories along the Adriatic. United Croatia stands in defense of its highest national values, in gratitude and legendary Croat faithfulness, firmly with you, Fuehrer, and with your invincible armed forces.[2]

The Germans were careful, however, to mention only "territories taken away from Croatia," and Kasche avoided answering Pavelić's question about Istria and Fiume.[3] Leaving the issue open for the moment, Pavelić signed a decree on September 10 annulling the offer of the Crown of Tomislav to the Duke of Spoleto.[4] On the same day he gave a speech at the square outside *Banski dvori*, in which he called on all Croats who had left their homes because of "Italian brutalities" – a conciliatory reference to Dalmatians in the ranks of Tito's Partisans – to return to their homes and surrender arms, in return for an unconditional amnesty.[5]

On September 11 Pavelić signed a decree on the abrogation of the Rome Agreements.[6] They were signed when both contracting parties had been committed to "the New Order in Europe," the decree stated. By signing unilateral armistice with the enemy Italy had forfeited that status, and Croatia felt released from any obligations resulting from the Treaties. An anti-Italian press campaign was simultaneously launched. It was based on the claim that Italians to the west and Serbs to the east were Croatia's mortal enemies, similar in their depravity and racial inferiority, identical in their objectives.

---

[1] Krizman (1983) Vol. I, p. 114.

[2] T-120, roll 212, No. 3832. Pavelić to Hitler, 9 September 1943.

[3] In another telegram to Hitler on September 13 Pavelić reduced his claims to eastern Istria and Fiume. He was unaware that Hitler had already decided to keep the area under German control.

[4] *Hrvatski narod*, Vol. V, No. 831, 11 September 1943.

[5] *Hrvatski narod*, Vol. V, No. 830, 10 September 1943.

[6] *Hrvatski narod*, Vol. V, No. 831, 11 September 1943.

Pavelić also made a number of moves that were supposed to demonstrate his readiness to broaden the base of his regime. A few days before the fall of Italy he appointed an obscure lawyer from Bosnia, Nikola Mandić, as prime minister. Pavelić remained the head of state (*Poglavnik*), of course, and it was obvious that Mandić – a man in his late seventies, with no strong connections in Zagreb – would not be allowed to exercise much influence.[1] Perhaps of

greater significance was the appointment of General Miroslav Navratil (l.), an avid Germanophile, as armed forces minister. A veteran pilot from the First World War, Navratil held that professional soldiers, and not Ustaša "colonels," should control the Croatian armed forces. As a former Yugoslav officer he was disliked and mistrusted by the latter.[2]

In addition Pavelić indirectly put out feelers to the HSS. Confidential talks involved Mandić and Lorković on the government-Ustaša side and HSS politicians Košutić, Pernar and Andres. The latter three were allowed, for the first time since April 1941, to visit Maček who was interned at his estate in Kupinec and permanently guarded by a detachment of two hundred Ustašas. Pavelić even hinted that he would appoint Košutić as prime minister, only if the HSS agreed to join the

---

[1] As a junior apprentice at Mandić's law office, Miljenko Ristić (a well-known Sarajevo jurist in the post-war period) in early September 1943 was unexpectedly asked by his boss: "Would you, Miljenko, as a Serb, condone my acceptance of this offer?" Ristić was surprised by the question, but replied promptly that he would rather have Mandić, a man who does not hate Serbs, in a position of influence than one of the common "bloodsuckers" (*krvoloci*). In his opinion Mandić had never been a sworn Ustaša; that in itself ensured that he would never be able to exercise any real power in Zagreb. He was probably selected merely in order to demonstrate the irrelevance of the post. (Ristić to the author, Belgrade, July 1994).

[2] The NDH had a total of five ministers or acting ministers nominally in charge of defense:

June 1, 1941, to September 9, 1942: Marshal Slavko Kvaternik, Minister of the Home Guard (Domobranstvo);

September 9, 1942, to October 10, 1943: General Vilko Begić (Acting Minister of the Armed Forces);

October 11, 1943, to February 1,1944: General Miroslav Navratil (Minister of the Armed Forces);

February 1,1944, to August 30, 1944: General Ante Vokić (Minister of the Armed Forces); August 30, 1944, to May 15, 1945: Vice-Admiral Nikola Steinfel (Minister of the Armed Forces).

government.[1] Those talks came to naught, however. Košutić and his party colleagues knew that Pavelić did not intend to give up any real power, but simply to exploit the HSS as a means of gaining greater legitimacy and popular support for his regime. Besides, their policy of wait-and-see entirely relied on an eventual Allied landing on the Adriatic Coast and precluded any move that would leave them open to the charge of collaboration with a compromised regime, dependent on the obviously losing side in the war.

While Pavelić was interested in window dressing of *his* regime, a group of younger leaders within the Ustaša movement regarded the mood of emergency in September 1943 as an opportune moment to seek serious political reforms. Their objective was to uphold Croatian independence in the uncertain times ahead by limiting Pavelić's power and increasing the role of non-Ustaša political forces, primarily the HSS. The most prominent among whom were Mladen Lorković and Vladko Košak; their group also included Mile Starčević and Matija Kovačić. They had never been on good terms with the *Ras* clique of former émigrés, and were not known for unbridled genocidal zeal towards the Serbs that characterized the latter.

The "reformers" were distressed that Pavelić had selected Mandić as his prime minister, seeing this as a sure sign that he did not want any serious changes in his regime. They tended their resignations which Pavelić refused to accept. After a brief experiment with limited reforms Pavelić opted for complete reliance on a Germanvictory externally and on his trusted colonels (above) domestically. His discardingt of any scenario involving Maček was accompanied by renewed public accusations against the HSS as Masons and Anglophiles, "Yugoslavs" and enemies of Germany. An Abwehr report ascribed this to Pavelić's desire to obtain clear statement of German support when he found himself under pressure at home.[2] In this way he made it impossible for Lorković's group to pursue a "moderate" course without breaking with him. Lorković was not prepared to go that far at that time.

---

[1] For Kasche's detailed report on contacts with the HSS, see T-120, roll 212, No. 3865. Kasche to the foreign ministry, 13 September 1943.

[2] Kazimirović, op. cit., p. 176.

5. Neubacher's Mission

An attempt to bring about a real change of government in Zagreb in the aftermath of the Italian armistice was made by Herman Neubacher, who was appointed Ribbentrop's special plenipotentiary in the southeast in August 1943. This Viennese politician (former mayor of Vienna) and diplomat was well acquainted with the situation in the Balkans. In Hitler's eyes he enjoyed the reputation not only of an able official but also of a brilliant person. He was widely considered the most talented Austrian National-Socialist, highly educated, well read and acquainted with a broad range of issues from economics to literature.

According to the instructions from Hitler personally, Neubacher's primary task in the former Yugoslavia was to "politically organize national anti-Communist forces and guide them politically in their struggle against Communist bands." He alone was empowered "to negotiate with the leaders of the bands, accept or reject them." No German political or military officer in the Balkans during the war enjoyed such wide powers as Herman Neubacher. Belatedly and reluctantly, the argument that political problems could not be resolved by military means alone was accepted in Berlin.

Neubacher quickly joined the burgeoning ranks of Pavelić's enemies. He soon prepared a plan for comprehensive pacification of the area. It was, as he put it, "aimed against the continued existence of Pavelić's regime." His intentions were not unknown to the government circles in Zagreb, in which he was regarded, in his own words, "as the Enemy of the State No 1."[1] Small wonder, considering that besides removing the Ustašas from power in Zagreb Neubacher proposed the creation of a "greater-Serbian federation" – to include Montenegro, the Sanjak and an outlet to the Adriatic – with Nedić at its helm. Neubacher (above) expected his plans to result in a far-reaching pacification of the entire area of former Yugoslavia. By finally rectifying the Carthaginian peace imposed on the Serbs in 1941 and

---

[1] Neubacher, op. cit. p. 155. timely interventions in the Athens Exchange in 1942-44 from a modest cashe of gold entrusted to him by the Reichsbank, Neubacher was able to stave off the collapse of the financial system in occupied Greece.

giving them a place under the German sun, he hoped to drive a wedge in the Communist "zip" (*Reisverschluss*) that threatened to tear apart the Balkans from Slovenia in the north-west to Greece in the south-east.

Neubacher's main problem was Hitler's lack of commitment to the concept. Hitler approved in principle, but warned him not to go too far in appeasing the Serbs. In his words Germany should not allow a nation with "a sense of political mission" to become predominant in the Balkans, "and the Serbs are" – Hitler warned – "one such nation. They have shown that they possess great state-creating energy... so I have serious reasons not to encourage this nation in its ambitions."[1] With Hitler's qualified support Neubacher nevertheless proceeded to develop a more conciliatory German attitude towards the Serbs in general and the Četniks in particular. He had an extensive network of contacts in Belgrade, which he chose as his headquarters. He understood the predicament of General Milan Nedić and tried to ease it by arranging the latter's visit to Hitler in September 1943, but the results were disappointing. His contacts with the Royalist resistance were potentially compromising for both parties yet Neubacher developed and cultivated them, too, aware that a new Balkan strategy was essential in the period of Germany's increasing military weakness and strategic vulnerability.

The limits of Neubacher's powers became visible when in late 1943 he renewed his insistence that a lasting understanding with Mihailović was needed. This was rejected by Ribbentrop in early 1944. As the Red Army pushed its way back to the Soviet western border (map, opp. p.), the foreign minister warned Neubacher that "Germany waged the war in the Balkans in order to destroy, once for all, the Serbian hotbed of unrest... We therefore have no interest in re-igniting the greater-Serbian spirit..."[2]

Neubacher did not give up, and his efforts were heartily supported by many German political and military circles, from the SS to Glaise, Rendulic and Löhr.[3] Unhappy with the way in which all previous initiatives to unseat Pavelić seemed to flounder, Neubacher sent his confident Robert Kronholz to Zagreb. Kronholz, former Austrian consul-general in Belgrade, was to get in touch with the HSS and explore the possibility of establishing an alternative government. He had two illicit meetings with prominent HSS representatives,

---

[1] ibid. p. 160.

[2] ADAP, E, VII, pp. 374-375. Ribbentrop to Neubacher, 29 January 1944.

[3] Thanks to Neubacher the Propaganda Department in late 1943 received instructions not to use the word "Ustaša" in the press articles at all. German intelligence reports from Zagreb noted concern in Ustaša ranks about sudden German benevolence towards Serbia.

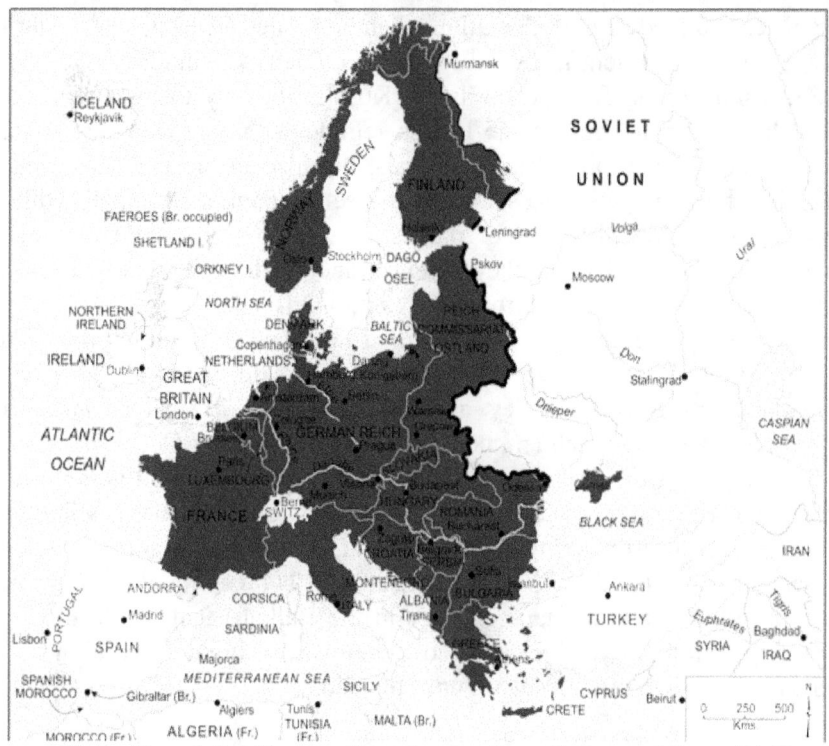

August Košutić and Bariša Smoljan, in the flat of General Pero Blašković.[1] Kronholz's suggestion that the HSS should form a government was rejected by Košutić outright. He proposed the formation of a non-party "government of civil servants" instead, and the removal of Pavelić and the Ustašas. Kronholz appeared unconvinced, insisting that "everyone in Croatia is aligned in some way by now." Košutić and Smoljan countered by quoting several names of various public figures, university professors, lawyers and *Domobran* generals (Prpić, Marić) who could be considered.[2] During the second meeting they produced a list with about twenty names of persons free of political party affiliations which could be acceptable to the HSS as candidates for a new government.

Kronholz returned to Belgrade and reported to Neubacher. Also present was Croatia's *Staatenbilder* Edmund Veesenmayer, then based in Budapest.[3]

---

[1] For eyewitness accounts of Kronholz's mission, see Krizman (1983), Vol. I, p. 272.

[2] Their statements to Tito's investigators are contained in a report prepared in 1948 (*Put izdaje dr Mačeka i družine*), A-VII, NDH, I.O.10, No. reg. 1/3-1-580.

[3] ibid, p. 228. Statement by Blašković's widow.

Neubacher had made a miscalculation when he invited Veesenmayer, who felt upstaged and was resentful of the Austrian's extensive authority. He alerted Pavelić's minister in Budapest, Vladko Košak, not only to the existence of Neubacher's plan to replace the Ustaša regime with a government of civil servants, experts and non-Ustaša generals, but also to the fact that a list of names had been prepared. Košak promptly sent a courier to Zagreb with the news and with Košutić's list of names. It was to prove fatal for several persons who had no idea that they had been included. Pavelić alerted Kasche, who raised alarm with Ribbentrop, yet again, on his behalf.

Neubacher's initiative was thus killed even before it got off the ground due to Veesenmayer's indiscretion. Pavelić was safe, yet again, due to the ambivalence of German policy and rivalry among its institutions. Hitler wanted Neubacher to reach an understanding with the non-Communist Serbs, but did not want to appease those Serbs too much, and wanted nothing to do with the most prominent of those non-Communist Serbs, General Mihailović. He wanted to do "something" about Croatia, but did not want to go all the way and replace Pavelić. With the onset of 1944 Germany still lacked a coherent political and military strategy in the Balkans that would match its decreasing ability to produce desired outcomes by brute force alone. That problem was to remain unresolved until the end.

XII
Decline and Fall

1. *"Zone of Operations Adriatic Littoral"*

On 12 September 1943, in a daring commando raid, Otto Skorzeny freed Mussolini from Gran Sasso. The Duce's return to the scene (albeit in a reduced form) and the activity of Austrian Gauleiters in the area of the northern Adriatic, had a profound effect on the German attitude towards Pavelić's territorial demands. Even before the eventual change of heart in Berlin, it had become obvious that the expected political advantage to the NDH from the Italian armistice would not materialize.

As German units advanced to the Adriatic coast, large areas of Bosnia and continental Croatia which had been cleared of Partisans in the first half of 1943 came under Tito's control yet again. The situation was especially alarming in northern Bosnia, where mining centers of Lukavac and Kreka fell to the Partisans, and in Croatia's breadbasket, Slavonija. Most of that year's bumper harvest could not be collected by the NDH authorities.[1] The failure of political initiatives aimed at limiting Pavelić's power had a demoralizing effect on the middle classes which had opted for waiting in 1941. The strengthening of the Partisan movement by large stocks of captured Italian arms and supplies removed hope that Tito's men could be tempted to accept Pavelić's offer of amnesty.[2] After September 1943 the Croats started to join Tito's ranks in significant numbers for the first time.

On October 5 the NDH government asked that its troops be deployed along the Dalmatian coast and in the cities. German-Croat tensions on this issue were soon apparent. NDH minister Edo Bulat sent a telegram to Pavelić while on his way to Split claiming that the Germans had simply abandoned his group. Melodramatically he wrote that those guilty for his predicament "would be responsible before history!"[3] At the same time, the Germans started using the Fascist militia in Yugoslav areas *outside* Zara and Fiume.[4]

The first Croatian territorial demand directly rejected by the Germans concerned the only fjord in the Mediterranean and a natural naval base, the Bay (Bocca) of Cattaro. The OKW tolf Ribbentrop that it was categorically

---

[1] T-501, roll 264, No. 01955/43. Glaise's report to the OKW, 2 October 1943.

[2] T-501, roll 267. Report from Zagreb dated 4 October 1943.

[3] T-501, roll 267. Bulat's telegram to Pavelić; copy to Glaise, received 5 October 1943.

[4] T-501, roll 264, No. 61980/43. Glaise to Army Group F, 5 October 1943.

opposed to the transfer of that strategically vital area to the Croats: until the end of the war military considerations had to take precedence. Neubacher seconded this view, commenting that "the introduction of the present incurable Croatian disorder" into the area of Kotor was politically undesirable as well as strategically unjustified. His view was that the Bay had to remain "one hundred percent German military-administrative area."[1]

Alarmed by the news, Budak instructed all NDH representatives in Germany to embark on a lobbying campaign aimed at securing for Croatia the coastal area "from Istria to Budva." The goal was "to obtain from the Führer a general order to all German officers in our area, that Kotor, all islands, Zadar and Rijeka belong to Croatia, and that there is no way Italy could have any business there." The NDH government was particularly upset by some German officers openly declaring that they would rather see coastal territory under the control of "anyone *but* the Ustašas": "such acts force our people to join Partisans ... and to fight against German and Croatian liberating units. A lot of blame is with the ill-informed German officers."[2]

The next blow to Ustaša hopes came from Ribbentrop himself. He warned Pavelić (inspecting an Ustaša unit, r.) on October 9 against pursuing Croatian propaganda about Fiume, and spelled out in no uncertain terms the German view that the whole coastal zone was an insurgent area in which German forces had to fight hard.[3] It was, in other words, a German zone of operations, which meant that anti-insurgent action and prevention of an Anglo-Saxon invasion were the first priority. The Fuehrer could not devote himself to the secondary "state-legal issues" while fighting was going on. It would be more useful for the Croats to concentrate their energy on regaining "predominantly Croatian areas" (i.e. the former *Zone I*), than on propagating additional territorial demands.

---

[1] T-120, roll 212, No. 1155. Neubacher to the foreign ministry, 9 October 1943.

[2] A-VII, NDH, Box 257, Reg. no. 45/5-2. Budak to Rušinović, 9 October 1943.

[3] T-120, roll 212, No. 1628. Ribbentrop to Kasche, 9 October 1943.

In the event, in the immediate aftermath of Italy's capitulation German field commands did not allow even token NDH units to show the flag in any coastal sector, Zone I included. When Hermann Neubacher talked to Lorković in Zagreb on October 13, 1943, this was one of the chief Ustaša complaints to Ribbentrop's newly-appointed plenipotentiary.[1] At the same time, as Lorković pointed out, German commands gladly deployed Fascist Italians and Četniks alongside their own units throughout the area supposedly liberated for Croatia while no Croat units were allowed into the area. The complaint was not unfounded: It is remarkable how quickly German field commands started treating Četniks in a manner similar to that of their Italian predecessors. Lorković's complaint to Neubacher was to no avail, however. Neubacher had plans of his own about Četniks, plans which were very different from the hopes and ambitions of the Ustaša government.

Unaware of Ribbentrop's warning to Pavelić to refrain from territorial demands, Minister Ratković spoke to Secretary Steengracht on October 15. In accordance with Budak's instructions he recalled Hitler's "generous decision" to transfer "Croat areas along the Adriatic" to the NDH. He repeated the request that German military authorities "be instructed from the highest instance" that the entire coast with all islands, including Fiume, Zara and the Bay of Kotor, would be finally incorporated into the NDH.[2] His interlocutor maintained a perfect reserve.

The issue came to a head in mid-October when a group of some four hundred NDH police officers and administrative personnel, headed by an assistant secretary of state at the NDH interior ministry, one Kamenarović, attempted to reach Fiume via Trieste.[3] Their goal was to establish NDH authority in the city. It coincided with the establishment of the "Zone of Operations Adriatic Littoral" (*Operationszone Adriatisches Küstenland*, above) by the Germans in the northern Adriatic. The zone embraced large areas of northeastern Italy (Belluno, Venezia Giulia, the former *Provinzia di Lubiana*, Istria, Fiume with Sušak and all surrounding areas, and the islands of Krk, Rab and Pag). It was placed under the political authority of the Gauleiter of Carinthia, Rainer, who became its high commissioner.

The refusal of the Germans to let Kamenarović's group through – it was turned back to Zagreb at the border with Slovenia – opened the Ustašas' eyes

---

[1] T-501, roll 265. Kasche's notes on Neubacher's talks with Lorković, 13 October 1943.

[2] T-120, roll 212, Staatssekretär No. 471. Steengracht's note of 15 October 1943.

[3] Taking the route via Trieste more than doubled the distance that had to be covered on their journey, but taking the main road from Zagreb to Fiume via Jastrebarsko, Karlovac and Delnice (85 miles in all) entailed risking Partisan ambushes.

to reality. Lorković spoke to Kasche on October 19, the latter reported, using "uniquely sharp language." He said that if the areas under Rainer's control were not to be given to the NDH, then the earlier Italian annexation would merely be replaced by the German one.[1] Kasche (as was his habit) recommended acceptance of the Croatian demands. He was unaware, however, that the initiative in the former Habsburg lands annexed by Italy after 1918 was firmly in the hands of the Austrians: Gauleiters Rainer and Hofer were only its most visible executors on the ground.[2] Increasingly appreciative of the Habsburg heritage as the war went on, and especially after the Italian armistice, Hitler confided to Glaise that Trieste and Fiume should eventually become the Reich's commercial ports, while the Bay of Cattaro [Kotor] would be the main German naval base in the Mediterranean.[3]

Foreign minister Budak sent a long letter to Kasche on 21 October 1943, making an appeal to the German minister to work towards the incorporation of all Croat-inhabited coastal territories into the NDH.[4] Budak recalled Hitler's "promise" of September 8, and in an almost desperate tone urged Kasche, "a tested friend of Croatia and the Croat people," to seek a solution which would be in line with that promise. Budak warned of "the gravest consequences" of disappointment which German measures would cause among most Croats. The NDH minister in Berlin, Ratković, made a formal *demarche* in the same tone to Steengracht on 22 October.[5]

This time the Croats were given a short shrift. Steengracht stated that he regarded their complaints as "inappropriate": Croatia was an insurgent area, and military considerations had absolute precedence. It was not done to raise the issue of frontiers in an area where the Wehrmacht was trying hard to establish peace and order. Steengracht told Ratković that Kasche had already been instructed to inform the NDH government accordingly. Kasche's habitual reluctance to convey any bad news from Berlin to his Ustaša hosts had already earned him another warning from Ribbentrop that his duty in Zagreb was to represent the interests of the Reich, and not those of the NDH, and that considerations of "justice" could not play any role. As for the status of the Croats vis-à-vis the Reich, Ribbentrop was brief and explicit:

---

[1] T-120, roll 212, No. 4497. Kasche to the foreign ministry, 19 October 1943.

[2] For the "Austrians' revenge" of 1943-1944, see Rusinow, op. cit.

[3] See Kazimirović, op. cit., p. 179.

[4] A-VII, NDH, Box 233a, No. Reg. 91/1-1. Budak's letter to Kasche, 21 October 1943.

[5] T-120, roll 212, Staatssekretär No. 497. Steengracht's note on the meeting with Ratković, 22 October 1943.

The Croatian government is not allowed in any way to make any demands of us, or to make its desires known to us, even if they are justified. The reality is such that the Croatian government must be satisfied with whatever it gets, as even that will be entirely thanks to the force of German arms.[1]

As far as Germany was concerned, the issue was finally resolved by Ribbentrop's *Note for the Führer* of October 26, 1943, which annulled Kasche's promises to Pavelić of September 8.[2] This was too much for Budak to stomach. He sent a rambling telegram to Ratković, which marked the end of his ministerial career when it was intercepted and deciphered by the Germans. Budak asked his minister in Berlin to tell the Germans that "the new Serbophile course of German policy is catastrophic not only for Croatia, but also for Germany, and a mortal blow, for ever, to the political morality and to Croatian-German relations."

Hitler's decision on territories of September 8 had been communicated to Pavelić, who made it public – only to see those lands returned to the Italians, albeit under firm German control. In Budak's words, "such action against us can hardly find precedent in political history." Budak's melodramatic tone apart, his chagrin was understandable. It was humiliating for Pavelić to

announce with much fanfare the inclusion of all Croat-inhabited coastal areas in the NDH (l.), only to have them denied a month later. By over-reacting, the Ustaša foreign minister showed his failure to grasp that, in late 1943, the Independent State of Croatia was merely a cloutless satellite of the Reich. The removal of Italy from the equation reduced the maneuvering space for the NDH regime.

The gap between reality and Budak's pretenses caused irritation in Berlin. Commenting with characteristic sarcasm on the Ustašas' tendency to take themselves too seriously, Glaise told Hitler on September 5: "*Mein Fuehrer*, the Croats are a primitive nation. They are not able, as we Germans are, to penetrate the deeper meaning of things. Therefore, they look at a

---

[1] ADAP, E, VI, pp. 579-582. Ribbentrop to Kasche, 23 September 1943.

[2] PA Bonn, Nachlass S. Kasche, Box 10. Ribbentrop's note for Hitler, 26 October 1943.

situation not by its substance, but by its outside appearances." To this Hitler "smiled with understanding." But the treatment of the Croat regime over the *Operationszone* prompted even Glaise to call it degrading: "it passed every boundary of what can be expected even from the most miserable 'ally' if we still want to keep him with us."

Ribbentrop was unmoved. As he had noted a month earlier, the NDH owed everything to Germany and was not to be allowed to ask for anything – not even to make its "desires" known. Before the summer of 1943 the NDH could enjoy a limited autonomy of action for as long as there was a German-Italian rivalry to exploit. At the critical moment of Badoglio's armistice the Germans were prepared to promise Pavelić anything to secure his reliability. Mussolini's return to the scene, however, made it impractical for Germany to sanction any formal adjustments to Italy's pre-1941 borders. Such sanction was additionally unlikely in view of the fact that Mussolini was himself at the mercy of the Germans, who could no longer pretend to take "no political interest" in Croatia. Any territorial and administrative adjustment was going to be seen as the will of the Germans, both in Zagreb and at Salò.

Finally, to those German officials who effected *de facto* annexation of the coastal "Zone of Operations" to the Reich, it was preferable to retain existing Italian administrative structure, rather than to risk the introduction of the Ustašas with their "incurable chaos." With the disappearance of the Axis, Germany could give up even the pretence of partnership with the Ustašas. The creation of *Operationszone Adriatisches Kuesteland* was a clear sign that by the autumn of 1943 the NDH, and the movement which ruled it, had ceased to be even a semi-autonomous actor on the political scene of occupied Europe.

2. Croatian Policy Review in Berlin

Tito's fortunes took a lasting turn for the better after September 1943. Swiftly reacting to the armistice and aided by the sympathetic attitude of Italian commanders, his forces captured arms and equipment enabling the Partisan army to grow to some 200,000 men, perhaps half of that number front-line fighters. By late November he felt confident enough to convene the "Anti-Fascist Council of National Liberation" (AVNOJ) in the town of Jajce in Bosnia, a quasi-legislative body under complete Communist control which provided the pseudo-constitutional cover for Tito's intended takeover of post-war Yugoslavia. Confident that he could finally give up his hitherto effective tactic of constant movement, he established his headquarters at Drvar, in northwestern Bosnia. In this Communist stronghold from the early days of the uprising in the summer of 1941 he felt secure from sudden intrusion amidst the gorges and passes of the Dinaric Alps.

By late 1943 Tito was assured not only of Soviet commitment, which often had to remain discrete, but also of British support. Winston Churchill had been badly wrong about Gallipoli in the spring of 1915 and just as wrong about Greece in the spring of 1941. He nevertheless had an enduring obsession with finding strategic opportunities in the Balkans. This left him open to the suggestion that the Partisans – who could certainly fight well – were far more effective than was plausible. At the same time there were several Communist double agents in British intelligence who were in a position to pass upwards what Churchill seemed to want to hear.[1] The conspirators worked, from two geographically and operationally different centers, to reinforce his conviction that the Partisans, and hence *not* the Četniks, were tying down large numbers of Axis 'divisions.'[2]

By the end of 1943, Field Marshal Maximilian von Weichs (l.), Löhr's replacement as the Wehrmacht supreme commander in the Balkans (*Oberbefehlshaber Südost*, OB SO), argued that "Tito is our most dangerous enemy." Weichs was finding his many tasks beyond his powers to fulfil, and was concerned about the security of the 750-mile long railway upon which his troops depended for present sustenance and future retreat. His position was aggravated early in 1944 when two of his divisions were sent to Kesselring in Italy, and then four more were sent to occupy Hungary in March. During the early part of 1944 Weichs mounted a series of "special operations" with the object of wiping out the guerrillas in

---

[1] Two key men were John Cairncross at Bletchley Park, who worked on German Army intelligence related to the Balkans, and James Klugmann, the Special Operations desk officer in Cairo who doctored agents' reports from the Balkans on a daily basis to favor Tito.

[2] On British exaggeration of Partisan record, see Vane Ivanović, *Memoirs of a Yugoslav.* London: Harcourt Brace Jovanovich, 1977. The signals sent by Klugmann, who was an intimate of the traitors Anthony Blunt, Kim Philby, and Guy Burgess at Cambridge in the late 1930s, became public in 1997 and confirmed earlier claims that Klugmann was principally responsible for the massive wartime sabotage of the Mihailović supply operation and for keeping from London information about the impressive activities of his forces in the fight against the Germans. Cf. Andrew Boyle, *The Climate of Treason.* London: Hutchinson, 1979.

particular areas. Each time their activity flared up with renewed vigor once the attack had passed.[1]

While the soldiers were struggling to retain control, Kasche kept sending his optimistic reports about "consolidation" of the Ustaša state. His views were totally at odds with the views of Weichs and Neubacher in Belgrade, Glaise in Zagreb, Rendulic at Vrnjačka Banja (in central Serbia), and a myriad of SS, police, labor, NSDAP and other German officials throughout the Balkans. Not for the first time Hitler decided to have this "double-track" reporting ended, and ordered a policy review of the entire Croatian issue. To clear the Balkan mist, in the NDH and elsewhere, Jodl's deputy, Colonel-General Walter Warlimont, was sent to the Balkans in January 1944.

Shortly before Warlimont's visit to Zagreb Pavelić decided to replace his armed forces minister Navratil, whose appointment – five months earlier – met with wholehearted German approval.[2] Glaise and Weichs were shocked by the news, which they saw as a sign that the Poglavnik was going to further weaken *Domobranstvo* and return to the policy of favoring Ustaša units. General Glaise acted energetically against Pavelić's decision. Initially at least, even Kasche thought it somewhat inappropriate to remove a man who left had an excellent impression on Hitler.

However, Pavelić won over Kasche with the assertion that Navratil was ideologically not sound: he was "neglecting the Ustaša militia" and had "surrounded himself at the Ministry with a clique of pro-Yugoslav oriented officers." On January 29 Navratil was replaced by Ante Vokić (above), a hitherto little-known Ustaša officer from Bosnia. Glaise's defeat in the dispute over Navratil marked the beginning of a new phase in his relations with Pavelić, which was to culminate with Glaise's departure from Zagreb in September 1944.

Warlimont arrived in Zagreb at the height of the controversy over Navratil, on January 17, 1944. He stayed at Glaise's villa and was thoroughly

---

[1] Ralph Bennett: "Knight's Move at Drvar." *Journal of Contemporary History*, Vol. 22 (1987).

[2] BA/MAF, RH 31/III/4. Abwehr assessment of Navratil, 26 November 1943.

briefed by him. Warlimont also had an *ad hoc* meeting with Pavelić, whom he described to Glaise as "a perfidious Oriental." The Ustaša made three specific requests: the setting up of "village guards," to be armed by the Germans; the creation of a single German command with headquarters in Croatia for all Wehrmacht units in the NDH (which were commanded from Serbia); and the abandonment of German support for the Četniks in Dalmatia.[1] The Germans decided that "village guards" had to be linked with Kammerhofer's organization and under control of local German commanders. The old Ustaša complaint that the command of German troops in Croatia was in Serbia was rejected again on grounds of strategic necessity. As for the Četniks, Weichs decided to do nothing.

Warlimont returned from the Balkans fully committed to the views of Glaise with regard to Croatia. On January 22 he presented his findings to Hitler, who agreed with them. On March 9 he attended a conference at Hitler's headquarters. In the presence of Ribbentrop and Kasche he sharply contradicted Kasche's assertion that conditions in the NDH were improving. Warlimont outlined the activity of Tito's forces, unbroken and strengthened in spite of large operations against him. He mentioned the catastrophic transport situation, with one third of railways in the NDH permanently out of use and the rest subject to ambushes and raids; and the collapse of Croatian agriculture, so that the country had to import foodstuffs from Germany.[2] Warlimont compared Pavelić's government performance unfavorably to Tito's ability to administer territories under Communist control. He also said that the combat value of both Ustaša and Domobran forces was negligible: along the Adriatic coast they could not be used at all, and against the "bands" only if their units were led by German officers. Warlimont strongly opposed any increase of Ustaša influence in military matters, and especially any

---

[1] See Krizman (1983), Vol. I, p. 269.

[2] G. Fricke, op. cit., pp. 159-160.

"spoiling of German-Croatian units" (*Legionnaires*, above) by Ustaša elements and the proposed creation of autonomous Croat village guards.

Hitler supported Warlimont's assessment. When Kasche tried to intervene he was cut short and told that the temporary lull in Partisan activity is not a sign of real pacification; the flaring up of insurgent activity was to be expected soon. Hitler also warned against any "unlimited and disorganized" setting up of village guards, which would simply turn into Tito's arms suppliers. His decision was communicated to Weichs on 18 March. The spring of 1944 was Kasche's low point: his "line," it seemed, was rejected at the top. He also received yet another admonition from Ribbentrop that he tended to look at the Croatian situation too much through Ustaša eyes and take for granted what they told him.[1]

The Ustaša authorities were concerned, and attempted to influence the thrust of German policy with a diplomatic mini-offensive of their own. They prepared several verbal notes for the German foreign ministry. One was devoted to the tendency of the German press to write about "Croats from Bosnia of Islamic faith" without mentioning their Croat nationality, but calling them "Muslims," "Bosnians" and in some cases even "Serbs."[2] Another complained that Germany allowed the NDH railway network to deteriorate while huge bills for transit through Croatia remained unpaid.

In a long memorandum (February 5, 1944) the Ustaša government warned that Croatia could soon become, yet again, the exposed rampart (*antemurale*) of Europe.[3] Therefore "the Croatian citizen, and especially the Croatian soldier, must not be shaken in his faith and his trust in the new European order, within which his state should take the sovereign position which is due to it." The specific complaints in the memorandum were manifold. General Rendulic still commanded all forces in Croatia from his headquarters in Serbia. The Croatian authorities could not exercise control over their own units. Some German commanders carried out reprisals against Croat civilians and property, which sometimes caused "dismay and shock." Croatian towns and entire sectors were abandoned by the Wehrmacht without giving prior notice to the NDH authorities and with no regard for consequences. Especially irksome to Pavelić was the "arbitrary setting up of units recruited from the local population, and the parallel prevention or disruption of local recruitment by the NDH." From Pavelić's point of viw the

---

[1] PA, Nachlass Kasche, Bd. 10. Ribbentrop to Kasche, 13 April 1944.
[2] A-VII, NDH, Box 268, No. Reg. 1/4-32. *Note verbale* of 31 January 1944.
[3] A-VII, NDH, Box 233a, No. Reg. 20/1-1. Memorandum of 5 February 1944.

sorest issue concerned the Četniks and what the memorandum called "the continuum of the notorious policy of the Second Italian Army." On February 10, 1944, two additional formal complaints were sent from Zagreb to Berlin. The first was a summary of Ustaša complaints in connection with the 13th SS Volunteer Division, and in particular its designation as a "Bosnian-Herzegovinian," rather than Croatian, combat unit.[1] The second was a long round-up of Ustaša objections to the creation of the Zone of Operations in the northern Adriatic. It singled out for criticism the inclusion into the said Zone not only of "mainly Croat-inhabited territories which were taken by Italy in 1918-1923" but even of some areas (Krk, Sušak, Bakar, Čabar) which had belonged to Yugoslavia before April 1941.[2]

The Ustaša diplomatic offensive did not yield any results. There is no record of a single German reply to the verbal notes and memoranda, and there was no change in actual German policy on any of the issues raised. A final attempt was made by Pavelić on March 1, 1944, when his premier Mandić and foreign minister Perić visited Hitler at Klassheim. Their pitch focused on fresh assurances to the German leader that the NDH was finally on the road to consolidation and pacification. They proceeded to raise the issues discussed with Warlimont in Zagreb and elaborated in the verbal notes and memoranda presented to Berlin.[3] Hitler remained indifferent and did not reply.

At a follow-up meeting at the German legation in Zagreb two days later the Croats were told that Hitler had turned down their request to move Rendulic's headquarters from Serbia to Croatia. He approved arms deliveries for the new Croatian "auxilliary gendarmerie" (village guards), but this program was to proceed only "in close liaison" with the Reichsführer's plenipotentiary in Croatia, Police Chief Kammerhofer. The distribution of arms would be entrusted to Glaise. Strengthening of Ustaša units could proceed only if this was not done at the expense of regular *Domobranstvo* brigades. The Inspector-General of the NDH armed forces, German General Juppe (above)

---

[1] A-VII, NDH, Box 264, No. Reg. 6/5-16. Memorandum of 10 February 1944.

[2] KTB, Bd. IV/1, pp. 739-740.

[3] On Mandić's visit to Hitler see his statement to interrogators (A-VII, SUP Zagreb).

was instructed accordingly.[1] Territorial issues were not mentioned; Kasche had brought them up, but yet again Hitler was aloof.[2]

A month later the Ustaša authorities were reminded that Berlin no longer considered Croatia a sovereign state. In the first week of April 1944 German units carried out mass reprisals against civilians in the area of Sinj, in the Dalmatian hinterland.[3] Pavelić's foreign minister Stijepo Perić instructed Tomislav Sambugnach, the NDH chargé d'affaires in Berlin, to file a protest with the Wilhelmstrasse. Sambugnach composed a clumsy note in which he demanded investigation and "further demanded" (*des Weiteren wird verlangt*) "public punishment of the condemned culprits on the spot of the massacre."[4]

When Ribbentrop was shown the note he went into a fit of rage. He ordered his ministry to return the document, to warn Pavelić that this was no way to talk to the Greater German Reich, and "to seek satisfaction." Kasche personally handed to the Poglavnik Ribbentrop's message that it was no longer possible for him to communicate with Perić. Pavelić immediately dismissed his foreign minister.[5] Poor Sambugnach was recalled from Berlin. Furthermore, although it eventually transpired that the massacre of two hundred Croat civilians near Sinj was not carried out by any "Četniks" in German uniforms – as was originally claimed by the Ustašas – but by German soldiers belonging to the Seventh SS Division *Prinz Eugen*, the handling of the affair resulted in the Germans being furious and the Croats turning defensive. Perić's successor  Mehmed Alajbegović, an obscure Muslim lawyer from Bosnia (above), sent an abjectly apologetic letter to Ribbentrop which marked the end of the affair.[6]

In the spring of 1944 it seemed that Kasche's days in Zagreb were numbered: Glaise informed Jodl in early May that the change at the German

---

[1] T-50, roll 264, No. 0421/44. Kasche to Weichs, 3 March 1944.

[2] A-VII, SUP Zagreb, MF-5. Kasche's statement to interrogators.

[3] A-VII, NDH, Box 268, No. Reg. 13/4-17. Perić to Sambugnach, 8 April 1944.

[4] A-VII, NDH, Box 268, No. Reg. 13/4-19. NDH Note to the Foreign Ministry of the Reich, 11 April 1944.

[5] A-VII, NDH, I.O. 9, No. Reg. 5/2-1. Košak's statement to interrogators, 1947.

[6] A-VII, NDH, Kut. 233a, No. Reg. 35/1-1. Alajbegović to Ribbentrop, 10 May 1944.

legation was imminent.[1] The ascendent Wehrmacht line was also apparent during a visit which the new NDH armed forces minister, Ante Vokić, paid to the Fuehrer's Headquarters on 16 April 1944.[2] In line with Hitler's decision of 9 March the OKW Operations Department reiterated that, in considering Croatian requests, there was "no room for any concessions or understanding."

3. The "Affair" of Lorković and Vokić

During 1944 all German satellites in eastern-central Europe made attempts to get off the doomed Nazi bandwagon. The least successful, and the most half-hearted attempt of all was made in the NDH by interior minister Mladen Lorković and armed forces minister Ante Vokić.[3]

The first signs of discord between Lorković and Pavelić were apparent in the second half of 1943. Lorković was disappointed by Pavelić's lukewarm response to his efforts to open talks with the HSS and possibly broaden the base of the regime after Mussolini's fall. Lorković had established contact with three senior HSS figures who had remained at large after Maček's internment: the party vice-president, August Košutić, and two former deputies, Ljudevit Tomašić and Ivanko Farolfi. This group had avoided any move until that time that could compromise them in the eyes of the Western Allies, on whom they counted as the ultimate arbiters of the fate of Croatia. In the fall of 1943, however, the Partisan movement in the NDH was ceasing to be an overwhelmingly Serb affair. It started attracting increasing numbers of Croats who were tempted to join the side that looked like winning. This threatened to undermine the base of HSS support and created the mood of urgency among Maček's aides. Although the initiative to draw the HSS into government came to naught, Lorković continued to display greater concern about the tide of events than his colleagues. Pavelić and his émigré old guard were reconciled to sharing the destiny of Germany come what may. Their view that there was nothing to hope for from the Allies was essentially correct, but a passive posture was at odds with Lorković's temperament.

After Ante Vokić was appointed minister of armed forces early in 1944 Lorković soon befriended him. Vokić, a simple but dynamic newcomer from Bosnia, and Lorković, the educated scion of an old Zagreb family, started to think the unthinkable, unlike the rest of the mediocre Ustaša top leadership.

---

[1] T-501, roll 264. Glaise to Jodl, 12 May 1944.

[2] For details on Vokić's visit, see: KTB, Bd IV/1, pp. 742 on.

[3] For a detailed account of the "affair" see Krizman (1983), Vol. II, pp. 78-139.

They saw a possible Allied landing on the Adriatic not as a threat but as a possible opportunity to follow in Badoglio's footsteps, change sides at the right moment and thus save an independent Croatian state. The role of the Domobranstvo figured prominently in this scenario. Vokić soon established and cultivated nuerous contacts in the officer corps. In late spring and early summer of 1944 he embarked on a series of confidential conferences with senior officers to probe their views through hints, allusions, and eventually frank discussions about the future.

While Vokić was working on the military, Lorković sought foreign connections in Switzerland, in Bari and at the Vatican. The gist of the plan was the removal of the Poglavnik and the replacement of the regime by a HSS-led government, the disarming of German units by the Domobrans, and an invitation to the Allies to land unopposed on the Dalmatian coast. The plan attracted support from several HSS leaders, the most prominent of whom were Ivanko Farolfi, Ljudevit Tomašić, Josip Torbar and Ivan Pernar. The HSS deputy chairman August Košutić also maintained contact with Lorković, initially through the former Prefect in Knin and representative to the Second Italian Army, David Sinčić. In May 1944 Lorković confided to Sinčić that in his opinion Germany had lost the war, and added that – according to his confidential sources – the British were planning an amphibious landing in the Balkans.[1] Lorković was right on the overall estimate. Hopelessly wrong on the specific prediction of British plans, he went on to suggest that the time had come for the HSS to become active and do what it could for the Croat people. Lorković asked Sinčić to talk to Košutić and inform him of the situation: the talks originally initiated yet quickly aborted in September 1943 had to be continued. A meeting wasarranged and jointly agreed messages were sent to would-be intermediaries.

The Allies were unwilling to respond, however. Had an initiative of this kind come at the time of Italy's pending collapse, a year earlier, the prospects perhaps would have been more promising. By the late spring and early summer of 1944 it was conclusively decided that there would be no Allied landing on the eastern Adriatic – a key premise of the putative plan. There were also political obstacles. In addition to the near-impossibility of reconciling an independent Croatian state with their stated Allied war aim of re-establishing Yugoslavia, both Britain and the United States were equally loath to enter into dialogue with the representatives of a regime identified by its extreme brutality. By mid-1944, in London and in Washington, it was

---

[1] Matković, op. cit., p. 92.

regarded as common knowledge that "as many as 700,000 victims, most of them Serbs, had been killed at the Ustasha death camps ... by the most ruthless and primitive methods, including mass shootings, clubbings, and decapitation."[1] President Roosevelt (with King Peter in 1942, below) was shocked by the atrocities. He expressed puzzlement at how the Serbs could ever be expected to live again in the same state with the Croats. When British Foreign Secretary Anthony Eden visited the White House in March 1943 to review Allied war aims, he was presented with President Roosevelt's "oft-repeated opinion" that the antagonism between the Croats and the Serbs ruled out their being in the same state. Furthermore, Roosevelt opined that the Croats were fit to be placed under some kind of "international trusteeship." He expressed similar views to Secretary of State Hull in October 1943 on the eve of Hull's departure for Moscow for the Foreign Ministers Conference.[2]

In view of such sentiments at the top of the political ladder it is unsurprising that Allied operatives in neutral countries were not interested in Lorković's emissaries: "the Croatian Ustasha regime... was not a significant target of Allied intelligence activities nor did it gain the attention of diplomatic policy-makers."[3] British intelligence operatives in Istanbul passed the message to Zagreb that their support for Tito and the reestablishment of Yugoslavia were beyond doubt after the Teheran Conference, the first meeting of the "Big Three." Therefore no dialogue was possible on any other basis and any action in Croatia was exclusively the business of those planning it.[4] The response from Rome was hardly more encouraging.[5]

---

[1] *The Fate of the Wartime Ustasha Treasury*. Report prepared by the United States Information Agency and issued by the U.S. Department of State on 2 June 1998.

[2] FRUS, 1943, vol. I, p. 543.

[3] Ibid.

[4] See also Vlaho Raić. *Saveznici i NDH*. Buenos Aires, 1960.

[5] In Switzerland some contacts were supposedly attempted through the famous sculptor, Ivan Meštrović, but his credibility in the West was compromised by that time. Even his old friend Professor R.W. Seton-Watson of London University was weary of contact with him.

As a former HSS activist who had entered Pavelić's service, David Sinčić was sent by Lorković's circle to probe the Vatican and find some Allied agents in Rome, but he returned empty-handed.[1] No more successful were attempts by two NDH trade officials in Zurich, Josip Cabas and Mirko Lamer.[2] In Madrid the Croatian envoy, Count Petar Pejacsevich, cultivated the image of an Anglophile opposed to the Ustašas and ready to consider any offer. He made many hints, but to no avail.[3]

While the Allies remained completey reserved, some encouragement to Lorković may have come from Glaise, who had had doubts about Germany's prospects at least since Stalingrad.[4] It is uncertain whether he was acquainted with the attempted *Putsch* against Hitler of 20 July, although he appears to have been tacitly sympathetic to its perpetrators.[5] By the late summer of 1944 the writing was on the wall, in the wake of a series of major German military disasters. The defeat in France, the collapse of the Army Group Center (*Operation Bagration*) in the East, and the loss of Finland, Romania and Bulgaria in quick succession, indicated that the days of the Reich were indeed numbered.

Lorković kept Pavelić informed of what he, Vokić and others were trying to do. There was no "conspiracy" (*urota*) and certainly no "coup attempt" (*pokušaj puča*). While ostensibly approving their plans, Pavelić used the information to arrest the "plotters." Most were eventually killed by Luburić's Ustaša Defense. He also used it to denounce Glaise to the Germans and to consolidate his own position. According to Košak, who was close to Lorković and privy to his plans, Pavelić's feigned his support for the project with the sole purpose of learning as many details as possible to use against Lorković and his group in due course.

---

[1] A-VII, NDH, Kut. I.O.9, No. Reg. 6/7-1-187. Sinčić's statement to interrogators, 1947.

[2] Cabas arranged the transfer of 1,400 kg of gold stolen by the Ustašas from their victims or looted from the Yugoslav National Bank to Switzerland in 1944. After the war he offered his services to the Yugoslav Communist regime. According to the U.S. Information Agency report on Ustaša treasury (June 1998), U.S. intelligence officers knew "that all the puppet Croatian government funds moved to Switzerland had been controlled by Dr. Josip Cabas, an official of the Croatian Ministry of National Economy and later the Chief of the Croatian Commercial delegation in Switzerland. After the war Cabas reportedly sought to use the Ustasha funds, amounting to 12-16 million Swiss francs, to purchase arms for the Communist Yugoslav Government, but the Swiss resisted, preferring to use the funds to pay old debts."

[3] A-SSIP, Izbeglička vlada - ministarstvo inostranih poslova, F-1, Pov. br. 1087. Višacki to Ninčić, Madrid, no date but probably March 1942.

[4] Matija Kovačić. *Od Radića do Pavelića*. Munich-Barcelona: KHR, 1970.

[5] A-VII, NDH, SUP-Zgb, MF-4. Košak's statement to interrogators.

On August 21, 1944, Pavelić unexpectedly asked Kasche to come to his private residence without delay. He told the German minister that he had information according to which Lorković and Vokić "no longer believed in a successful outcome of the war and wanted to abandon the alliance with Germany by the Croatian Government."[1] Because of his own loyalty to Germany, Pavelić continued, he would have to part ways with those ministers. He added that the same suspicion existed with regard to the Minister in Berlin, Košak, who would be replaced and subjected to identical proceedings. Last but by no means least, Pavelić told Kasche that he would have to demand the replacement of General Glaise, as the latter, in his talks with Vokić and Lorković, had expressed doubts about the successful outcome of the war.

Pavelić's intention was to get rid both of his domestic detractors – whose conflict with the *Ras* coterie of the hard-line Ustaša émigrés was as old as the NDH itself – and of Glaise, whose low esteem for the *Poglavnik* and his regime was common knowledge. On both fronts he found a willing accomplice in Kasche, who said that he would have to see Ribbentrop: a matter of such magnitude could only be discussed in person. Pavelić told Kasche that the day of reckoning with the "defeatists" would be at the end of the month, and requested that the border of the Reich be sealed for three days to stop any suspects from trying to make their way to Switzerland.

Having prepared the ground with his faithful Ustaša Colonels (of whom he often said that each was more valuable to him "than a hundred university professors") Pavelić called a cabinet meeting at his villa in North Zagreb on August 30. In front of his ministers he accused Lorković and Vokić of high treason: "I cannot and will not tolerate this, and I am taking all their responsibilities away from them herewith."[2] Both supposed traitors were dismayed by Pavelić's words. Lorković soon regained his composure: grasping Pavelić's duplicity, he even behaved with a touch of irony. Not so his friend and fellow "plotter" Vokić, who kept asking, with tears in his eyes: "Why now all this, when he [Pavelić] knew all along?"[3] He kept repeating "I don't understand, I don't understand," and several times said that he "would not have started anything" had Pavelić not given his approval.

An ad-hoc Ustaša "special tribunal" was convened immediately. Both accused claimed that they were not guilty because Pavelić had been told of their every step. Pavelić confirmed that he had been told of their plans, but –

---

[1] PA Bonn, Nachlass Kasche, Bd 10.
[2] Mato Rajković. "Iza kulisa 'puča' Lorković-Vokić." *Vjesnik*, Zagreb, 4 December 1965.
[3] A-VII, Kut. I.O. 9, No. Reg. 7/7-1-18. Statement by Moškov to interrogators, 1947.

as he put it – he merely "wanted to see just how far these gentlemen would go." Lorković and Vokić (shown taking a report before his downfall, below) were initially interned in two provincial towns (Koprivnica and Novi Marof, respectively), and later taken to the prison at Lepoglava. They and about a dozen other actors in the "conspiracy" (Farolfi, Tomašić, and several high-ranking officers) were murdered in the last days of April 1945 by Luburić's *Obrana* acting on Pavelić's orders. Their graves are unknown. The entire episode was a nasty skeleton in Pavelić's cupboard that was to haunt him and his apologists in the émigré diaspora in later years.

The "affair" boils down to the question of Pavelić's motives and integrity. If he knew what the two ministers were up to – and it is beyond doubt that he did know – then it appears that he acted in bad faith at a time when the state was in mortal danger. If his primary motive was to keep personal power until the bitter end, then the systemic dysfunctionality of his motivation pattern is fully confirmed. In August 1944 Pavelić showed that he would rather have the NDH slide to its doom with himself at the helm, than allow for an alternative – however slim its chances of success – which entailed his ouster  from power. In the assessment of a man who was constantly by his side, the commander of his bodyguard, Ante Moškov, Pavelić was "unable to reconcile himself to the thought that he could be left aside, with an uncertain personal fate." This is the clue to Pavelić's actions both before and during the war, including notably his behavior in April-May 1941, during the talks with Italy over Dalmatia.

It is probable, that the outcome for Croatia would not have been different even if the Poglavnik had not clamped down on the non-existent "conspiracy." Unlike Finland, Romania, Bulgaria, or Hungary, the Ustaša state lacked all essential political and geo-strategic prerequisites for an action similar to those attempted by Admiral Horthy in the spring, or King Michael of Romania in the summer of 1944. The reasons were threefold:

1. The very existence of the Croatian Ustaša state lacked legitimacy in the eyes of the Allies, who were by 1944 firmly committed to Tito, and who had just engineered his "coalition" with the Yugoslav government-in-exile. The U.S. Office of War Information had categorized the Ustaša by that time as "collaborationists" and "war criminals" to be punished by international action.[1] Any attempt to seek Western political support for a Croatian solution outside Yugoslavia was *a priori* doomed.

2. The strategic prerequisite for such an initiative was an Anglo-American landing on the eastern Adriatic coast. By 1944 the mythical *iskrcavanje* had become the only hope of diverse non-Communist groups in Yugoslavia. As no invasion of the Balkans was planned (much to Churchill's chagrin), the pivotal point in Lorković's and Vokić's strategy was absent.

3. Pavelić's self-rule had created a climate of fear and instilled inhibitions among his associates against acting on their own. Those free from such restraints were outside the decision-making circle. This meant that psychological conditions for Lorković's initiative maturing into a successful "coup" were also lacking.

The "affair" of Lorković and Vokić was no more than an internal political episode in the final phase of the NDH. It was intended by its perpetrators to be an action of strategic, even European significance, but its external effect was negligible. The manner of its ending signified Pavelić's determination to remain at the helm, even if "his" Croatia was doomed to share the fate of the Reich.

4. Glaise Defeated

Both Pavelić and Kasche had strong reasons for wanting to remove Glaise from his post. Ever since the summer of 1941 they were aware of the suave Austrian's personal and professional antipathy for everything that the Ustašas stood for. Glaise's contempt and loathing for Pavelić and his inner circle was common knowledge, both in Germany and in Zagreb. Kasche resented Glaise as a social and intellectual superior and an arch-rival, the key obstacle to the Nazi minister's single-minded attempts to promote an unreservedly pro-Ustaša line in Berlin. The "affair" of Lorković and Vokić provided both Pavelić and Kasche with an opportunity to engineer the downfall of the turbulent general, with Pavelić taking the lead and Kasche eagerly following.

---

[1] Department of State, Historical Policy Research Project No. 61, "United States Policy Toward the Ustashi," RG 59, Decimal Files, 740.00116-EW

Glaise's idiosyncratic nature, his ability to get away with a degree of independent thinking even in Hitler's presence, is unique in the annals of the Third Reich. Hitler liked him and allowed him liberties of which Keitel or Jodl could not dream. His eventual departure from Zagreb was not due to the intrigue which Pavelić and Kasche set in motion in the last week of August 1944, but to his own loathing for both of them. In an old-fashioned manner of speaking Glaise was not "defeated"; he gave up in disgust. He was a gentleman, and he had his standards.

It all commenced with Pavelić's "confidential" remark to Kasche on August 21, 1944, that Glaise had made defeatist remarks to Lorković and Vokić. As Glaise recorded in his diary, fully informed only after the event,

> Kasche, being in equal measure stupid and evil, reacted impossibly: he asked Pavelić for a written statement of accusation against a German General! This was immediately provided. The Poglavnik simultaneously requested that Hitler be informed of everything. Instead of informing me immediately of accusations against me, Kasche put the written denunciation in his pocket, bid a cordial farewell to me and went to Berlin to submit the accusation against my person.[1]

Before leaving to see Ribbentrop on 23 August Kasche met Pavelić one more time. The two acted, in spirit and in fact, like co-conspirators in a plot against Glaise. Kasche suggested that it might be useful if he took with him a written document about the case and especially about the alleged role of Glaise. Pavelić was happy to oblige. In Kasche's recollection, "the Poglavnik duly penned a draft letter. He asked that this letter should under no circumstances get into the hands of the OKW, because he was afraid that this could have unpleasant consequences..."[2] The letter, in Pavelić's handwriting and in German, stated that "General Glaise specifically told Minister Lorković that the war was lost."[3] This was an accusation that, if proven, carried the death sentence, especially after the plot of 20 July. Of this both Pavelić and Kasche were fully aware. They tried to destroy Glaise, both professionally and physically.

When Kasche arrived at Ribbentrop's headquarters, Ritter – who as ambassador at the foreign ministry was Kasche's immediate superior – expressed doubts about the affair. He pointed out that the minister should have spoken to Glaise before leaving Zagreb. Kasche replied that he wanted,

---

[1] Glaise's diary, quoted in Kazimirović, op. cit., p. 315.
[2] Kasche's statement to interrogators, doc. cit.
[3] Pavelić's letter dated 22 August 1944. PA Bonn, Nachlass Kasche, H302, 134/136.

above all, to avoid any rumors about the affair becoming public. Disingeniously, he added that he also wanted to avoid any disruption of Glaise's current negotiations with the Croats on military cooperation.[1]

In the evening of August 25 Ribbentrop received Kasche. When told of the affair he was not impressed and commented that Glaise was a "cafe politician" who enjoyed talking off the top of his head, which the Croats used for their ends. Guessing that Glaise's well known anti-Ustaša views may have impacted the spin in Zagreb, he asked Kasche if Pavelić had political objectives of his own in this affair, to which Kasche replied that he was convinced of the authenticity of Pavelić's information. Ribbentrop took Pavelić's letter and told Kasche that he would inform Hitler.

When the following day (August 26) Kasche came to see Ribbentrop again, the foreign minister flatly stated that he could not present the matter to Hitler without hearing Glaise's side of the story first. He said that otherwise Hitler would see the whole affair as an impropriety and low denunciation. Kasche begged to differ by saying that he wanted to avoid the "usual official routes" and that he hoped for a decision by the Fuehrer which would take into account the "dynamic personality" of General Glaise. Ribbentrop interrupted Kasche sharply, saying that "it was not up to Kasche to worry about the policy of the Reich." It was conducted by the Fuehrer and himself, Ribbentrop added grandly, and Kasche was there simply to carry out his orders: "Within the framework of world politics Croatia is an entirely insignificant matter, and Kasche must get used to this. [The Reich Minister] is sick and tired of arguing with Kasche over such issues, and being forced to stand behind Kasche's stubbornness."[2] In the end Ribbentrop completely lost his self-control and started shouting at Kasche, but eventually calmed down and ordered him to go back and hear what Glaise had to say before making a formal report. On his return to Zagreb (29 August) Kasche first went to Pavelić. He was shown materials to support the charges that were being prepared against Lorković and Vokić, including a four-page handwritten statement by Vokić's one-time friend, Ustaša officer Štitić.[3] Pavelić stated that he would act against Lorković and Vokić the following day (30 August), and that some sixty arrests were to be carried out. On 31 August, at 5 a.m. the SD representative in Zagreb SS-*Obersturmbannfuehrer* Hermann called Kasche to tell him that Pavelić's plan had been carried out smoothly. Lorković and Vokić were dealt with in

---

[1] PA Bonn, NAK, Bd. 10.

[2] As quoted in Krizman (1983), Vol. II, p. 85.

[3] Ibid. p. 86.

Pavelić's villa, while various HSS and military "fellow conspirators" were being apprehended all over Zagreb.

It was only at that point that Kasche finally invited Glaise, who had noticed the minister's "cool and distant posture." By contrast – Glaise later remembered – in the last week of August, while Kasche was in Germany, "[Pavelić] behaved in an extraordinarily cordial and pleasant manner towards me, so that I could not imagine that mean stab in my back which he had engineered with the help of his friend Kasche."[1] Kasche and Glaise met on August 31 at 12 noon. Their conversation initially focused on the events in Zagreb of the previous night, but then Kasche went to the crux of the matter. In Glaise's recollection:

> He gave me a personal memorandum containing Pavelić's accusations against me in connection with my talks with Lorković. Certain points in Kasche's note were identical with the Poglavnik's letter, which Kasche had provoked [Pavelić] to write. Of Pavelić's letter, the proof of Kasche's deviousness, I only learnt later at the OKW.

Glaise flatly denied Pavelić's accusations ("which were based 100 percent on tête-à-tête conversations"). Deeply indignant he warned Kasche that he could not talk with a grown-up man in such manner. Glaise then left abruptly, but returned the following day to inform Kasche that it was no longer possible for him to discuss the matter directly with the minister, and that he would have to use "official channels." Glaise reiterated his indignation at Kasche's role in the affair. He added that, after Pavelić's grossly improper behavior, it was impossible for him to continue as the armed forces representative in Zagreb. Also on September 1 Glaise sent a telex to Weichs and Löhr, informing them of "an apparently unbridgeable schism" which had developed between him and Pavelić, "unfortunately not without the fault of the German Minister." This had made it impossible for him to represent the interests of the Wehrmacht, either personally or through Kasche. He asked to be allowed to report to Keitel in person.[2]

On September 7 Glaise left Zagreb for good, "with a raised head and a broken heart" as he put it. He had no choice: although Kasche's and Pavelić's accusations were not proven, and were not believed in Berlin, he could not stay unless both Kasche and Pavelić were removed.[3] Just before his departure

---

[1] Glaise's diary, quoted in Kazimirović, op. cit., p. 317.

[2] BA, MAF, RH 31/iii/11. Glaise to Weichs, Löhr, 1 September 1944.

[3] PA Bonn, NAK, Bd. 10/6. Kasche to Ribbentrop, 5 September 1944.

he sent a courier to Kasche with a handwritten letter, warning against the danger of rekindled "raw Ustaša terror."[1] He feared the triumph of the old *Ras* clique. An early sign was the murder of Lorković's friend Milutin Jurčić, who was dragged out of his apartment in the middle of the night, butchered by the *Obrana* men acting on the orders of Vjekoslav Luburić (below), and left in the street with a macabre note attached to the knife protruding from his body: *Job Vacancy: New Director of Public Security Wanted.*

In Berlin Keitel greeted Glaise cordially but admitted that he did not want to be too involved in "an eminently political affair." Glaise said that there were only two alternatives. Either Hitler would inform Pavelić that he [Glaise] enjoyed the Fuehrer's fullest confidence, in which case he would stay in Zagreb; or else Glaise was to be sacrificed, in which case his departure should be made as dignified as possible. Keitel agreed, while Ribbentrop avoided further involvement "in a matter of interest only to the OKW." The final decision on Glaise came on September 26, a week after Pavelić's fourth and final visit to Hitler. Weichs informed all German authorities in the southeast that, commencing on that day, Glaise was removed from his post in Croatia and transferred to the reserve. Keitel tried to comfort the old general by telling him he should be pleased that he "would not have to witness the shameful end of that miserable state."[2]

Having lost the battle but saved his face – as he put it – Glaise obtained satisfaction from Hitler, who awarded him the Knight's Cross (*Ritterkreuz*) with swords. Keitel gave him the decoration saying that he hoped "the unpleasant aftertaste was thereby removed," which Glaise may have felt about departure from Zagreb.

---

[1] PA Bonn, NAK, Bd. 10/6. Glaise to Kasche, 6 September 1944.

[2] "I replied – *jawohl!*" Glaise wrote in his diary, "but that was not true. I could not get over it that Kasche was still down there, playing a great man and a victor, in spite of his bad faith not only towards me, but also towards the German Army."

5. The Last Ally

Pavelić's success in disposing of Lorković's group as well as Glaise coincided with a strategic shift in the Balkans which radically weakened Germany's defenses but further contributed to the strengthening of Pavelić's position in Berlin. With the loss of Romania and Bulgaria and the arrival of the Red Army into the Pannonian Plain, the importance of Croatia to the defense of the heartland of the Reich increased rapidly. This precluded any further search for an alternative to Pavelić, who in late August and early September 1944 won the final victory in his fight to obtain unreserved support from Hitler. To the German leadership, the NDH turned from "a bothersome child" into the last remaining ally in the area.[1] This led to the abdication of any policy based on the removal of the Ustašas, their regime and methods.

Pavelić sealed his victory with a speech at the Chamber of Labor (*Radnička komora*) in Zagreb, on September 7. He said that the Croats should devote themselves to the defense of their homeland, and leave broader issues - such as "the conduct of the war" - to the Germans: "My duty is to look after what is going on here, in our country... And what is going elsewhere, there must be someone who is looking after that too. And we know that there is, and if I were to bother about events on the other side of the Carpathians, woe unto our fatherland."[2] Any hope of further combinations with the Allies was dispelled when Pavelić went on to declare that he would greet the British "with guns." In his closing remarks he charted the course that the NDH would follow until the end: "The Croats have never blemished their honor in their history. We will not do so now either. Our road is determined. We chose it not three, but 30 years ago, since 1918. We shall endure with our ally, and we shall win with our ally. The Croat people will not betray itself, and therefore it will not betray its ally." In the ensuing days he embarked on a series of morale-boosting visits to the provincial garrisons (opp. p.)

Hitler's readiness to allow the sacrifice of Glaise effectively ended discussions about possible alternatives to Pavelić. This decision was the result of necessity rather than choice. He had no illusions about Kasche's assessment of the situation in Croatia. On September 17, 1944 he remarked that "Kasche is prone to fantasy": "One can be wrong ten degrees, twenty, even fifty degrees. But when a man is ninety degrees wrong, something is badly out of order. However, when he is all of 180 degrees wrong, totally

---

[1] Bogdan Krizman. "Vodstvo Trećeg Reicha i raskorak u ocjenjivanju situacije u Hrvatskoj (1941-1944)." *Jugoslovenski istorijski časopis*, 3-4/1975, p. 115.

[2] A-VII, NDH, Box 293, No. 1/1-36. Leaflet *S Poglavnikom do pobjede*.

wrong – well, that is a masterpiece!"[1] Yet Hitler's scope was limited by events outside his control. This was apparent in Pavelić's fourth and, as it turned out, last visit to Hitler, at the *Wolfschanze* on September 18, 1944. Hitler opened the meeting by describing the difficult position of Germany in the Balkans which necessitated evacuation of southern Greece and the Aegean islands.[2] It was crucial to defend the positions in Hungary and the Iron Gate-Vardar valley line. Asked about Croatia Pavelić stated that the country had gone through a period of crisis recently, under the impact of the collapse of Romania and Bulgaria. The Lorković-Vokić case he presented as a problem with some Croatian intellectuals, including members of the government, who had lost faith in final victory and wanted to enable the British to get into Croatia before the Russians. There was a lot of enemy propaganda in Zagreb, he went on, rumors about the fall and arrest of the Poglavnik, and some weakening of morale among Domobrans, especially among those officers

who had served in the old Yugoslav army. This caused some units, misled by such officers, to go over to the enemy. Pavelić claimed that the Partisans were much weaker than before, as 30,000 of them – he asserted – had accepted the offer of amnesty and returned to their homes. He also claimed that the mood of the Croat people was "absolutely positive." The faith in victory was undiminished among the people, it was only weakened among intellectuals. The people were not interested in their speculations, but followed their instinct for preservation and wanted to continue the struggle. Pavelić asserted that the best way to fight Tito was to strengthen the organization and arm the Ustašas, if need be at the expense of the regular army. To disarm the *Domobranstvo* in order to give arms to the Ustašas was "politically impossible," however. Therefore, Pavelić asked Hitler to supply more arms to the NDH specifically earmarked for the Ustaša units. Hitler replied that this was not possible in view of the demands posed by the crises in the east, west and southeast, but praised Pavelić's ability to

---

[1] KTB, IV/2 1945. pp. 1637-1639.

[2] For Paul Schmidt's records see Andreas Hillgruber (ed.). *Staatsmaenner und Diplomaten bei Hitler. Vertrauliche Aufzeichnungen und Unterredungen mit Vertretern des Auslandes 1939-1944*. Teil 2, 1942-1944. Frankfurt a.M. 1970, pp. 506-519.

rely on his Ustašas at all times. He said that Croatia was "the only place in the Balkans which had a national government which enjoyed the full support and confidence of the Reich."

In subsequent talks with Keitel Pavelić reiterated his determination to rely solely on the Ustašas. He said he would gradually merge the Domobrans into Ustaša units (a "mixed" platoon, below). He also said that he would renew "energetic" treatment of the Orthodox population, and to this end he requested Keitel's help for the arming and training of two Ustaša divisions.

The new course in Zagreb was fully endorsed by Hitler, as evidenced by Keitel's circular sent to field commands on the day of Pavelić's departure from Germany, September 19. He conveyed Hitler's latest instructions for co-operation with the NDH armed forces and institutions. It had two key points:

1. The Ustaša movement was the political foundation of the state and of the armed forces of Croatia. German armed forces in Croatia had to adapt, uniformly and unconditionally, to the Ustaša course and to support it.

2. The state leadership of Croatia saw in the Četnik movement a danger to the survival of the NDH. The Wehrmacht therefore must stop all co-operation with the Četniks in Croatia. Wherever necessary the Ustašas were to be assisted in disarming the Četniks.[1]

The new course was immediately felt on the ground. The Military-Economic Staff South-East reported from Belgrade that changes in Croatia "have resulted in an intensified Ustaša course, with German approval. As a consequence there is renewed total animosity towards the Orthodox population."[2] Glaise's worst fears were coming true: the clique of Ustaša colonels was no longer just a shadowy force. Its members were given formal posts that had been kept out of their reach for as long as the OKW and the SS had the upper hand.

---

[1] T-120, roll 1757, No. 0011434/44 Kdos. Keitel's circular of 19 September 1944.

[2] A-VII, *Zbornik*, XII/4, pp. 599-601. Report of 19 September 1944.

Having won his battle with the OKW, Kasche turned his guns on Himmler's plenipotentiary in Croatia, Konstantin Kammerhofer. In the first detailed report following Pavelić's return from Germany and the official endorsement of the renewed pro-Ustaša course by Hitler, Kasche hastened to make scathing attacks on Kammerhofer's "lack of cooperation with the Croatian police and armed forces." He asked that Kammerhofer be appointed police attache at the German legation, which would make him Kasche's subordinate.[1] Although this was not accepted, Kammerhofer's role in the final months of the NDH was less conspicuous. It was unusual, if not unique, to see an outside agency score a success *against*

the SS autonomy at that late stage. Hard-line Ustašas were back with a vengeance. Internal security (RAVSIGUR) was entrusted to Erih Lisak, the gendarmerie to Vilko Pečnikar while the post of the chief of staff of NDH armed forces was given to Tomislav Sertić (top). All of them were

blood-stained Ustaša émigrés in the same league with Luburić, Herenčić, Moškov, Servatzy and Boban (above). Those eight men – led by Pavelić - held the real power in the NDH, or what was left of it, until the bitter end.

Pavelić's fatalistic course was also reflected in the Ustaša foreign ministry. Periodic "Foreign Political Reports" prepared by the Ministry no longer contained previously common references to the reports of possible separate peace between Germany and the Allies. Instead, the salient feature of NDH diplomats and analysts after September 1944 was their insistence on the "inevitable" and "imminent" clash between the Anglo-Americans and the Soviet Union, as well as officially sanctioned optimism about the overall situation. This sometimes bordered on the absurd. A report dated 23 October

---

[1] T-120, roll 1077, GRs-160/44. Kasche to the Foreign Ministry, 29 September 1944.

1944 stated that Germany seeks to maintain the existing position in order to gain time, "to manufacture new weapons in sufficient quantities, and to use them to reverse the situation on the battlefields... An outline of the dispute among the allies is increasingly clear."[1] In November 1944 a report by the Ustaša foreign ministry was even more surreally optimistic:

> There are considerable real prospects for Germany. Further struggle will inevitably bring to the surface ever more sharply the weaknesses in the enemy camp, which surely exist due to fatigue and great losses... Mounting enemy losses on a daily basis will convince the enemy that further struggle does not make sense, especially on German territory."[2]

The subdued manner in which Goebbels hinted at new secret weapons was described in an NDH foreign ministry report as a proof that "this is no sign of skepticism, but of self-confidence and real assurance which does not require any propagandistic spin." Typically, the conclusion was that "Germany most certainly will not lose this war, but on the contrary it will win, which is to say it will force *both* enemy camps to a favorable peace."

At this same time German troops started evacuating large tracts of territory; these were immediately taken over by the Partisans. Before the end of 1944 this happened in central and southern Dalmatia, eastern Herzegovina, Srem and eastern Bosnia. This caused the morale of the Ustašas to waver, especially when local German commanders failed to provide sufficient prior notification of their withdrawal.[3] The official explanation was that retreats were unfortunate but temporary measures, to be reversed in due course. By early November 1944 the Ustaša propaganda allowed for the possibility that the entire country would be overrun. "Even if it happens that Croatia is temporarily occupied by the enemy," a foreign ministry report stated,

> It is clear that the decision on the war's outcome will not come here, and that our events will not have great significance for the overall decision. After the anticipated successful conclusion of this war Croatia will be reestablished with all its rights and in its entirety, and this is precisely what the Croatian national idea, embodied in Ustašism, is seeking and struggling for.[4]

---

[1] A-VII, NDH, Kut. 3/2-1. *Vanjskopolitički pregled br. 10 MVP NDH*, 23 October 1944.

[2] A-VII, NDH, Kut. 279, No. 4/2-1. *Vanjskopolitički pregled br. 11 MVP*, 4 November 1944.

[3] On the fall of the garrison at Travnik, see Vrančić (1985), op. cit. Vol. II.

[4] A-VII, NDH, Kut. 279, No. 4/2-1. *Vanjskopolitički pregled br. 11 MVP*, 4 November 1944.

The Germans offered to accommodate a number of Croats threatened by Titošs forces. The NDH government replied with a lengthy memorandum for the government of the Reich. It intended to move "the national and state core" – not only the armed forces, but government members and officials, civil servants and their families, war invalids, prominent members of the Ustaša movement, former state officials, "artists, national creators and intellectuals... persons that in the opinion of the government of Croatia need protection," etc.[1] The Germans replied that the evacuees (government officials, civil servants, and their families) could not exceed three hundred. The Ustaša government in reponse asked that this number should be at least doubled.[2]

With the Partisans entering Belgrade on the backs of Soviet tanks on October 20 and Tito at the helm of the "new Yugoslavia," the atmosphere of doom in Zagreb was reinforced by evacuations of Volksdeutsche communities from the eastern areas of the NDH. Even Kasche was forced to remark in a report to Ribbentrop that "the government [of the NDH] must be kept on course. Its understanding of the situation is fatalistic, rather than optimistic."[3] Even though the main fronts were temporarily stabilized in the last three months of 1944, there were few grounds for any "optimism" as 1945 approached. One straw which the Ustašas attempted to grab in late 1944 and early 1945 was the idea of a Danubian confederation, or that of a Central European Catholic bloc. Old Habsburg legitimist notions were quietly revived, and the initial impetus to such plans was apparently given by Lorković himself during his "conspiratorial" contacts in the spring and summer of 1944. His plan to take Croatia out of the Nazi camp was closely linked with the Danubian solution. In that case "Croatia would have a chance to get onto the side of the Allies, like Badoglio's government in Italy, to save its independence, and to become a partner in a Danubian federation, which would include Austria, Czechoslovakia, Hungary and Slovenia."[4] Lorković's messengers never managed to get beyond low-level operatives of Allied intelligence services, however. In the last phase of the war there were many different "Danubian" projects, all of them doomed because they depended on their acceptance by the Allies. The proponents of the concept shared a horror at the prospect of the Red Army marching into the heart of Europe. The

---

[1] A-VII, NDH, Kut.233a, No.Reg. 43/1-1-8. Memorandum dated 15 November 1944.

[2] A-VII, NDH, Kut. 257, No. Reg. 34/5-3, SVT-1032/44. Alajbegović to Košak, no date.

[3] T-120, roll 1025, No. 2119. Kasche to Ribbentrop, 7 November 1944.

[4] L. Toncic-Sorin. *Erfuellte Träume*. Vienna 1982, p. 98.

Moscow Conference put an early end to much speculation in October 1943, when the Allies came out in favor of re-established Austria.

While Lorković was disgraced and finally killed by Pavelić, a series of articles broadly supportive of the idea of the Danubian confederation appeared in Zagreb in the winter of 1945 with at least tacit approval of the regime.[1] Such articles discussed at length the importance of Croat-inhabited lands to the West and ancient and modern links between Croatia and Western Europe. Geopolitical arguments all aimed at promoting the thesis that Croatia was too valuable o the West to be abandoned to Tito's Communists. In some clerical circles the preferred plan envisaged a Catholic bloc of nations, which would serve as a new *cordon sanitaire* between the Soviets and the West.[2] But for all their eloquence the authors of such articles were merely talking to themselves. They went to a lot of trouble to say things between the lines that could not be uttered loudly, let alone written. Their efforts had no impact outside the NDH, however, or outside the narrow circle in Zagreb who read and commented on them.

The only group apparently untouched by the doomsday atmosphere of early 1945 were the hard-line Ustašas, ever more tightly gathered around their Poglavnik (r.) and finally in near-complete control of their shrinking domain. Their renewed policy of anti-Serb terror excluded any possibility of a tactical truce in order to fight the almost-victorious common enemy. In pursuance of such policy Ustaša units even had engaged in armed confrontations with the Germans, while trying to get hold of Serbs in German uniform, or Serbs in German-controlled units, and kill them.[3] Such incidents, literally unthinkable only a few months earlier, resulted in a sharply worded note from Ribbentrop to Pavelić in December

---

[1] Characteristic are several articles by Milivoj Magdić in Spremnost, 1944-1945.

[2] Cf. statement by one Dizdar ("Ustaštvo"): A-VII, NDH, I.O. 10-f.3, 1-216, pp. 30-31.

[3] T-120, roll 1025, Büro RAM 1197/44 R. Ribbentrop to Kasche, 16 December 1944.

1944.¹ [see Appendix] The posture of Ustaša veterans in the final months was in line with Eugen Kvaternik's statement to Branko Pešelj three years earlier: "We may lose the war, but there will be no more Serbs in Croatia, and whoever comes after us will have to take it from there."

The new fanaticism of the leadership in Zagreb indicated that while in the past there had been a two-track German policy towards the Ustašas – that of Glaise, and that of Kasche – in the final period there was a two-track policy of the Ustašas towards the Germans. The first track officially mobilized all remaining Croatian resources for the "total war." Prime Minister Mandić announced on December 11, 1944, a "general people's mobilization" and the papers pledged every last ounce of energy for the war effort. By the end of the year Pavelić reorganized the armed forces. Ustaša and Domobran units were merged, and integration was practiced even at platoon and squad level (below). The new conscripts were subjected to "political education," aimed to imbue them with the Ustaša spirit. There was a further increase in the exaltation of the Poglavnik as "the leader of the people" at the head of the "armed Croat nation." Key command posts in the reorganized force – which numbered over 200,000 men in early 1945 – were given to Ustaša officers. Papers were also filled with frightening notices of executions of Domobran men and officers who were caught deserting or trying to cross to the Partisans.

The other, hidden track of Ustaša policy was revealed in the events of late 1944 and early 1945. The terrorist, murderous core within the Ustaša leadership regained all of the ground lost in late 1942, and returned to its old agenda of fighting an *anti-Serb*, rather than a *pro-German* war. The victory of one side or another in that war was less important to them than the ethnic composition of Croatia that would emerge from the war. To persevere with the policy of killing Serbs had precedence over "pragmatic" considerations of

---

¹ As a result Pavelić was forced to accept, on 21 December, an unhindered passage of Djujić's Četniks from Lika to Slovenia.
A-VII, NDH, Kut. 2339, No. Reg. 48-1/1. Pavelić's circular of 21 December 1944.

holding front lines and conserving scarce resources. The renewed fanaticism was apparent in February 1945 in Pavelić's response to papal legate Marcone's complaint that "many arbitrary death sentences were still being carried out in the NDH, often without any trial." It was not the executions that were disturbing the peace, Pavelić replied, but but "the acts of sabotage and crimes of those elements that act against the Croatian people and state under the Bolshevik leadership."

The regime's priorities were on display as late as March 1945, when elite Ustaša units were withdrawn from the front in Srem to destroy a large group of typhoid-plagued, demoralized and exhausted Montenegrin Četniks, led by Pavle Djurišić, who were trying to make their way to Slovenia across the NDH. They were destroyed, Djurišić and his officers taken prisoner and killed, while the rank-and-file were drafted into a "Montenegrin army" under Ustaša protégé Sekula Drljević. Within weeks Tito's forces broke through; the front in Srem had collapsed, and the road to Zagreb was wide open.

6. In Search of a Miracle

The Yalta Conference (February 4-11, 1945) should have ended the illusions of the most stubborn optimist in the Ustaša camp. The details were known to the NDH foreign ministry immediately from the Allied press.[1] The collapse of German fronts was in full swing. A massive Soviet offensive in the second half of January brought the Red Army to the Oder, an hour's drive from the capital of the Reich. The fall of Budapest opened the road to Vienna. A lull in the West, after the German counteroffensive in the Ardennes ran out of steam, was obviously temporary. Massive air raids on Germany were continuing unabated, and culminated in the destruction of Dresden (13-14 February). The end was obviously near, and NDH diplomats in the Reich reported on the signs of the collapse of German morale. The consul in Essen, Gredelj, reported in February that "people are cautious in their statements, being afraid of persecution... Party members are now saying that they were forced to join. The leadership is criticized, by the military as well." The consul in Munich, Machiedo, stated in his political report for February that "among the population one notices deep depression, and there is a lot of talk of dissatisfaction in the armed forces, of the threat of famine, and so on."[2]

---

[1] A-VII, NDH, Kut.269, No. Reg. 1/4-1. Foreign ministry, report on Yalta conference.

[2] Gredelj's report: A-VII, NDH, Kut. 304, No. Reg. 2/8-3. Machiedo's report: A-VII, NDH, Kut. 305, No. Reg. 6/3-1.

The Ustaša foreign minister, Alajbegović, told Pavelić that after the Yalta conference (below) Tito was fully empowered by the Allies to take the entire territory of Yugoslavia, with their material assistance but without their direct intervention. Pavelić refused to accept this appraisal as accurate, saying that "difficulties were already apparent in Belgrade [...] which he saw as the result of the agreement between Tito and Šubašić. Insisting on this detail Pavelić wanted to belittle the importance of the agreements at Yalta with regard to Yugoslavia, or the NDH."[1] By the beginning of March, however, Pavelić felt compelled to respond to the decisions at Yalta, which were common knowledge thanks to the BBC. Amidst rumors and advancing enemies on March 8 the NDH government issued a proclamation rejecting the Allies' position on Yugoslavia. The statement asserted "a fundamental right of every civilised nation to live in its independent state":

> On the basis of no principle, including even those formally accepted by the Yalta conference participants, can anyone deny the right to self-determination to the Croat people, to its freedom paid with heavy losses and a people's uprising [sic!] and to its independence in its own state. The decisions and advice coming from the conference at Yalta, insofar as they concern the Croat people and state, are in contradiction with history, with law, and the will of the Croat people. Therefore, the Croat people, as a mature and politically developed nation, reject them resolutely. An attempt to carry them out must be made with brutal force alone, together with attempts to falsify the will of the Croat people.[2]

On the same day Pavelić convened the ceremonial "Ustaša council" (*Doglavničko vieće*), which issued a brief statement in support of the above principles. But since it was obvious that statements and proclamations by the NDH government and Ustaša elders would not have much impact on anyone, Pavelić enlisted the support of the Roman Catholic Church in Croatia. In March 1945, following the NDH government statement in response to Yalta, the campaign started with a commemorative assembly in Zagreb devoted to "Catholic priests killed by the hand of the enemy."[3] At the ensuing Easter student assembly Stepinac delivered a sermon in which he stated:

> If all nations have the right to secure their life and independence, then it is impossible to impose a solution contrary to the popular will of the Croat people either [...] We do not hesitate to declare that the Croat people will reject any

---

[1] A-VII, NDH, Kut.I.O.9, No.Reg.4/5-1-155. Statement by Alajbegović to investigators.
[2] A-VII, NDH, Kut. 290, No. Reg. 4/4/-2. NDH government statement of 8 March 1945.
[3] See *Katolički list*, Zagreb 1945, No. 12-13, 29 March 1945, pp. 99-100.

regime, be it of the extreme left or right, which does not take into account and respect in the fullest possible sense its thousand-year-old Catholic tradition. Such a regime would represent no one among the Croat people, or just an insignificant minority imposed by force.[1]

The climax of Stepinac's last-minute support of Pavelić's crumbling edifice was the message to the faithful by the Catholic episcopate of 24 March 1945. This document provided the endorsement of the NDH and its government and an "explanation"of the predicament in which the nation had found itself. It denied any responsibility of the Catholic Church in Croatia "for the present bloody reckoning in our Fatherland."[2]

The bishops reiterated the standard tenet of Ustaša ideology that "the Croats' continuity of millenium-old statehood was interrupted, by force, only between 1918 and 1941, creating an illegal situation for the Croat people." The decisions at Yalta "are in total contradiction with history, with law, and with the will of the Croat people." The bishops ended with a ringing assertion that "during the Second World War this will was expressed and realized in our own State" and that "nobody has the right to accuse any citizen of the State of Croatia because they respect this immutable will of the Croat People, to which it has the right both by God's laws and those of men."

The initiative for the bishops' message came from Pavelić, and the remaining resources of the diminishing state were engaged to bring all bishops still in Ustaša-controlled territory to Zagreb.[3] That this document was intended for external consumption is apparent from the fact that it mentions "the world community" twice, and its translations into German, French and English were immediately sent to the few remaining foreign legations in Zagreb and NDH consulates in the Reich. The effect was again negligible, however. In addition, the back-up from the Vatican was not forthcoming. The day was too advanced for the Holy See to try any such action of its own, and "the world community" – by which the bishops presumably meant the Allies – did not react.

The battle for Berlin was coming to a close, Americans and Russians had met in the heart of the Reich, but Pavelić's intentions still remained unknown. All his "initiatives" in the spring of 1945 came to naught. A flood of refugees and troops was pouring into Zagreb and its vicinity following the collapse of the front in Srem (April 17). No attempt was made to regroup at the

---

[1] ibid. pp. 95-97.

[2] ibid. pp. 93-95.

[3] See Krizman (1983), Vol. II, pp. 266-268.

"Zvonimir Line," an ufinished network of fortified points east of Zagreb that had been heralded as Croatia's Maginot Line. On April 28 at 2 a.m. Pavelić summoned his senior commanders and high-ranking Ustašas to tell them that further resistance was impossible since German troops were withdrawing from the NDH and the fronts were collapsing.[1] There was no mention of any contact with the Allies, but Pavelić hinted to his close aides that arrangements were being made "to withdraw to the line where we can lay arms under honorable conditions and await further developments." Pavelić said he was hoping for an "imminent and inevitable" clash between Western allies and the Red Army, in which case the remaining German forces would side with the Anglo-Americans, and the Croats would join them.[2]

Even those who doubted this scenario, notably Vladko Maček, nevertheless expected that the British would accept the surrender of Croatian troops, place them in camps, and keep them as a compact entity. Maček thought that Croatian soldiers could subsequently become a trump card to be taken into account in the forthcoming political combinations.[3] In the last few days before withdrawal Maček was allowed contact with his followers, and after consulting several leading HSS figures he decided to leave the country with the retreating NDH units and government.[4]

The decision to evacuate Zagreb and retreat to Austria was made on May 5 late in the evening.[5] The withdrawal was executed in stages by regiment-sized units over the next three days. It was complete in increasing disarray by May 9. Later that day Tito's troops entered the city without firing a shot. On the eve of departure the Ustaša government addressed a long memorandum to Field Marshal Alexander ("Allied Headquarters Mediterranean, present location unknown"). Signed by all ministers, it contained the usual arguments in favor of the continued existence of an independent Croat state.[6] In a covering letter attached to the memorandum, Prime Minister Mandić requested the Allied General Staff to send a military mission to Zagreb "to ascertain the military and political situation now prevailing here." Vjekoslav

---

[1] A-VII, NDH, SUP-Zagreb, MF-23. Vjekoslav Servatzy, "Autobiografija."

[2] A-VII, NDH, Kut. I.O.9, Br. reg. 3a/2-1-9. Statement by V. Židovec to interrogators.

[3] A-VII, NDH, Kut.I.O.9, No. reg. 1/4-1-117. Statement by A. Moškov to interrogators.

[4] On details of Maček's departure, see: Branko Pešelj, "S predsjednikom Mačkom u emigraciju." *Hrvatska revija*, Munich, Vol. XX, No. 4 (December 1970).

[5] Matija Kovačić, *Od Radića do Pavelića* (op. cit.), pp. 237-238.

[6] For the full text of the Memorandum see: Jerome Jareb and Ivo Omrčanin, "Croatian Government's Memorandum to the Allied Headquarters Mediterranean, May 4, 1945." *Journal of Croatian Studies*, New York, Vol. XXI (1980), pp. 120-143.

Vrančić was dispatched in search of Alexander's headquarters but never got there, however: he was taken prisoner by the British. His memorandum was sent to London, but only to the Foreign Office Research Department.[1]

In terms of sheer ineptitude both the memorandum itself, and the manner in which it was sent, were typical of a "diplomacy" devoid of coherence, strategy, and even down-to-earth logistics. The Allies were suddenly invited to send a fact-finding mission as the NDH government was packing to leave and the area under its control was reduced to the capital city. The long-winded memorandum (translated into poor English) reiterated those same points contained in several previous propaganda exercises of the NDH regime. Finally, the man selected to hand the memorandum to Alexander, Vrančić, left Zagreb in his full Ustaša uniform. No prior contact with the Allies existed and he was supposed to get through to the unknown place where the Allied headquarters was situated. An obvious exercise in futility, Vrančić's "mission" was just another smokescreen thrown by Pavelić to conceal from his entourage the fact that there would be no bridge across the abyss to which they were about to be taken.

The dispatch of Vrančić with the Memorandum was the last political act of the government of the Independent State of Croatia. Within days, most of its retreating soldiers, civil servants, ministers and public figures were refused surrender by the British at Bleiburg, in Carinthia, and turned back to Tito. Tens of thousands were summarily executed on their return.

Pavelić and many of his inner circle managed to get away, however, largely thanks to the Vatican. The Croatian-run College of San Girolamo degli Illirici in Rome became the nerve center of Ustaša underground that helped Pavelić and many of his top aides to escape to Latin America. It was run by a brotherhood of Croatian priests, the *confraternita di San Girolamo*, which issued identity cards with false names to the fugitives.[2] These operations were controlled by the secretary of the College, Fr Dr. Krunoslav Draganović, "who was also an Ustasha colonel and former official of the Croat 'Ministry for Internal Colonization,' the agency responsible for the confiscation of Serb property. [Draganović was] regarded by U.S. intelligence officers as 'Ante Pavelic's alter ego'"[3]

---

[1] Vjekoslav Vrančić. *S bielom zastavom preko Alpa. U misiji hrvatske državne vlade za predaju hrvatskih oružanih snaga.* Buenos Aires, 1953.

[2] Public Records Office, War Office Files, WO 204/11574. British intelligence identified Croatian priest Dominic Mandić as the Vatican representative to San Girolamo.

[3] *The Fate of the Wartime Ustasha Treasury*, op. cit. Report quotes CIA Operational Files on Draganović from 1947 to 1968.

Pavelić, members of his inner circle, and hundreds of other ranking Ustašas who were shrewd or lucky enough to escape the destiny of their less fortunate countrymen at Bleiburg, got away and lived to provide the core of the second, post-1945 Ustaša emigration. Bleiburg, the bloody *finis* of the Independent State of Croatia in May 1945, was the final outcome of Pavelić's chronic opportunism. He commenced his agitation in 1927 by offering Croatian land and sovereignty as a bargaining chip to potential foreign sponsors, and continued it by complying with their demands. He started his rule in 1941 by sacrificing Croatian territories to secure his power; he was to end it in 1945 by sacrificing the Croatian army to secure his escape. The massacre of some 50,000 Ustašas, Domobrans and fleeing Croat civilians the Partisans carried out in the aftermath of their surrender at Bleiburg in May 1945 "marked the end to the dialectic of violence that had been initiated by the Ustasha genocidal program in 1941. The Ustashe had launched a fanatical ideological war that had to end in either a complete Ustasha (and Nazi) victory, or their eradication."[1]

Pavelić led his army to doom, incessantly insinuating that he knew what he was doing. The outcome prompted even his former loyal followers to conclude that his fundamental motives concerned his personal power to the exclusion of all other considerations.

The ill-fated Vrančić "mission," and the clumsy memorandum for Alexander, provided a suitable backdrop for the downfall of the Ustaša state. An apt comment, with a tinge of prophecy, was annotated by some long-dead Foreign Office Research Department official on May 18, 1945:

> The signatures of all the members of the Croat puppet Govt. on one document will be something of a curiosity for the future historians. There seems to be nothing of interest in the long memorandum. [...] Croatia may be heard of again some day, but for the present it is finished.

---

[1] Bartulin, op. cit., p. 414.

XIII
Conclusion

The range of moral and political issues raised by the Ustaša movement and the regime it established in the Independent State of Croatia is akin to that facing a student of the Third Reich. In both cases, a political group, organized into a regime, exceeded the bounds of previously conventional morality by devoting extraordinary resources to mass murder based on the victims' race, creed or ethnicity. In both cases most *ordinary* Germans and *ordinary* Croats – those not directly affiliated with the regime, or overtly supportive of its goals and methods – opted for passive acquiescence, ranging from apathy to *Schadenfreude*. Many of them subsequently claimed an ignorance of the magnitude of the crimes, regardless of the wealth of evidence to inform the curious. In both cases only a small minority was directly involved in the killing. The members of that minority had reason to believe that many *ordinary* people shared their eliminationist attitudes yet lacked the stomach for doing what needed to be done. In both cases the perpetrators understood why it had to be done; the mass murder made sense to them.

There are intriguing differences. The Nazis subjected ordinary Germans to relentless anti-Semitic indoctrination for almost a decade prior to the final, exterminationist phase of 1942-45. The anti-Serb propaganda campaign conducted by the Ustaša regime preceded the beginning of its own exterminationist campaign by weeks rather than months. In both cases modern racial myths were blended with a mix of pre-existing myths, stereotypes and prejudices, thus preparing ordinary people to internalize the dehumanization and subsequent liquidation of the victims. In Croatia, however, the collective indoctrination preceding the mass murder could be so much shorter because the soil was more receptive to the seed.

The Ustaša movement had its roots in the political tradition based on Croatia's *state rights*, which included the key claim that no inhabitants of Croatia were exempt from the jurisdiction of its political and legal institutions. For the upholders of this view, the Serbs of the Military Border were unwelcome aliens for as long as they insisted on retaining their distinct name, their autonomous legal status vis-à-vis Civil Croatia, and their Orthodox faith. An obsessive aristocratic resentment at Grenzer privileges was passed on from one generation to another, and became democratized after the collapse of feudalism in 1848.

At the historical root of the Ustaša bloodbath lay a centuries-old striving of the Croatian elite to impose legal and religious homogeneity and to reestablish political obedience. A culturally homogeneous nation-state could not be created from the diversity of nationalities without ethnic cleansing, however. The notion of a racially distinct national community with an exclusive claim to its land was the necessary ingredient to make such a project not only possible but emotionally and culturally legitimate. That notion was eventually articulated in the aftermath of 1848, in the period of rapid modernization, with *the Serb* as the essential 'other' at its center. The old distaste for *the Vlach* of the Croatian Estates was re-defined in surprisingly modern terms by the "father of the nation," Ante Starčević. He articulated *eliminationist anti-Serbism* and thus created the necessary political culture for the Ustaša project of *exterminationist Serbophobia*.

Unlike Fascism and Nazism, which were dynamic, Ante Pavelić aimed for a *stable* situation: his project entailed the creation of a nationally homogeneous, Serb-free, Croat state. His movement's ideology was meant to serve that project, not to give it meaning. Its task was to justify and celebrate, rather than explain and develop. That ideologyt had never amounted to much more than a half-baked mix of historical and racial myths peppered with rudimentary geopolitics and sweeping ethno-cultural generalizations. It was produced *ad-hoc* (mainly in the aftermath of April 10) by some two-dozen men of dubious credentials motivated by nationalist fixations. It was neither interesting nor original.

What also set the Ustašas apart from both Nazis and Fascists was the degree to which their anti-Serb animus defined their emotional as well as cultural self perception, their very *Croatness*. This set the movement apart from all other political forces in Croatia, and notably the HSS. The Ustašas postulated a demonic concept of *the Serb* which made any compromise impossible. Limited sovereignty and amputation of territory was preferable. Pavelić's perception of Croatia's interests was consistent with his basic assumptions, eventually turning him into Mussolini's "Balkan pawn" in the latter's own words.

The NDH was an Axis creation but it possessed certain attributes of *de facto* statehood. It was an *actor*. Although the scope and quality of its statehood kept diminishing as the war progressed, it was nevertheless more than a mere extension of the policy dictated in Berlin or Rome. The existence of rivalries and divergent interests between the Axis powers enhanced the scope for autonomous action. Pavelić needed that scope to pursue his project, if possible unhindered by German or Italian meddling. His mix of genocidal brutality, racism and despotism was hardly an "ideology." The raw power of the mélange was nevertheless able to remove the old restraints of civility and turn the NDH into a pandemonium of bloody anarchy. Up to half a million civilians were murdered. About four-fifths of them were Serbs; the balance, in almost equal thirds, was made up of Croatia's Jews, Gypsies, and politically unreliable *Aryans*.

The system of occupation in the Yugoslav lands was an improvisation, hastily conceived and weakened by intra-Axis differences. A destabilizing factor was Hitler's desire to impose a Carthaginian peace on the Serb nation, but without allocating sufficient resources for the purpose. The fuse was lit, west of the Drina, by a wave of terror for which Pavelić felt authorized by Hitler in June 1941. Most German authorities in the Balkans were horrified by the massacres and became antagonistic to the Pavelić regime. The Italian army was even more hostile, and by virtue of its greater political autonomy it succeeded in having the zone of Italian occupation successively extended to the demarcation line with Germany.

Hitler's unwillingness to get rid of Pavelić was initially inspired by the desire to maintain an institutionalized chaos, which the Ustašas duly provided. Later on there was no alternative. The HSS was unwilling to compromise itself in the eyes of the Allies, especially when it became clear that Germany would lose the war. After September 1943 even such limited degree of Ustaša policy-making, which had been made possible by the intra-Axis rivalry, was no longer allowed. As Ribbentrop put it, "the Croats are not to make even their wishes known to us."

In the final year of the war the Ustaša regime revived its anti-Serb zeal, confirming that all along it was fighting an *anti-Serb*, rather than a *pro-German* war. With the outcome of the war no longer in doubt, in that final year the number of Croats in the ranks of Communist resistance finally exceeded the number of the western Serbs. They saw what the would-be conspirators of the summer of 1944 could not accept: that the NDH was as doomed as Mgr. Tiso's Slovakia. It expired with a whimper at Bleiburg in May 1945. There was no last stand, no Siege of Sziget, as Pavelić's leaderless soldiers were disarmed and unceremoniously marched back to an uncertain and often tragic fate.

His power secure and absolute, Tito tried to force all "Yugoslavs" to invest their memories of the war into the common bank of the *National Liberation Struggle* (NOB) and *Fascist Terror* as equal shareholders, and to draw the common dividend of *brotherhood and unity*. Tito's edifice thus came to be built on three fictions:
1. The myth of the constituent nations' equal contribution to the Partisan victory in the 'National Liberation Struggle.'

2. The myth of all ethnic groups' equal suffering under the 'occupiers and their domestic servants.'
3. The equating of the Četniks with Pavelić's Ustašas as politically and morally equivalent.

The Serbs were not allowed to be personalized as victims and the Ustašas were seldom named as perpetrators. Countless markers and monuments in Lika, Kordun, Banija, or Bosnia and Herzegovina memorialized the "victims of the terror by occupiers and their domestic servants," followed by long columns of Serbian names. The state narrative could not prevent or outweigh the impact of personal and family ones, however, which for the Serbs became part of an underground national narrative.

While politically expedient for the Communist dictator, this policy assured that there would be no atonement and no internal reconciliation. It curtailed public discussion and scholarly discourse on the Ustaša legacy; "The West, meanwhile, bankrolled prominent Ustaše reborn as anti-communist agents, while America's popular consciousness all but forgot about the Balkans until Yugoslavia imploded."[1] The new communist regime was not, of course, officially anti-Serb; but its principle of 'brotherhood and unity' had as its chief practical consequence a massive official coverup of Ustaša crimes in the name of ideological *Gleichschaltung*. The anti-Serb tenor of the Comintern's pre-war slogans about royal Yugoslavia was reflected in the assumptions on which the second, Communist Yugoslavia was based. Two provinces, Kosovo-Metohija and Vojvodina, were granted autonomy within Serbia, but the Serbs of the old Military Border did not get anything approaching autonomy within Croatia.

Tito's Yugoslavia was built not on the principle of a-nationality or supra-nationality, but on arbitrary territorial adjudications which would have been impossible at any point between 1918 and 1941. The Serbs of western Yugoslavia, who had provided the core fighting force of the Partisan movement, were assured that those arrangements did not matter since the Yugoslav state remained in place. The Serbs in the Croatian Communist Party, indoctrinated in Partisan ranks, provided the middle-ranking *apparat* but they were not present at the top. They were in the forefront of enforcing ideological rigidity among their own people, by imposing collectivization of agriculture and preventing the rebuilding of Orthodox churches. In the name of *brotherhood and unity* they even opposed the exhumation of the bodies of

---

[1] Michele Frucht Levy, op. cit.

Ustaša victims from mass graves and mountain pits for proper funeral. De-Nazification never took place in Croatia.

The Serb-Croat conflict of the 1990s grew from elements which should now be familiar. The Communist *apparat* in Croatia and the police force were disproportionately Serb. This was resented by Croats, just as Serb privileges had been resented before 1881. As the Croatian Communist Party became more nationalistic, this became consequential; and when Communism failed, nationalism detonated. The Serbs were identified as the bearers of the Communist revolution itself.

In 1990-91 it was hardly imaginable that the Serbs should not take up arms against a regime in Zagreb which was reviving the symbols, slogans, and atmosphere of the Ustaša state. Their fears were kindled by the government of Franjo Tudjman which came to power in April 1990 after the first multiparty election since 1938. It was composed of nationalists whose stated goal was to reconcile the legacy of the Croatian Partisans and their Ustaša opponents. Tudjman's successor as president, Stjepan Mesić, thus declared that Croatia had scored a victory twice in the Second World War, first in 1941 and then again in 1945.[1] Tudjman readily affirmed that the NDH reflected the legitimate, *centuries-old aspirations of the Croat people*.[2]

The war which broke out in August 1991 had the traumatic collective memory of the NDH as its key cause. Its final act came on August 4, 1995, when *Operation Storm* was launched by the Croatian army and police. Its political objectives became evident over a decade later, when the Yugoslav War Crimes Tribunal at The Hague released a transcript of Tudjman's meeting with his top military commanders and civilian aides at the Adriatic island of Brioni on July 31, 1995. "We have to inflict such blows," Tudjman announced, "that the Serbs will to all practical purposes disappear." It is important that those civilians set out, he went on, "and then the army will

---

[1] "In the Second World War, the Croats won twice and we have no reason to apologise to anyone. What they ask of the Croats the whole time, 'Go kneel in Jasenovac...' - we don't have to kneel in front of anyone for anything! We won twice and all the others only once. We won on 10 April when the Axis Powers recognized Croatia as a state and we won for the second time because we sat after the war, again with the winners, at the victors' table." (Croatian news agency HINA in English, BBC Monitoring Europe, December 10, 2006) Five days later the Speaker of the Croatian parliament said on TV that he and then-president Mesić might have "possibly sung songs celebrating notorious Ustaša commanders Jure [Francetić] and [Rafael] Boban" during the 1990s. (HINA in English, BBC Monitoring Europe, December 15, 2006) It would have been unthinkable for a German politician, in the first decade of the 21st century, to be suspected of a similar transgression and yet to remain in office.

[2] Speech at the First HDZ Convention, February 26, 1990.

follow them, and when the columns set out they will have a psychological impact on each other ... This means giving them a way out, while pretending to guarantee civil rights etcetera."[1] This strategic design was firmly rooted in 1941. The result was the biggest act of ethnic cleansing in post-1945 Europe. An area the size of New Jersey, inhabited by over half a million people a century ago, was literally depopulated. Of those left behind, "many have been shot in the back of the head or had throats slit, others have been mutilated... Serb lands continue to be torched and looted."[2] Virtually all Serb villages had been destroyed and many corpses left unburied.[3]

To most Croats this was but the final act of a war of Serbian aggression and Croatian Defense of the Motherland. The power of this narrative became evident in April 2011, when tens of thousands of people took to the streets to protest the conviction of two Croatian generals by the UN war crimes tribunal in The Hague.[4] A rational verdict on the crimes against the Serbs remains as unlikely in today's Croatia as it was seven decades ago.[5] The collective refusal to judge immoral acts *as such,* separate from some alleged context, does not bode well either for Croatia or for its neighbors.

Tudjman's vision behind the *Storm*, a Serb-free Croatia, indicated that the legacy of 1941 was alive. A week after it was all over, at a rally in Knin, Tudjman announced, "There can be no return to the past, to the times when [Serbs] were spreading cancer in the heart of Croatia, a cancer that was destroying the Croatian national being." Those same words could have been uttered at a rally in the spring of 1941. Tudjman gloated in the "ignominious disappearance" of the Krajina Serbs, "as if they have never lived here." His predecessors of 1941-45 would have approved.

What happens in the Balkans is seldom due to the Balkans alone. The interests, preferences and strategic designs of the great powers matter as greatly in our own time as they did during the Second World War or during the Seven-Year War. Tudjman felt authorized from Washington and Bonn to proceed with his final solution in the Krajina no less than Pavelić had felt authorized to pursue *fifty years of intolerance* after visiting Hitler in June

---

[1] ICTY Case No. IT-02-54-T, Exhibit No. PC11A of June 26, 2003.

[2] "Croats Burn and Kill with a Vengeance." Robert Fisk, *The Independent*, 4 September 1995.

[3] "Helsinki Committee Reports on Krajina Operations." Hartmut Fiedler, Österreich 1 Rundfunk, 21 August 1995.

[4] Especially problematic is the Tribunal's use of the concept of *Joint Criminal Enterprise* – a blunt legal tool with Kafkaesque implications.

[5] The Croatian Army chief chaplain, Bishop Juraj Jezerinac, compared the predicament of generals Gotovina and Markač to the suffering of Jesus Christ.

1941[1] Tudjman's goals were recapitulated with precision on August 23, 1995, in the aftermath of the *Storm*: "Military force can be a most effective means for solving the internal needs of the state... It is necessary for military command precisely to become one of the most efficient components of our state policies in solving the demographic situation of Croatia."[2]

The Ustaša legacy is a *Serbenfrei* Croatia. It is kept alive not only by the skinhead fringe at Thompson's concerts and the Black Legion lookalikes at Bad Blue Boys' soccer rallies, but also by the political, academic, ecclesiastical, cultrual and media establishments. They, too, have internalized a host of similar assumptions and preferences, but they no longer require explicit symbolism and terminology of seven decades ago. Steadily reduced from a quarter of Croatia's population before 1914 to a sixth after 1945 and a seventh in 1991, the Serbs today account for fewer than five percent.

Europe may have moved beyond blood-and-soil atavism, west of the Oder at least, but in the Balkans the old heart of darkness keeps beating. After the decline of higher cynicism in the name of Human Progress, benevolent tolerance by the "international community" of that legacy reflects the ascent of higher cynicism in the name of Human Rights. Some important Westerners may prefer *to look forward*, to forget, minimize, or even deny, the fruits of the Croatian Holocaust of 1941-45 and its revived legacy of 1995.[3] The endeavor is flawed. Sins unatoned for will continue coming back to haunt us. To paraphrase a warning about another ghost from Europe's not too distant past,[4] we are not yet finished with Pavelić.

---

[1] Former U.S. Ambassador in Zagreb Peter Galbraith, testifying at The Hague, dismissed claims that Croatia had engaged in ethnic cleansing, "because most of the population had already fled when the Croatian army and police arrived."

[2] *Feral Tribune*, Split, July 18, 2003.

[3] The U.S. Department of State human rights report on Croatia (March 11, 2010) thus states matter-of-factly that Jasenovac was "the site of the largest concentration camp in Croatia during World War II, where *thousands* of Serbs, Jews, and Roma were killed" [emphasis added]. This claim is the exact moral and factual equivalent of asserting that "tens of thousands" of Jews and others were killed in Auschwitz or Treblinka.

[4] *Wir sind mit Hitler noch lange nicht fertig.* John Lukacs, *The Hitler of History*. New York: Vintage Books, 1998, p. 1.

APPENDIXES

APPENDIX I: Anfuso's minutes of the meeting between Ciano and Pavelić in Rome, 23 January 1940 (DDI, 9, III, pp. 162-164)

Count Ciano met Pavelić on 23 January 1940 in the presence of Marquis Bombelles and Anfuso. He asked Pavelić detailed questions on the possibility of uprising in Croatia, the spread of his movement, Dr. Pavelić's intentions regarding the form of government that can be given to Croatia, as well as possible Serbian reaction to the planned Croat uprising.

Pavelić said that he was certain of the uprising's success. He confirmed the need that Italian troops, 30 thousand strong, enter Croatia as soon as the uprising takes place in Zagreb, in smaller towns and villages. He added that the Serbs would then have no alternative but to withdraw to the area of the old Kingdom of Serbia. Pavelić thinks that the uprising will inevitably lead to the collapse of the Yugoslav system created by the treaties of 1919. If that process is not to be accelerated, it may be necessary that Italian troops enter Belgrade and install a government, headed if possible by Stojadinović, which would negotiate with Italy and determine Serbia's new frontiers.

Prompted by Count Ciano's question, Pavelić says that in his opinion Italian troops could successfully enter Kosovo and extend the sovereignty of the Kingdom of Albania over that area. Pavelić confirms what Count Ciano has stated: that the Serbs have always feared the Albanians' armed action and irredentism. As for the fate of Slovenia, Pavelić accepts Count Ciano's opinion that will necessarily adapt to the new regime which the Croat people will set up together with Italy. Slovenia is needed by Croatia's economy, its people have always lived in harmony with the Croats, and it will have to accept the situation created by Italy. Pavelić thinks that an eventual cession of Maribor to Germany may represent natural compensation to German interests in Slovenia. He does not conceal that the proclamation of an independent Croatian state in union with Italy would represent a blow that would halt Germanic designs, but he finds Italy's support indispensable to Catholic Croatia if German intentions in the Adriatic are to be frustrated. Pavelić also points out the importance to Italy of the major Slovene coal mine at Trbovlje.

Count Ciano agrees with Pavelić on the terms of the insurgent movement and approves the tactic of Croatian national-Fascists. He also asks Pavelić not to hurry with his action because of obvious international reasons, and to wait for a signal from Rome, so that the uprising does not start prematurely. On Count Ciano's demand, Pavelić formulates the following points:

1. Croatia will be an independent state;
2. The Croat State will be in a monetary and customs union with Italy;
3. The Croat State will have its national Croat army, "Domobranstvo" (what the Austrians used to call *Heimwehren*, and the Hungarians *Honved*);
4. The Croat State will enter a personal union with the Kingdom of Italy.

In connection with the last point Dr. Pavelić expresses agreement with Count Ciano on the desirability of the personal union between the Kingdom of Italy and the

Kingdom of Croatia, but also thinks it is necessary to keep the possibility of such personal union secret at first, so as not to provide Serbian propaganda with ammunition. Realization of this union will be easy once Italy is definitely established in Croatia. [...]

Count Ciano mentions what could be the state profile of Croatia linked to Italy by personal union: ministries, administrative autonomy, Italian minister of foreign affairs, part of the Government Croatian and a joint Supreme Military Committee. Pavelić agrees.

It is agreed that insurgent action will proceed as follows:

1. Proclamation of Croatian independence in Zagreb by... Pavelić, creation of a Croatian government, call on Italian troops to intervene to preserve Croatia's independence.

2. Entry of Italian troops into Croatia led by the Ustašas presently in Italy. First objective – Zagreb; final objective, in case of Serb resistance, the confluence of the Sava and the Danube [i.e. Belgrade] or the Iron Gate.

3. Complete possession of Croatia, proclamation of personal union.

The situation that may emerge in Yugoslavia as a consequence of Croatia's independence is considered, and probable future of other provinces is mentioned: Montenegro, because of its Slav character, could be constituted as a separate state, Slovenia would stay Croatian [sic!], while Italy would get islands facing Zara so that the city may gain free access to the sea. It is agreed that Count Bombelles personally reports to Ciano at the end of the following month, while Dr Pavelić will intensify his contacts with the Foreign Minister, who will continue to provide him with all the means for successful direction of his movement which has so far scored real political successes.

(The document bears Mussolini's signature)

APPENDIX II: The "Croatian National Committee" Appeal to the Italian Foreign Minister, Zagreb, June 1940 (DDI, 9, VI, #848)

We, the undersigned members of the Croatian National Committee for Liberation and Establishment of the Independent State of Croatia, as representatives of the Croat national organization, address the following APPEAL to Your Excellency:

In 1918 the Croat people was forcibly included into the so-called Yugoslav state, indeed contrary to its clear desire for independence and autonomy.

The Croat nation is aware of its millenium-old state and national individuality, since its state independence dates from the seventh century. The Croats have maintained their national identity and state independence through the centuries in a more or less clear form until the end of the world war. In 1918 Serbia, aided by Western democracies, completely eradicated any state or national identity by annexing our territory and holding the Croat nation under the hegemony of Belgrade.

From 1918 onwards, the Croat people has fought by all available means to rid itself of the foreign yoke. After cruel acts of violence and persecution, known to the whole world, which the Belgrade government committed against the Croat nation, the regime in Belgrade was forced to grant the Croats some sort of autonomy, but even that only under the pressure of international events and the threat of war.

However, this autonomy is only formal, since after a year it has not fulfilled a single promise, and the constitutional agreements have not been carried through. This autonomy, purely formal as it is, has no lasting importance, since the Belgrade regime can revoke it at any moment, as soon as the international situation is changed. Furthermore, this false autonomy does not embrace the whole Croat territory, but only a part of it. Finally, this false autonomy does not reflect the aspirations of the Croat people; for it wants a more complete national and state independence.

The Croat nation is no longer willing to endure such state of affairs, but it has decided to reestablish its sovereignty over its entire historical and ethnic territory. The Croat nation belongs to the Western civilization and owes such progress to the centuries of cultural contacts, to its orientation towards the Appennine Peninsula and the Italian nation. [It is with that nation that] it links its own fate, physically by the Adriatic Sea and spiritually by the community of culture, civilization and religion.

Before this wealth is completely destroyed, both spiritual and material, in which our country is so rich, the Croat nation has decided to cut off decisively all links with Serbia and to cede from so-called Yugoslavia, which is nothing but an extended Serbia created by the dictate of Versailles.

With this decision, the Croat nation addresses its great neighbor, Fascist Italy, and asks for help in the struggle for liberation. Therefore we, the undersigned delegates of the Croat national organization from all Croat regions, gathered within the National Committee for the Liberation and Establishment of the Croatian State, freely address Your Excellency. We ask that you interpret our desires to the Duce of the great and glorious Fascist Italy, to which we appeal for help. [We appeal that] Italy sends her tried and invincible army to defend the holy and just cause of the Croat nation against the barbaric Serb intrusion and that of their allies, so that we can, under Italy's auspices, reestablish the thousand-year-old Independent State of Croatia. It had always been and will always remain the first barrier of Western culture and civilization in this area of eternal struggle against the barbarian penetration from the East. This would establish true peace here, and secure civilized life not only for the Croat people but also for other nations which are equally suffering in this part of Europe from the imposed, unjust and artificial political situation.

The Croat nation expects with complete confidence the great act of liberation worthy only of the great Duce and the mighty nation of Fascism, which points the way to all the nations of the world to a new path of justice and a new life.

Obedient to our Leader and ready to carry out his orders, we address this Appeal to Your Highness, and express to the Duce and to you our admiration and gratitude.

[Attached: 66 signatures of the Committee members "from the city of Zagreb, from upper Croatia, Lika, Slavonija, Dalmatia, and Bosnia-Herzegovina"]

APPENDIX III: Statement by the "Home Ustaša" group obtained by the Reich Foreign Ministry plenipotentiary Veesenmayer on 5 April 1941, and addressed to the government of the Reich (DGFP, D, 12, No. 270.)

A meeting was held of a number of deputies and officials of the *Banovina* of Croatia, representatives of Croat cultural and commercial institutions, representatives of all strata of people from all historical Croat provinces, without difference or party allegiance, in Zagreb on 31 March 1941. A detailed discussion considered the political situation in the aftermath of the coup perpetrated in Belgrade on 27 March.

It was unanimously concluded that, after that event, peaceful life, national expansion and development is no longer possible within Yugoslavia for the Croat people. Within the Serb nation there is a strong will to take Yugoslavia to war with Germany, while the Croat nation wants peace with Germany and cooperation with it. The Serb nation is opposed to the new order in Europe, while the Croat people has a deeper understanding for the new, more just European order and wants that order. Serbian people's representatives are in the service of British policy, which out of its own self-interest wishes to instigate disorder, chaos and war in the Balkans, while the Croat people does not want to serve the interests of England, which had always supported Serb hegemony over Croatia.

It is therefore determined

- That the Croat people has maintained a strong political, cultural and economic link with the German people for centuries;
- That the Croat people has enjoyed its statehood for centuries, and the Serb mastery, imposed and aided by Western democracies, had never been accepted;
- That within the Croat nation there is belief and hope that it can count on the full support of Germany in the creation of a free and independent Croat state, since one of Germany's war aims is to secure to all nations of Europe free national development and expansion. Thus the following was unanimously agreed:

1. Yugoslavia has ceased to exist. An independent Croat state is being created. It embraces historical and ethnic Croat lands: Croatia with Medjimurje, Slavonia, Dalmatia, Bosnia and Hercegovina, and the Croat part of Vojvodina;

2. Until the constitution, or the law on state authority is enacted, legislative power is in the hands of the new Croat people's government in Zagreb;

3. This conclusion is forwarded to the Government of the Reich, with the request that the recognition of the Croat state by other Axis states be effected;

4. In order to protect independence and self-reliance of the newly-created Croat state, representatives of the Croat people, on behalf of the entire people, request from the government of the Reich its immediate protection and help.

In the capital city of Zagreb on 31 March 1941. Plenipotentiary signatories.

[NB: According to Veesenmayer's covering note, the statement was in fact signed by only five people, two HSS "rightists" (Tortić and Lamešić) and three "nationalists" - Kvaternik, Lorković, and Edo Bulat, who was belatedly included as a "representative" of Dalmatia.]

APPENDIX IV: Kvaternik's proclamation of the Independent State of Croatia and Maček's statement, read on Zagreb radio on 10 April 1941

Croatian people,
Divine providence and the will of our ally, centuries-long hard struggle of the Croat people and the great self-sacrifice of our Poglavnik Dr. Antun Pavelić, and the Ustaša movement in our country and abroad, have determined that today, on the eve of the Resurrection of the Son of God, our independent Croat State also be resurrected.

I invite all Croats, wherever they are, and especially all officers, NCOs and men of the armed forces and police, to maintain complete order and to report immediately their present location to the Command of the Armed Forces in Zagreb; and that all members of the armed forces immediately take the oath of allegiance to the independent Croat state and its Poglavnik. Today I assumed the state authority and command over the entire armed forces as the Poglavnik's plenipotentiary.

God and the Croats - For Homeland On Guard!
Slavko Kvaternik

After Kvaternik's proclamation the announcer read Maček's statement:

Croatian people: Colonel Slavko Kvaternik, the leader of the nationalist movement in the country, proclaimed today a free and independent Croatian state in the entire territory of the Croat nation and thereupon as of today he assumes power.

I call on all Croats to obey the new authorities. I enjoin all members of the Croat Peasant Party to remain calm, and all members of district administrations to remain at their posts and sincerely to cooperate with the new government.

In Zagreb, 10 April 1941. Dr. Vladko Maček

APPENDIX V: Pavelić's speech at a public rally in Zagreb, 21 May 1941[1]

When in 1918 the enemy, due to then prevailing circumstances, stepped in to subjugate the Croat people, our people put up resistance with such means as were then available. When the enemy realized that its methods were not sufficient and strong enough, then twelve years ago he applied new means of force and violence to sweep the Croat people from the face of the Earth, to eliminate the last trace of its national individuality and its statehood. Then the Ustaša movement emerged among the Croat people. It was clear to me that we could not fight the tyrant with a prayer book in our hands. Therefore, I started the movement that would apply the painful medicine to the painful wound. Violence used against Croats was stopped by violence. No nation in history has achieved liberty with folk songs, but with blood and deadly weapons. It was clear to us that a captive and disarmed people could never

---

[1] *Hrvatski narod*, Vol. III, No. 99, Zagreb, 22 May 1941

achieve liberty without assistance and support of another friendly people. Therefore, preparations for liberation followed those two paths.

Another world war broke out because it had to, because Europe and the world could live on the basis of paper peace treaties. [...] We have been waiting for such moment. It has arrived and brought us liberation [assisted] by our will, our awareness, our faith, our sacrifices, our struggle, our organization, our great - we can confidently claim – glorious military feats, carried out in the last days of the sinister Yugoslavia. Liberation of the Croat people, and the establishment of the Independent State of Croatia, have been brought about by the two great Axis nations, led by two great leaders. For this, we are grateful to them. For this, the Croat people will be eternally grateful to them. [...]

Following its recognition our state had to have its frontiers determined. And again thanks to the leaders of the two great friendly peoples, the Croat people today has already roughly determined frontiers in two most important parts of the country. In this area we had to make some sacrifices. But a nation unable to make sacrifices is unable to live. I am certain, and all of you can be certain, and the whole Croat people can be certain, that every Croat who remains outside the frontiers of the Independent State of Croatia will have his name preserved, his language, his nationality, his culture and household!

It was different when there had been no Croat state. But the very existence of the Independent State of Croatia, her sovereignty, her friendly relations with her great neighbors, those very facts are the guarantee that those Croats who remain outside our frontiers. Their number, thank God, is not great, and that those Croats will remain an integral part of the Croat people. I am openly telling you that this is completely in accordance with the intentions of our great friend Benito Mussolini. When we were concluding treaties on frontiers, we were not striking bargains - that used to be done by those politicians who were not representatives of the free people and of an Independent State. We concluded treaties as representatives of a free and sovereign people. Other frontiers will be determined soon, to the great satisfaction of the entire Croat people. Croatia's Independent State is already greater than it had ever been in history!

[...] The Croatian State will be set up on the basis of traditions of the Croat people, and on the most modern principles pursued by our great friends and allies. In their case, such principles demonstrated that they alone are capable of providing order, work, bread and normal life. Ustaša brothers! Our internal political order will be such that people can decide by itself, in a sovereign manner, on all its vital issues, without so-called democracy or political speculations. [...] The Croat peasant nation, according to the Ustaša principles, is not only the source of all good for itself, it is also the subject and bearer of all power and authority in the Croatian state. Croatia's Independent State is, and will be, only the organ that serves Croatia's peasants and workers. [...] We find our place in the New European Order as a free people and as the Independent State of Croatia. This order was initiated and created by the two great leaders of friendly nations, and they will, God willing, soon complete it to the well-being and happiness of all European nations.

Ustaša brothers! The Croat people have had enemies, and they will always have them. But we were not afraid of them even when we had no freedom and no weapons; we are even less afraid of them now that we are completely free, and when there is the Croat rifle on the gallant Croat shoulder! We shall defend our national and state freedom with our lives, always. We shall not allow enemies of the Croat people to work against it, to poison it from within. We shall not allow them to spit on the spilt blood of Croat martyrs, we shall not allow them - and as you know we are not allowing them – to exploit and squander the fruits of labor of Croat peasants and workers.

The times when the Croat nation was but an object, are over. The Croat nation is the master now, and everything else will be *its* object. These are not promises, but clear indications of our intentions. They are being applied and will be carried out. I shall carry them out! And everyone knows that until now I have fulfilled all my promises!

APPENDIX VI: German note of 16 December 1944 on Ustaša crimes[1]

The Government of the Reich has learnt with greatest surprise of a host of incidents involving members of the Ustaša militia who had committed unprecedented transgressions against members of the German armed forces. The matter concerns, among others, the following incidents:
1. For some time now, the Ustaša brigade from Jasenovac has been searching trains and columns in the area of Novska-Dubica. On such occasions soldiers and military escort of non-German nationality, in Wehrmacht uniforms and with German travel documents, have been arrested and forcefully taken to the camp at Jasenovac. To objections by German officers and railway station commanders, the Ustaša side has partly responded with the threat of arms (deploying armored scout cars etc.).
2. On 23 and 24 November 1944, near Jasenovac, the Ustaša brigade searched a German transport of wounded soldiers belonging to Field Hospital 615. In a brutal manner they took away members of [Ljotić's] Serbian Volunteer Corps, threatening to use arms in the process. They also mistreated wounded Germans.
3. On 3 December 1944 a transport of German soldiers consisting of soldiers convicted by the Divisional Court to various sentences to be served in the Reich, which included five Croats, had the escorting guard removed by force. A protest by the attendant German military-judicial officer was unsuccessful. An Ustaša lieutenant, who did not give his name, said that the Ustašas from Jasenovac would liberate every Croat Legionnaire sentenced by German military organs and sent to serve his sentence in the Reich.
4. Not far from the railway station at Zagreb, and at the station itself, on 7 December 1944, heavily armed members of an Ustaša unit – I n spite of the

---

[1] T-120, roll 1025. Buro RAM 1197/44

protest by a German NCO accompanying the group – dragged out of a train 36 officers and men belonging to the Serbian Volunteer Corps and shot them on the spot. [They] were on their way to Rijeka, having taken part in combat on the side of a German army group.

The Commander South-East has already protested most vigorously with the Poglavnik through military channels and asked that the culprits be punished, and that a special order be issued to prevent repetition of such incidents in the future. The Government of the Reich is prompted to tell on its part the following to the Poglavnik:

The Government of the Reich cannot regard acts, such as those committed by the members of Ustaša militia, as soldierly actions. In its estimate, this is undisciplined and irresponsible behavior by criminal elements. The fact that participating Ustaša officers and soldiers dared, in one instance in Zagreb itself, to break into German military transports and to threaten even members of the Wehrmacht with arms, is so unprecedented that the Government of the Reich will under no circumstances tolerate such outrages. On the contrary, it must expect that now, in a country which owes its state existence exclusively to the blood of German soldiers, its leader will immediately undertake most effective measures to end such incidents once for all.

The Government of the Reich further expects that its demands for exemplary punishment of all culprits be met without delay, as already demanded by the Commander South-East. [It also expects] that the Croatian side will acquaint the German Legation in Zagreb and the Commander South-East with the sentences and all relevant details.

Sources and Bibliography

A. Primary sources

1. German documents on microfilm, listed and catalogued in the Guides to German Records Microfilmed at Alexandria, Virginia (Washington DC: National Archives Records Office):

    a. Microcopy T-501, Records of German Field Commands, Occupied Territories and Others. Rolls 250, 256, 264-268, 351 and 352 deal with various aspects of the occupation and resistance in the Balkans.

    b. Microcopies T-311...T-315, Records of Army Groups E and F (Heeresgruppen E, F in rolls 175, 176 and 197, mainly relevant to the closing stages of the war) and Records of German Field Commands.

2. Politisches Archiv, Auswärtiges Amt, PA/AA): Office of the Minister (Büro RAM, i.e. Reichsaussenminister - Kroatien); Office of the Secretary of State (Büro Staatssekretär - Jugoslawien Bd 3, Kroatien Bd 1-4). All on NA Microfilm T-120, Rolls 120, 197, 199, 200, 208 and 212.

3. The War Archive in Vienna (Kriegsarchiv Wien, KAW) contains the papers of Glaise von Horstenau (B/67) and Alexander Loehr (B/521).

4. Published collections: *Akten zur Deutschen Auswärtigen Politik 1918-45.*(ADAP) E, 1 (Göttingen, 1969). 2 (1972). *Documents on German Foreign Policy 1918-45* (DGFP) D, 12 vols, (London, 1962)

5. The Federal Archive – Military Archive in Freiburg (Bundesarchiv – Militärarchiv in Freiburg, BA/MAF) has the official papers of Glaise, Loehr and other German generals in the Balkans.

6. George O. Kent, *A Catalog of Files and Microfilms of the German Foreign Ministry Archives, 1920-1945*. Stanford, CA: Hoover Institution, 1966, Vol. 3.

7. Paul N. Hehn (ed.). *The German Struggle against Yugoslav Guerillas in World War II: German Counter-Insurgency in Yugoslavia 1941-1943*. East European Quarterly, Boulder. Distributed by Columbia University Press, New York 1975.

8. International Military Tribunal. *The Trial of Major War Criminals (Proceedings)*. Vol. 10. Nuremberg: IMT, 1946. Contains the interrogation of Ribbentrop in 1946, with information on the Axis policy in Yugoslavia.

9. National Archives, Washington D.C.: microfilmed records of the Italian High Command (Comando Supremo) and the Second Army Command (Comando 2. Armata) classified as Microcopy T-821. Rolls 53, 54, 64, 66, 70, 232, 285-290, 294, 297, 298, 395, 398-400, 410, 448, 474, 497 and 503 contain material on the relations of the Italian Army with the Četniks and the NDH.

10. *Documenti diplomatici italiani*. IX, 2 (Rome, 1958). 3 (1959).

11. National Archives, Washington D.C., Record Group 59 DD. 860H.00 and 860H.01 for reports concerning Croatia from the U.S. Legation in Belgrade, the Consulate in Zagreb and U.S. diplomats in Budapest until mid-1941.

12. Public Records Office (PRO) London, FO/371. Foreign Office documents relevant to Yugoslav affairs during the Second World War.

13. Arhiv Saveznog sekretarijata za spoljne poslove (ASSIP): Ministry of Foreign Affairs of the Independent State of Croatia (Ministarstvo vanjskih poslova Nezavisne Države Hrvatske, MVP NDH).

14. ASSIP, Royal Yugoslav Government in Exile, Ministry for Foreign Affairs (Ministarstvo inostranih poslova, F-1, F-2, F4); and Presidency of the Council of Ministers (Predsedništvo Ministarskog saveta, F-1, F-2) have reports on Croatia from Yugoslav diplomats in neutral capitals.

15. Arhiv Jugoslavije (AJ). Fond Milana Stojadinovića (the papers of Milan Stojadinović). Contains documents on the Yugoslav-Italian relations in the late 1930s and on the Croat question at home.

16. Fond izbegličke vlade (Royal Yugoslav Government in Exile documents) deposited in the Yugoslav Archive in Belgrade (AJ). Material covered in: Krizman, Bogdan, and Petranović, Branko. *Jugoslovenske vlade u izbeglištvu.* 2 vols. (1941-43, 1943-45). Belgrade-Zagreb: Arhiv Jugoslavije/Globus, 1981.

17. Institute of Military History, Belgrade (Vojnoistorijski institut, V.I.I.; fond VII/NDH). Abundant material on the NDH in boxes (*kutije*), including statements by captured officials after the war.

18. V.I.I. *Zbornik dokumenata i podataka o Narodno-oslobodilačkom ratu naroda Jugoslavije.* 13 vols in 128 parts. Belgrade: Vojnoistorijski institut 1949. Arranged regionally and topically. The documentary source for the Partisan version of war in Yugoslavia. Contains Ustaša documents and translations of German and Italian ones.

19. *Das Kriegstagebuch des Oberkommandos der Wehrmacht* (KTB/OKW - War Diary, German High Command), III/5.

B. Secondary Sources

Aarons, Mark and Loftus, John. *The Unholy Trinity.* New York: St. Martins, 1991.

Anfuso, Filippo. *Roma, Berlino, Salo (1936-1945).* Milan: Edizione Garzanti, 1950.

Bakic-Hayden, Milica. "Nesting Orientalisms: The Case of the Former Yugoslavia." *Slavic Review* 54.4 (Winter, 1995): 917-931.

Banac, Ivo. *The National Question in Yugoslavia: Origins, History, Politics.* Ithaca and London: Cornell University Press, 1984.

Barriot, Patrick & Crépin, Eve. *On assassine un peuple: les Serbes de Krajina.* Paris: L'Age d'Homme, 1995.

Basta, Milan. *Agonija i slom NDH*. Belgrade, 1971.

Bataković, Dušan T. "The National Integration of the Serbs and Croats: A Comparative Analysis." *Dialogue* (Paris), No. 7-8, September 1994.

Bauer, Yehuda. *The Holocaust in Historical Perspective*. London: Sheldon, 1978.

Biber, Dušan. "Ustaše i Treći rajh. Prilog problematici jugoslovensko-nemačkih odnosa 1933-1939." *Jugoslovenski istorijski časopis*, 2-1964.

Boban, Ljubo. *Maček i politika Hrvatske seljačke stranke, 1928-1941*. Two volumes. Zagreb: Liber, 1974.

Bracewell, C.W. *The Uskoks of Senj: Piracy, Banditry and Holy War in the sixteenth-century Adriatic* Cornell University Press, 1992.

Broucek, Peter. *Ein General im Zweilicht. Die Erimerungen Edmund Glaise von Horstenau*. Vienna-Cologne-Graz: Boehlhaus Nachf., 3 Vols (1980, 1983, 1988). Vol. 3 includes Glaise's Zagreb diary.

Cannistraro, Pilip (ed.). *Historical Dictionary of Fascist Italy*. Westport, Connecticut-London: Greenwood Press, 1982.

Ciano, Galeazzo. *Diario 1937-43*. Ed. by Renzo De Felice. Milan: Rizzoli, 1980.

"Croatia," in *Shoah Resource Center*. Jerusalem: The International School for Holocau-st Studies at Yad Vashem, 2005.

Dedijer, Vladimir. *The Yugoslav Auschwitz and the Vatican: The Croatian Massacre of the Serbs During World War II* Buffalo, N.Y., 1992

Deakin, William. *The Brutal Friendship: Mussolini, Hitler and the Fall of Italian Fascism*. New York: Harper and Row, 1962.

- *The Embattled Mountain*. London - New York - Toronto, 1971.

Diklić, Momčilo. *Srpsko pitanje u Hrvatskoj, 1941-1950*. Beograd: Zora, 2004

Djilas, Milovan. *Wartime*. New York: Harcourt Brace Jovanovich, 1977.

Djuretić, Veselin. *Saveznici i jugoslovenska ratna drama: Izmedju nacionalnih i ideoloških izazova*. 2 vols. Belgrade: SANU, 1985.

Dragnich, Alex N. *The First Yugoslavia: Search for a Viable Political System*. Stanford, California: Hoover Institution Press, 1983.

- *Serbs and Croats: The Struggle in Yugoslavia*. New York: Harcourt, Brace. 1992.

Dvorniković, Vladimir. *Karakterologija Jugoslavena*. Beograd: Gregorić, 1939.

Falconi, Carlo. *The Silence of Pius XII*. Boston: Little, Brown and Co., 1970.

Fortis, Abbe Alberto. *Travels Into Dalmatia*. New York: Cosimo Classics, 2007. A contemporary reprint of an 18th century classic.

Fricke, Gert. *Kroatien 1941-1944: Die "Unabhaengige Staat" in der Sicht des Deutschen Bevollmaechtigen Generals in Agram, Glaise v. Horstenau*. Freiburg/i. Breisgau: Rombach Verlag, 1972.

Gligorijević, Branislav. "Politički život na prostoru RSK (1918-1941)" in *Republika Srpska Krajina*, Belgrade 1996.

Hagen, Walter. *Die Geheime Front*. Wien: Niebelungen Verlag, 1950. In English: *The Secret Front - the Story of Nazi Political Espionage*. London: Weidenfeld and Nicholson, 1953. "Hagen" is the alias of Wilhelm Hoettl.

Hammel, E.A. "Demography and the Origins of the Yugoslav Civil War." *Anthropology Today* 9 (1): 4-9 (February 1993), Royal Anthropological Institute of Great Britain and Ireland.

Robert M. Hayden, *Recounting the Dead: The Rediscovering and Redefinition of Wartime Massacres in Late- and Post-Communist Yugoslavia* (in Rubie S. Watson (ed.): *Memory, History, and Opposition Under State Socialism*, Santa Fe, New Mexico, School of American Research Press, 1994, pp. 167-201.

Hlinicka, Karl. *Das Ende auf dem Balkan 1944/45: Die Militaerische Raeumung Jugoslawiens durch die Deutsche Wehrmacht*. Goettingen: Musterscheudt, 1970.

Hollins, David. *Austrian Frontier Troops, 1740-98*. Oxford: Osprey Publishing, 2005.

Hory, Ladislaus, and Broszat, Martin. *Der kroatische Ustascha-Staat, 1941-1945*. Stuttgart: Deutsche Verlags-Anstalt, 1964.

Hoptner, Jacob B: *Yugoslavia in Crisis, 1934-1941*. New York: Columbia UP, 1962.

Horvat, Josip. *Zivjeti u Hrvatskoj: Zapisi iz nepovrata*. Zagreb: Liber, 1983.

Istorija srpskog naroda, Beograd: Srpska književna zadruga, 10 vols.

Ivanović, Vane. *Memoirs of a Yugoslav*. New York and London: Harcourt Brace Jovanovich, 1977.

Janković, Djordje. *Tradicionalna kultura Srba u Srspkoj Krajini i Hrvatskoj*. Beograd: Etnografski muzej, 2000.

Jareb, Jere. *Pola stoljeca hrvatske politike*. Buenos Aires: Hrvatska Revija, 1960.

Jelić-Butić, Fikreta. *Ustaše i Nezavisna Država Hrvatska*. Zagreb: Globus, 1977.

Jukić, Ilija. *The Fall of Yugoslavia*. New York: Harcourt Brace Jovanovich 1974.

Kazimirović, Vasa. *NDH u svetlu nemačkih dokumenata i dnevnika Gleza fon Horstenau 1941-1944*. Belgrade: Narodna knjiga, 1987.

Kiszling, Rudolf. *Die Kroaten: Der Schichsalweg eines Südslawenvolkes*. Graz-Cologne: Verlag Hermann Boehlhaus, 1956.

Krestić, Vasilije. *Through Genocide to Greater Croatia*, Belgrade: BIGZ, 1997.

Krizman, Bogdan. *Korespondencija Stjepana Radića, 1885-1918.* Zagreb Zagreb: Sveučilište – Institut za hrvatsku povijest, 1972.

- *Ante Pavelić i ustaše.* Zagreb: Globus, 1987.

- *NDH izmedju Hitlera i Mussolinija.* Zagreb: Globus, 1980.

- *Ustaše i Treći Reich.* Two volumes. Zagreb: Globus, 1983.

Kukuljević Sakcinski, Ivan. *Književnici u Hrvatah u prvoj polovini XVII vieka.* Zagreb 1868.

Lederer, Ivo. *Yugoslavia at the Paris Peace Conference.* New Haven and London: Yale University Press, 1963.

Levy, Michele Frucht. "'The Last Bullet for the Last Serb': The Ustasha Genocide against Serbs: 1941-1945." *Nationalities Papers* 37, No. 6 (2009), pp. 807-837.

Lowe, C.J. and Marzari, F. *Italian Foreign Policy, 1870-1940.* London and Boston: Routledge and Kegan Paul, 1975.

Lukacs, John. *The Hitler of History.* New York: Vintage Books, 1998.

MacDonald, David. *Balkan Holocausts? Serbian and Croatian Victim-Centered Propaganda and the War in Yugoslavia.* Manchester University Press, 2002.

Martin, David. *The Web of Disinformation: Churchill's Yugoslav Blunder.* San Diego and New York: Harcourt, Brace, Jovanovich, 1990.

Matković, Hrvoje. *Povijest Nezavisne Države Hrvatske.* Zagreb: Naklada P.I.P. 2002.

Mažuran, I. *Popis naselja i stanovnistva u Slavoniji 1698. godine*, vol. 2, JAZU, Osijek, 1988.

Milaš, Bishop Nikodim. *Documenta spectantia historiam Dalmatiae et Istriae a XV usgue ad XIX saeculum.* Zara 1894.

Milazzo, Matteo J. *The Chetnik Movement and the Yugoslav Resistance.* Baltimore and London: The Johns Hopkins University Press, 1975.

Miletić, Antun. *Koncentracioni logor Jasenovac 1941-1945.* Beograd: Narodna knjiga, 1986.

Miller, Nicholas J. *Between Nation and State: Serbian Politics in Croatia Before the First World War.* University of Pittsburgh Press, 1997

Neubacher, Hermann. *Sonderaufrag Südost 1940-1945. Bericht eines fliegenden Diplomaten.* Goettingen: Muster-Schmidt-Verlag, 1957.

Novak, Viktor. *Magnum Crimen: Pola vijeka klerikalizma u Hrvatskoj.* Zagreb, 1948.

Nyström, Kerstin. "The Holocaust and Croatian National Identity: An Uneasy Relationship." *The Holocaust on Post-War Battlefields: Genocide as Historical*

Culture. Eds. Klas-Göran Karlsson and Ulf Zander. Malmö: Sekel Bokförlag, 2006: pp. 259-314.

Orlow, Dietrich. *The Nazis in the Balkans: A Case Study of Totalitarian Politics*. University of Pittsburgh Press, 1968.

Paris, Edmund. *Genocide in Satellite Croatia: A Record of Racial and Religious Persecutions and Massacres*. Chicago, 1962.

Pavlinović, Mihovio. *Misao hrvatska i misao srbska u Dalmaciji, od godine 1848 do godine 1882*. Zadar, 1882.

Pavlovich, Paul. *History of the Serbian Orthodox Church*. Toronto: Serbica, 1989.

Pavlowitch, Stevan. *Unconventional Perceptions of Yugoslavia 1940-1945*. East European Monographs. New York: Columbia University Press, 1985.

Plećaš-Nitonja, Nikola. *Požar u Krajini*. Chicago 1975.

Plenča, Dušan. *Kninska ratna vremena 1850-1946*. Zagreb: Globus, 1986.

Rendulic, Lothar. *Gekämpft, gesiegt, geschlagen*. Welsermühl Verlag, Wels und Heidelberg, 1952.

Ribar, Dr. Ivan. *Iz moje političke suradnje, 1901-1965*. Zagreb: Naprijed, 1965.

Roberts, Walter R. *Tito, Mihailović and the Allies 1941-1945*. (2nd ed.). Durham, North Carolina, 1987.

Rothenberg, Gunther E. *The Military Border in Croatia 1740-1881*. Chicago and London: The University of Chicago Press, 1966.

Schechtman, Joseph. *The Mufti and the Führer: The Rise and Fall of Haj Amin el-Husseini*. New York: Thomas Yoseloff, 1965.

Šišić, Ferdo. *Povijesti hrvatskoga naroda*. Zagreb, 1916.

- "O stogodišnjici Ilirskog pokreta." *Ljetopis Jugoslavenske akademije*, Zagreb, Vol. 49-1936.

Srbi u Hrvatskoj: Naseljavanje, broj i teritorijalni razmeštaj. Belgrade: Univerzitet u Beogradu, 1993.

Starčević, Ante. *Razgovori*. Djela, Vol 3. Zagreb 1894.

Steinberg, Jonathan. "Types of Genocide: Croatians, Serbs, and Jews, 1941-1945," in David Cesarani, *The Final Solution: Origins and Implementation*. Routledge 1996.

- *All or nothing: the Axis and the Holocaust 1941-1943*. London, 1990.

Stillman, Edmund. *The Balkans*. New York: Time-Life Books, 1967.

Stenton, Michael. *Radio London and Resistance in Occupied Europe: British Political Warfare 1939-1943*. Oxford University Press, 2000.

Stojadinović, Milan. *Ni rat ni pakt: Jugoslavija izmedju dva rata.* Buenos Aires: El Economista, 1963.

Sufflay, Milan. *Hrvatska u svjetlu svjetske historije i politike.* Zagreb, 1928.

Tanner, Marcus. *Croatia: A Nation Forged in War.* New Haven: Yale University Press, 1997.

Taylor, Scott & Nolan, Brian. *Tested Metal.* Ottawa: Esprit de Corps, 1998

Tomasevich, Jozo. *The Chetniks.* Stanford University Press, 1975.

Trifkovic, Srdja. *Ustaša: Croatian Separatism and European Politics, 1929-1945.* London: The Lord Byron Foundation, 1998.

- "Rivalry Between Germany and Italy in Croatia, 1942-1943." *The Historical Journal,* Vol. 34, No. 4 (1993).

- "Yugoslavia in Crisis: Europe and the Croatian Question 1939-41." *European History Quarterly.* Vol. 23 (1993), No. 4, pp. 529-561.

- "The First Yugoslavia and Origins of Croatian Separatism." *East European Quarterly.* Vol. 24, No 3, September 1992, pp. 345-370.

Van Creveld, Martin. *Hitler's Strategy 1940-1941: The Balkan Clue.* Cambridge University Press 1973.

Voinovitch, Louis. *Dalmatia and the Yugoslav Movemen.* London: George Allen & Unwin, 1920.

West, Rebecca. *Black Lamb and Grey Falcon.* Penguin Classics, 2007.

Wilson, Peter H. *The Thirty Years War: Europe's Tragedy.* Cambridge, MA: The Belknap Press, 2009.

Winnifrith, T. J. *The Vlachs: The History of a Balkan People,* London: Palgrave MacMillan, 1987.

Žerjavić, Vladimir. *Gubici stanovništva Jugoslavije u Drugom svjetskom ratu.* Zagreb: Jugoslavensko viktimološko društvo, 1989.

The Author

Srdja (Serge) Trifkovic has a BA in international relations from the University of Sussex, a BA in political science from the University of Zagreb, and a doctorate in history from the University of Southampton. In the course of a long career combining journalism with academia he has worked for the BBC in London, the Voice of America in Washington D.C., and since 1999 as foreign affairs editor of *Chronicles* magazine. His previous books in English include:

The Krajina Chronicle: A Short History of Serbs in Croatia, Slavonia and Dalmatia. Chicago-Ottawa-London: The Lord Byron Foundation, 2010

Defeating Jihad: How the war on terrorism may yet be won, in spite of ourselves. Boston, MA: Regina Orthodox Press, 2007.

Peace in the Promised Land: A Realist Scenario (editor & contributor). Rockford, IL: Chronicles Press, 2006.

The Sword of the Prophet. Islam: History, Theology, Impact on the World. Boston, MA: Regina Orthodox Press, 2002.

Ustaša: Croatian Separatism and European Politics, 1929-1945. London: The Lord Byron Foundation, 1998 (first edition).

* * * * *

The Lord Byron Foundation for Balkan Studies

www.Balkanstudies.org

was founded by the late Sir Alfred Sherman in 1994 as a non-partisan research center devoted to studying the Balkan Peninsula in all its aspects. The Foundation's research, publications and conferences are designed to correct the current trend of public commentary, which tends, systematically, not to understand events but to construct a version of Balkan rivalries that fits daily political requirements. The Foundation is named after a great Western poet who gave his life in the fight to free Balkan Christians from Islamic rule. This choice reflects its belief in the essential unity of our civilization. The work of The Lord Byron Foundation is based on the acceptance that the cause of tolerance in a perennially troubled region can never be advanced by misrepresentation or by the sentimental lapse of seriousness that often characterizes Western discourse on the region.

> **Publication of this book was supported by a grant from the Hilandar Foundation. The opinions and findings expressed in this book are those of the author and do not necessarily reflect the views of the sponsors.**

www.ingramcontent.com/pod-product-compliance
Lightning Source LLC
Chambersburg PA
CBHW052134230426
43671CB00009B/1249